REACT
KEY CONCEPTS

Consolidate your knowledge of React's
core features

Maximilian Schwarzmüller

‹packt›

REACT KEY CONCEPTS

Author: Maximilian Schwarzmüller

Reviewer: Cihan Yakar

Senior Editor: Megan Carlisle

Acquisitions Manager: Bridget Kenningham

Acquisitions Editor: Sneha Shinde

Production Editor: Shantanu Zagade

Editorial Board: Vijin Boricha, Megan Carlisle, Ketan Giri, Heather Gopsill, Akin Babu Joseph, Bridget Kenningham, Manasa Kumar, Alex Mazonowicz, Monesh Mirpuri, Aaron Nash, Abhishek Rane, Brendan Rodrigues, Ankita Thakur, Nitesh Thakur, and Jonathan Wray

First published: December 2022

Production reference: 2100123

ISBN: 978-1-80323-450-2

Published by Packt Publishing Ltd.
Livery Place, 35 Livery Street
Birmingham B3 2PB, UK

Table of Contents

Preface   i

Chapter 1: React – What and Why   1

Introduction 2

What Is React? 2

The Problem with "Vanilla JavaScript" 4

React and Declarative Code 8

    How React Manipulates the DOM 12

Introducing Single Page Applications 14

    Creating a React Project 14

Summary and Key Takeaways 17

    What's Next? 17

    Test Your Knowledge! 18

Chapter 2: Understanding React Components and JSX   21

Introduction 22

What Are Components? 22

    Why Components? 23

    The Anatomy of a Component 24

    What Exactly Are Component Functions? 27

What Does React Do with All These Components? 28

    Built-in Components 32

    Naming Conventions 33

JSX vs HTML vs Vanilla JavaScript 34

    Using React without JSX 36

    JSX Elements Are Treated like Regular JavaScript Values 38

    JSX Elements Must Be Self-Closing 40

Outputting Dynamic Content 41

    When Should You Split Components? 41

Summary and Key Takeaways 43

    What's Next? 43

    Test Your Knowledge! 44

Apply What You Learned 44

    Activity 2.1: Creating a React App to Present Yourself 44

    Activity 2.2: Creating a React App to Log Your Goals for This Book 45

Chapter 3: Components and Props   49

Introduction 50

Not There Yet 50

Using Props in Components 51

    Passing Props to Components 51

    Consuming Props in a Component 52

Components, Props, and Reusability 53

    The Special "children" Prop 54

    Which Components Need Props? 55

How to Deal with Multiple Props 56

    Spreading Props 57

    Prop Chains/Prop Drilling 59

Summary and Key Takeaways 60

    What's Next? 60

Test Your Knowledge! 61

Apply What You Learned 61

Activity 3.1: Creating an App to Output Your Goals for This Book 61

Chapter 4: Working with Events and State — 65

Introduction 66

What's the Problem? 66

How Not to Solve the Problem 67

A Better Incorrect Solution 69

Properly Reacting to Events 71

Updating State Correctly 73

A Closer Look at useState() 75

A Look under the Hood of React 76

Naming Conventions 78

Allowed State Value Types 78

Working with Multiple State Values 79

Using Multiple State Slices 80

Managing Combined State Objects 82

Updating State Based on Previous State Correctly 84

Two-Way Binding 88

Deriving Values from State 90

Working with Forms and Form Submission 92

Lifting State Up 94

Summary and Key Takeaways 98

What's Next? 99

Test Your Knowledge! 99

Apply What You Learned 99

    Activity 4.1: Building a Simple Calculator 100

    Activity 4.2: Enhancing the Calculator 101

Chapter 5: Rendering Lists and Conditional Content   103

Introduction 104

What Are Conditional Content and List Data? 104

Rendering Content Conditionally 106

    Different Ways of Rendering Content Conditionally 109

        Utilizing Ternary Expressions..109

        Abusing JavaScript Logical Operators 112

        Get Creative!..113

        Which Approach Is Best?...114

    Setting Element Tags Conditionally 114

Outputting List Data 116

    Mapping List Data 119

    Updating Lists 121

A Problem with List Items 124

    Keys to the Rescue! 127

Summary and Key Takeaways 129

    What's Next? 129

    Test Your Knowledge! 130

Apply What You Learned 130

    Activity 5.1: Showing a Conditional Error Message 130

    Activity 5.2: Outputting a List of Products 131

Chapter 6: Styling React Apps 135

Introduction 136

How Does Styling Work in React Apps? 136

    Using Inline Styles 140

    Setting Styles via CSS Classes 142

    Setting Styles Dynamically 144

    Conditional Styles 146

    Combining Multiple Dynamic CSS Classes 148

    Merging Multiple Inline Style Objects 149

    Building Components with Customizable Styles 150

        Customization with Fixed Configuration Options 151

    The Problem with Unscoped Styles 152

Scoped Styles with CSS Modules 152

    The styled-components Library 156

    Using Other CSS or JavaScript Styling Libraries and Frameworks 158

Summary and Key Takeaways 159

    What's Next? 160

    Test Your Knowledge! 160

Apply What You Learned 160

    Activity 6.1: Providing Input Validity Feedback
upon Form Submission 160

    Activity 6.2: Using CSS Modules for Style Scoping 162

Chapter 7: Portals and Refs   165

Introduction 166

A World without Refs 166

Refs versus State 170

Using Refs for More than DOM Access 172

    Forwarding Refs 175

    Controlled versus Uncontrolled Components 181

React and Where Things End up in the DOM 184

    Portals to the Rescue 187

Summary and Key Takeaways 189

    What's Next? 190

    Test Your Knowledge! 190

Apply What You Have Learned 190

    Activity 7.1: Extract User Input Values 191

    Activity 7.2: Add a Side-Drawer 192

Chapter 8: Handling Side Effects   197

Introduction 198

What's the Problem? 198

Understanding Side Effects 200

    Side Effects Are Not Just about HTTP Requests 202

Dealing with Side Effects with the useEffect() Hook 204

    How to Use useEffect() 205

Effects and Their Dependencies 207

    Unnecessary Dependencies 209

    Cleaning Up after Effects 212

    Dealing with Multiple Effects 216

Functions as Dependencies 217

Avoiding Unnecessary Effect Executions 223

Effects and Asynchronous Code 230

Rules of Hooks 231

Summary and Key Takeaways 232

What's Next? 233

Test Your Knowledge! 233

Apply What You Learned 233

Activity 8.1: Building a Basic Blog 234

Chapter 9: Behind the Scenes of React and Optimization Opportunities 237

Introduction 238

Revisiting Component Evaluations and Updates 238

What Happens When a Component Function Is Called 241

The Virtual DOM vs the Real DOM 242

State Batching 245

Avoiding Unnecessary Child Component Evaluations 247

Avoiding Costly Computations 252

Utilizing useCallback() 256

Avoiding Unnecessary Code Download 259

Reducing Bundle Sizes via Code Splitting (Lazy Loading) 260

Strict Mode 267

Debugging Code and the React Developer Tools 268

Summary and Key Takeaways 272

What's Next? 273

Test Your Knowledge! 273

Apply What You Learned 274

Activity 9.1: Optimize an Existing App 274

Chapter 10: Working with Complex State   279

Introduction 280

A Problem with Cross-Component State 280

Using Context to Handle Multi-Component State 285

Providing and Managing Context Values 286

Using Context in Nested Components 290

Changing Context from Nested Components 293

Getting Better Code Completion 294

Context or "Lifting State Up"? 295

Outsourcing Context Logic into Separate Components 295

Combining Multiple Contexts 297

Limitations of useState() 298

Managing State with useReducer() 300

Understanding Reducer Functions 301

Dispatching Actions 303

Summary and Key Takeaways 306

What's Next? 306

Test Your Knowledge! 307

Apply What You Learned 307

Activity 10.1: Migrating an App to the Context API 307

Activity 10.2: Replacing useState() with useReducer() 309

Chapter 11: Building Custom React Hooks   313

Introduction 314

Why Would You Build Custom Hooks? 314

    What Are Custom Hooks? 317

    A First Custom Hook 318

Custom Hooks: A Flexible Feature 321

    Custom Hooks and Parameters 322

    Custom Hooks and Return Values 324

A More Complex Example 326

Summary and Key Takeaways 335

    What's Next? 335

    Test Your Knowledge! 336

Apply What You Learned 336

    Activity 11.1: Build a Custom Keyboard Input Hook 336

Chapter 12: Multipage Apps with React Router   341

Introduction 342

One Page Is Not Enough 342

Getting Started with React Router and Defining Routes 343

    Adding Page Navigation 347

    From Link to NavLink 352

    Route Components versus "Normal" Components 357

From Static to Dynamic Routes 361

    Extracting Route Parameters 364

    Creating Dynamic Links 366

    Navigating Programmatically 368

Redirecting 372

    Nested Routes 372

    Handling Undefined Routes 376

    Lazy Loading 377

Summary and Key Takeaways 378

    What's Next? 379

    Test Your Knowledge! 380

Apply What You Learned 380

    Activity 12.1: Creating a Basic Three-Page Website 380

    Activity 12.2: Enhancing the Basic Website 382

Chapter 13: Managing Data with React Router   385

Introduction 386

Data Fetching and Routing Are Tightly Coupled 386

    Sending HTTP Requests without React Router 388

Loading Data with React Router 390

    Enabling These Extra Router Features 395

    Loading Data for Dynamic Routes 397

    Loaders, Requests, and Client-Side Code 399

Layouts Revisited 401

    Reusing Data across Routes 407

Handling Errors 409

Onward to Data Submission 411

    Working with action() and Form Data 415

    Returning Data Instead of Redirecting 418

    Controlling Which <Form> Triggers Which Action 421

    Reflecting the Current Navigation Status 421

Submitting Forms Programmatically 423

Behind-the-Scenes Data Fetching and Submission 426

Deferring Data Loading 429

Summary and Key Takeaways 432

What's Next? 433

Test Your Knowledge! 433

Apply What You Learned 434

Activity 13.1: A To-Dos App 434

Chapter 14: Next Steps and Further Resources   439

Introduction 440

How Should You Proceed? 440

Interesting Problems to Explore 441

Build a Shopping Cart..441

Build an Application's Authentication System (User Signup and Login) ...442

Build an Event Management Website..443

Common and Popular React Libraries 444

Other Resources 445

Beyond React for Web Applications 445

Final Words 446

Appendix   449

Index   549

PREFACE

ABOUT THE BOOK

As the most popular JavaScript library for building modern, interactive user interfaces, React is an in-demand framework that'll bring real value to your career or next project. But like any technology, learning React can be tricky, and finding the right teacher can make things a whole lot easier.

Maximilian Schwarzmüller is a bestselling instructor who has helped over two million students worldwide learn how to code, and his latest React video course (React—The Complete Guide) has over six hundred thousand students on Udemy.

Max has written this quick-start reference to help you get to grips with the world of React programming. Simple explanations, relevant examples, and a clear, concise approach make this fast-paced guide the ideal resource for busy developers.

This book distills the core concepts of React and draws together its key features with neat summaries, thus perfectly complementing other in-depth teaching resources. So, whether you've just finished Max's React video course and are looking for a handy reference tool, or you've been using a variety of other learning material and now need a single study guide to bring everything together, this is the ideal companion to support you through your next React projects. Plus, it's fully up to date for React 18, so you can be sure you're ready to go with the latest version.

ABOUT THE AUTHOR

Maximilian Schwarzmüller is a professional web developer and bestselling online course instructor. Having learned to build websites and web user interfaces the hard way with just HTML, CSS, and (old-school) JavaScript, he embraced modern frontend frameworks and libraries like Angular and React right from the start.

Having the perspective of a self-taught freelancer, Maximilian started teaching web development professionally in 2015. On Udemy, he is now one of the most popular and biggest online instructors, teaching more than 2mn students worldwide. Students can become developers by exploring more than 40 courses, most of those courses being bestsellers in their respective categories. In 2017, together with a friend, Maximilian also founded Academind to deliver even more and better courses to even more students. For example, Academind's "React – The Complete Guide" course is the bestselling React course on the Udemy platform, reaching more than 500,000 students.

Besides helping students from all over the world as an online instructor, Maximilian never stopped working as a web developer. He still loves exploring and mastering new technologies, building exciting digital products, and sharing his knowledge with fellow developers. He's driven by his passion for good code and engaging websites and apps. Beyond web development, Maximilian also works as a mobile app developer and cloud expert. He holds multiple AWS certifications, including the "AWS Certified Solutions Architect – Professional" certification.

Apart from his courses on Udemy, Maximilian also publishes free tutorial videos on Academind's YouTube channel (https://youtube.com/c/academind) and articles on academind.com. You can also follow him on Twitter (@maxedapps).

AUDIENCE

This book is designed for developers who already have some familiarity with React basics. It can be used as a standalone resource to consolidate understanding or as a companion guide to a more in-depth course. To get the most value from this book, it is advised that readers have some understanding of the fundamentals of JavaScript, HTML, and CSS.

PROSPECTIVE TABLE OF CONTENTS

Chapter 1, React – What and Why, will re-introduce the reader to React.js. Assuming that React.js is not brand-new to the reader, this chapter will clarify which problems React solves, which alternatives exist, how React generally works, and how React projects may be created.

Chapter 2, Understanding React Components and JSX, will explain the general structure of a React app (a tree of components) and how components are created and used in React apps.

Chapter 3, Components and Props, will ensure that readers are able to build reusable components by using a key concept called "props".

Chapter 4, Working with Events and State, will cover how to work with state in React components, which different options exist (single state vs multiple state slices) and how state changes can be performed and used for UI updates.

Chapter 5, Rendering Lists and Conditional Content, will explain how React apps can render lists of content (e.g. list of user posts) and conditional content (e.g. alert if incorrect values were entered into an input field).

Chapter 6, Styling React Apps, will clarify how React components can be styled and how styles can be applied dynamically or conditionally, touching on popular styling solutions like vanilla CSS, styled components, and CSS modules for scoped styles.

Chapter 7, Portals and Refs, will explain how direct DOM access and manipulation is facilitated via the "refs" feature which is built-into React. In addition, readers will learn how Portals may be used to optimize the rendered DOM element structure.

Chapter 8, Handling Side Effects, will discuss the **useEffect** hook, explaining how it works, how it can be configured for different use-cases and scenarios, and how side effects can be handled optimally with this React hook.

Chapter 9, Behind the Scenes of React and Optimization Opportunities, will take a look behind the scenes of React and dive into core topics like the virtual DOM, state update batching and key optimization techniques that help developers avoid unnecessary re-render cycles (and thus improve performance).

Chapter 10, Working with Complex State, will explain how the advanced React hook **useReducer** works, when and why you might want to use it and how it can be used in React components to manage more complex component state with it. In addition, React's Context API will be explored and discussed in-depth, allowing developers to manage app-wide state with ease.

Chapter 11, Building Custom React Hooks, will explain how developers can build their own, custom React hooks and what the advantage of doing so is.

Chapter 12, Multipage Apps with React Router, will explain what React Router is and how this extra library can be used to build multipage experiences in a React single-page-application.

Chapter 13, Managing Data with React Router, will dive deeper into React Router and explore how this package can also help with fetching and managing data.

Chapter 14, Next Steps and Further Resources, will further cover the core and "extended" React ecosystem and which resources may be helpful for next steps.

CONVENTIONS

Code words in text, database table names, folder names, filenames, file extensions, pathnames, dummy URLs, user input, and Twitter handles are shown as follows: "Store the paragraph element reference in a constant named **paragraphElement**."

Words that you see on the screen, for example, in menus or dialog boxes, also appear in the text like this: "In the header with the navigation bar you will find the following components: the navigation items (**Login** and **Profile**) and the **Logout** button."

A block of code is set as follows:

```
const buttonElement = document.querySelector('button');
const paragraphElement = document.querySelector('p');
function updateTextHandler() {
  paragraphElement.textContent = 'Text was changed!';
}
buttonElement.addEventListener('click', updateTextHandler);
```

New terms and important words are shown like this: "It is currently used by over 5% of the top 1,000 websites and compared to other popular frontend JavaScript frameworks like Angular, React is leading by a huge margin, when looking at key metrics like weekly package downloads via **npm** (**Node Package Manager**), which is a tool commonly used for downloading and managing JavaScript packages."

SETTING UP YOUR ENVIRONMENT

Before you can successfully install React.js on your system, you will need to ensure you have the following software installed:

Node.js and **npm** (included with your installation by default)

These are available for download at https://nodejs.org/en/.

The home page of this site should automatically provide you with the most recent installation options for your platform and system. For more options, select `Other Downloads` (the first of three links visible beneath each of your default options). This will open a new page through which you can explore all installation choices for all main platforms, as shown in the screenshot below:

LTS	Current	
Recommended For Most Users	Latest Features	
Windows Installer	**macOS Installer**	**Source Code**
node-v17.9.0-x86.msi	node-v17.9.0.pkg	node-v17.9.0.tar.gz

	32-bit	64-bit
Windows Installer (.msi)	32-bit	64-bit
Windows Binary (.zip)	32-bit	64-bit
macOS Installer (.pkg)	64-bit / ARM64	
macOS Binary (.tar.gz)	64-bit	ARM64
Linux Binaries (x64)	64-bit	
Linux Binaries (ARM)	ARMv7	ARMv8
Source Code	node-v17.9.0.tar.gz	

Figure 0.1: Download Node.js source code or pre-built installer

At the bottom of this page, you will find a bullet list of available resources should your system require specialised instructions, including guidance on Node.js installation via source code and node package manager.

Once you have downloaded Node.js through this website, find the **.pkg** file in your downloads folder. Double-click this file to open the **Install Node.js** pop-up window, then simply follow given instructions to complete your installation.

INSTALLING REACT.JS

React.js projects can be created in various ways, including custom-built project setups that incorporate webpack, babel and other tools. The easiest and recommended way is the usage of the **create-react-app** command though. This book uses this method. The creation of a react app will be covered in *Chapter 1, React.js – What and Why*, but you may refer to this section for step-by-step instructions on this task.

> **NOTE**
>
> For further guidance regarding the installation and setup of your React.js environment, resources are available at the following:
> https://reactjs.org/docs/getting-started.html

Perform the following steps to install React.js on your system:

1. Open your terminal (Powershell/command prompt for Windows; bash for Linux).

2. Use the make directory command to create a new project folder with a name of your choosing (e.g. **mkdir react-projects**) and navigate to that directory using the change directory command (e.g. **cd react-projects**).

3. Enter the following command prompt to create a new project directory within this folder:

```
npx create-react-app my-app
```

4. Grant permission when prompted to install all required files and folders needed for basic React setup. This may take several minutes.

5. Once completed, navigate to your new directory using the cd command:

```
cd my-app
```

6. Open a terminal window in this new project directory and run the following command to start a Node.js development server and lauch a new browser to preview your app locally:

npm start

7. This should open a new browser window automatically, but if it does not, open your browser manually type **http://localhost:3000** in the address/location bar to navigate to **localhost:3000**, as shown in the screenshot below:

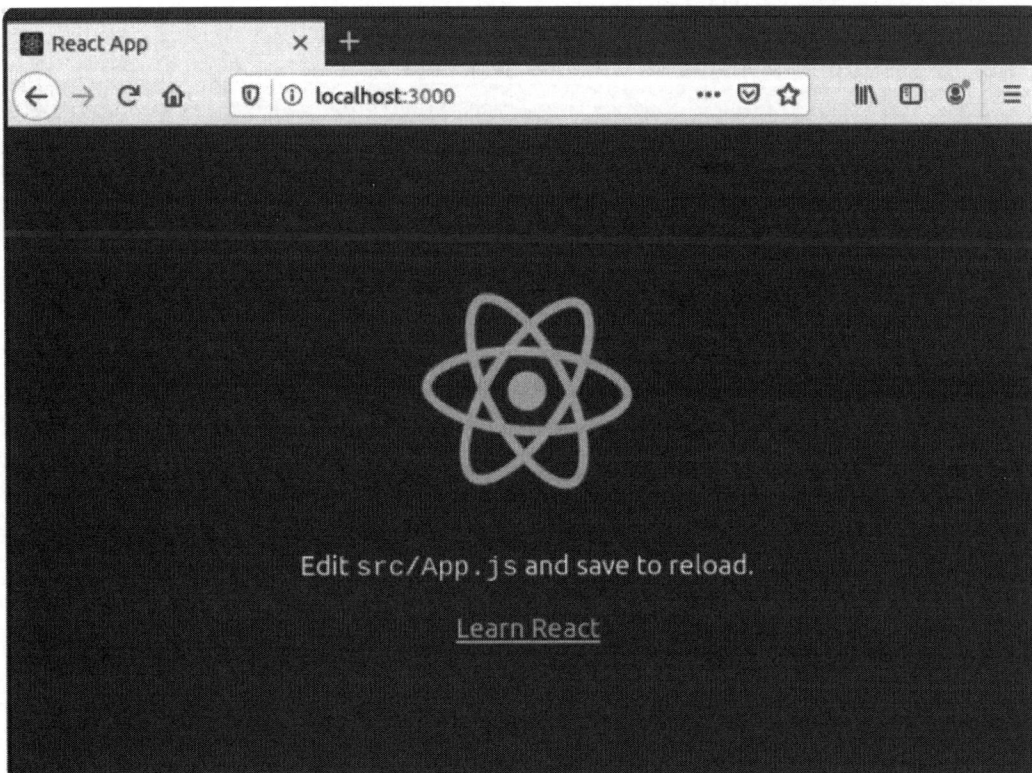

Figure 0.2: Access React App in Your Browser

8. When you are ready to stop development for the time being, use **Ctrl** + **C** in the same terminal as in step 6 to quit running your server. To relaunch it, simply run the **npm start** command in that terminal once again. Keep the process started by **npm start** up and running while developing, as it will automatically update the website loaded on **localhost:3000** with any changes you make.

DOWNLOADING THE CODE BUNDLE

Download the code files from GitHub at https://packt.link/leoCT. Refer to these code files for the complete code bundle.

GET IN TOUCH

Feedback from our readers is always welcome.

General feedback: If you have any questions about this book, please mention the book title in the subject of your message and email us at customercare@packtpub.com.

Errata: Although we have taken every care to ensure the accuracy of our content, mistakes do happen. If you have found a mistake in this book, we would be grateful if you could report this to us. Please visit www.packtpub.com/support/errata and complete the form.

Piracy: If you come across any illegal copies of our works in any form on the Internet, we would be grateful if you could provide us with the location address or website name. Please contact us at copyright@packt.com with a link to the material.

If you are interested in becoming an author: If there is a topic that you have expertise in and you are interested in either writing or contributing to a book, please visit authors.packtpub.com.

PLEASE LEAVE A REVIEW

Let us know what you think by leaving a detailed, impartial review on O'Reilly or Amazon. We appreciate all feedback. It helps us continue to make great products and help aspiring developers build their skills. Please spare a few minutes to give your thoughts. It makes a big difference to us.

DOWNLOAD A FREE PDF COPY OF THIS BOOK

Thanks for purchasing this book!

Do you like to read on the go but are unable to carry your print books everywhere? Is your eBook purchase not compatible with the device of your choice?

Don't worry, now with every Packt book you get a DRM-free PDF version of that book at no cost.

Read anywhere, any place, and on any device. Search, copy, and paste code from your favorite technical books directly into your application.

The perks don't stop there; you can get exclusive access to discounts, newsletters, and great free content in your inbox daily.

Follow these simple steps to get the benefits:

1. Scan the QR code or visit the link below:

https://packt.link/free-ebook/9781803234502

2. Submit your proof of purchase.

3. That's it! We'll send your free PDF and other benefits to your email directly.

1

REACT — WHAT AND WHY

LEARNING OBJECTIVES

By the end of this chapter, you will be able to do the following:

- Describe what React is and why you would use it
- Compare React to web projects built with just JavaScript
- Create new React projects

INTRODUCTION

React.js (or just **React**, as it's also called and as it'll be referred to for the majority of this book) is one of the **most popular frontend JavaScript libraries**—maybe even the most popular one, according to a 2021 Stack Overflow developer survey. It is currently used by over 5% of the top 1,000 websites and compared to other popular frontend JavaScript frameworks like Angular, React is leading by a huge margin, when looking at key metrics like weekly package downloads via **npm** (**Node Package Manager**), which is a tool commonly used for downloading and managing JavaScript packages.

Though it is certainly possible to write good React code without fully understanding how React works and why you're using it, you should always aim to understand the tools you're working with as well as the reasons for picking a certain tool in the first place.

Therefore, before considering anything about its core concepts and ideas or reviewing example code, you first need to understand **what** React actually is and why it exists. This will help you understand how React works internally and why it offers the features it does.

If you already know why you're using React, why solutions like React in general are being used instead of **vanilla JavaScript** (i.e. JavaScript without any frameworks or libraries, more on this in the next section), and what the idea behind React and its syntax is, you may of course skip this section and jump ahead to the more practice-oriented chapters later in this book.

But if you only *think* that you know it and are not 100% certain, you should definitely follow along with this chapter first.

WHAT IS REACT?

React is a JavaScript library, and if you take a look at the official webpage (Official React website and documentation: https://reactjs.org), you learn that it's actually a *"JavaScript library for building user interfaces"*.

But what does this mean?

It should be clear what JavaScript is and why you use JavaScript in the browser (React is mostly a browser-side JavaScript library). JavaScript allows you to add interactivity to your website since, with JavaScript, you can react to user events and manipulate the page after it was loaded. This is extremely valuable as it allows you to build highly interactive web user interfaces.

But what is a "library" and how does React help with "building user interfaces"?

While you can have philosophical discussions about what a library is (and how it differs from a framework), the pragmatic definition of a library is that it's a collection of functionalities that you can use in your code to achieve results that would normally require more code and work from your side. Libraries help you write better and shorter code and enable you to implement certain features more quickly. In addition, since you can focus on your "core business logic", you not only move faster but are also likely to produce better code since you don't have to reinvent the wheel for problems that have been solved before by others.

React is such a library—one that focuses on providing functionalities that help you create interactive and reactive user interfaces. Indeed, React deals with more than web interfaces (i.e. websites loaded in browsers). You can also build native mobile devices with React and React Native, which is another library that utilizes React under the hood. No matter which platform you're targeting though, creating interactive user interfaces with just JavaScript can quickly become very complex and overwhelming.

> **NOTE**
>
> The focus of this book is on React in general, and for simplicity, the focus lies on React for websites. With projects like React Native, you can also use React to build user interfaces for native mobile apps. The React concepts covered in this book still apply, no matter which target platform is chosen. But examples will focus on React for web browsers.

THE PROBLEM WITH "VANILLA JAVASCRIPT"

Vanilla JavaScript is a term commonly used in web development for referring to "JavaScript without any frameworks or libraries". That means, you write all the JavaScript on your own, without falling back to any libraries or frameworks that would provide extra utility functionalities. When working with vanilla JavaScript, you especially don't use major frontend frameworks or libraries like React or Angular.

Using vanilla JavaScript generally has the advantage, that visitors of a website have to download less JavaScript code (as major frameworks and libraries typically are quite sizeable and can quickly add 50+ kb of extra JavaScript code that has to be downloaded).

The downside of relying on vanilla JavaScript is, that you, as the developer, must implement all functionalities from the ground up on your own. This can be error-prone and highly time consuming. Therefore, especially more complex user interfaces and websites can quickly become very hard to manage with vanilla JavaScript.

React simplifies the creation and management of such user interfaces by moving from an imperative to a declarative approach. Though this is a nice sentence, it can be hard to grasp if you haven't worked with React or similar frameworks before. To understand it and the idea behind "imperative vs declarative approaches" and why you might want to use React instead of just vanilla JavaScript, it's helpful to take a step back and evaluate how vanilla JavaScript works.

Here's a short code snippet that shows how you could handle the following user interface actions with vanilla JavaScript:

1. Add an event listener to a button to listen for "click" events.

2. Replace the text of a paragraph with new text once a click on the button occurs.

```javascript
const buttonElement = document.querySelector('button');
const paragraphElement = document.querySelector('p');

function updateTextHandler() {
  paragraphElement.textContent = 'Text was changed!';
}

buttonElement.addEventListener('click', updateTextHandler);
```

This example is deliberately kept simple, so it's probably not looking too bad or overwhelming. It's just a basic example to show how code is generally written with vanilla JavaScript (a more complex example will be discussed below). But even though this example is very straightforward and easy to digest, working with vanilla JavaScript will quickly reach its limits for feature-rich user interfaces and the code to handle various user interactions therefore also becomes more complex. Code can quickly grow significantly, and therefore maintaining it can become a challenge.

In the preceding example, code is written with vanilla JavaScript and, therefore, imperatively. This means that you write instruction after instruction, and you describe every step that needs to be taken in detail.

The code shown above could be translated to these more human-readable instructions:

1. Look for an **HTML** element of type **button** to obtain a reference to the first button on the page.

2. Create a constant (i.e., a data container) named **buttonElement** that holds that button reference.

3. Repeat step 1 but get a reference to the first element that is of type of **p**.

4. Store the paragraph element reference in a constant named **paragraphElement**.

5. Add an event listener to the **buttonElement** that listens for **click** events and triggers the **updateTextHandler** function whenever such a **click** event occurs.

6. Inside the **updateTextHandler** function, use the **paragraphElement** to set its **textContent** to **"Text was changed!"**.

Do you see how every step that needs to be taken is clearly defined and written out in the code?

This shouldn't be too surprising because that is how most programming languages work: you define a series of steps that must be executed in order. It's an approach that makes a lot of sense because the order of code execution shouldn't be random or unpredictable.

But when working with user interfaces, this imperative approach is not ideal. Indeed, it can quickly become cumbersome because, as a developer, you have to add a lot of instructions that despite adding little value, cannot simply be omitted. You need to write all the DOM (**Document Object Model**) instructions that allow your code to interact with elements, add elements, manipulate elements. etc.

Your core business logic (e.g., deriving and defining the actual text that should be set after a click) therefore often makes up only a small chunk of the overall code. When controlling and manipulating web user interfaces with JavaScript, a huge chunk (often the majority) of your code is frequently made up of DOM instructions, event listeners, HTML element operations, and UI state management.

Therefore, you end up describing all the steps that are required to interact with the UI technically **and** all the steps that are required to derive the output data (i.e., the desired final state of the UI).

> **NOTE**
>
> This book assumes that you are familiar with the DOM (Document Object Model). In a nutshell, the DOM is the "bridge" between your JavaScript code and the HTML code of the website with which you want to interact. Via the built-in DOM **API**, JavaScript is able to create, insert, manipulate, delete, and read HTML elements and their content.
>
> You can learn more about the DOM in this article: https://academind.com/tutorials/what-is-the-dom.

Modern web user interfaces are often quite complex, with lots of interactivity going on behind the scenes. Your website might need to listen for user input in an input field, send that entered data to a server to validate it, output a validation feedback message on the screen, and show an error overlay modal if incorrect data is submitted.

This is not a complex example in general, but the vanilla JavaScript code for implementing such a scenario can be overwhelming. You end up with lots of DOM selection, insertion, and manipulation operations, as well as multiple lines of code that do nothing but manage event listeners. And keeping the DOM updated, without introducing bugs or errors, can be a nightmare since you must ensure that you update the right DOM element with the right value at the right time. Below, you will find a screenshot of some example code for the described use-case.

> **NOTE**
>
> The full, working, code can be found on GitHub at https://packt.link/tLSLU.

If you take a look at the JavaScript code in the screenshot (or in the linked repository), you will probably be able to imagine how a more complex user interface is likely to look.

Figure 1.1. An example JavaScript code file that contains over 100 lines of code for a fairly trivial user interface

This example JavaScript file already contains roughly 110 lines of code. Even after minifying ("minifying" means that code is shortened automatically, e.g. by replacing long variable names with shorter ones and removing redundant whitespace; in this case via https://javascript-minifier.com/) it and splitting the code across multiple lines thereafter (to count the raw lines of code), it still has around 80 lines of code. That's a full 80 lines of code for a simple user interface with only basic functionality. The actual business logic (i.e., input validation, determining if and when overlays should be shown, and defining the output text) only makes up a small fraction of the overall codebase—around 20 to 30 lines of code, in this case (around 20 after minifying).

That's roughly 75% of code spent on pure DOM interaction, DOM state management, and similar boilerplate tasks.

As you can see by these examples and numbers, controlling all the UI elements and their different states (e.g., whether an info box is visible or not) is a challenging task and trying to create such interfaces with just JavaScript often leads to complex code that might even contain errors.

That's why the imperative approach, wherein you must define and write down every single step, has its limits in situations like this. This is the reason why React provides utility functionalities that allow you to write code differently: with a declarative approach.

> **NOTE**
>
> This is not a scientific paper, and the preceding example is not meant to act as an exact scientific study. Depending on how you count lines and which kind of code you consider to be "core business logic", you will end up with higher or lower percentage values. The key message doesn't change though: Lots of code (in this case most of it) deals with the DOM and DOM manipulation—not with the actual logic that defines your website and its key features.

REACT AND DECLARATIVE CODE

Coming back to the first, simple, code snippet from above, here's that same code snippet, this time using React:

```javascript
import { useState } from 'react';

function App() {
  const [outputText, setOutputText] = useState('Initial text');

  function updateTextHandler() {
    setOutputText('Text was changed!');
  }

  return (
    <>
      <button onClick={updateTextHandler}>Click to change text</button>
      <p>{outputText}</p>
```

```
      </>
    );
}
```

This snippet performs the same operations as the first did with just vanilla JavaScript:

1. Add an event listener to a button to listen for **click** events (now with some React-specific syntax: **onClick={...})**.

2. Replace the text of a paragraph with new text once the click on the button occurred.

Nonetheless, this code looks totally different—like a mixture of JavaScript and HTML. And indeed, React uses a syntax extension called **JSX** (i.e., JavaScript with embedded XML). For the moment, it's enough to understand that this JSX code will work because of a **pre-processing** step that's part of the build workflow of every React project.

Pre-processing means that certain tools, which are part of React projects, analyze and transform the code before its deployed. This allows for development-only syntax like JSX which would not work in the browser and is therefore transformed to regular JavaScript before deployment. (You'll get a thorough introduction into JSX in *Chapter 2, Understanding React Components and JSX.*)

In addition, the snippet shown above contains a React specific feature: State. State will be discussed in greater detail later in the book (*Chapter 4, Working with Events and State* will focus on handling events and state with React). For the moment, you can think of this state as a variable that, when changed, will trigger React to update the user interface in the browser.

What you see in the preceding example is the "declarative approach" used by React: You write your JavaScript logic (e.g., functions that should eventually be executed), and you combine that logic with the HTML code that should trigger it or that is affected by it. You don't write the instructions for selecting certain DOM elements or changing the text content of some DOM elements. Instead, with React and JSX, you focus on your JavaScript business logic and define the desired HTML output that should eventually be reached. This output can and typically will contain dynamic values that are derived inside of your main JavaScript code.

In the preceding example, **outputText** is some state managed by React. In the code, the **updateTextHandler** function is triggered upon a click, and the **outputText** state value is set to a new string value (**'Text was changed!'**) with help of the **setOutputText** function. The exact details of what's going on here will be explored in *Chapter 4*.

The general idea, though, is that the state value is changed and, since it's being referenced in the last paragraph (**<p>{outputText}</p>**), React outputs the current state value in that place in the actual DOM (and therefore on the actual web page). React will keep the paragraph updated, and therefore, whenever **outputText** changes, React will select this paragraph element again and update its **textContent** automatically.

This is the declarative approach in action. As a developer, you don't need to worry about the technical details (for example, selecting the paragraph, updating its **textContent**). Instead, you will hand this work off to React. You will only need to focus on the desired end state(s) where the goal simply is to output the current value of **outputText** in a specific place (i.e., in the second paragraph in this case) on the page. It's React's job of doing the "*behind the scenes*" work of getting to that result.

It turns out that this code snippet isn't shorter than the vanilla JavaScript one; indeed, it's actually even a bit longer. But that's only the case because this first snippet was deliberately kept simple and concise. In such cases, React actually adds a bit of overhead code. If that were your entire user interface, using React indeed wouldn't make too much sense. Again, this snippet was chosen because it allows us to see the differences at a glance. Things change if you take a look at the more complex vanilla JavaScript example from before) and compare that to its React alternative.

> **NOTE**
>
> Referenced code can be found on GitHub at http://packt.link/tLSLU and https://packt.link/YkpRa, respectively.

```javascript
1   import { useState } from 'react';
2
3   function validateEmail(enteredEmail) {
4     // In reality, we might be sending the entered email address to a backend API to check if a user with that email exists already
5     // Here, this is faked with help of a promise wrapper around some dummy validation logic
6
7     const promise = new Promise(function (resolve, reject) {
8       if (enteredEmail === 'test@test.com') {
9         reject(new Error('Email exists already'));
10      } else {
11        resolve();
12      }
13    });
14
15    return promise;
16  }
17
18  function validatePassword(enteredPassword) {
19    if (enteredPassword.trim().length < 6) {
20      throw new Error('Invalid password - must be at least 6 characters long.');
21    }
22  }
23
24  function App() {
25    const [emailIsValid, setEmailIsValid] = useState(true);
26    const [passwordIsValid, setPasswordIsValid] = useState(true);
27    const [modalData, setModalData] = useState(null);
28
29    async function validateInputHandler(inputType, event) {
30      const enteredValue = event.target.value;
31
32      let validationFn = validateEmail;
33      if (inputType === 'password') {
34        validationFn = validatePassword;
35      }
36
37      let isValid = true;
38
39      try {
40        await validationFn(enteredValue);
41      } catch (error) {
42        isValid = false;
43      }
44
45      if (inputType === 'email') {
46        setEmailIsValid(isValid);
47      } else {
48        setPasswordIsValid(isValid);
49      }
50    }
51
52    function submitFormHandler(event) {
53      event.preventDefault();
54
55      let title = 'An error occurred!';
56      let message = 'Invalid input values - please check your entered values.';
57
58      if (emailIsValid && passwordIsValid) {
59        title = 'Success!';
60        message = 'User created successfully!';
61      }
62
63      setModalData({
64        title: title,
65        message: message,
66      });
67    }
68
69    function closeModal() {
70      setModalData(null);
71    }
72
73    return (
74      <>
75        {modalData && <div className='backdrop' onClick={closeModal}></div>}
76        {modalData && (
77          <aside className='modal'>
78            <header>
79              <h2>{modalData.title}</h2>
80            </header>
81            <section>
82              <p>{modalData.message}</p>
83            </section>
84            <section className='modal__actions'>
85              <button onClick={closeModal}>Okay</button>
86            </section>
87          </aside>
88        )}
89        <header>
90          <h1>Create a New Account</h1>
91        </header>
92        <main>
93          <form onSubmit={submitFormHandler}>
94            <div className='form-control'>
95              <label htmlFor='email'>Email</label>
96              <input
97                type='email'
98                id='email'
99                onBlur={validateInputHandler.bind(null, 'email')}
100               />
101               {!emailIsValid && <p>This email is already taken!</p>}
102             </div>
103             <div className='form-control'>
104               <label htmlFor='password'>Password</label>
105               <input
106                 type='password'
107                 id='password'
108                 onBlur={validateInputHandler.bind(null, 'password')}
109               />
110               {!passwordIsValid && (
111                 <p>Password must be at least 6 characters long!</p>
112               )}
113             </div>
114             <button>Create User</button>
115           </form>
116         </main>
117         <footer>
118           <p>(c) Maximilian Schwarzmüller</p>
119           <p>
120             This is just a dummy example - not a fully functional website or
121             anything like that.
122           </p>
123         </footer>
124       </>
125     );
126   }
127
128   export default App;
```

Figure 1.2. The code snippet from before, now implemented via React.

It's still not short because all the JSX code (i.e., the HTML output) is included in the JavaScript file. If you ignore pretty much the entire right side of that screenshot (since HTML was not part of the vanilla JavaScript files either), the React code gets much more concise. But, most importantly, if you take a closer look at all the React code (also in the first, shorter snippet), you will notice that there are absolutely no operations that would select DOM elements, create or insert DOM elements, or edit DOM elements.

And this is the core idea of React. You don't write down all the individual steps and instructions; instead, you focus on the "big picture" and the desired end state(s) of your page content. With React, you can merge your JavaScript and markup code without having to deal with the low-level instructions of interacting with the DOM like selecting elements via **document.getElementById()** or similar operations.

Using this declarative approach, instead of the imperative approach with vanilla JavaScript, allows you, the developer, to focus on your core business logic and the different states of your HTML code. You don't need to define all the individual steps that have to be taken (like "adding an event listener", "selecting a paragraph", etc.), and this simplifies the development of complex user interfaces tremendously.

> **NOTE**
>
> It is worth emphasizing that React is not a great solution if you're working on a very simple user interface. If you can solve a problem with a few lines of vanilla JavaScript code, there is probably no strong reason to integrate React into the project.

Looking at React code for the first time, it can look very unfamiliar and strange. It's not what you're used to from JavaScript. Still, it is JavaScript—just enhanced with this JSX feature and various React-specific functionalities (like State). It may be less confusing if you remember that you typically define your user interface (i.e., your content and its structure) with HTML. You don't write step-by-step instructions there either, but rather create a nested tree structure with HTML tags. You express your content, the meaning of different elements, and the hierarchy of your user interface by using different HTML elements and by nesting HTML tags.

If you keep this in mind, the "traditional" (vanilla JavaScript) approach of manipulating the UI should seem rather odd. Why would you start defining low-level instructions like *"insert a paragraph element below this button and set its text to <some text>"* if you don't do that in HTML at all? React in the end brings back that HTML syntax, which is far more convenient when it comes to defining content and structure. With React, you can write dynamic JavaScript code side-by-side with the UI code (i.e., the HTML code) that is affected by it or related to it.

HOW REACT MANIPULATES THE DOM

As mentioned earlier, when writing React code, you typically write it as shown above: You blend HTML with JavaScript code by using the JSX syntax extension.

It is worth pointing out that JSX code does not run like this in browsers. It instead needs to be pre-processed before deployment. The JSX code must be transformed to regular JavaScript code before being served to browsers. The next chapter will take a closer look at JSX and what it's transformed to. For the moment, though, simply keep in mind that JSX code must be transformed.

Nonetheless, it is worth knowing that the code to which JSX will be transformed will also not contain any DOM instructions. Instead, the transformed code will execute various utility methods and functions that are built-into React (in other words, those that are provided by the React package that needs to be added to every React project). Internally, React creates a virtual DOM-like tree structure that reflects the current state of the user interface. This book takes a closer look at this abstract, virtual DOM and how React works in *Chapter 9, Behind the Scenes of React and Optimization Opportunities*. Therefore, React (the library) splits its core logic across two main packages:

- The main **react** package

- And the **react-dom** package

The main react package is a third-party JavaScript library that needs to be imported into a project to use React's features (like JSX or state) there. It's this package that creates this virtual DOM and derives the current UI state. But you also need the **react-dom** package in your project if you want to manipulate the DOM with React.

The **react-dom** package, specifically the **react-dom/client** part of that package, acts as a "translation bridge" between your React code, the internally generated virtual DOM, and the browser with its actual DOM that needs to be updated. It's the **react-dom** package that will produce the actual DOM instructions that will select, update, delete, and create DOM elements.

This split exists because you can also use React with other target environments. A very popular and well-known alternative to the DOM (i.e., to the browser) would be React Native, which allows developers to build native mobile apps with help of React. With React Native, you also include the react package into your project, but in place of **react-dom**, you would use the **react-native** package. In this book, "React" refers to both the react package and the "bridge" packages (like **react-dom**) .

> **NOTE**
>
> As mentioned earlier, this book focuses on React itself. The concepts explained in this book, therefore, will apply to both web browsers and websites as well as mobile devices. Nonetheless, all examples will focus on the web and react-DOM since that avoids introducing extra complexity.

INTRODUCING SINGLE PAGE APPLICATIONS

React can be used to simplify the creation of complex user interfaces, and there are two main ways of doing that:

1. Manage parts of a website (e.g., a chat box in the bottom left corner).

2. Manage the entire page and all user interaction that occurs on it.

Both approaches are viable, but the more popular and common scenario is the second one: Using React to manage the entire web page, instead of just parts of it. This approach is more popular because most websites that have complex user interfaces, have not just one complex element but multiple elements on their pages. Complexity would actually increase if you were to start using React for some website parts without using it for other areas of the site. For this reason, it's very common to manage the entire website with React.

This doesn't even stop after using React on one specific page of the site. Indeed, React can be used to handle URL path changes and update the parts of the page that need to be updated in order to reflect the new page that should be loaded. This functionality is called "routing" and third-party packages like **react-router-dom** (see *Chapter 12, Multipage Apps with React Router*), which integrate with React, allow you to create a website wherein the entire user interfaces is controlled via React.

A website that does not just use React for parts of its pages but instead for all subpages and for routing is called a **"Single Page Application" (SPA)** because it consists of only one HTML file (typically named **index.html**) which is used to initially load the React JavaScript code. Thereafter, the React library and your React code take over and control the actual user interface. This means that the entire user interface is created and managed by JavaScript via React and your React code.

CREATING A REACT PROJECT

To work with React, the first step is the creation of a React project. This can be done in multiple ways, but the most straightforward and easiest way is to use the **create-react-app** utility command line tool. This is a tool maintained by (parts of) the React team, and you can install it as a **Node.js** package via the **Node Package Manager (npm)**. Once installed, this tool can be used to create a project folder that comes with React pre-installed, as well as some other tools, such as the **Jest** package for automated testing.

You need a project setup like this because you typically use features like JSX which wouldn't work in the browser without prior code transformation. Therefore, as mentioned earlier, a pre-processing step is required, and the React project created via **create-react-app** includes such a step as part of the code build workflow.

To create a project with **create-react-app**, you must have Node.js installed—preferably the latest (or latest **LTS**) version. You can get the official Node.js installer for all operating systems from https://nodejs.org/. Once you have installed Node.js, you will also gain access to the built-in **npm** and **npx** commands, which you can use to utilize the **create-react-app** package to create a new project.

You can run the following command inside of your command prompt (Windows), bash (Linux), or terminal (macOS) program. Just make sure that you navigated (via **cd**) into the folder in which you want to create your new project.

```
npx create-react-app my-react-project
```

This command will create a new subfolder with a basic React project setup (i.e., with various files and folders) in the place where you ran it. You should run it in some path on your system where you have full read and write access and where you're not conflicting with any system or other project files.

The exact project structure (that is, the file names and folder names) may vary over time, but generally, every new React project contains a couple of key files and folders:

- A **src/** folder that contains the main source code files for the project:
- An **index.js** file which is the main entry script file that will be executed first
- An **App.js** file which contains the root component of the application (you'll learn more about components in the next chapter)
- Various styling (***.css**) files that are imported by the JavaScript files
- Other files, like code files for automated tests
- A **public/** folder which contains static files that will be part of the final website:
- This folder may contain static images like favicons
- The folder also contains an **index.html** file which is the single HTML page of this website

- **package.json** and **package-lock.json** are files that manage third-party dependencies of your project

- Production dependencies like **react** or **react-dom**

- Development dependencies like **jest** for automated tests

> **NOTE**
>
> **package.json** is the file in which you actually manage packages and their versions. **package-lock.json** is created automatically (by **Node.js**). It locks in exact dependency and sub-dependency versions, whereas **package.json** only specifies version ranges. You can learn more about these files and package versions on https://docs.npmjs.com/.

- The **node_modules** folder holds the actual third-party package code of the packages that are listed in the **package.json** file. This **node_modules** folder can be deleted since you can recreate it by running **npm** install inside of the project folder

Most of the React code will be written in the **App.js** file or custom components that will be added to the project. This book will explore components in the next chapter.

> **NOTE**
>
> The **node_modules** folder can become very big since it contains all projects dependencies and dependencies of dependencies. Therefore, it's typically not included if projects are shared with other developers or pushed to GitHub. The **package.json** file is all you need. By running **npm install**, the **node_modules** folder will be recreated locally.

Once the project is created, you can start writing your code. To preview your code on a live website locally on your system, you can **run npm** start inside of the project folder. This will start a built-in development server that pre-processes, builds, and hosts your React-powered SPA. This process should normally open the preview page in a new browser tab automatically. If that doesn't happen, you can manually open a new tab and navigate to **localhost:3000** there (unless you see a different address as output in the window where you executed **npm start**, in which case, use the address that's shown after you ran **npm start**).

The preview website that opens up will automatically reload and reflect code changes whenever you save changes to your code.

When you're done with development for the day, you can quit the running development server process via **CTRL + C** (in the command prompt or terminal window where you started it via **npm start**). To continue development and get back that live preview website, you can always restart it by running **n**pm start (inside of the project folder) again.

SUMMARY AND KEY TAKEAWAYS

- React is a library, though it's actually a combination of two main packages: **react** and **react-dom**.

- Though it is possible to build non-trivial user interfaces without React, simply using vanilla JavaScript to do so can be cumbersome, error-prone, and hard to maintain.

- React simplifies the creation of complex user interfaces by providing a declarative way to define the desired end state(s) of the UI.

- **Declarative** means that you define the target user interface content and structure, combined with different states (e.g., *"is a modal open or closed?"*), and you leave it up to React to figure out the appropriate DOM instructions.

- The react package itself derives UI states and manages a virtual DOM. It's "bridges" like **react-dom** or **react-native** that translate this virtual DOM into actual UI (DOM) instructions.

- With React, you can build Single Page Applications (SPAs), meaning that React is used to control the entire user interface on all pages as well as the routing between pages.

- React projects can be created with help of the **create-react-app** package, which provides a readily configured project folder and a live preview development server.

WHAT'S NEXT?

At this point, you should have a basic understanding of what React is and why you might consider using it, especially for building non-trivial user interfaces. You learned how to create new React projects with create-react-app, and you are now ready to dive deeper into React and the actual key features it offers.

In the next chapter, you will learn about a concept called **components** which are the fundamental building blocks of React apps. You will learn how components are used to compose user interfaces and why those components are needed in the first place. The next chapter will also dive deeper into JSX and explore how it is transformed to regular JavaScript code and which kind of code you could write alternatively to JSX.

TEST YOUR KNOWLEDGE!

Test your knowledge about the concepts covered in this chapter by answering the below questions. You can then compare your answers to example answers that can be found here: https://packt.link/ENPda.

1. What is React?

2. Which advantage does React offer over vanilla JavaScript projects?

3. What's the difference between imperative and declarative code?

4. What is a Single-Page-Application (SPA)?

5. How can you create new React projects and why do you need such a more complex project setup?

2

UNDERSTANDING REACT COMPONENTS AND JSX

LEARNING OBJECTIVES

By the end of this chapter, you will be able to do the following:

- Define what exactly **components** are
- Build and use components effectively
- Utilize common naming conventions and code patterns
- Describe the relation between components and JSX
- Write JSX code and understand why it's used
- Write React components without using JSX code
- Write your first React apps

INTRODUCTION

In the previous section, you learned about React in general, what it is and why you could consider using it for building user interfaces. You also learned how to create React projects with the help of **npx create-react-app**.

In this chapter, you will learn about one of the most important React concepts and building blocks: React as above, components. You will learn that components are reusable building blocks which are used to build user interfaces. In addition, JSX code will be discussed in greater detail so that you will be able to use the concept of components and JSX to build your own, first, basic React apps.

WHAT ARE COMPONENTS?

A key concept of React is the usage of so-called components. **Components** are reusable building blocks which are combined to compose the final user interface. For example, a basic website could be made up of a header that includes a navigation bar and a main section that includes an authentication form.

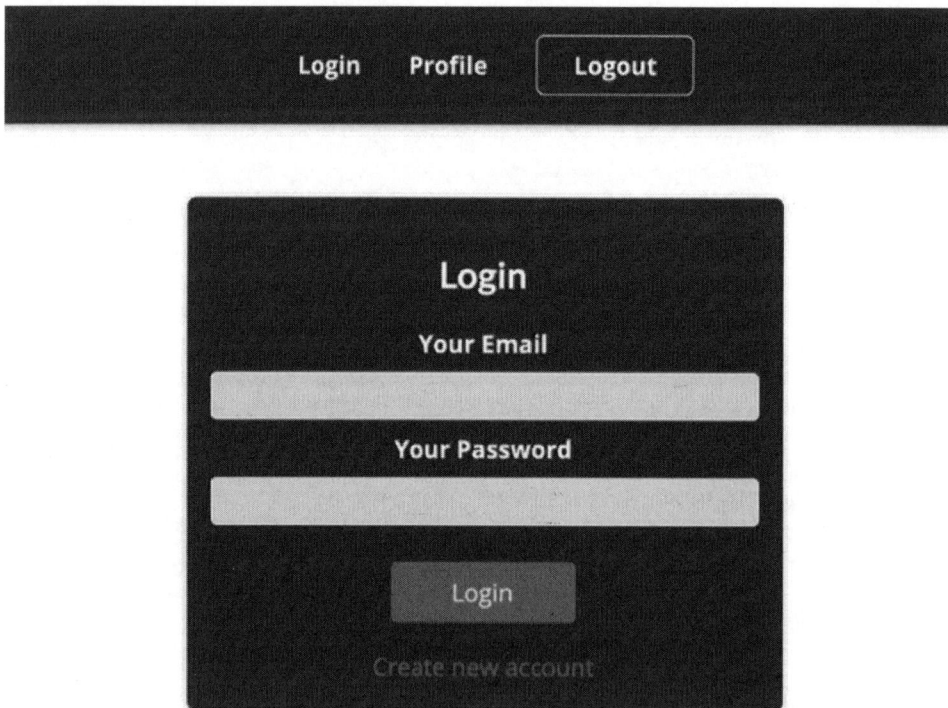

Figure 2.1 An example authentication screen with navigation bar.

If you look at this example page, you might be able to identify various building blocks (i.e., components). Some of these components are even reused.

In the header with the navigation bar you will find the following components:

- The navigation items (**Login** and **Profile**)
- The **Logout** button

Below this, the main section displays the following:

- The container that contains the authentication form
- The input elements
- The confirmation button
- A link to switch to the **New Account** page

Please note that some components are nested inside other components—i.e., components are also made up of other components. That's a key feature of React and similar libraries.

WHY COMPONENTS?

No matter which web page you look at, they are all made up of building blocks like this. It's not a React-specific concept or idea. Indeed, HTML itself "thinks" in components if you take a closer look. You have elements like **<img>**, **<header>**, **<nav>**, etc. And you combine these elements to describe and structure your website content.

But React **embraces** this idea of breaking a web page into reusable building blocks because this is an approach that allows developers to work on small, manageable chunks of code. It's easier and more maintainable than working on a single, huge HTML (or React code) file.

That's why other libraries—both frontend libraries like React or Angular as well as backend libraries and templating engines like **EJS (Embedded JavaScript templates)**—also embrace components (though the names might differ, you also find *"partials"* or *"includes"* as common names).

> **NOTE**
>
> EJS is a popular templating engine for JavaScript. It's especially popular for backend web development with NodeJS.

When working with React, it's especially important to keep your code manageable and work with small, reusable components because React components are not just collections of HTML code. Instead, a React component also encapsulates JavaScript logic and often also CSS styling. For complex user interfaces, the combination of markup (JSX), logic (JavaScript) and styling (CSS) could quickly lead to large chunks of code, thus making it difficult to maintain that code. Think of a large HTML file that also includes JavaScript and CSS code. Working in such a code file wouldn't be a lot of fun.

To make a long story short, when working in a React project, you will work with lots of components. You will split your code into small, manageable building blocks and then combine these components to form the overall user interface. It's a key feature of React.

> **NOTE**
>
> When working with React, you should embrace this idea of working with components. But technically, they're optional. You could, theoretically, build very complex web pages with one single component alone. It would not be much fun, and it would not be practical, but it would technically be possible without any issues.

THE ANATOMY OF A COMPONENT

Components are important. But what exactly does a React component look like? How do you write React components on your own?

Here's an example component:

```
import { useState } from 'react';

function SubmitButton() {
  const [isSubmitted, setIsSubmitted] = useState(false);

  function submitHandler() {
    setIsSubmitted(true);
  };

  return (
    <button onClick={submitHandler}>
      { isSubmitted ? 'Loading...' : 'Submit' }
```

```
    </button>
  );
};


export default SubmitButton;
```

Typically, you would store a code snippet like this in a separate file (e.g., a file named **SubmitButton.js**, stored inside a **/components** folder which in turn resides in the **/src** folder of your React project) and import it into other component files that need this component. For example, the following component imports the component defined above and uses it in its **return** statement to output the **SubmitButton** component:

```
import SubmitButton from './submit-button';


function AuthForm() {
  return (
    <form>
      <input type="text" />
      <SubmitButton />
    </form>
  );
};


export default AuthForm;
```

The import statements you see in these examples are standard JavaScript import statements with one extra twist: the file extension (**.js** in this case) can be omitted in most React projects (like the one created via **npx create-react-app**). **import** and **export** are standard JavaScript keywords that help with splitting related code across multiple files. Things like variables, constants, classes, or functions can be exported via **export** or **export default** so that they can then be used in other files after **import**ing them there.

> **NOTE**
>
> If the concept of splitting code into multiple files and using **import** and **export** is brand-new to you, you might want to dive into more basic JavaScript resources on this topic first. For example, MDN has an excellent article that explains the fundamentals, which you can find at https://developer.mozilla.org/en-US/docs/Web/JavaScript/Guide/Modules.

Of course, the components shown in these examples are highly simplified and also contain features that you haven't learned about yet (e.g. `useState()`). But the general idea of having standalone building blocks that can be combined should be clear.

When working with React, there are two alternative ways to define components:

Class-based components (or "**class components**"): components defined via the `class` keyword

Functional components (or "**function components**"): components that are defined via regular JavaScript functions

In all the examples covered in this book thus far, components were built as JavaScript functions. As a React developer, you have to use one of these two approaches as React expects components to be functions or classes.

> **NOTE**
>
> Until late 2018, you had to use class-based components for certain kinds of tasks—specifically for components that use state internally. (State will be covered later in the book). However, in late 2018, a new concept was introduced: **React Hooks**. This allows you to perform all operations and tasks with functional components. Consequently, class-based components are on their way out and not covered in this book.

In the examples above, there are a couple of other noteworthy things:

- The component functions carry capitalized names (e.g., `SubmitButton`)
- Inside the component functions, other "inner" functions can be defined (e.g., `submitHandler`)
- The component functions return *HTML-like* code (JSX code)
- Features like `useState()` can be used inside the component functions
- The component functions are exported (via `export default`)
- Certain features (like `useState` or the custom component, `SubmitButton`) are imported via the `import` keyword

The following sections will take a closer look at these different concepts that make up components and their code.

WHAT EXACTLY ARE COMPONENT FUNCTIONS?

In React, components are functions (or classes, but as mentioned above, those aren't relevant anymore).

A function is a regular JavaScript construct, not a React-specific concept. This is important to note. React is a JavaScript library and therefore **uses JavaScript features** (like functions); React is **not a brand-new programming language**.

When working with React, regular JavaScript functions can be used to encapsulate HTML (or, to be more precise, JSX) code and JavaScript logic that belongs to that markup code. However, it depends on the code you write in a function, whether it qualifies to be treated as a React component or not. For example, in the code snippets above, the **submitHandler** function is also a regular JavaScript function, but it's not a React component. The following example shows another regular JavaScript function that doesn't qualify as a React component:

```
function calculate(a, b) {
  return {sum: a + b};
};
```

Indeed, a function will be treated as a component and can therefore be used like a HTML element in JSX code if it returns a **renderable** value (typically JSX code). This is very important. You can only use a function as a React component in JSX code if it is a function that returns something that can be rendered by React. The returned value technically doesn't have to be JSX code, but in most cases, it will be. You will see an example for non-JSX code being returned later in the book, in *Chapter 7, Portals and Refs*.

In the code snippet where functions named **SubmitButton** and **AuthForm** were defined, those two functions qualified as React components because they both returned JSX code (which is code that can be rendered by React, making it renderable). Once a function qualifies as a React component, it can be used like a HTML element inside of JSX code, just as **<SubmitButton />** was used like a (self-closing) HTML element.

When working with vanilla JavaScript, you of course typically call functions to execute them. With functional components, that's different. React calls these functions on your behalf, and therefore, as a developer, you use them like HTML elements inside of this JSX code.

> ### NOTE
>
> When referring to renderable values, it is worth noting that by far the most common value type being returned or used is indeed JSX code—i.e., markup defined via JSX. This should make sense because, with JSX, you can define the HTML-like structure of your content and user interface.
>
> But besides JSX markup, there are a couple of other key values that also qualify as renderable and therefore could be returned by custom components (instead of JSX code). Most notably, you can also return strings or numbers as well as arrays that hold JSX elements or strings or numbers.

WHAT DOES REACT DO WITH ALL THESE COMPONENTS?

If you follow the trail of all components and their **import + export** statements to the top, you will find a **root.render(...)** instruction in the main entry script of the React project. Typically, this main entry script can be found in the index.js file, located in the project's **src/** folder. This **render()** method, which is provided by the React library (to be precise, by the **react-dom** package), takes a snippet of JSX code and interprets and executes it for you.

The complete snippet you find in the root entry file (**index.js**) typically looks like this:

```
import React from 'react';
import ReactDOM from 'react-dom/client';

import './index.css';
import App from './App';

const root = ReactDOM.createRoot(document.getElementById('root'));
root.render(<App />);
```

The exact code you find in your new React project might look slightly different.

It may, for instance, include an extra **<StrictMode>** element that's wrapped around **<App>**. **<StrictMode>** turns on extra checks that can help catch subtle bugs in your React code. But it can also lead to confusing behavior and unexpected error messages, especially when experimenting with React or learning React. As this book is primarily interested in the coverage of React core features and key concepts, **<StrictMode>** will not be covered.

To follow along smoothly then, cleaning up a newly created **index.js** file to look like the code snippet above is a good idea.

The **createRoot()** method instructs React to create a new **entry point** which will be used to inject the generated user interface into the actual HTML document that will be served to website visitors. The argument passed to **createRoot()** therefore is a pointer to a DOM element that can be found in **index.html**—the single page that will be served to website visitors.

In many cases, **document.getElementById('root')** is used as an argument. This built-in vanilla JavaScript method yields a reference to a DOM element that is already part of the **index.html** document. Therefore, as a developer, you must ensure that such an element with the provided **id** attribute value (**root**, in this example) exists in the HTML file into which the React app script is loaded. In a default React project created via **npx create-react-app**, this will be the case. You can find a **<div id="root">** element in the **index.html** file in the **public/** folder.

This **index.html** file is a relatively empty file which only acts as a shell for the React app. React just needs an entry point (defined via **createRoot()**) which will be used to attach the generated user interface to the displayed website. The HTML file and its content therefore do not directly define the website content. Instead, the file just serves as a starting point for the React application, allowing React to then take over and control the actual user interface.

Once the root entry point has been defined, a method called **render()** can be called on the root object created via **createRoot()**:

```
root.render(<App />);
```

This **render()** method tells React which content (i.e., which React component) should be injected into that root entry point. In most React apps, this is a component called **App**. React will then generate appropriate DOM-manipulating instructions to reflect the markup defined via JSX in the **App** component on the actual webpage.

This **App** component is a component function that is imported from some other file. In a default React project, the **App** component function is defined and exported in an **App.js** file which is also located in the **src/** folder.

This component, which is handed to **render()** (**<App />**, typically), is also called the **root component** of the React app. It's the main component that is rendered to the DOM. All other components are nested in the JSX code of that **App** component or the JSX code of even more nested descendent components. You can think of all these components building up a tree of components which is evaluated by React and translated into actual DOM-manipulating instructions.

> ### NOTE
>
> As mentioned in the previous chapter, React can be used on various platforms. With the **react-native** package, it could be used to build native mobile apps for iOS and Android. The **react-dom** package which provides the **createRoot()** method (and therefore implicitly the **render()** method) is focused on the browser. It provides the "bridge" between React's capabilities and the browser instructions that are required to bring the UI (described via JSX and React components) to life in the browser. If you would build for different platforms, replacements for **ReactDOM.createRoot()** and **render()** are required (and of course such alternatives do exist).

Either way, no matter whether you use a component function like an HTML element inside of JSX code of other components or use it like an HTML element that's passed as an argument to the **render()** method, React takes care of interpreting and executing the component function on your behalf.

Of course, this is not a new concept. In JavaScript, functions are first-class objects, which means that you can pass functions as arguments to other functions. This is basically what happens here, just with the extra twist of using this JSX syntax which is not a default JavaScript feature.

React executes these component functions for you and translates the returned JSX code into DOM instructions. To be precise, React traverses the returned JSX code and dives into any other custom components that might be used in that JSX code until it ends up with JSX code that is only made up of native, built-in HTML elements (technically, it's not really HTML, but that will be discussed later in this chapter).

Take these two components as an example:

```
function Greeting() {
  return <p>Welcome to this book!</p>;
};

function App() {
  return (
    <div>
      <h2>Hello World!</h2>
      <Greeting />
    </div>
  );
};


const root = ReactDOM.createRoot(document.getElementById('app'));
root.render(<App />);
```

The **App** component uses the **Greeting** component inside its JSX code. React will traverse the entire JSX markup structure and derive this final JSX code:

```
root.render((
  <div>
    <h2>Hello World!</h2>
    <p>Welcome to this book!</p>
  </div>
), document.getElementById('app'));
```

And this code would instruct React and ReactDOM to perform the following DOM operations:

- Create a **<div>** element

- Inside that **<div>**, create two child elements: **<h2>** and **<p>**

- Set the text content of the **<h2>** element to **'Hello World!'**

- Set the text content of the **<p>** element to **'Welcome to this book!'**

- Insert the **<div>** with its children into the already-existing DOM element which has the **id 'app'**

This is a bit simplified, but you can think of React handling components and JSX code as described above.

> **NOTE**
>
> React doesn't actually work with JSX code internally. It's just easier to use as a developer. Later, in this chapter, you will learn what JSX code gets transformed to and how the actual code, with which React works, looks like.

BUILT-IN COMPONENTS

As shown in the earlier examples, you can create your own, custom components by creating functions that return JSX code. And indeed, that's one of the main things you will do all the time as a React developer: you create component functions. Lots of component functions.

But ultimately, if you would merge all JSX code into just one big snippet of JSX code, as shown in the last example above, you would end up with a chunk of JSX code that includes only standard HTML elements like **<div>**, **<h2>**, **<p>**, and so on.

When using React, you don't create brand-new HTML elements that the browser would be able to display and handle. Instead, you create components that **only work inside the React environment**. Before they reach the browser, they have been evaluated by React and "translated" into DOM-manipulating JavaScript instructions (like **document.append(...)**).

But keep in mind that all this JSX code is a feature that's not part of the JavaScript language itself. It's basically **syntactical sugar** (i.e., a simplification regarding the code syntax) provided by the React library and the project setup you're using to write React code. Therefore, elements like **<div>**, when used in JSX code, also **aren't normal HTML elements** because you **don't write HTML code**. It might look like that, but it's inside a **.js** file and it's not HTML markup. Instead, it's this special JSX code. It is important to keep this in mind.

Therefore, these **<div>** and **<h2>** elements you see in all these examples are also just React components in the end. But they are not components built by you, but instead provided by React (or to be precise, by ReactDOM).

When working with React, you therefore always end up with these primitives—these built-in component functions that are later translated to browser instructions that generate and append or remove normal DOM elements. The idea behind building custom components is to group these elements together such that you end up with reusable building blocks that can be used to build the overall UI. But, in the end, this UI is made up of regular HTML elements.

> **NOTE**
>
> Depending on your level of frontend web development knowledge, you might have heard about a web feature called **Web Components**. The idea behind this feature is that you can indeed build brand-new HTML elements with vanilla JavaScript.
>
> As mentioned, React does not pick up this feature; you don't build new custom HTML elements with React.

NAMING CONVENTIONS

All component functions that you can find in this book carry names like **SubmitButton**, **AuthForm**, or **Greeting**.

You can generally name your React functions however you want—at least in the file where you are defining them. But it is a common convention to use the **PascalCase** naming convention, wherein the first character is uppercase and multiple words are grouped into one single word (**SubmitButton** instead of **Submit Button**), where every "subword" then starts with another uppercase character.

In the place where you define your component function, it is only a naming convention, not a hard rule. However, it **is** a requirement in the place where you **use** the component functions—i.e., in the JSX code where you embed your own custom components.

You can't use your own custom component like this:

```
<greeting />
```

React forces you to use an uppercase starting character for your own custom component names, when using them in JSX code. This rule exists to give React a clear and easy way of telling custom components apart from built-in components like **<div>** etc. React only needs to look at the starting character to determine whether it's a built-in element or a custom component.

Besides the names of the actual component functions, it is also important to understand file naming conventions. Custom components are typically stored in separate files that live inside a **src/components/** folder. However, this is not a hard rule. The exact placement as well as folder name is up to you, but it should be somewhere inside the **src/** folder. Using a folder named **components/** is the standard though.

Where it is the standard to use **PascalCase** for the component functions, there is no general default regarding the file names. Some developers prefer **PascalCase** for file names as well; and, indeed, in brand-new React projects, created as described in this book, the **App** component can be found inside a file named **App.js**. Nonetheless, you will also encounter many React projects where components are stored in files that follow the **kebap-case** naming convention. (All-lowercase, multiple words are combined into a single word via a dash.) With this convention, component functions could be stored in files named **submit-button.js**, for example.

Ultimately, it is up to you (and your team) which file naming convention you want to follow. In this book, **PascalCase** will be used for file names.

JSX VS HTML VS VANILLA JAVASCRIPT

As mentioned above, React projects typically contain lots of JSX code. Most custom components will return JSX code snippets. You can see this in all the examples shared thus far, and you will see in basically every React project you will explore, no matter whether you are using React for the browser or for other platforms like **react-native**.

But what exactly is this JSX code? How is it different from HTML? And how is it related to vanilla JavaScript?

JSX is a feature that's not part of vanilla JavaScript. What can be confusing, though, is that it's also not directly part of the React library.

Instead, JSX is syntactical sugar that is provided by the build workflow that's part of the overall React project. When you start the development web server via **npm start** or build the React app for production (i.e., for deployment) via **npm run build**, you kick off a process that transforms this JSX code back to regular JavaScript instructions. As a developer, you don't see those final instructions but React, the library, actually receives and evaluates them.

So, what does the JSX code get transformed to?

In the end, all JSX snippets get transformed into calls to the **React.createElement(…)** method.

Here's a concrete example:

```
function Greeting() {
  return <p>Hello World!</p>;
};
```

The JSX code returned by this component would be translated into the following vanilla JavaScript code:

```
function Greeting() {
  return React.createElement('p', {}, 'Hello World!');
};
```

createElement() is a method built into the React library. It instructs React to create a paragraph element with **'Hello World!'** as child content (i.e., as inner, nested content). This paragraph element is then created internally first (via a concept called **virtual DOM**, which will be discussed later in the book, in *Chapter 9*, *Behind The Scenes Of React and Optimization Opportunities*). Thereafter, once all elements for all JSX elements have been created, the virtual DOM is translated into real DOM-manipulating instructions that are executed by the browser.

> **NOTE**
>
> It has been mentioned before that React (in the browser) is actually a combination of two packages: **react** and **react-dom**.
>
> With the introduction of **React.createElement(…)**, it's now easier to explain how these two packages work together: React creates this virtual DOM internally and then passes it to the **react-dom** package. This package then generates the actual DOM-manipulating instructions that must be executed in order to update the web page such that the desired user interface is displayed there.
>
> As mentioned, this will be covered in greater detail in *Chapter 9*.

The middle parameter value (**{ }**, in the example) is a JavaScript object that may contain extra configuration for the element that is to be created.

Here's an example where this middle argument becomes important:

```
function Advertisement() {
  return <a href="https://my-website.com">Visit my website</a>;
};
```

This would be transformed to the following:

```
function Advertisement() {
  return React.createElement(
    'a',
    { href: ' https://my-website.com ' },
    'Visit my website'
  );
};
```

The last argument that's passed to **React.createElement(...)** is the child content of the element—i.e., the content that should be between the element's opening and closing tags. For nested JSX elements, nested **React.createElement(...)** calls would be produced:

```
function Alert() {
  return (
    <div>
      <h2>This is an alert!</h2>
    </div>
  );
};
```

This would be transformed like this:

```
function Alert() {
  return React.createElement(
    'div', {}, React.createElement('h2', {}, 'This is an alert!')
  );
};
```

USING REACT WITHOUT JSX

Since all JSX code gets transformed to these native JavaScript method calls anyways, you can actually build React apps and user interfaces with React without using JSX.

You can skip JSX entirely if you want to. Instead of writing JSX code in your components and all the places where JSX is expected, you can simply call **React. createElement(...)**.

For example, the following two snippets will produce exactly the same user interface in the browser:

```
function App() {
  return (
    <p>Please visit my <a href="https://my-blog-site.com">Blog</a></p>
  );
};
```

The preceding snippet will ultimately be the same as the following:

```
function App() {
  return React.createElement(
    'p',
    {},
    [
      'Please visit my ',
      React.createElement(
        'a',
        { href: 'https://my-blog-site.com' },
        'Blog'
      )
    ]
  );
};
```

Of course, it's a different question whether you would want to do this. As you can see in this example, it's way more cumbersome to rely on **React.createElement(...)** only. You end up writing a lot more code and deeply nested element structures will lead to code that can become almost impossible to read.

That's why, typically, React developers do use JSX. It's a great feature that makes building user interfaces with React way more enjoyable. But it is important to understand that it's neither HTML nor a vanilla JavaScript feature, but that it instead is some syntactical sugar that gets transformed to these **React.createElement(...)** calls behind the scenes.

JSX ELEMENTS ARE TREATED LIKE REGULAR JAVASCRIPT VALUES

Because JSX is just syntactical sugar that gets transformed to **React. createElement()** calls, there are a couple of noteworthy concepts and rules you should be aware of:

- JSX elements are just **regular JavaScript values** (functions, to be precise) in the end

- The same rules that apply to all JavaScript values also apply to JSX elements

- As a result, in a place, where only one value is expected (e.g., after the **return** keyword), you must only have one JSX element

This code would cause an error:

```
function App() {
  return (
    <p>Hello World!</p>
    <p>Let's learn React!</p>
  );
};
```

The code might look valid at first, but it's actually incorrect. In this example, you would return two values instead of just one. That is not allowed in JavaScript.

For example, the following non-React code would also be invalid:

```
function calculate(a, b) {
  return (
    a + b
    a - b
  );
};
```

You can't return more than one value. No matter how you write it.

Of course, you can return an array or an object though. For example, this code would be valid:

```
function calculate(a, b) {
  return [
    a + b,
    a - b
  ];
};
```

It would be valid because you only return one value: an array. This array than contains multiple values as arrays typically do. That would be fine and the same would be the case if you used JSX code:

```
function App() {
  return [
    <p>Hello World!</p>,
    <p>Let's learn React!</p>
  ];
};
```

This kind of code would be allowed since you are returning one array with two elements inside of it. The two elements are JSX elements in this case, but as mentioned earlier, JSX elements are just regular JavaScript values. Thus, you can use them anywhere, where values would be expected.

When working with JSX, you won't see this array approach too often though—simply because it can become annoying to remember wrapping JSX elements via square brackets. It also looks less like HTML which kind of defeats the purpose and core idea behind JSX (it was invented to allow developers to write HTML code inside of JavaScript files).

Instead, if sibling elements are required, as in these examples, a special kind of wrapping component is used: a React **fragment**. That's a built-in component that serves the purpose of allowing you to return or define sibling JSX elements.

```
function App() {
  return (
    <>
      <p>Hello World!</p>
      <p>Let's learn React!</p>
    </>
  );
};
```

This special **<>**...**</>** element is available in most modern React projects (like the one that is created via **npx create-react-app**), and you can think of it wrapping your JSX elements with an array behind the scenes. Alternatively, you can also use **<React.Fragment>**...**</React.Fragment>**. This built-in component is always available.

The parentheses (**()**) that are wrapped around the JSX code in all these examples are required to allow for nice multiline formatting. Technically, you could put all your JSX code into one single line, but that would be pretty unreadable. In order to split the JSX elements across multiple lines, just as you typically do with regular HTML code in **.html** files, you need those parentheses; they tell JavaScript where the returned value starts and ends.

Since JSX elements are regular JavaScript values (after being translated to **React. createElement(**...**)** calls, at least), you can also use JSX elements in all the places where values can be used.

Thus far, that has been the case for all these **return** statements, but you can also store JSX elements in variables or pass them as arguments to other functions.

```
function App() {
  const content = <p>Stored in a variable!</p>; // this works!
  return content;
};
```

This will be important once you dive into slightly more advanced concepts like conditional or repeated content—something that will be covered later in the book, of course.

JSX ELEMENTS MUST BE SELF-CLOSING

Another important rule related to JSX elements is that they must be self-closing if there is no content between the opening and closing tags.

```
function App() {
  return <img src="some-image.png" />;
};
```

In regular HTML, you would not need that forward backslash at the end. Instead, regular HTML supports void elements (i.e., **<img src="**...**">**). You can add that forward slash there as well, but it's not mandatory.

When working with JSX, these forward slashes are mandatory, if your element doesn't contain any child content.

OUTPUTTING DYNAMIC CONTENT

Thus far, in all these examples, the content that was returned was static. It was content like **`<p>Hello World!</p>`**—which of course is content that never changes. It will always output a paragraph that says, **`'Hello World!'`**.

At this point in the book, you don't yet have any tools to make the content more dynamic. To be precise, React requires that state concept (which will be covered in a later chapter) to change the content that is displayed (e.g. upon user input or some other event).

Nonetheless, since this chapter is about JSX, it is worth diving into the syntax for outputting dynamic content, even though it's not yet dynamic.

```
function App() {
  const userName = 'Max';
  return <p>Hi, my name is {userName}!</p>;
};
```

This example technically still produces static output since **`userName`** never changes; but you can already see the syntax for outputting dynamic content as part of the JSX code. You use opening and closing curly braces (**`{...}`**) with a JavaScript expression (like the name of a variable or constant, as is the case here) between those braces.

You can put any valid JavaScript expression between those curly braces. For example, you can also call a function (e.g. **`{getMyName()}`**) or do simple inline calculations (e.g. **`{1 + 1}`**).

You can't add complex statements like loops or **`if`**-statements between those curly braces though. Again, standard JavaScript rules apply. You output a (potentially) dynamic value, and therefore, anything that produces a single value is allowed in that place.

WHEN SHOULD YOU SPLIT COMPONENTS?

As you work with React and learn more and more about it, and as you dive into more challenging React projects, you will most likely come up with one very common question: "*When should I split a single React component into multiple, separate components?*".

Because, as mentioned earlier in this chapter, React is all about components, and it is therefore very common to have dozens, hundreds or even thousands of React components in a single React project.

When it comes to splitting a single React component into multiple smaller components, there is no hard rule you must follow. As mentioned earlier, you could put all your UI code into one single, large component. Alternatively, you could create a separate custom component for every single HTML element and piece of content that you have in your UI. Both approaches are probably not that great. Instead, a good rule of thumb is to create a separate React component for every **data entity** that can be identified.

For example, if you're outputting a "to do" list, you could identify two main entities: the individual to-do item and the overall list. In this case, it could make sense to create two separate components instead of writing one bigger component.

The advantage of splitting your code into multiple components is that the individual components stay manageable because there's less code per component and component file.

However, when it comes to splitting components into multiple components, a new problem arises: how do you make your components reusable and configurable?

```
import Todo from './todo';

function TodoList() {
  return (
    <ul>
      <Todo />
      <Todo />
    </ul>
  );
};
```

In this example, all "to-dos" would be the same because we use the same **<Todo />** component which can't be configured. You might want to make it configurable by either adding custom attributes (**<Todo text="Learn React!" />**) or by passing content between the opening and closing tags (**<Todo>Learn React!</Todo>**).

And, of course, React supports this. In the next course chapter, you will learn about a key concept called **props** which allows you to make your components configurable like this.

SUMMARY AND KEY TAKEAWAYS

- React embraces **components**: reusable building blocks that are combined to define the final user interface

- Components must return **renderable** content, typically JSX code which defines the HTML code that should be produced in the end

- React provides a lot of built-in components: besides special components like `<>...</>` you get components for all standard HTML elements

- To allow React to tell custom components apart from built-in components, custom component names have to start with capital characters, when being used inside of JSX code (typically, `PascalCase` naming is used therefore)

- JSX is neither HTML nor a standard JavaScript feature, instead it's **syntactical sugar** provided by build workflows that are part of all React projects

- You could replace JSX code with `React.createElement(...)` calls; but since this leads to significantly more unreadable code, it's typically avoided.

- When using JSX elements, you must not have sibling elements in places where single values are expected (e.g., directly after the `return` keyword)

- JSX elements must always be self-closing, if there is no content between the opening and closing tags

- Dynamic content can be output via curly braces (e.g., `<p>{someText}</p>`)

- In most React projects, you split your UI code across dozens or hundreds of components which are then exported and imported in order to be combined again

WHAT'S NEXT?

In this chapter, you learned a lot about components and JSX. The next chapter builds up on this key knowledge and explains how you can make components reusable by making them configurable.

Before you continue, you can also practice what you learned up this point by going through the questions and exercises below.

TEST YOUR KNOWLEDGE!

Test your knowledge about the concepts covered in this chapter by answering the below questions. You can then compare your answers to example answers that can be found here: https://packt.link/iSHGL.

1. What's the idea behind using components?

2. How can you create a React component?

3. What turns a regular function into a React component function?

4. Which core rules should you keep in mind regarding JSX elements?

5. How is JSX code handled by React and ReactDOM?

APPLY WHAT YOU LEARNED

With this and the previous chapter, you have all the knowledge you need to create a React project and populate it with some first, basic components.

Below, you'll find your first two activities for this book:

ACTIVITY 2.1: CREATING A REACT APP TO PRESENT YOURSELF

Suppose you are creating your personal portfolio page, and as part of that page, you want to output some basic information about yourself (e.g., your name or age). You could use React and build a React component that outputs this kind of information, as outlined in the following activity.

The aim is to create a React app as you learned it in the previous chapter (i.e., create it via **npx create-react-app**, run **npm start** to start the development server) and edit the **App.js** file such that you output some basic information about yourself. You could, for example output your full name, address, job title or other kinds of information. In the end, it is up to you what content you want to output and which HTML elements you choose.

The idea behind this first exercise is that you practice project creation and working with JSX code.

The steps are as follows:

1. Create a new React project via **npx create-react-app**.

2. Edit the App.js file in the **/src folder** of the created project and return JSX code with any HTML elements of your choice to output basic information about yourself.

You should get output like this in the end:

Hi, this is me - Max!

Right now, I am 32 years old and I live in Munich.

My full name is Maximilian Schwarzmüller and I am a web developer as well as top-rated, bestselling online course instructor.

Figure 2.2: The final activity result—some user information being output on the screen.

> **NOTE**
>
> The solution to this activity can be found on page 450.

ACTIVITY 2.2: CREATING A REACT APP TO LOG YOUR GOALS FOR THIS BOOK

Suppose you are adding a new section to your portfolio site, where you plan to track your learning progress. As part of this page, you plan to define and output your main goals for this book (e.g., *"Learn about key React features"*, *"Do all the exercises"* etc.).

The aim of this activity is to create another new React project in which you add **multiple new components**. Each goal will be represented by a separate component, and all these goal components will be grouped together into another component that lists all main goals. In addition, you can add an extra header component that contains the main title for the webpage.

The steps to complete this activity are as follows:

1. Create a new React project via **npx create-react-app**.

2. Inside the new project, create a **components** folder which contains multiple component files (for the individual goals as well as for the list of goals and the page header).

3. Inside the different component files, define and export multiple component functions (**FirstGoal**, **SecondGoal**, **ThirdGoal**, etc.) for the different goals (one component per file).

4. Also, define one component for the overall list of goals (**GoalList**) and another component for the page header (**Header**).

5. In the individual goal components, return JSX code with the goal text and a fitting HTML element structure to hold this content.

6. In the **GoalList** component, import and output the individual goal components.

7. Import and output the **GoalList** and **Header** components in the root App component (replace the existing JSX code).

You should get the following output in the end:

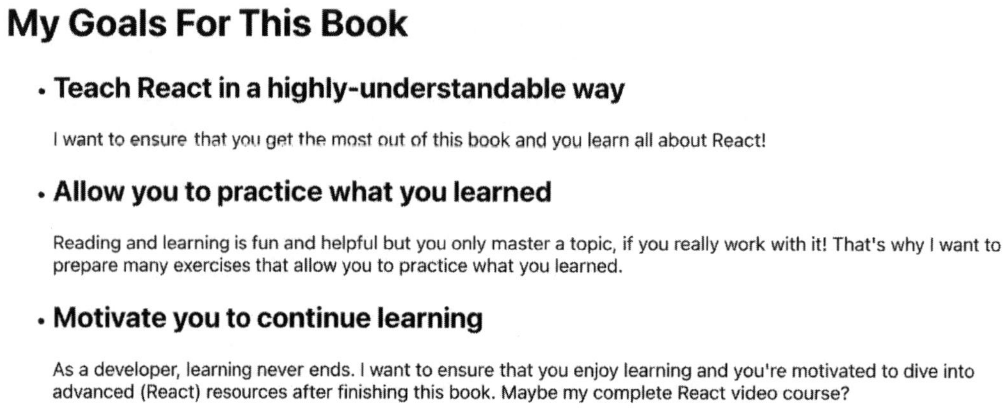

My Goals For This Book

• Teach React in a highly-understandable way

I want to ensure that you get the most out of this book and you learn all about React!

• Allow you to practice what you learned

Reading and learning is fun and helpful but you only master a topic, if you really work with it! That's why I want to prepare many exercises that allow you to practice what you learned.

• Motivate you to continue learning

As a developer, learning never ends. I want to ensure that you enjoy learning and you're motivated to dive into advanced (React) resources after finishing this book. Maybe my complete React video course?

Figure 2.3: The final page output, showing a list of goals.

> **NOTE**
>
> The solution to this activity can be found on page 451.

3

COMPONENTS AND PROPS

LEARNING OBJECTIVES

By the end of this chapter, you will be able to do the following:

- Build reusable React components

- Utilize a concept called **Props** to make components configurable

- Build flexible user interfaces by combining components with props

INTRODUCTION

In the previous chapter, you learned about the key building block of any React-based user interface: **components**. You learned why components matter, how they are used, and how you may build components yourself.

You also learned about JSX, which is the HTML-like markup that's typically returned by component functions. It's this markup that defines what should be rendered on the final web page (in other words, which HTML markup should end up on the final web page that is being served to visitors).

NOT THERE YET

But up to this point, those components haven't been too useful. While you could use them to split your web page content into smaller building blocks, the actual reusability of these components was pretty limited. For example, every course goal that you might have as part of an overall course goal list would go into its own component (if you decided to split your web page content into multiple components in the first place).

If you think about it, this isn't too helpful: it would be much better if different list items could share one common component and you would just configure that one component with different content or attributes—just like how HTML works.

When writing plain HTML code and describing content with it, you use reusable HTML elements and configure them with different content or attributes. For example, you have one **<a>** HTML element, but thanks to the **href** attribute and the element child content, you can build an endless amount of different anchor elements that point at different resources, as in the following snippets:

```
<a href="https://google.com">Use Google</a>
<a href="https://academind.com">Browse Free Tutorials</a>
```

These two elements use the exact same HTML element (**<a>**) but lead to totally different links that would end up on the web page (pointing to two totally different websites).

To fully unlock the potential of React components, it would therefore be very useful if you could configure them just like regular HTML elements. And it turns out that you can do exactly that—with another key React concept called **props**.

USING PROPS IN COMPONENTS

How do you use props in your components? And when do you need them?

The second question will be answered in greater detail a little bit later. For the moment, it's enough to know that you typically will have some components that are reusable that therefore need props and some components that are unique that might not need props.

The "how" part is the more important part at this point.

And this part can be split into two complementary problems:

1. Passing props to components

2. Consuming props in a component

PASSING PROPS TO COMPONENTS

How would you expect props and component configurability to work if you were to design React from the ground up?

Of course, there would be a broad variety of possible solutions, but there is one great role model that can be considered: HTML. As mentioned above, when working with HTML, you pass content and configuration either between element tags or via attributes.

And fortunately, React components work just like HTML elements when it comes to configuring them. Props are simply passed as attributes (to your component) or as child data between component tags, and you can also mix both approaches:

- `<Product id="abc1" price="12.99" />`

- `<FancyLink target="https://some-website.com">Click me</FancyLink>`

For this reason, configuring components is quite straightforward—at least, if you look at them from the consumer's angle (in other words, at how you use them in JSX).

But what about defining component functions? How are props handled in those functions?

CONSUMING PROPS IN A COMPONENT

Imagine you're building a **GoalItem** component that is responsible for outputting a single goal item (for example, a course goal or project goal) that will be part of an overall goals list.

The parent component JSX markup could look like this:

```
<ul>
  <GoalItem />
  <GoalItem />
  <GoalItem />
</ul>
```

Inside **GoalItem**, the goal (no pun intended) would be to accept different goal titles so that the same component (**GoalItem**) can be used to output these different titles as part of the final list that's displayed to website visitors. Maybe the component should also accept another piece of data (for example, a unique ID that is used internally).

```
That's how the GoalItem component could be used in JSX, as in the
following example:
<ul>
  <GoalItem id="g1" title="Finish the book!" />
  <GoalItem id="g2" title="Learn all about React!" />
</ul>
```

Inside the **GoalItem** component function, the plan would probably be to output dynamic content (in other words, the data received via props) like this:

```
function GoalItem() {
  return <li>{title} (ID: {id})</li>;
}
```

But this component function would not work. It has a problem: **title** and **id** are never defined inside that component function. This code would therefore cause an error because you're using a variable that wasn't defined.

Of course, it shouldn't be defined inside the **GoalItem** component, though, because the idea was to make the **GoalItem** component reusable and receive different **title** and **id** values *from outside the component* (i.e., from the component that renders the list of **<GoalItem>** components).

React provides a solution for this problem: a special parameter value that will be passed into every component function automatically by React. This is a special parameter that contains the extra configuration data that is set on the component in JSX code, called the **props** parameter.

The preceding component function could (and should) be rewritten like this:

```
function GoalItem(props) {
  return <li>{props.title} (ID: {props.id})</li>;
}
```

The name of the parameter (**props**) is up to you, but using **props** as a name is a convention because the overall concept is called **props**.

To understand this concept, it is important to keep in mind that these component functions are not called by you somewhere else in your code, but that instead, React will call these functions on your behalf. And since React calls these functions, it can pass extra arguments into the functions when calling them.

This **props** argument is indeed such an extra argument. React will pass it into every component function, irrespective of whether you defined it as an extra parameter in the component function definition. Though, if you didn't define that **props** parameter in a component function, you, of course, won't be able to work with the props data in that component.

This automatically provided **props** argument will always contain an object (because React passes an object as a value for this argument), and the properties of this object will be the "attributes" you added to your component inside the JSX code where the component is used.

That's why in this **GoalItem** component example, custom data can be passed via attributes (**<GoalItem id="g1"** ... **/>**) and consumed via the **props** object and its properties (**<li>{props.title}</li>**).

COMPONENTS, PROPS, AND REUSABILITY

Thanks to this props concept, components become *actually* reusable, instead of just being *theoretically* reusable.

Outputting three **<GoalItem>** components without any extra configuration could only render the same goal three times since the goal text (and any other data you might need) would have to be hardcoded into the component function.

By using props as described above, the same component can be used multiple times with different configurations. That allows you to define some general markup structure and logic once (in the component function) but then use it as often as needed with different configurations.

And if that sounds familiar, that is indeed exactly the same idea as for regular JavaScript (or any other programming language) functions. You define logic once, and you can then call it multiple times with different inputs to receive different results. It's the same for components—at least when embracing this props concept.

THE SPECIAL "CHILDREN" PROP

It was mentioned before that React passes this **props** object automatically into component functions. That is the case, and, as described, this object contains all the attributes you set on the component (in JSX) as properties.

But React does not just package your attributes into this object; it also adds another extra property into the props object: the special **children** property (a built-in property whose name is fixed, meaning you can't change it).

The **children** property holds a very important piece of data: the content you might have provided between the component's opening and closing tags.

Thus far, in the examples shown above, the components were mostly self-closing. **<GoalItem id="..." title="..." />** holds no content between the component tags. All the data is passed into the component via attributes.

There is nothing wrong with this approach. You can configure your components with attributes only. But for some pieces of data and some components, it might make more sense and be more logical to actually stick to regular HTML conventions and pass that data between the component tags instead. And the **GoalItem** component is actually a great example.

Which approach looks more intuitive?

1. **<GoalItem id="g1" title="Learn React" />**

2. **<GoalItem id="g1">Learn React</GoalItem>**

You might determine that the second option looks a bit more intuitive and in line with regular HTML because, there, you would also configure a normal list item like this: `<li id="li1">Some list item</li>`.

While you have no choice when working with regular HTML elements (you can't just add a **goal** attribute to a **`<li>`** just because you want to), you do have a choice when working with React and your own components. It simply depends on how you consume props inside the component function. Both approaches can work, depending on that internal component code.

Still, you might want to pass certain pieces of data between component tags, and the special **children** property allows you to do just that. It contains any content you define between the component opening and closing tags. Therefore, in the case of example 2 (in the list above), **children** would contain the string **"Learn React"**.

In your component function, you can work with the **children** value just as you work with any other prop value:

```
function GoalItem(props) {
  return <li>{props.children} (ID: {props.id})</li>;
}
```

WHICH COMPONENTS NEED PROPS?

It was mentioned before already, but it is extremely important: **Props are optional!**

React will always pass **prop** data into your components, but you don't have to work with that **prop** parameter. You don't even have to define it in your component function if you don't plan on working with it.

There is no hard rule that would define which components need **props** and which don't. It comes with experience and simply depends on the role of a component.

You might have a general **Header** component that displays a static header (with a logo, title, and so on), and such a component probably needs no external configuration (in other words, no "attributes" or other kinds of data passed into it). It could be self-contained, with all the required values hardcoded into the component.

But you will also often build and use components like the **GoalItem** component (in other words, components that do need external data to be useful). Whenever a component is used more than once in your React app, there is a high chance that it will utilize props. However, the opposite is not necessarily true. While you will have one-time components that don't use props, you absolutely will also have components that are only used once in the entire app and still take advantage of props. As mentioned, it depends on the exact use case and component.

Throughout this book, you will see plenty of examples and exercises that will help you gain a deeper understanding of how to build components and use props.

HOW TO DEAL WITH MULTIPLE PROPS

As shown in the preceding examples, you are not limited to only one prop per component. Indeed, you can pass and use as many props as your component needs—no matter if that's 1 or 100 (or more) props.

Once you do create components with more than just two or three props, a new question might come up: do you have to add all those props individually (in other words, as separate attributes)? Or can you pass fewer attributes that contain grouped data, such as arrays or objects?

And indeed, you can. React allows you to pass arrays and objects as prop values as well. In fact, any valid JavaScript value can be passed as a prop value!

This allows you to decide whether you want to have a component with 20 individual props ("attributes") or just one "big" prop. Here's an example of where the same component is configured in two different ways:

```
<Product title="A book" price={29.99} id="p1" />
// or
const productData = {title: 'A book', price: 29.99, id: 'p1'}
<Product data={productData} />
```

Of course, the component must also be adapted internally (in other words, in the component function) to expect either individual or grouped props. But since you're the developer, that is, of course, your choice.

Inside the component function, you can also make your life easier.

There is nothing wrong with accessing prop values via **props.XYZ**, but if you have a component that receives multiple props, repeating **props.XYZ** over and over again could become cumbersome and make the code a bit harder to read.

You can use a default JavaScript feature to improve readability: **object destructuring**.

Object destructuring allows you to extract values from an object and assign those values to new variables or constants in a single step:

```
const user = {name: 'Max', age: 29};
const {name, age} = user; // <-- this is object destructuring in action
console.log(name); // outputs 'Max'
```

You can therefore use this syntax to extract all prop values and assign them to equally named variables directly at the start of your component function:

```
function Product({title, price, id}) { // destructuring in action
  … // title, price, id are now available as variables inside this function
}
```

You don't have to use this syntax, but it can make your life easier.

> **NOTE**
>
> When using object destructuring to extract prop values, it is worth noting that this only works if **single-value** props were passed to the component. You can also extract grouped props, but there you only have one property to destructure: the attribute that contains the grouped data.
>
> For more information on object destructuring, MDN is a great place to dive deeper. You can access this at https://developer.mozilla.org/en-US/docs/Web/JavaScript/Reference/Operators/Destructuring_assignment.

SPREADING PROPS

Imagine you're building a custom component that should act as a "wrapper" around some other component— a built-in component, perhaps.

For instance, you could be building a custom **Link** component that should return a standard **<a>** element with some custom styling (covered in *Chapter 6, Styling React Apps*) or logic added:

```
function Link({children}) {
  return <a target="_blank" rel="noopener noreferrer">{children}</a>
};
```

This very simple example component returns a pre-configured **<a>** element. This custom **Link** component configures the anchor element such that new pages are always opened in a new tab. In place of the standard **<a>** element, you could be using this **Link** component in your React app to get that behavior out of the box for all your links.

But this custom component suffers from a problem: it's a wrapper around a core element, but by creating your own component, you remove the configurability of that core element. If you were to use this **Link** component in your app, how would you set the **href** prop to configure the link destination?

You might try the following:

```
<Link href="https://some-site.com">Click here</Link>
```

However, this example code wouldn't work because **Link** doesn't accept or use a **href** prop.

Of course, you could adjust the **Link** component function such that a href prop is used:

```
function Link({children, href}) {
   return <a href={href} target="_blank" rel="noopener
noreferrer">{children}</a>
};
```

But what if you also wanted to ensure that the **download** prop could be added if needed?

Well, it's true that you can always accept more and more props (and pass them on to the **<a>** element inside your component), but this reduces the reusability and maintainability of your custom component.

A better solution is to use the standard JavaScript spread operator (i.e., the **. . .** operator) and React's support for that operator when working with components.

For example, the following component code is valid:

```
function Link({children, config}) {
   return <a {...config} target="_blank" rel="noopener
noreferrer">{children}</a>
};
```

In this example, **config** is expected to be a JavaScript object (i.e., a collection of key-value pairs). The spread operator (**. . .**), when used in JSX code on a JSX element, converts that object into multiple props.

Consider this example **config** value:

```
const config = { href: 'https://some-site.com', download: true };
```

In this case, when spreading it on **<a>**, (i.e., **<a {...config}>**), the result would be the same as if you had written this code:

```
<a href="https://some-site.com" download={true}>
```

The behavior and pattern can be used to build reusable components that should still maintain the configurability of the core element they may be wrapping. This helps you avoid long lists of pre-defined, accepted props and improves the reusability of components.

PROP CHAINS/PROP DRILLING

There is one last phenomenon that is worth noting when learning about props: "prop drilling" or "prop chains".

This isn't an official term, but it's a problem every React developer will encounter at some point. It occurs when you build a slightly more complex React app that contains multiple layers of nested components that need to send data to each other.

For example, assume that you have a **NavItem** component that should output a navigation link. Inside that component, you might have another nested component, **AnimatedLink**, that outputs the actual link (maybe with some nice animation styling).

The **NavItem** component could look like this:

```
function NavItem(props) {
  return <div><AnimatedLink target={props.target} text="Some text" /></
div>;
}
```

And **AnimatedLink** could be defined like this:

```
function AnimatedLink(props) {
  return <a href={props.target}>{props.text}</a>;
}
```

In this example, the **target** prop is passed through the **NavItem** component to the **AnimatedLink** component. The **NavItem** component must accept the **target** prop because it must be passed on to **AnimatedLink**.

That's what prop drilling/prop chains is all about: you forward a prop from a component that doesn't really need it to another component that *does* need it.

Having some prop drilling in your app isn't necessarily bad and you can definitely accept it. But if you should end up with longer chains of props (in other words, multiple **pass-through components**), you can use a solution that will be discussed in *Chapter 10, Working with Complex States*.

SUMMARY AND KEY TAKEAWAYS

- Props are a key React concept that makes components configurable and therefore reusable.

- Props are automatically collected and passed into component functions by React.

- You decide (on a per-component basis) whether you want to use the props data (an object) or not.

- Props are passed into components like attributes or, via the special `children` prop, between the opening and closing tags.

- Since you are writing the code, it's up to you how you want to pass data via props. Between the tags or as attributes? A single grouped attribute or many single-value attributes? It's up to you.

WHAT'S NEXT?

Props allow you to make components configurable and reusable. Still, they are rather static. Data and therefore the UI output doesn't change. You can't react to user events like button clicks.

But the true power of React only becomes visible once you do add events (and reactions to them).

In the next chapter, you will learn how you can add event listeners when working with React and you will learn how you can react (no pun intended) to events and change the (invisible and visible) state of your application.

TEST YOUR KNOWLEDGE!

Test your knowledge regarding the concepts covered in this chapter by answering the following questions. You can then compare your answers to the example answers that can be found here: https://packt.link/ekAg6.

1. Which "problem" do props solve?

2. How are props passed into components?

3. How are props consumed inside a component function?

4. Which options exist for passing (multiple) props into components?

APPLY WHAT YOU LEARNED

With this and the previous chapters, you now have enough basic knowledge to build truly reusable components.

Below, you will find an activity that allows you to apply all the knowledge, including the new props knowledge, you have acquired up to this point:

ACTIVITY 3.1: CREATING AN APP TO OUTPUT YOUR GOALS FOR THIS BOOK

This activity builds upon *Activity 2.2, "Create a React app to log your goals for this book"* from the previous chapter. If you followed along there, you can use your existing code and enhance it by adding props. Alternatively, you can also use the solution provided as a starting point accessible through the following link: https://packt.link/8tvm6.

The aim of this activity is to build reusable **GoalItem** components that can be configured via props. Every **GoalItem** component should receive and output a goal title and a short description text with extra information about the goal.

The steps are as follows:

1. Complete the second activity from the previous chapter.

2. Replace the hardcoded goal item components with a new configurable component.

3. Output multiple goal components with different titles and descriptions (configured via props).

The final user interface could look like this:

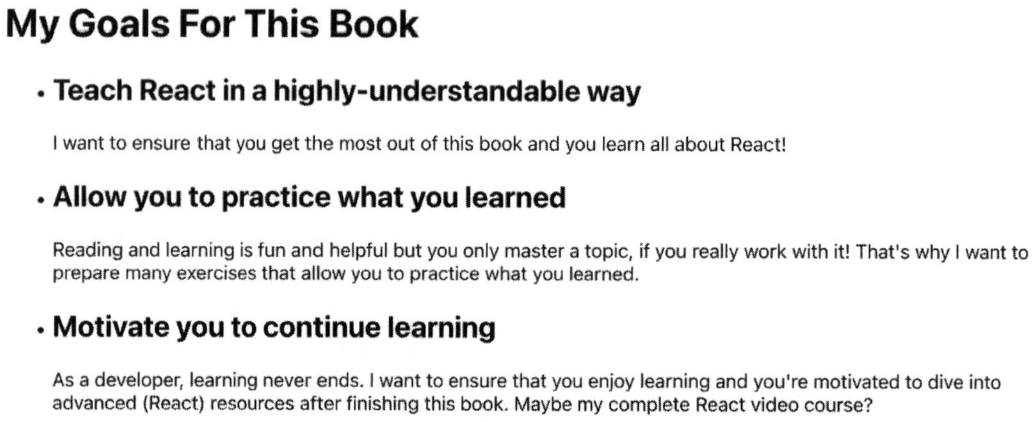

My Goals For This Book

- **Teach React in a highly-understandable way**

  I want to ensure that you get the most out of this book and you learn all about React!

- **Allow you to practice what you learned**

  Reading and learning is fun and helpful but you only master a topic, if you really work with it! That's why I want to prepare many exercises that allow you to practice what you learned.

- **Motivate you to continue learning**

  As a developer, learning never ends. I want to ensure that you enjoy learning and you're motivated to dive into advanced (React) resources after finishing this book. Maybe my complete React video course?

Figure 3.1: The final result: Multiple goals output below each other

> **NOTE**
>
> The solution to this activity can be found on page 455.

4

WORKING WITH EVENTS AND STATE

LEARNING OBJECTIVES

By the end of this chapter, you will be able to do the following:

- Add user event handlers (for example, for reacting to button clicks) to React apps.

- Update the UI via a concept called **state**.

- Build real dynamic and interactive UIs (that is, so that they are not static anymore).

INTRODUCTION

In the previous chapters, you learned how to build UIs with the help of React **components**. You also learned about **props**—a concept and feature that enables React developers to build and reuse configurable components.

These are all important React features and building blocks, but with these features alone, you would only be able to build static React apps (that is, web apps that never change). You would not be able to change or update the content on the screen if you only had access to those features. You also would not be able to react to any user events and update the UI in response to such events (for instance, to show an overlay window upon a button click).

Put in other words, you would not be able to build real websites and web applications if you were limited to just components and props.

Therefore, in this chapter, a brand-new concept is introduced: state. State is a React feature that allows developers to update internal data and trigger a UI update based on such data adjustments. In addition, you will learn how to react (no pun intended) to user events such as button clicks or text being entered into input fields.

WHAT'S THE PROBLEM?

As outlined previously, at this point in the book, there is a problem with all React apps and sites you might be building: they're static. The UI can't change.

To understand this issue a bit better, take a look at a typical React component, as you are able to build it up to this point in the book:

```
function EmailInput() {
  return (
    <div>
      <input placeholder="Your email" type="email" />
      <p>The entered email address is invalid.</p>
    </div>
  );
};
```

This component might look strange though. Why is there a **<p>** element that informs the user about an incorrect email address?

Well, the goal might be to show that paragraph only if the user *did* enter an incorrect email address. That is to say, the web app should wait for the user to start typing and evaluate the user input once the user is done typing (that is, once the input loses focus). Then, the error message should be shown if the email address is considered invalid (for example, an empty input field or a missing @ symbol).

But at the moment, with the React skills picked up thus far, this is something you would not be able to build. Instead, the error message would always be shown since there is no way of changing it based on user events and dynamic conditions. In other words, this React app is a static app, not dynamic. The UI can't change.

Of course, changing UIs and dynamic web apps are things you might want to build. Almost every website that exists contains some dynamic UI elements and features. Therefore, that's the problem that will be solved in this chapter.

HOW NOT TO SOLVE THE PROBLEM

How could the component shown previously be made more dynamic?

The following is one solution you could come up with. (*Spoiler, the code won't work, so you don't need to try running it!*)

```
function EmailInput() {
  return (
    <div>
      <input placeholder="Your email" type="email" />
      <p></p>
    </div>
  );
};


const input = document.querySelector('input');
const errorParagraph = document.querySelector('p');


function evaluateEmail(event) {
  const enteredEmail = event.target.value;
  if (enteredEmail.trim() === '' || !enteredEmail.includes('@')) {
    errorParagraph.textContent = ' The entered email address is
invalid.';
  } else {
```

```
    errorParagraph.textContent = '';
  }
};


input.addEventListener('blur', evaluateEmail);
```

This code won't work, because you can't select React-rendered DOM elements from inside the same component file this way. This is just meant as a dummy example of how you could try to solve this. That being said, you could put the code below the component function some place where it does execute successfully (for example, into a **setTimeout()** callback that fires after a second, allowing the React app to render all elements onto the screen).

Put in the right place, this code will add the email validation behavior described earlier in this chapter. Upon the built-in **blur** event, the **evaluateEmail** function is triggered. This function receives the **event** object as an argument (automatically, by the browser), and therefore the **evaluateEmail** function is able to parse the entered value from that **event** object via **event.target.value**. The entered value can then be used in an **if** check to conditionally display or remove the error message.

> **NOTE**
>
> All the preceding code that deals with the **blur** event (such as **addEventListener**) and the **event** object, including the code in the **if** check, is standard JavaScript code. It is not specific to React in any way.
>
> If you find yourself struggling with this non-React code, it's strongly recommended that you dive into more vanilla JavaScript resources (such as the guides on the MDN website at https://developer.mozilla.org/en-US/docs/Web/JavaScript) first.

But what's wrong with this code, if it would work in some places of the overall application code?

It's imperative code! That means you are writing down step-by-step instructions on what the browser should do. You are not declaring the desired end state; you are instead describing a way of getting there. And it's not using React.

Keep in mind that React is all about controlling the UI and that writing React code is about writing declarative code—instead of imperative code. Revisit *Chapter 2, What Is React?*, if that sounds brand new to you.

You could achieve your goal by introducing this kind of code, but you would be working against React and its philosophy (React's philosophy being that you declare your desired end state(s) and let React figure out how to get there). A clear indicator of this is the fact that you would be forced to find the right place for this kind of code in order for it to work.

This is not a philosophical problem, and it's not just some weird hard rule that you should follow. Instead, by working against React like this, you will make your life as a developer unnecessarily hard. You are neither using the tools React gives you nor letting React figure out how to achieve the desired (UI) state.

That does not just mean that you spend time on solving problems you wouldn't have to solve. It also means that you're passing up possible optimizations React might be able to perform under the hood. Your solution is very likely not just leading to more work (that is, more code) for you; it also might result in a buggy result that could also suffer from suboptimal performance.

The example shown previously is a simple one. Think about more complex websites and web apps, such as online shops, vacation rental websites, or web apps such as Google Docs. There, you might have dozens or hundreds of (dynamic) UI features and elements. Managing them all with a mixture of React code and standard vanilla JavaScript code will quickly become a nightmare. Again, refer to *Chapter 2* of this book to understand the merits of React.

A BETTER INCORRECT SOLUTION

The naïve approach discussed previously doesn't work well. It forces you to figure out how to make the code run correctly (for example, by wrapping parts of it in some `setTimeout()` call to defer execution) and leads to your code being scattered all over the place (that is, inside of React component functions, outside of those functions, and maybe also in totally unrelated files). How about a solution that embraces React, like this:

```
function EmailInput() {
  let errorMessage = '';


  function evaluateEmail(event) {
    const enteredEmail = event.target.value;
    if (enteredEmail.trim() === '' || !enteredEmail.includes('@')) {
```

```
      errorMessage = ' The entered email address is invalid.';
    } else {
      errorMessage = '';
    }
  };

  const input = document.querySelector('input');

  input.addEventListener('blur', evaluateEmail);

  return (
    <div>
      <input placeholder="Your email" type="email" />
      <p>{errorMessage}</p>
    </div>
  );
};
```

This code again would not work (even though it's technically valid JavaScript code). Selecting JSX elements doesn't work like this. It doesn't work because **document. querySelector('input')** executes before anything is rendered to the DOM (when the component function is executed for the first time). Again, you would have to delay the execution of that code until the first render cycle is over (you would therefore be once again working against React).

But even though it still would not work, it's closer to the correct solution.

It's closer to the ideal implementation because it embraces React way more than the first attempted solution did. All the code is contained in the component function to which it belongs. The error message is handled via an **errorMessage** variable that is output as part of the JSX code.

The idea behind this possible solution is that the React component that controls a certain UI feature or element is also responsible for its state and events. You might identify two important keywords of this chapter here!

This approach is definitely going in the right direction, but it still wouldn't work for two reasons:

- Selecting the JSX **<input>** element via **document. querySelector('input')** would fail.

- Even if the input could be selected, the UI would not update as expected.

These two problems will be solved next—finally leading to an implementation that embraces React and its features. The upcoming solution will avoid mixing React and non-React code. As you will see, the result will be easier code where you have to do less work (that is, write less code).

PROPERLY REACTING TO EVENTS

Instead of mixing imperative JavaScript code such as **document. querySelector('input')** with React-specific code, you should fully embrace React and its features.

And since listening to events and triggering actions upon events is an extremely common requirement, React has a built-in solution. You can attach event listeners directly to the JSX elements to which they belong.

The preceding example would be rewritten like this:

```
function EmailInput() {
  let errorMessage = '';

  function evaluateEmail(event) {
    const enteredEmail = event.target.value;
    if (enteredEmail.trim() === '' || !enteredEmail.includes('@')) {
      errorMessage = 'The entered email address is invalid.';
    } else {
      errorMessage = '';
    }
  };

  return (
    <div>
      <input placeholder="Your email" type="email" onBlur={evaluateEmail}
/>
      <p>{errorMessage}</p>
    </div>
  );
};
```

The **onBlur** prop was added to the built-in input element. This prop is made available by React, just as all these base HTML elements (such as **<input>** and **<p>**) are made available as components by React. In fact, all these built-in HTML components come with their standard HTML attributes as React props (plus some extra props, such as the **onBlur** event handling prop).

React exposes all standard events that can be connected to DOM elements as **onXYZ** props (where **XYZ** is the event name, such as **blur** or **click**, starting with a capital character). You can react to the **blur** event by adding the **onBlur** prop. You could listen to a **click** event via the **onClick** prop. You get the idea.

> **NOTE**
>
> For more information on standard events see https://developer.mozilla.org/en-US/docs/Web/Events#event_listing.

These props require values to fulfill their job. To be precise, they need a pointer to the function that should be executed when the event occurs. In the preceding example, the **onBlur** prop receives a pointer to the **evaluateEmail** function as a value.

> **NOTE**
>
> There's a subtle difference between **evaluateEmail** and **evaluateEmail()**. The first is a pointer to the function; the second actually executes the function (and yields the return value, if any). Again, this is not something specific to React but a standard JavaScript concept. If it's not clear, this resource explains it in greater detail: https://developer.mozilla.org/en-US/docs/Web/Events#event_listing.

By using these event props, the preceding example code will now finally execute without throwing any errors. You could verify this by adding a **console.log('Hello');** statement inside the **evaluateEmail** function. This will display the text **'Hello'** in the console of your browser developer tools, whenever the input loses focus:

```
function EmailInput() {
  let errorMessage = '';

  function evaluateEmail(event) {
    console.log('Hello');
    const enteredEmail = event.target.value;
    if (enteredEmail.trim() === '' || !enteredEmail.includes('@')) {
      errorMessage = 'The entered email address is invalid.';
    } else {
```

```
      errorMessage = '';
    }
  };

  return (
    <div>
      <input placeholder="Your email" type="email" onBlur={evaluateEmail}
/>
      <p>{errorMessage}</p>
    </div>
  );
};
```

In the browser console, this looks as follows:

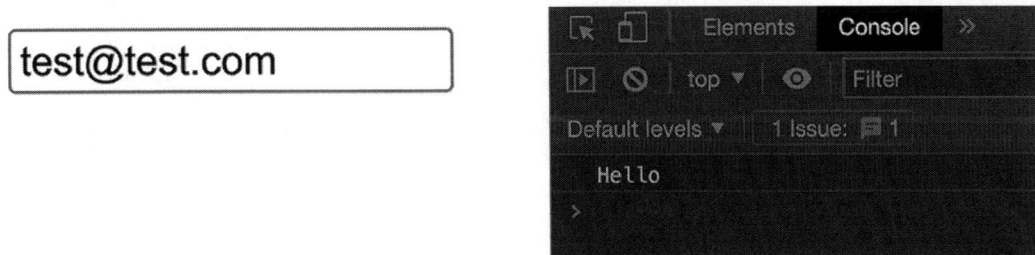

Figure 4.1: Displaying some text in the browser console upon removing focus from the input field

This is definitely one step closer to the best possible implementation, but it also still won't produce the desired result of updating the page content dynamically.

UPDATING STATE CORRECTLY

By now, you understand how to correctly set up event listeners and execute functions upon certain events. What's missing is a feature that forces React to update the visible UI on the screen and the content that is displayed to the app users.

That's where React's **state** concept comes into play. Like props, state is a key concept of React, but whereas props are about receiving external data inside a component, state is about managing and updating **internal data**. And, most importantly, whenever such state is updated, React goes ahead and updates the parts of the UI that are affected by the state change.

Here's how state is used in React (of course, the code will then be explained in detail afterward):

```
import { useState } from 'react';
```

```
function EmailInput() {
  const [errorMessage, setErrorMessage] = useState('');

  function evaluateEmail(event) {
    const enteredEmail = event.target.value;
    if (enteredEmail.trim() === '' || !enteredEmail.includes('@')) {
      setErrorMessage('The entered email address is invalid.');
    } else {
      setErrorMessage('');
    }
  };

  return (
    <div>
      <input placeholder="Your email" type="email" onBlur={evaluateEmail}
/>
      <p>{errorMessage}</p>
    </div>
  );
};
```

Compared to the example code discussed earlier in this chapter, this code doesn't look much different. But there is a key difference: the usage of the **useState()** Hook.

Hooks are another key concept of React. These are special functions that can only be used inside of React components (or inside of other Hooks, as will be covered in *Chapter 11, Building Custom React Hooks*). Hooks add special features and behaviors to the React components in which they are used. For example, the **useState()** Hook allows a component (and therefore, implicitly React) to set and manage some state that is tied to this component. React provides various built-in Hooks, and they are not all focused on state management. You will learn about other Hooks and their purposes throughout this book.

The **useState()** Hook is an extremely important and commonly used Hook as it enables you to manage data inside a component, which, when updated, tells React to update the UI accordingly.

That is the core idea behind state management and this state concept: state is data, which, when changed, should force React to re-evaluate a component and update the UI if needed.

Using Hooks such as **useState()** is pretty straightforward: You import them from **'react'** and you then call them like a function inside your component function. You call them like a function because, as mentioned, React Hooks are functions—just special functions (from React's perspective).

A CLOSER LOOK AT USESTATE()

How exactly does the **useState()** Hook work and what does it do internally?

By calling **useState()** inside a component function, you register some data with React. It's a bit like defining a variable or constant in vanilla JavaScript. But there is something special: React will track the registered value internally, and whenever you update it, React will re-evaluate the component function in which the state was registered.

React does this by checking whether the data used in the component changed. Most importantly, React validates whether the UI needs to change because of changed data (for example, because a value is output inside the JSX code). If React determines that the UI needs to change, it goes ahead and updates the real DOM in the places where an update is needed (for example, changing some text that's displayed on the screen). If no update is needed, React ends the component re-evaluation without updating the DOM.

React's internal workings will be discussed in great detail later in the book, in *Chapter 9, Behind the Scenes of React and Optimization Opportunities*).

The entire process starts with calling **useState()** inside a component. This creates a state value (which will be stored and managed by React) and ties it to a specific component. An initial state value is registered by simply passing it as a parameter value to **useState()**. In the preceding example, an empty string (' ') is registered as a first value:

```
const [errorMessage, setErrorMessage] = useState('');
```

As you can see in the example, **useState()** does not just accept a parameter value. It also returns a value: an array with exactly two elements.

The preceding example uses **array destructuring**, which is a standard JavaScript feature that allows developers to retrieve values from an array and immediately assign them to variables or constants. In the example, the two elements that make up the array returned by **useState()** are pulled out of that array and stored in two constants (**errorMessage** and **setErrorMessage**). You don't have to use array destructuring when working with React or **useState()**, though.

You could also write the code like this instead:

```
const stateData = useState('');
const errorMessage = stateData[0];
const setErrorMessage = stateData[1];
```

This works absolutely fine, but when using array destructuring, the code stays a bit more concise. That's why you typically see the syntax using array destructuring when browsing React apps and examples. You also don't have to use constants; variables (via **let**) would be fine as well. As you will see throughout this chapter and the rest of the book, though, the variables won't be reassigned, and so using constants makes sense (but it is not required in any way).

> **NOTE**
>
> If array destructuring or the difference between variables and constants sounds brand new to you, it's strongly recommended that you refresh your JavaScript basics before progressing with this book. As always, MDN provides great resources for that (see http://packt.link/3B8Ct for array destructuring, https://packt.link/hGjqL for information on the **let** variable, and https://packt.link/TdPPS for guidance on the use of **const**.)

As mentioned before, **useState()** returns an array with exactly two elements. It will always be exactly two elements—and always exactly the same kind of elements. The first element is always the current state value, and the second element is a function that you can call to set the state to a new value.

But how do these two values (the state value and the state-updating function) work together? What does React do with them internally? And how are these two array elements used (by React) to update the UI?

A LOOK UNDER THE HOOD OF REACT

React manages the state values for you, in some internal storage that you, the developer, can't directly access. Since you often do need access to a state value (for instance, some entered email address, as in the preceding example), React provides a way of reading state values: the first element in the array returned by **useState()**. The first element of the returned array holds the current state value. You can therefore use this element in any place where you need to work with the state value (for example, in the JSX code to output it there).

In addition, you often also need to update the state—for example, because a user entered a new email address. Since you don't manage the state value yourself, React gives you a function that you can call to inform React about the new state value. That's the second element in the returned array.

In the example shown before, you call **setErrorMessage('Error!')** to set the **errorMessage** state value to a new string (**'Error!'**).

But why is this managed like this? Why not just use a standard JavaScript variable that you can assign and reassign as needed?

Because React must be informed whenever there's a state that impacts the UI changes. Otherwise, the visible UI doesn't change at all, even in cases where it should. React does not track regular variables and changes to their values, and so they have no influence on the state of the UI.

The state-updating function exposed by React (that second array element returned by **useState()**) *does* trigger some internal UI-updating effect though. This state-updating function does more than set a new value; it also informs React that a state value changed, and that the UI might therefore be in need of an update.

So, whenever you call **setErrorMessage('Error!')**, React does not just update the value that it stores internally; it also checks the UI and updates it when needed. UI updates can involve anything from simple text changes up to the complete removal and addition of various DOM elements. Anything is possible there!

React determines the new target UI by rerunning (also called re-evaluating) any component functions that are affected by a state change. That includes the component function that executed the **useState()** function that returned the state-updating function that was called. But it also includes any child components, since an update in a parent component could lead to new state data that's also used by some child components (the state value could be passed to child components via props).

It's important to understand and keep in mind that React will re-execute (re-evaluate) a component function if a state-updating function was called in the component function or some parent component function. Because this also explains why the state value returned by **useState()** (that is, the first array element) can be a constant, even though you can assign new values by calling the state-updating function (the second array element). Since the entire component function is re-executed, **useState()** is also called again (because all the component function code is executed again) and hence a new array with two new elements is returned by React. And the first array element is still the current state value.

However, as the component function was called because of a state update, the current state value now is the updated value.

This can be a bit tricky to wrap your head around, but it is how React works internally. In the end, it's just about component functions being called multiple times by React. Just as any JavaScript function can be called multiple times.

NAMING CONVENTIONS

The **useState()** Hook is typically used in combination with array destructuring, like this:

```
const [enteredEmail, setEnteredEmail] = useState('');
```

But when using array destructuring, the names of the variables or constants (**enteredEmail** and **setEnteredEmail**, in this case) are up to you, the developer. Therefore, a valid question is how you should name these variables or constants. Fortunately, there is a clear convention when it comes to React and **useState()**, and these variable or constant names.

The **first element** (that is, the current state value) should be named such that it describes what the state value is all about. Examples would be **enteredEmail**, **userEmail**, **providedEmail**, just **email**, or similar names. You should avoid generic names such as **a** or **value** or misleading names such as **setValue** (which sounds like it is a function—but it isn't).

The **second element** (that is, the state-updating function) should be named such that it becomes clear that it is a function and that it does what it does. Examples would be **setEnteredEmail** or **setEmail**. In general, the convention for this function is to name it **setXYZ**, where **XYZ** is the name you chose for the first element, the current state value variable. (Note, though, that you start with an uppercase character, as in **setEnteredEmail**, not **setenteredEmail**.)

ALLOWED STATE VALUE TYPES

Managing entered email addresses (or user input in general) is indeed a common use case and example for working with state. But you're not limited to this scenario and value type.

In the case of entered user input, you will often deal with string values such as email addresses, passwords, blog posts, or similar values. But any valid JavaScript value type can be managed with the help of **useState()**. You could, for example, manage the total sum of multiple shopping cart items—that is, a number—or a Boolean value (for example, *"did a user confirm the terms of use?"*).

Besides managing primitive value types, you can also store and update reference value types such as objects and arrays.

> **NOTE**
>
> If the difference between primitive and reference value types is not entirely clear, it's strongly recommended that you dive into this core JavaScript concept before proceeding with this book through the following link: https://academind.com/tutorials/reference-vs-primitive-values.

React gives you the flexibility of managing all these value types as state. You can even switch the value type at runtime (just as you can in vanilla JavaScript). It is absolutely fine to store a number as the initial state value and update it to a string at a later point in time.

Just as with vanilla JavaScript, you should, of course, ensure that your program deals with this behavior appropriately, though there's nothing technically wrong with switching types.

WORKING WITH MULTIPLE STATE VALUES

When building anything but very simple web apps or UIs, you will need multiple state values. Maybe users can not only enter their email but also a username or their address. Maybe you also need to track some error state or save shopping cart items. Maybe users can click a "Like" button whose state should be saved and reflected in the UI. There are many values that change frequently and whose changes should be reflected in the UI.

Consider this concrete scenario: you have a component that needs to manage both the value entered by a user into an email input field and the value that was inserted into a password field. Each value should be captured once a field loses focus.

Since you have two input fields that hold different values, you have two state values: the entered email and the entered password. Even though you might use both values together at some point (for example, to log a user in), the values are not provided simultaneously. In addition, you might also need every value to stand alone, since you use it to show potential error messages (for example, *"password too short"*) while the user is entering data.

Scenarios like this are very common, and therefore, you can also manage multiple state values with the **useState()** Hook. There are two main ways of doing that:

1. Use multiple **state slices** (multiple state values)

2. Using one single, *big* state object

USING MULTIPLE STATE SLICES

You can manage multiple state values (also often called **state slices**), by simply calling **useState()** multiple times in your component function.

For the example described previously, a (simplified) component function could look like this:

```
function LoginForm() {
  const [enteredEmail, setEnteredEmail] = useState('');
  const [enteredPassword, setEnteredPassword] = useState('');

  function emailEnteredHandler(event) {
    setEnteredEmail(event.target.value);
  };

  function passwordEnteredHandler(event) {
    setEnteredPassword(event.target.value);
  };

  // Below, props are split across multiple lines for better readability
  // This is allowed when using JSX, just as it is allowed in standard
HTML
  return (
    <form>
      <input
        type="email"
        placeholder="Your email"
        onBlur={emailEnteredHandler} />
      <input
        type="password"
        placeholder="Your password"
        onBlur={passwordEnteredHandler} />
    </form>
  );
};
```

In this example, two state slices are managed by calling **useState()** twice. Therefore, React registers and manages two state values internally. These two values can be read and updated independently from each other.

> **NOTE**
>
> In the example, the functions that are triggered upon events end with **handler** (**emailEnteredHandler** and **passwordEnteredHandler**). This is a convention used by some React developers. Event handler functions end with ...**handler** to make it clear that these functions are executed upon certain (user) events. This is not a convention you have to follow. The functions could have also been named **updateEmail**, **updatePassword**, **handleEmailUpdate**, **handlePasswordUpdate**, or anything else. If the name is meaningful and follows some stringent convention, it's a valid choice.

You can register as many state slices (by calling **useState()** multiple times) as you need in a component. You could have one state value, but you could also have dozens or even hundreds. Typically, though, you will only have a couple of state slices per component since you should try to split bigger components (which might be doing lots of different things) into multiple smaller components to keep them manageable.

The advantage of managing multiple state values like this is that you can update them independently. If the user enters a new email address, you only need to update that email state value. The password state value doesn't matter for your purposes.

A possible disadvantage could be that multiple state slices—and therefore multiple **useState()** calls—leads to lots of lines of code that might bloat your component. As mentioned before though, you typically should try to break up big components (that handle lots of different slices of state) into multiple smaller components anyways.

Still, there is an alternative to managing multiple state values like this: you can also manage a single, *merged* state value object.

MANAGING COMBINED STATE OBJECTS

Instead of calling **useState()** for every single state slice, you can go for one *big* state object that combines all the different state values:

```
function LoginForm() {
  const [userData, setUserData] = useState({
    email: '',
    password: ''
  });

  function emailEnteredHandler(event) {
    setUserData({
      email: event.target.value,
      password: userData.password
    });
  };

  function passwordEnteredHandler(event) {
    setUserData({
      email: userData.email,
      password: event.target.value
    });
  };

  // ... code omitted, because the returned JSX code is the same as
before
};
```

In this example, **useState()** is called only once, and the initial value passed to **useState()** is a JavaScript object. The object contains two properties: **email** and **password**. The property names are up to you, but they should describe the values that will be stored in the properties.

useState() still returns an array with exactly two elements. That the initial value is an object does not change anything about that. The first element of the returned array is now just an object instead of a string (as it was in the examples shown earlier). As mentioned before, any valid JavaScript value type can be used when working with **useState()**. Primitive value types such as strings or numbers can be used just as you would reference value types such as objects or arrays (which, technically, are objects of course).

The state-updating function (**setUserData**, in the preceding example) is still a function created by React that you can call to set the state to a new value. And you wouldn't have to set it to an object again, though that is typically the default. You don't change value types when updating the state, unless you have a good reason for doing so (though, technically, you are allowed to switch to a different type any time).

> **NOTE**
>
> In the preceding example, the way the state-updating function is used is not entirely correct. It would work but it does violate recommended best practices. You will learn later in this chapter why this is the case and how you should use the state-updating function instead.

When managing state objects as shown in the preceding example, there's one crucial thing you should keep in mind: you must always set all properties the object contains, even the ones that didn't change. This is required because, when calling the state-updating function, you *tell* React which new state value should be stored internally.

Thus, any value you pass as an argument to the state-updating function will overwrite the previously stored value. If you provide an object that contains only the properties that changed, all other properties will be lost since the previous state object is replaced by the new one, which contains fewer properties.

This is a common pitfall and therefore something you must pay attention to. For this reason, in the example shown previously, the property that is not changed is set to the previous state value—for example, **email: userData.email**, where **userData** is the current state snapshot and the first element of the array returned by **useState()**, while setting **password** to **event.target.value**.

It is totally up to you whether you prefer to manage one state value (that is, an object grouping together multiple values) or multiple state slices (that is, multiple **useState()** calls) instead. There is no right or wrong way and both approaches have their advantages and disadvantages.

However, it is worth noting that you should typically try to break up *big* components into smaller ones. Just as regular JavaScript functions shouldn't do too much work in a single function (it is considered a good practice to have separate functions for different tasks), components should focus on one or only a few tasks per component as well. Instead of having a huge **<App />** component that handles multiple forms, user authentication, and a shopping cart directly in one component, it would be preferable to split the code of that component into multiple smaller components that are then combined together to build the overall app.

When following that advice, most components shouldn't have too much state to manage anyway, since managing many state values is an indicator of a component doing *too much work*. That's why you might end up using a few state slices per component, instead of large state objects.

UPDATING STATE BASED ON PREVIOUS STATE CORRECTLY

When learning about objects as state values, you learned that it's easy to accidentally overwrite (and lose) data because you might set the new state to an object that contains only the properties that changed—not the ones that didn't. That's why, when working with objects or arrays as state values, it's important to always add the existing properties and elements to the new state value.

And, in general, setting a state value to a new value that is (at least partially) based on the previous state is a common task. You might set **password** to **event.target. value** but also set **email** to **userData.email** to ensure that the stored email address is not lost due to updating a part of the overall state (that is, because of updating the password to the newly entered value).

That's not the only scenario where the new state value could be based on the previous one though. Another example would be a **counter** component—for example, a component like this:

```
function Counter() {
  const [counter, setCounter] = useState(0);

  function incrementCounterHandler() {
    setCounter(counter + 1);
  };

  return (
    <>
      <p>Counter Value: {counter}</p>
```

```
            <button onClick={incrementCounterHandler}>Increment</button>
        </>
    );
};
```

In this example, a **click** event handler is registered for **<button>** (via the **onClick** prop). Upon every click, the counter state value is incremented by **1**.

This component would work, but the code shown in the example snippet is actually violating an important best practice and recommendation: state updates that depend on some previous state should be performed with the help of a function that's passed to the state-updating function. To be precise, the example should be rewritten like this:

```
function Counter() {
    const [counter, setCounter] = useState(0);

    function incrementCounterHandler() {
        setCounter(function(prevCounter) { return prevCounter + 1; });
        // alternatively, JS arrow functions could be used:
        // setCounter(prevCounter => prevCounter + 1);
    };

    return (
        <>
            <p>Counter Value: {counter}</p>
            <button onClick={incrementCounterHandler}>Increment</button>
        </>
    );
};
```

This might look a bit strange. It might seem like a function is now passed as the new state value to the state-updating function (that is, the number stored in **counter** is replaced with a function). But indeed, that is not the case.

Technically, a function *is* passed as an argument to the state-updating function, but React won't store that function as the new state value. Instead, when receiving a function as a new state value in the state-updating function, React will call that function for you and pass the latest state value to that function. Therefore, you should provide a function that accepts at least one parameter: the previous state value. This value will be passed into the function automatically by React, when React executes the function (which it will do internally).

The function should then also return a value—the new state value that should be stored by React. And since the function receives the previous state value, you can now derive the new state value based on the previous state value (for example, by adding the number 1 to it, but any operation could be performed here).

Why is this required, if the app worked fine before this change as well? It's required because in more complex React applications and UIs, React could be processing many state updates simultaneously—potentially triggered from different sources at different times.

When *not* using the approach discussed in the last paragraphs, the order of state updates might not be the expected one and bugs could be introduced into the app. Even if you know that your use case won't be affected and the app does its job without issue, it is recommended to simply adhere to the discussed best practice and pass a function to the state-updating function if the new state depends on the previous state.

With this newly gained knowledge in mind, take another look at an earlier code example:

```
function LoginForm() {
  const [userData, setUserData] = useState({
    email: '',
    password: ''
  });

  function emailEnteredHandler(event) {
    setUserData({
      email: event.target.value,
      password: userData.password
    });
  };

  function passwordEnteredHandler(event) {
    setUserData({
      email: userData.email,
      password: event.target.value
    });
```

```
  };


  // ... code omitted, because the returned JSX code is the same as
before
};
```

Can you spot the error in this code?

It's not a technical error; the code will execute fine, and the app will work as expected. But there is a problem with this code nonetheless. It violates the discussed best practice. In the code snippet, the state in both handler functions is updated by referring to the current state snapshot via **userData.password** and **userData. email**, respectively.

The code snippet should be rewritten like this:

```
function LoginForm() {
  const [userData, setUserData] = useState({
    email: '',
    password: ''
  });

  function emailEnteredHandler(event) {
    setUserData(prevData => ({
      email: event.target.value,
      password: prevData.password
    }));
  };

  function passwordEnteredHandler(event) {
    setUserData(prevData => ({
      email: prevData.email,
      password: event.target.value
    }));
  };


  // ... code omitted, because the returned JSX code is the same as
before
  // userData is not actively used here, hence you could get a warning
  // regarding that. Simply ignore it or start using userData
  // (e.g., via console.log(userData))
};
```

By passing an arrow function as an argument to **setUserData**, you allow React to call that function. React will do this automatically (that is, if it receives a function in this place, React will call it) and it will provide the previous state (**prevState**) automatically. The returned value (the object that stores the updated **email** or **password** and the currently stored **email** or **password**) is then set as the new state. The result, in this case, might be the same as before, but now the code adheres to recommended best practices.

> **NOTE**
>
> In the previous example, an arrow function was used instead of a "regular" function. Both approaches are fine though. You can use either of the two function types; the result will be the same.

In summary, you should always pass a function to the state-updating function if the new state depends on the previous state. Otherwise, if the new state depends on some other value (for instance, user input), directly passing the new state value as a function argument is absolutely fine and recommended.

TWO-WAY BINDING

There is one special usage of React's state concept that is worth discussing: **two-way binding**.

Two-way binding is a concept that is used if you have an input source (typically an **<input>** element) that sets some state upon user input (for instance, upon the **change** event) and outputs the input at the same time.

Here's an example:

```
function NewsletterField() {
  const [email, setEmail] = useState('');

  function changeEmailHandler(event) {
    setEmail(event.target.value);
  };

  return (
    <>
      <input
        type="email"
```

```
        placeholder="Your email address"
        value={email}
        onChange={changeEmailHandler} />
    </>
  );
};
```

Compared to the other code snippets and examples, the difference here is that the component does not just store the user input (upon the **change** event, in this case) but that the entered value is also output in the **<input>** element (via the default **value** prop) thereafter.

This might look like an infinite loop, but React deals with this and ensures that it doesn't become one. Instead, this is what's commonly referred to as two-way binding as a value is both set and read from the same source.

You may wonder why this is being discussed here, but it is important to know that it is perfectly valid to write code like this. And this kind of code could be necessary if you don't just want to set a value (in this case, the **email** value) upon user input in the **<input>** field but also from other sources. For example, you might have a button in the component that, when clicked, should clear the entered email address.

It might look like this:

```
function NewsletterField() {
  const [email, setEmail] = useState('');

  function changeEmailHandler(event) {
    setEmail(event.target.value);
  };

  function clearInputHandler() {
    setEmail(''); // reset email input (back to an empty string)
  };

  return (
    <>
      <input
        type="email"
        placeholder="Your email address"
        value={email}
        onChange={changeEmailHandler} />
      <button onClick={clearInputHandler}>Reset</button>
```

```
      </>
    );
  };
```

In this updated example, the **clearInputHandler** function is executed when **<button>** is clicked. Inside the function, the **email** state is set back to an empty string. Without two-way binding, the state would be updated, but the change would not be reflected in the **<input>** element. There, the user would still see their last input. The state reflected on the UI (the website) and the state managed internally by React would be different—a bug you absolutely must avoid.

DERIVING VALUES FROM STATE

As you can probably tell by now, state is a key concept in React. State allows you to manage data that, when changed, forces React to re-evaluate a component and, ultimately, the UI.

As a developer, you can use state values anywhere in your component (and in your child components, by passing state to them via props). You could, for example, repeat what a user entered like this:

```
function Repeater() {
  const [userInput, setUserInput] = useState('');

  function inputHandler(event) {
    setUserInput(event.target.value);
  };

  return (
    <>
      <input type="text" onChange={inputHandler} />
      <p>You entered: {userInput}</p>
    </>
  );
};
```

This component might not be too useful, but it will work, and it does use state.

Often, in order to do more useful things, you will need to use a state value as a basis to derive a new (often more complex) value. For example, instead of simply repeating what the user entered, you could count the number of entered characters and show that information to the user:

```
function CharCounter() {
  const [userInput, setUserInput] = useState('');

  function inputHandler(event) {
    setUserInput(event.target.value);
  };

  const numChars = userInput.length;

  return (
    <>
      <input type="text" onChange={inputHandler} />
      <p>Characters entered: {numChars}</p>
    </>
  );
};
```

Note the addition of the new **numChars** constant (it could also be a variable, via **let**). This constant is derived from the **userInput** state by accessing the **length** property on the string value that's stored in the **userInput** state.

This is important! You're not limited to working with state values only. You can manage some key value as state (that is, the value that will change) and derive other values based on that state value—such as, in this case, the number of characters entered by the user. And, indeed, this is something you will do frequently as a React developer.

You might also be wondering why **numChars** is a constant and outside of the **inputHandler** function. After all, that is the function that is executed upon user input (that is, upon every keystroke the user makes).

Keep in mind what you learned about how React handles state internally. When you call the state-updating function (**setUserInput**, in this case), React will re-evaluate the component to which the state belongs. This means that the **CharCounter** component function will be called again by React. All the code in that function is therefore executed again.

React does this to determine what the UI should look like after the state update; and, if it detects any differences compared to the currently rendered UI, React will go ahead and update the browser UI (that is, the DOM) accordingly. Otherwise, nothing will happen.

Since React calls the component function again, **useState()** will yield its array of values (current state value and state-updating function). The current state value will be the state to which it was set when **setUserInput** was called. Therefore, this new **userInput** value can be used to perform other calculations anywhere in the component function—such as deriving **numChars** by accessing the **length** property of **userInput**.

That's why **numChars** can be a constant. For this component execution, it won't be re-assigned. A new value might only be derived when the component function is executed again in the future (that is, if **setUserInput** is called again). And in that case, a brand-new **numChars** constant would be created (and the old one would be discarded).

WORKING WITH FORMS AND FORM SUBMISSION

State is commonly used when working with forms and user input. Indeed, most examples in this chapter dealt with some form of user input.

Up to this point, all examples focused on listening to user events that are directly attached to individual input elements. That makes sense because you will often want to listen to events such as keystrokes or an input losing focus. Especially when adding input validation (that is, checking entered values), you might want to use input events to give website users useful feedback while they're typing.

But it's also quite common to react to the overall form submission. For example, the goal could be to combine the input from various input fields and send the data to some backend server. How could you achieve this? How can you listen and react to the submission of a form?

You can do all these things with the help of standard JavaScript events and the appropriate event handler props provided by React. Specifically, the **onSubmit** prop can be added to **<form>** elements to assign a function that should be executed once a form is submitted. In order to then handle the submission with React and JavaScript, you must ensure that the browser won't do its default thing and generate (and send) an HTTP request automatically.

As in vanilla JavaScript, this can be achieved by calling the **preventDefault()** method on the automatically generated event object.

Here's a full example:

```
function NewsletterSignup() {
  const [email, setEmail] = useState('');
  const [agreed, setAgreed] = useState(false);

  function updateEmailHandler(event) {
    // could add email validation here
    setEmail(event.target.value);
  };

  function updateAgreementHandler(event) {
    setAgreed(event.target.checked); // checked is a default JS boolean
property
  };

  function signupHandler(event) {
    event.preventDefault(); // prevent browser default of sending a Http
request

    const userData = {userEmail: email, userAgrees: agreed};
    // doWhateverYouWant(userData);
  };

  return (
    <form onSubmit={signupHandler}>
      <div>
        <label htmlFor="email">Your email</label>
        <input type="email" id="email" onChange={updateEmailHandler}/>
      </div>
      <div>
        <input type="checkbox" id="agree"
onChange={updateAgreementHandler}/>
        <label htmlFor="agree">Agree to terms and conditions</label>
      </div>
    </form>
  );
};
```

This code snippet handles form submission via the **signupHandler()** function that's assigned to the built-in **onSubmit** prop. User input is still fetched with the help of two state slices (**email** and **agreed**), which are updated upon the inputs' change events.

NOTE

In the preceding code example, you might've noticed a new prop that wasn't used before in this book: **htmlFor**. This is a special prop, built into React and the core JSX elements it provides. It can be added to **<label>** elements in order to set the **for** attribute for these elements. The reason it is called **htmlFor** instead of just **for** is that, as explained earlier in the book, JSX looks like HTML but isn't HTML. It's JavaScript under the hood. And in JavaScript, **for** is a reserved keyword for **for** loops. To avoid problems, the prop is therefore named **htmlFor**.

LIFTING STATE UP

Here's a common scenario and problem: you have two components in your React app and a change or event in component A should change the state in component B. To make this less abstract, consider the following simplified example:

```
function SearchBar() {
  const [searchTerm, setSearchTerm] = useState('');

  function updateSearchTermHandler(event) {
    setSearchTerm(event.target.value);
  };

  return <input type="search" onChange={updateSearchTermHandler} />;
};

function Overview() {
  return <p>Currently searching for {searchTerm}</p>;
};

function App() {
  return (
    <>
```

```
        <SearchBar />
        <Overview />
      </>
  );
};
```

In this example, the **Overview** component should output the entered search term. But the search term is actually managed in another component—namely, the **SearchBar** component. In this simple example, the two components could of course be merged into one single component, and the problem would be solved. But it's very likely that when building more realistic apps, you'll face similar scenarios but with way more complex components. Breaking components up into smaller pieces is considered a good practice, since it keeps the individual components manageable.

Having multiple components depend on some shared piece of state is therefore a scenario you will face frequently when working with React.

This problem can be solved by *lifting state up*. When lifting state up, the state is not managed in either of the two components that use it—neither in **Overview**, which reads the state, nor in **SearchBar**, which sets the state—but in a shared ancestor component instead. To be precise, it is managed in the **closest** shared ancestor component. Keep in mind that components are nested into each other and thus a "tree of components" (with the **App** component as the root component) is built up in the end.

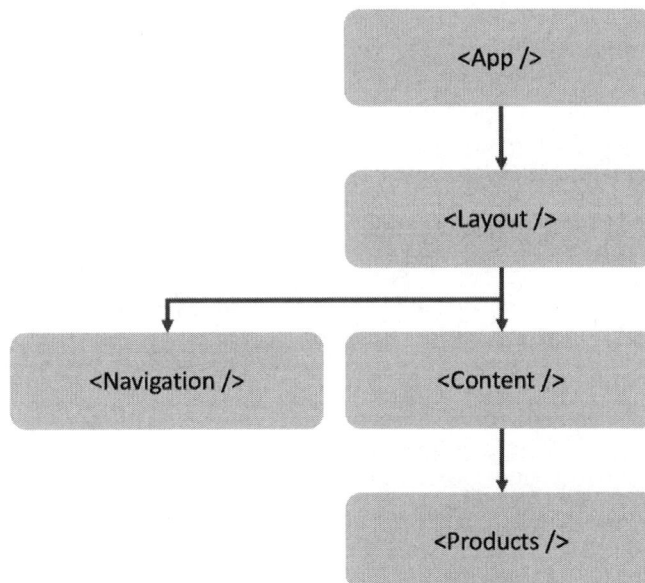

Figure 4.2: An example component tree

In the previous simple code example, the **App** component is the closest (and, in this case, only) ancestor component of both **SearchBar** and **Overview**. If the app was structured as shown in the figure, with state set in **Navigation** and used in **Products**, **Layout** would be the closest ancestor component.

State is lifted up by using props in the components that need to manipulate (that is, set) or read the state, and by registering the state in the ancestor component that is shared by the two other components. Here's the updated example from previously:

```
function SearchBar(props) {
  return <input type="search" onChange={props.onUpdateSearch} />;
};


function Overview({currentTerm}) {
  return <p>Currently searching for {currentTerm}</p>;
};


function App() {
  const [searchTerm, setSearchTerm] = useState('');

  function updateSearchTermHandler(event) {
    setSearchTerm(event.target.value);
  };

  return (
    <>
      <SearchBar onUpdateSearch={updateSearchTermHandler} />
      <Overview currentTerm={searchTerm} />
    </>
  );
};
```

The code didn't actually change that much; it mostly moved around a bit. The state is now managed inside of the shared ancestor component and **App** component, and the two other components get access to it via props.

Three key things are happening in this example:

1. The **SearchBar** component receives a prop called **onUpdateSearch**, whose value is a function—a function created in the **App** component and passed down to **SearchBar** from **App**.

2. The **onUpdateSearch** prop is then set as a value to the **onChange** prop on the **<input>** element inside of the **SearchBar** component.

3. The **searchTerm** state (that is, its current value) is passed from **App** to **Overview** via a prop named **currentTerm**.

The first two points could be confusing. But keep in mind that, in JavaScript, functions are first-class objects and regular values. You can store functions in variables and, when using React, pass functions as values for props. And indeed, you could already see that in action at the very beginning of this chapter. When introducing events and event handling, functions were provided as values to all these **onXYZ** props (**onChange**, **onBlur**, and so on).

In this code snippet, a function is passed as a value for a custom prop (that is, a prop expected in a component created by you, not built into React). The **onUpdateSearch** prop expects a function as a value because the prop is then itself being used as a value for the **onChange** prop on the **<input>** element.

The prop is named **onUpdateSearch** to make it clear that it expects a function as a value and that it will be connected to an event. Any name could've been chosen though; it doesn't have to start with **on**. But it's a common convention to name props that expect functions as values and that are intended to be connected to events like this.

Of course, **updateSearch** is not a default event, but since the function will effectively be called upon the **change** event of the **<input>** element, the prop acts like a custom event.

With this structure, the state was lifted up to the **App** component. This component registers and manages the state. But it also exposes the state-updating function (indirectly, in this case, as it is wrapped by the **updateSearchTermHandler** function) to the **SearchBar** component. And it also provides the current state value (**searchTerm**) to the **Overview** component via the **currentTerm** prop.

Since child and descendent components are also re-evaluated by React when state changes in a component, changes in the **App** component will also lead to the **SearchBar** and **Overview** components being re-evaluated. Therefore, the new prop value for **searchTerm** will be picked up, and the UI will be updated by React.

No new React features are needed for this. It's only a combination of state and props. But depending on how these features are connected and where they are used, both simple and more complex app patterns can be achieved.

SUMMARY AND KEY TAKEAWAYS

- Event handlers can be added to JSX elements via **on[EventName]** props (for example, **onClick**, **onChange**).

- Any function can be executed upon (user) events.

- In order to force React to re-evaluate components and (possibly) update the rendered UI, state must be used.

- State refers to data managed internally by React, and a state value can be defined via the **useState()** Hook.

- React Hooks are JavaScript functions that add special features to React components (for example, the state feature, in this chapter).

- **useState()** always returns an array with exactly two elements:

- The **first element** is the current state value.

- The **second element** is a function to set the state to a new value (the *state-updating function*).

- When setting the state to a new value that depends on the previous value, a function should be passed to the state-updating function. This function then receives the previous state as a parameter (which will be provided automatically by React) and returns the new state that should be set.

- Any valid JavaScript value can be set as state—besides primitive values such as strings or numbers. This also includes reference values such as objects and arrays.

- If state needs to change because of some event that occurs in another component, you should *lift the state up* and manage it on a higher, shared level (that is, a common ancestor component).

WHAT'S NEXT?

State is an extremely important building block because it enables you to build truly dynamic applications. With this key concept out of the way, the next chapter will dive into utilizing state (and other concepts learned thus far) to render content conditionally and to render lists of content.

These are common tasks that are required in almost any UI or web app you're building, no matter whether it's about showing a warning overlay or displaying a list of products. The next chapter will help you add such features to your React apps.

TEST YOUR KNOWLEDGE!

Test your knowledge about the concepts covered in this chapter by answering the following questions. You can then compare your answers to examples that can be found at https://packt.link/Zu02Z.

1. What problem does state solve?

2. What's the difference between props and state?

3. How is state registered in a component?

4. Which values does the `useState()` Hook provide?

5. How many state values can be registered for a single component?

6. Does state affect components other than the component in which it was registered?

7. How should state be updated if the new state depends on the previous state?

8. How can state be shared across multiple components?

APPLY WHAT YOU LEARNED

With the new knowledge gained in this chapter, you are finally able to build truly dynamic UIs and React applications. Instead of being limited to hardcoded, static content and pages, you can now use state to set and update values and force React to re-evaluate components and the UI.

Here, you will find an activity that allows you to apply all the knowledge, including this new state knowledge, you have acquired up to this point.

ACTIVITY 4.1: BUILDING A SIMPLE CALCULATOR

In this activity, you'll build a very basic calculator that allows users to add, subtract, multiply, and divide two numbers with each other.

The steps are as follows:

1. Build the UI by using React components. Be sure to build four separate components for the four math operations, even though lots of code could be reused.

2. Collect the user input and update the result whenever the user enters a value into one of the two related input fields.

   Note that when working with numbers and getting those numbers from user input, you will need to ensure that the entered values are treated as numbers and not as strings.

The final result and UI of the calculator should look like this:

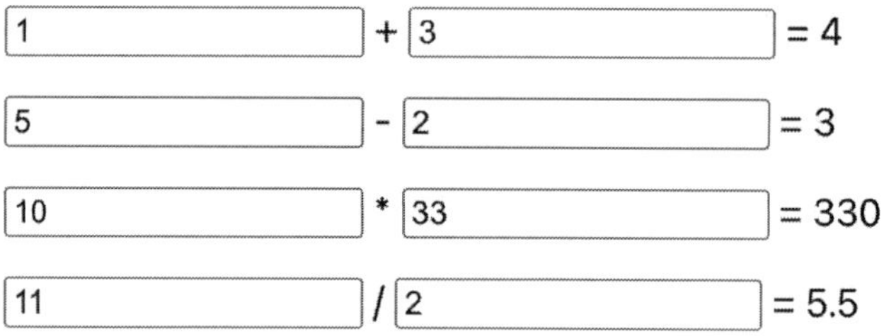

Figure 4.3: Calculator user interface

NOTE

The solution to this activity can be found on page 457.

ACTIVITY 4.2: ENHANCING THE CALCULATOR

In this activity, you'll build upon *Activity 4.1* to make the calculator built there slightly more complex. The goal is to reduce the number of components and build one single component in which users can select the mathematical operation via a drop-down element. In addition, the result should be output in a different component—that is, not in the component where the user input is gathered.

The steps are as follows:

1. Remove three of the four components from the previous activity and use one single component for all mathematical operations.

2. Add a drop-down element (**`<select>`** element) to that remaining component (between the two inputs) and add the four math operations as options (**`<option>`** elements) to it.

3. Use state to gather both the numbers entered by the user and the math operation chosen via the drop-down (it's up to you whether you prefer one single state object or multiple state slices).

4. Output the result in another component. (Hint: Choose a good place for registering and managing the state.)

The result and UI of the calculator should look like this:

Result: 15

Figure 4.4: User interface of the enhanced calculator

> **NOTE**
>
> The solution to this activity can be found on page 460.

5

RENDERING LISTS AND CONDITIONAL CONTENT

LEARNING OBJECTIVES

By the end of this chapter, you will be able to do the following:

- Output dynamic content conditionally.

- Render lists of data and map list items to JSX elements.

- Optimize lists such that React is able to efficiently update the user interface when needed.

INTRODUCTION

By this point in the book, you are already familiar with several key concepts, including components, props, state, and events, with which you have all the core tools you need to build all kinds of different React apps and websites. You have also learned how to output dynamic values and results as part of the user interface.

But there is one topic related to outputting dynamic data that has not yet been discussed in depth: outputting content conditionally and rendering list content. Since most (if not all) websites and web apps you build will require at least one of these two concepts, it is crucial to know how to work with conditional content and list data.

In this chapter, you will therefore learn how to render and display different user interface elements (and even entire user interface sections), based on dynamic conditions. In addition, you will learn how to output lists of data (such as a to-do list with its items) and render JSX elements dynamically for the items that make up a list. This chapter will also explore important best practices related to outputting lists and conditional content.

WHAT ARE CONDITIONAL CONTENT AND LIST DATA?

Before diving into the techniques for outputting conditional content or list content, it is important to understand what exactly is meant by those terms.

Conditional content simply means any kind of content that should only be displayed under certain circumstances. Examples are as follows:

- Error overlays that should only show up if a user submits incorrect data in a form

- Additional form input fields that appear once the user chooses to enter extra details (such as business details)

- A loading spinner that is displayed while data is sent or fetched to or from a backend server

- A side navigation menu that slides into view when the user clicks on a menu button

This is just a very short list of a few examples. You could, of course, come up with hundreds of additional examples. But it should be clear what all these examples are about in the end: visual elements or entire sections of the user interface that are only shown if certain conditions are met.

In the first example (an error overlay), the condition would be that a user entered incorrect data into a form. The conditionally shown content would then be the error overlay.

Conditional content is extremely common, since virtually all websites and web apps have some content that is similar or comparable to the preceding examples.

In addition to conditional content, many websites also output lists of data. It might not always be immediately obvious, but if you think about it, there is virtually no website that does not display some kind of list content. Again, here are some examples of list content that may be outputted on a site:

- An online shop displaying a grid or list of products

- An event booking site displaying a list of events

- A shopping cart displaying a list of cart items

- An orders page displaying a list of orders

- A blog displaying a list of blog posts—and maybe a list of comments below a blog post

- A list of navigation items in the header

An endless list (no pun intended) of examples could be created here. Lists are everywhere on the web. And, as the preceding examples show, many (probably even most) websites have multiple lists with various kinds of data on the same site.

Take an online shop, for example. Here, you would have a list (or a grid, which is really just another kind of list) of products, a list of shopping cart items, a list of orders, a list of navigation items in the header, and certainly a lot of other lists as well. This is why it is important that you know how to output any kind of list with any kind of data in React-driven user interfaces.

RENDERING CONTENT CONDITIONALLY

Imagine the following scenario. You have a button that, when clicked, should result in the display of an extra text box, as shown in the following diagram:

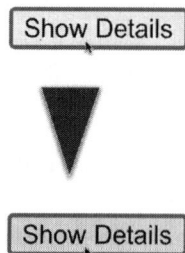

Figure 5.1: A button that, once clicked, reveals another element

This is a very simple example, but not an unrealistic one. Many websites have parts of the user interface that work like this. Showing extra information upon a button click (or some similar interaction) is a common pattern. Just think of nutrition information below a meal on a food order site or an FAQ section where answers are shown after selecting a question.

So, how could this scenario be implemented in a React app?

If you ignore the requirement of rendering some of the content conditionally, the overall React component could look like this:

```
function TermsOfUse() {
  return (
    <section>
      <button>Show Terms of Use Summary</button>
      <p>By continuing, you accept that we will not indemnify you for any
damage or harm caused by our products.</p>
    </section>
  );
}
```

This component has absolutely no conditional code in it, and therefore, both the button and the extra information box are shown all the time.

In this example, how could the paragraph with the terms-of-use summary text be shown conditionally (that is, only after the button is clicked)?

With the knowledge gained throughout the previous chapters, especially *Chapter 4, Working with Events and State*, you already have the skills needed to only show the text after the button is clicked. The following code shows how the component could be rewritten to show the full text only after the button is clicked:

```
import { useState } from 'react';

function TermsOfUse() {
  const [showTerms, setShowTerms] = useState(false);

  function showTermsSummaryHandler() {
    setShowTerms(true);
  }

  let paragraphText = '';

  if (showTerms) {
    paragraphText = 'By continuing, you accept that we will not indemnify
you for any damage or harm caused by our products.';
  }

  return (
    <section>
      <button onClick={showTermsSummaryHandler}>Show Terms of Use
Summary</button>
      <p>{paragraphText}</p>
    </section>
  );
}
```

Parts of the code shown in this snippet already qualify as conditional content. The **paragraphText** value is set conditionally, with the help of an **if** statement based on the value stored in the **showTerms** state.

But the **<p>** element itself is actually **not** conditional. It is always there, regardless of whether it contains a full sentence or an empty string. If you were to open the browser developer tools and inspect that area of the page, an empty paragraph element would be visible, as shown:

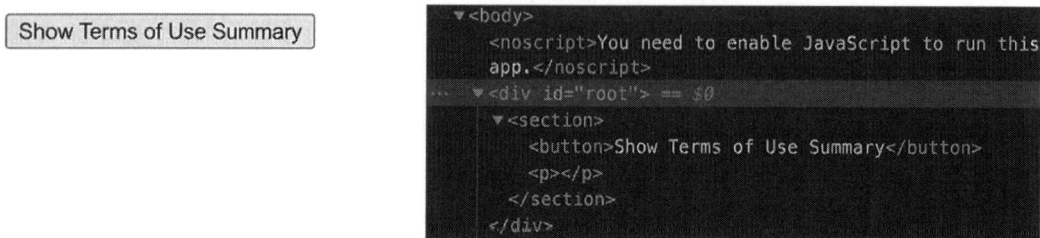

Figure 5.2: An empty paragraph element is rendered as part of the DOM

You can translate your knowledge about conditional values (such as the paragraph text) to conditional elements, however. Besides storing standard values such as text or numbers in variables, you can also store JSX elements in variables. This is possible because, as mentioned in *Chapter 1, React: What and Why*, JSX is just syntactic sugar. Behind the scenes, a JSX element is a standard JavaScript function that is executed by React. And, of course, the return value of a function call can be stored in a variable or constant.

With that in mind, the following code could be used to render the entire paragraph conditionally:

```
import { useState } from 'react';

function TermsOfUse() {
  const [showTerms, setShowTerms] = useState(false);

  function showTermsSummaryHandler() {
    setShowTerms(true);
  }

  let paragraph;

  if (showTerms) {
    paragraph = <p>By continuing, you accept that we will not indemnify
you for any damage or harm caused by our products.</p>;
  }

  return (
```

```
    <section>
      <button onClick={showTermsSummaryHandler}>Show Terms of Use
Summary</button>
      {paragraph}
    </section>
  );
}
```

In this example, if **showTerms** is **true**, the **paragraph** variable does not store text but instead an entire JSX element (the **<p>** element). In the returned JSX code, the value stored in the **paragraph** variable is outputted dynamically via **{paragraph}**. If **showTerms** is **false**, **paragraph** stores the value **undefined** and nothing is rendered to the DOM. Therefore, inserting **null** or **undefined** in JSX code leads to nothing being outputted by React. But if **showTerms** is **true**, the complete paragraph is saved as a value and outputted in the DOM.

This is how entire JSX elements can be rendered dynamically. Of course, you are not limited to single elements. You could store entire JSX tree structures (such as multiple, nested, or sibling JSX elements) inside variables or constants. As a simple rule, anything that can be returned by a component function can be stored in a variable.

DIFFERENT WAYS OF RENDERING CONTENT CONDITIONALLY

In the example shown previously, content is rendered conditionally by using a variable, which is set with the help of an **if** statement and then outputted dynamically in JSX code. This is a common (and perfectly fine) technique of rendering content conditionally, but it is not the only approach you can use.

Alternatively, you could also do the following:

- Utilize ternary expressions.
- *Abuse* JavaScript logical operators.
- Use any other valid JavaScript way of selecting values conditionally.

UTILIZING TERNARY EXPRESSIONS

In JavaScript (and many other programming languages), you can use ternary expressions as alternatives to **if** statements. Ternary expressions can save you lines of code, especially with simple conditions where the main goal is to assign some variable value conditionally.

Here is a direct comparison—first starting with a regular **if** statement:

```
let a = 1;
if (someCondition) {
  a = 2;
}
```

And here is the same logic, implemented with a ternary expression:

```
const a = someCondition ? 1 : 2;
```

This is standard JavaScript code, not React-specific. But it is important to understand this core JavaScript feature in order to understand how it can be used in React apps.

Translated to the previous React example, the paragraph content could be set and outputted conditionally with the help of ternary expressions like this:

```
import { useState } from 'react';

function TermsOfUse() {
  const [showTerms, setShowTerms] = useState(false);

  function showTermsSummaryHandler() {
    setShowTerms(true);
  }

  const paragraph = showTerms ? <p>By continuing, you accept that we will
not indemnify you for any damage or harm caused by our products.</p> :
null;

  return (
    <section>
      <button onClick={showTermsSummaryHandler}>Show Terms of Use
Summary</button>
      {paragraph}
    </section>
  );
}
```

As you can see, the overall code is a bit shorter than before, when an **if** statement was used. The paragraph constant contains either the paragraph (including the text content) or **null**. **null** is used as an alternative value because **null** can safely be inserted into JSX code as it simply leads to nothing being rendered in its place.

A disadvantage of ternary expressions is that readability and understandability may suffer—especially when using nested ternary expressions, like in the following example:

```
const paragraph = !showTerms ? null : someOtherCondition ? <p>By
continuing, you accept that we will not indemnify you for any damage or
harm caused by our products.</p> : null;
```

This code is difficult to read and even more difficult to understand. For this reason, you should typically avoid writing nested ternary expressions and fall back to **if** statements in such situations.

But, despite these potential disadvantages, ternary expressions can help you write less code in React apps, especially when using them inline, directly inside some JSX code:

```
import { useState } from 'react';

function TermsOfUse() {
  const [showTerms, setShowTerms] = useState(false);

  function showTermsSummaryHandler() {
    setShowTerms(true);
  }

  return (
    <section>
      <button>Show Terms of Use Summary</button>
      {showTerms ? <p>By continuing, you accept that we will not
indemnify you for any damage or harm caused by our products.</p> : null}
    </section>
  );
}
```

This is the same example as before, only now it's even shorter since here you avoid using the **paragraph** constant by utilizing the ternary expression directly inside of the JSX snippet. This allows for relatively lean component code, so it is quite common to use ternary expressions in JSX code in React apps to take advantage of this.

ABUSING JAVASCRIPT LOGICAL OPERATORS

Ternary expressions are popular because they enable you to write less code, which, when used in the right places (and avoiding nesting multiple ternary expressions), can help with overall readability.

Especially in React apps, in JSX code you will often write ternary expressions like this:

```
<div>
   {showDetails ? <h1>Product Details</h1> : null}
</div>
```

Or like this:

```
<div>
   {showTerms ? <p>Our terms of use ...</p> : null}
</div>
```

What do these two snippets have in common?

They are unnecessarily long, because in both examples, the else case (: **null**) must be specified, even though it adds nothing to the final user interface. After all, the primary purpose of these ternary expressions is to render JSX elements (**<h1>** and **<p>**, in the preceding examples). The else case (: **null**) simply means nothing is rendered if the conditions (**showDetails** and **showTerms**, respectively) are not met.

This is why a different pattern is popular among React developers:

```
<div>
   {showDetails && <h1>Product Details</h1>}
</div>
```

This is the shortest possible way of achieving the intended result, rendering only the **<h1>** element and its content if **showDetails** is **true**.

This code uses (or abuses) an interesting behavior of JavaScript's logical operators, and specifically of the **&&** (logical "and") operator. In JavaScript, the **&&** operator returns the second value (that is, the value after **&&**), if the first value (that is, the value before **&&**) is **true** or truthy (that is, not **false**, **undefined**, **null**, **0**, and so on).

For example, the following code would output **'Hello'**:

```
console.log(1 === 1 && 'Hello');
```

This behavior can be used to write very short expressions that check a condition and then output another value, as shown in the preceding example.

> **NOTE**
>
> It is worth noting that using `&&` can lead to unexpected results if you're using it with non-Boolean condition values (that is, if the value in front of `&&` holds a non-Boolean value). If `showDetails` were 0 instead of `false` (for whatever reason), the number 0 would be displayed on the screen. You should therefore ensure that the value acting as a condition yields `null` or `false` instead of arbitrary falsy values. You could, for example, force a conversion to a Boolean by adding `!!` (for example, `!!showDetails`). That is not required if your condition value already holds `null` or `false`.

GET CREATIVE!

At this point, you have learned about three different ways of defining and outputting content conditionally (regular `if` statements, ternary expressions, and using the `&&` operator). But the most important point is that React code is ultimately just regular JavaScript code. Hence, any approach that selects values conditionally will work.

If it makes sense in your specific use case and React app, you could also have a component that selects and outputs content conditionally like this:

```
const languages = {
  de: 'de-DE',
  us: ,en-US',
  uk: ,en-GB'
};


function LanguageSelector({country}) {
  return <p>Selected Language: {languages[country]}</p>
}
```

This component outputs either **'de-DE'**, **'en-US'**, or **'en-GB'** based on the value of the **country** prop. This result is achieved by using JavaScript's dynamic property selection syntax. Instead of selecting a specific property via the dot notation (such as **person.name**), you can select property values via the bracket notation. With that notation, you can either pass a specific property name (**languages['de-DE']**) or an expression that yields a property name (**languages[country]**).

Selecting property values dynamically like this is another common pattern for picking values from a map of values. It is therefore an alternative to specifying multiple `if` statements or ternary expressions.

And, in general, you can use any approach that works in standard JavaScript—because React is, after all, just standard JavaScript at its core.

WHICH APPROACH IS BEST?

Various ways of setting and outputting content conditionally have been discussed, but which approach is best?

That really is up to you (and, if applicable, your team). The most important advantages and disadvantages have been highlighted, but ultimately, it is your decision. If you prefer ternary expressions, there's nothing wrong with choosing them over the logical `&&` operator, for example.

It will also depend on the exact problem you are trying to solve. If you have a map of values (such as a list of countries and their country language codes), going for dynamic property selection instead of multiple `if` statements might be preferable. On the other hand, if you have a single **true/false** condition (such as **age > 18**), using a standard `if` statement or the logical `&&` operator might be best.

SETTING ELEMENT TAGS CONDITIONALLY

Outputting content conditionally is a very common scenario. But sometimes, you will also want to choose the type of HTML tag that will be outputted conditionally. Typically, this will be the case when you build components whose main task is to wrap and enhance built-in components.

Here's an example:

```
function Button({isButton, config, children}) {
  if (isButton) {
    return <button {...config}>{children}</button>;
  }
  return <a {...config}>{children}</a>;
};
```

This **Button** component checks whether the **isButton** prop value is truthy and, if that is the case, returns a **<button>** element. The **config** prop is expected to be a JavaScript object, and the standard JavaScript spread operator (**...**) is used to then add all key-value pairs of the **config** object as props to the **<button>** element. If **isButton** is not truthy (maybe because no value was provided for **isButton**, or because the value is **false**), the **else** condition becomes active. Instead of a **<button>** element, an **<a>** element is returned.

> **NOTE**
>
> Using the spread operator (**. . .**) to translate an object's properties (key-value pairs) into component props is another common React pattern (and was introduced in *Chapter 3, Components and Props*). The spread operator is not React-specific but using it for this special purpose *is*.
>
> When spreading an object such as **{link: 'https://some-url.com', isButton: false}** onto an **<a>** element (via **<a {...obj}>**), the result would be the same as if all props had been set individually (that is, **<a link="https://some-url.com" isButton={false}>**).
>
> This pattern is particularly popular in situations where you build custom *wrapper components* that wrap a common core component (e.g., **<button>**, **<input>**, or **<a>**) to add certain styles or behaviors, while still allowing for the component to be used in the same way as the built-in component (that is, you can set all the default props).

The **Button** component from the preceding example returns two totally different JSX elements, depending on the **isButton** prop value. This is a great way of checking a condition and returning different content (that is, conditional content).

But, by using a special React behavior, this component could be written with even less code:

```
function Button({isButton, config, children}) {
  const Tag = isButton ? 'button' : 'a';
  return <Tag {...config}>{children}</Tag>;
};
```

The special behavior is that tag names can be stored (as string values) in variables or constants, and that those variables or constants can then be used like JSX elements in JSX code (as long as the variable or constant name starts with an uppercase character, like all your custom components).

The **Tag** constant in the preceding example stores either the **'button'** or **'a'** string. Since it starts with an uppercase character (**Tag**, instead of **tag**), it can then be used like a custom component inside of JSX code snippets. React accepts this as a component, even though it isn't a component function. This is because a standard HTML element tag name is stored, and so React can render the appropriate built-in component. The same pattern could also be used with custom components. Instead of storing string values, you would store pointers to your custom component functions through the following:

```
import MyComponent from './my-component';
import MyOtherComponent from './my-other-component';


const Tag = someCondition ? MyComponent : MyOtherComponent;
```

This is another useful pattern that can help save code and hence leads to leaner components.

OUTPUTTING LIST DATA

Besides outputting conditional data, you will often work with list data that should be outputted on a page. As mentioned earlier in this chapter, some examples are lists of products, transactions, and navigation items.

Typically, in React apps, such list data is received as an array of values. For example, a component might receive an array of products via props (passed into the component from inside another component that might be getting that data from some backend API):

```
function ProductsList({products}) {
   // ... todo!
};
```

In this example, the products array could look like this:

```
const products = [
   {id: 'p1', title: 'A Book', price: 59.99},
   {id: 'p2', title: 'A Carpet', price: 129.49},
   {id: 'p3', title: 'Another Book', price: 39.99},
];
```

This data can't be outputted like this, though. Instead, the goal is typically to translate it into a list of JSX elements which fits. For example, the desired result could be the following:

```
<ul>
  <li>
    <h2>A Book</h2>
    <p>$59.99</p>
  </li>
  <li>
    <h2>A Carpet</h2>
    <p>$129.49</p>
  </li>
  <li>
    <h2>Another Book</h2>
    <p>$39.99</p>
  </li>
</ul>
```

How can this transformation be achieved?

Again, it's a good idea to ignore React and find a way to transform list data with standard JavaScript. One possible way to achieve this would be to use a **for** loop, as shown:

```
const transformedProducts = [];
for (const product of products) {
  transformedProducts.push(product.title);
}
```

In this example, the list of product objects (**products**) is transformed into a list of product titles (that is, a list of string values). This is achieved by looping through all product items in **products** and extracting only the **title** property from each product. This **title** property value is then pushed into the new **transformedProducts** array.

A similar approach can be used to transform the list of objects into a list of JSX elements:

```
const productElements = [];
for (const product of products) {
  productElements.push((
    <li>
```

```
      <h2>{product.title}</h2>
      <p>${product.price}</p>
    </li>
  ));
}
```

The first time you see code like this, it might look a bit strange. But keep in mind that JSX code can be used anywhere where regular JavaScript values (that is, numbers, strings, objects, and so on) can be used. Therefore, you can also **push** a JSX value onto an array of values. And since it's JSX code, you can also output content dynamically in those JSX elements (such as **<h2>{product.title}</h2>**).

This code is valid, and is an important first step toward outputting list data. But it is only the first step, since the current data was transformed but still isn't returned by a component.

How can such an array of JSX elements be returned then?

The answer is that it can be returned without any special tricks or code. JSX actually accepts array values as dynamically outputted values.

You can output the **productElements** array like this:

```
return (
  <ul>
    {productElements}
  </ul>
);
```

When inserting an array of JSX elements into JSX code, all JSX elements inside that array are outputted next to each other. So, the following two snippets would produce the same output:

```
return (
  <div>
    {[<p>Hi there</p>, <p>Another item</p>]}
  </div>
);

return (
  <div>
    <p>Hi there</p>
```

```
      <p>Another item</p>
   </div>
);
```

With this in mind, the **ProductsList** component could be written like this:

```
function ProductsList({products}) {
  const productElements = [];
  for (const product of products) {
    productElements.push((
      <li>
        <h2>{product.title}</h2>
        <p>${product.price}</p>
      </li>
    ));
  }

  return (
    <ul>
      {productElements}
    </ul>
  );
};
```

This is one possible approach for outputting list data. As explained earlier in this chapter, it's all about using standard JavaScript features and combining those features with JSX.

MAPPING LIST DATA

Outputting list data with **for** loops works, as you can see in the preceding examples. But just as with **if** statements and ternary expressions, you can replace **for** loops with an alternative syntax to write less code and improve component readability.

JavaScript offers a built-in array method that can be used to transform array items: the **map()** method. **map()** is a default method that can be called on any JavaScript array. It accepts a function as a parameter and executes that function for every array item. The return value of this function should be the transformed value. **map()** then combines all these returned, transformed values into a new array that is then returned by **map()**.

You could use **map()** like this:

```
const users = [
  {id: 'u1', name: 'Max', age: 35},
  {id: 'u2', name: 'Anna', age: 32}
];
const userNames = users.map(user => user.name);
// userNames = ['Max', 'Anna']
```

In this example, **map()** is used to transform the array of user objects into an array of usernames (that is, an array of string values).

The **map()** method is often able to produce the same result as that of a **for** loop, but with less code.

Therefore, **map()** can also be used to generate an array of JSX elements and the **ProductsList** component from before could be rewritten like this:

```
function ProductsList({products}) {
  const productElements = products.map(product => (
      <li>
        <h2>{product.title}</h2>
        <p>${product.price}</p>
      </li>
    )
  );

  return (
    <ul>
      {productElements}
    </ul>
  );
};
```

This is already shorter than the earlier **for** loop example. But, just as with ternary expressions, the code can be shortened even more by moving the logic directly into the JSX code:

```
function ProductsList({products}) {
  return (
    <ul>
      {products.map(product => (
        <li>
```

```
        <h2>{product.title}</h2>
        <p>${product.price}</p>
      </li>
    )
  )}
  </ul>
 );
};
```

Depending on the complexity of the transformation (that is, the complexity of the code executed inside the inner function, which is passed to the **map()** method), for readability reasons, you might want to consider not using this *inline* approach (such as when mapping array elements to some complex JSX structure or when performing extra calculations as part of the mapping process). Ultimately, this comes down to personal preference and judgment.

Because it's very concise, using the **map()** method (either with the help of an extra variable or constant, or directly *inline* in the JSX code) is the de facto standard approach for outputting list data in React apps and JSX in general.

UPDATING LISTS

Imagine you have a list of data mapped to JSX elements, and a new list item is added at some point. Or, consider a scenario in which you have a list wherein two list items swap places (that is, the list is reordered). How can such updates be reflected in the DOM?

The good news is that React will take care of that for you if the update is performed in a stateful way (that is, by using React's state concept, as explained in *Chapter 4, Working with Events and State*).

However, there are a couple of important aspects to updating (stateful) lists you should be aware of.

Here's a simplified example that would **not** work as intended:

```
import { useState } from 'react';

function Todos() {
  const [todos, setTodos] = useState(['Learn React', 'Recommend this book']);

  function addTodoHandler() {
    todos.push('A new todo');
```

```
  };

  return (
    <div>
      <button onClick={addTodoHandler}>Add Todo</button>
      <ul>
        {todos.map(todo => <li>{todo}</li>)}
      </ul>
    </div>
  );
};
```

Initially, two to-do items would be displayed on the screen (**<li>Learn React</li>** and **<li>Recommend this book</li>**). But once the button is clicked and **addTodoHandler** is executed, the expected result of another to-do item being displayed will not materialize.

This is because executing **todos.push('A new todo') will** update the **todos** array, but React won't notice it. Keep in mind that you must only update the state via the state updating function returned by **useState()**; otherwise, React will not re-evaluate the component function.

So how about this code?

```
function addTodoHandler() {
  setTodos(todos.push('A new todo'));
};
```

This is also incorrect because the state updating function (**setTodos**, in this case) should receive the new state (that is, the state that should be set) as an argument. But the **push()** method doesn't return the updated array. Instead, it mutates the existing array in place. Even if **push()** were to return the updated array, it would still be wrong to use the preceding code, because the data would be changed (mutated) behind the scenes before the state updating function would be executed. Technically, data would be changed before informing React about that change. Following the React best practices, this should be avoided.

Therefore, when updating an array (or, as a side note, an object in general), you should perform this update in an **immutable** way—i.e., without changing the original array or object. Instead, a new array or object should be created. This new array can be based on the old array and contain all the old data, as well as any new or updated data.

Therefore, the **todos** array should be updated like this:

```
function addTodoHandler() {
  setTodos(curTodos => [...curTodos, 'A new todo']);
  // alternative: Use concat() instead of the spread operator:
  // concat(), unlike push(), returns a new array
  // setTodos(curTodos => curTodos.concat('A new todo'));
};
```

By using **concat()** or a new array, combined with the spread operator, a brand-new array is provided to the state updating function. Note also that a function is passed to the state updating function, since the new state depends on the previous state.

When updating an array (or any object) state value like this, React is able to pick up those changes. Therefore, React will re-evaluate the component function and apply any required changes to the DOM.

> **NOTE**
>
> Immutability is not a React-specific concept, but it's a key one in React apps nonetheless. When working with state and reference values (that is, objects and arrays), immutability is extremely important to ensure that React is able to pick up changes and no "invisible" (that is, not recognized by React) state changes are performed.
>
> There are different ways of updating objects and arrays immutably, but a popular approach is to create new objects or arrays and then use the spread operator (. . .) to merge existing data into those new arrays or objects.

A PROBLEM WITH LIST ITEMS

If you're following along with your own code, you might've noticed that React actually shows a warning in the browser developer tools console, as shown in the following screenshot:

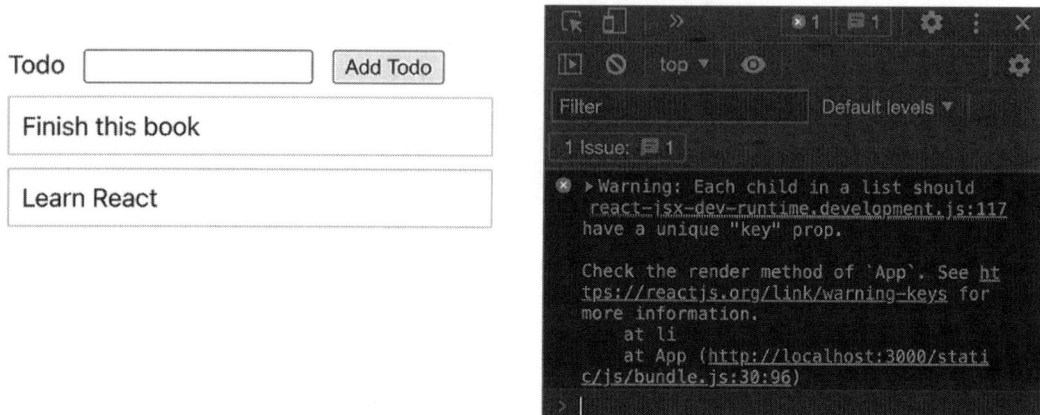

Figure 5.3: React sometimes generates a warning regarding missing unique keys

React is complaining about missing keys.

To understand this warning and the idea behind keys, it's helpful to explore a specific use case and a potential problem with that scenario. Assume that you have a React component that is responsible for displaying a list of items—maybe a list of to-do items. In addition, assume that those list items can be reordered and that the list can be edited in other ways (for example, new items can be added, existing items can be updated or deleted, and so on). Put in other words, the list is not static.

Consider this example user interface, in which a new item is added to a list of to-do items:

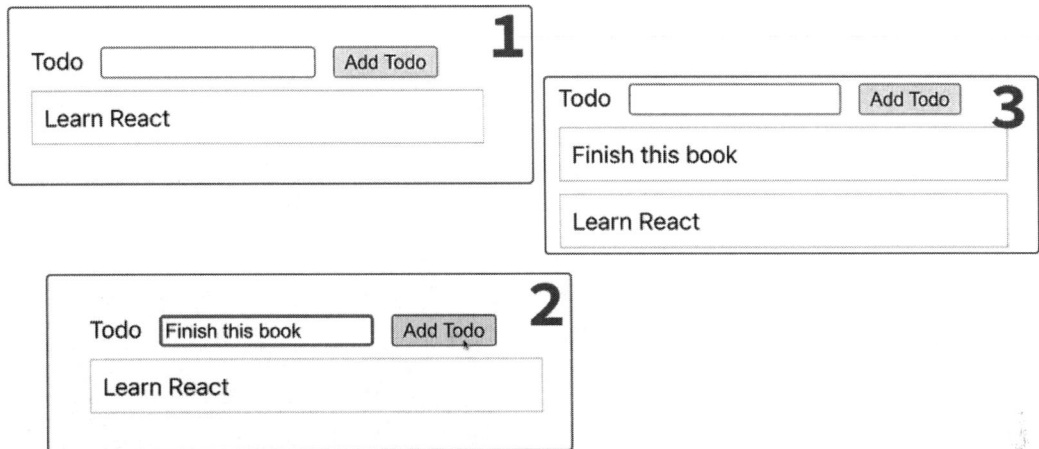

Figure 5.4: A list gets updated by inserting a new item at the top

In the preceding figure, you can see the initially rendered list (**1**), which is then updated after a user entered and submitted a new to-do value (**2**). A new to-do item was added to the top of the list (that is, as the first item of the list) (**3**).

> **NOTE**
>
> The example source code for this demo app can be found at
> https://packt.link/LsP33.

If you work on this app and open the browser developer tools (and then the JavaScript console), you will see the "missing keys" warning that has been mentioned before. This app also helps with understanding where this warning is coming from.

In the Chrome DevTools, navigate to the **Elements** tab and select one of the to-do items or the empty to-do list (that is, the **<ul>** element). Once you add a new to-do item, any DOM elements that were inserted or updated are highlighted by Chrome in the **Elements** tab (by flashing briefly). Refer to the following screenshot:

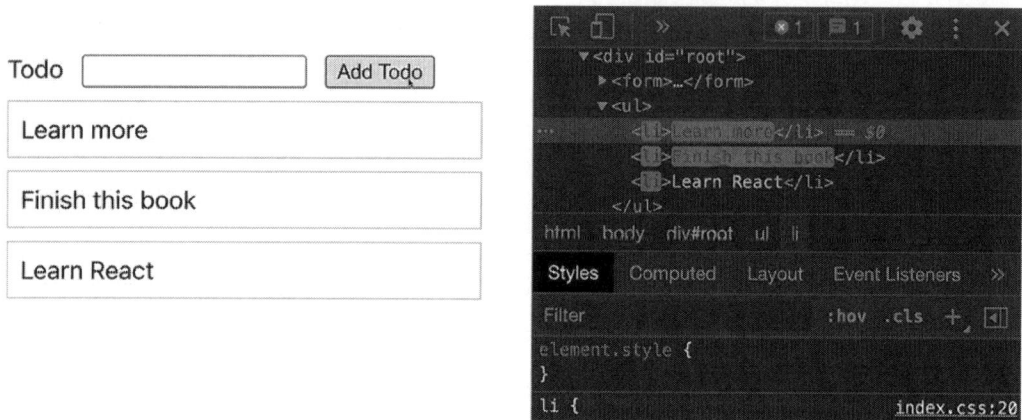

Figure 5.5: Updated DOM items are highlighted in the Chrome DevTools

The interesting part is that not only the newly added to-do element (that is, the newly inserted **<li>** element) is flashing. Instead, **all** existing **<li>** elements, which reflect existing to-do items that were not changed, are highlighted by Chrome. This implies that all these other **<li>** elements were also updated in the DOM—even though there was no need for that update. The items existed before, and their content (the to-do text) didn't change.

For some reason, React seems to destroy the existing DOM nodes (that is, the existing **<li>** items), just to then recreate them immediately. This happens for every new to-do item that is added to the list. As you might imagine, this is not very efficient and can cause performance problems for more complex apps that might be rendering dozens or hundreds of items across multiple lists.

This happens because React has no way of knowing that only one DOM node should be inserted. It cannot tell that all other DOM nodes should stay untouched because React only received a brand-new state value: a new array, filled with new JavaScript objects. Even if the content of those objects didn't change, they are technically still new objects (new values in memory).

As the developer, you know how your app works and that the content of the to-dos array didn't actually change that much. But React doesn't know that. Therefore, React determines that all existing list items (**<li>** items) must be discarded and replaced by new items that reflect the new data that was provided as part of the state update. That is why **all** list-related DOM nodes are updated (that is, destroyed and recreated) for every state update.

KEYS TO THE RESCUE!

The problem outlined previously is an extremely common one. Most list updates are incremental updates, not bulk changes. But React can't tell whether that is the case for your use case and your list.

That's why React uses the concept of **keys** when working with list data and rendering list items. Keys are simply unique **id** values that can (and should) be attached to JSX elements when rendering list data. Keys help React identify elements that were rendered before and didn't change. By allowing for the unique identification of all list elements, keys also help React to move (list item) DOM elements around efficiently.

Keys are added to JSX elements via the special built-in **key** prop that is accepted by every component:

```
<li key={todo.id}>{todo.text}</li>
```

This special prop can be added to all components, be they built-in or custom. You don't need to accept or handle the **key** prop in any way on your custom components; React will do that for you automatically.

The **key** prop requires a value that is unique for every list item. No two list items should have the same key. In addition, good keys are directly attached to the underlying data that makes up the list item. Therefore, list item indexes are poor keys because the index isn't attached to the list item data. If you reorder items in a list, the indexes stay the same (an array always starts with index **0**, followed by **1**, and so on) but the data is changed.

Consider the following example:

```
const hobbies = ['Sports', 'Cooking'];
const reversed = hobbies.reverse(); // ['Cooking', 'Sports']
```

In this example, **'Sports'** has the index **0** in the hobbies array. In the reversed array, its index would be **1** (because it's the second item now). In this case, if the index were used as a key, the data would not be attached to it.

Good keys are unique **id** values, such that every **id** belongs to exactly one value. If that value moves or is removed, its **id** should move or disappear with that value.

Finding good **id** values typically isn't a huge problem since most list data is fetched from databases anyway. No matter whether you're dealing with products, orders, users, or shopping cart items, it's all data that would typically be stored in a database. This kind of data already has unique **id** values since you always have some kind of unique identification criteria when storing data in databases.

Sometimes, even the values themselves can be used as keys. Consider the following example:

```
const hobbies = ['Sports', 'Cooking'];
```

Hobbies are string values, and there is no unique **id** value attached to individual hobbies. Every hobby is a primitive value (a string). But in cases like this, you typically won't have duplicate values as it doesn't make sense for a hobby to be listed more than once in an array like this. Therefore, the values themselves qualify as good keys:

```
hobbies.map(hobby => <li key={hobby}>{hobby}</li>);
```

In cases where you can't use the values themselves and there is no other possible key value, you can generate unique **id** values directly in your React app code. As a last resort, you can also fall back to using indexes; but be aware that this can lead to unexpected bugs and side effects if you reorder list items.

With keys added to list item elements, React is able to identify all items correctly. When the component state changes, it can identify JSX elements that were rendered before already. Those elements are therefore not destroyed or recreated anymore.

You can confirm this by again opening the browser DevTools to check which DOM elements are updated upon changes to the underlying list data:

Figure 5.6: From multiple list items, only one DOM element gets updated

After adding keys, when updating the list state, only the new DOM item is highlighted in the Chrome DevTools. The other items are (correctly) ignored by React.

SUMMARY AND KEY TAKEAWAYS

- Like any other JavaScript value, JSX elements can be set and changed dynamically, based on different conditions.

- Content can be set conditionally via **if** statements, ternary expressions, the logical "and" operator (**&&**), or in any other way that works in JavaScript.

- There are multiple ways to handle conditional content—any approach that would work in vanilla JavaScript can also be used in React apps.

- Arrays with JSX elements can be inserted into JSX code and will lead to the array elements being outputted as sibling DOM elements.

- List data can be converted into JSX element arrays via **for** loops, the **map()** method, or any other JavaScript approach that leads to a similar conversion.

- Using the **map()** method is the most common way of converting list data to JSX element lists.

- Keys (via the **key** prop) should be added to the list JSX elements to help React update the DOM efficiently.

WHAT'S NEXT?

With conditional content and lists, you now have all the key tools needed to build both simple and more complex user interfaces with React. You can hide and show elements or groups of elements as needed, and you can dynamically render and update lists of elements to output lists of products, orders, or users.

Of course, that's not all that's needed to build realistic user interfaces. Adding logic for changing content dynamically is one thing, but most web apps also need CSS styling that should be applied to various DOM elements. This book is not about CSS, but the next chapter will still explore how React apps can be styled. Especially when it comes to setting and changing styles dynamically or scoping styles to specific components, there are various React-specific concepts that should be familiar to every React developer.

TEST YOUR KNOWLEDGE!

Test your knowledge about the concepts covered in this chapter by answering the following questions. You can then compare your answers to examples that can be found at https://packt.link/QyB9E.

1. What is "conditional content"?

2. Name at least two different ways of rendering JSX elements conditionally.

3. Which elegant approach can be used to define element tags conditionally?

4. What's a potential downside of using only ternary expressions (for conditional content)?

5. How can lists of data be rendered as JSX elements?

6. Why should keys be added to rendered list items?

7. Give one example each for a good and a bad key.

APPLY WHAT YOU LEARNED

You are now able to use your React knowledge to change dynamic user interfaces in a variety of ways. Besides being able to change displayed text values and numbers, you can now also hide or show entire elements (or chunks of elements) and display lists of data.

In the following sections, you will find two activities that allow you to apply your newly gained knowledge (combined with the knowledge gained in the other book chapters).

ACTIVITY 5.1: SHOWING A CONDITIONAL ERROR MESSAGE

In this activity, you'll build a basic form that allows users to enter their email address. Upon form submission, the user input should be validated and invalid email addresses (for simplicity, here email addresses that contain no @ sign are being referred to here) should lead to an error message being shown below the form. When invalid email addresses are made valid, potentially visible error messages should be removed again.

Perform the following steps to complete this activity:

1. Build a user interface that contains a form with a label, an input field (of the text type—to make entering incorrect email addresses easier for demo purposes), and a submit button that leads to the form being submitted.

2. Collect the entered email address and show an error message below the form if the email address contains no @ sign.

The final user interface should look and work as shown here:

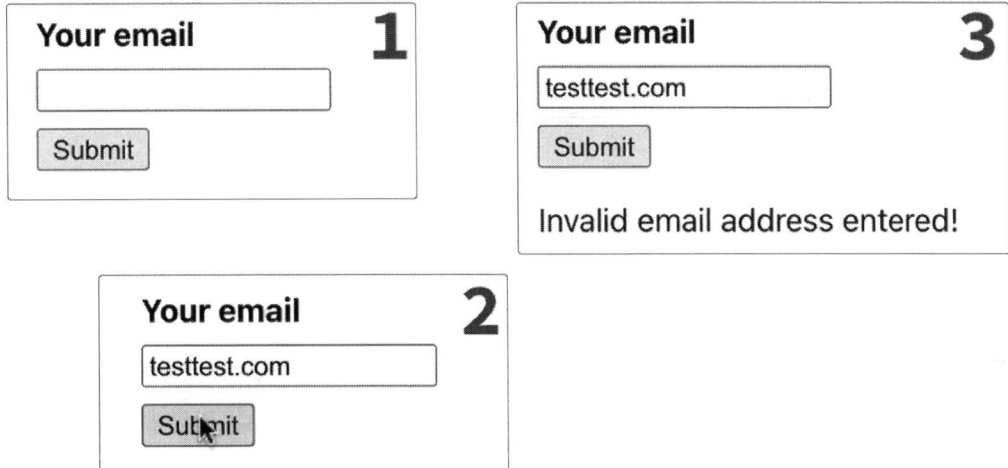

Figure 5.7: The final user interface of this activity

NOTE

The solution to this activity can be found on page 465.

ACTIVITY 5.2: OUTPUTTING A LIST OF PRODUCTS

In this activity, you will build a user interface where a list of (dummy) products is displayed on the screen. The interface should also contain a button that, when clicked, adds another new (dummy) item to the existing list of products.

Perform the following steps to complete this activity:

1. Add a list of dummy product objects (every object should have an ID, title, and price) to a React component and add code to output these product items as JSX elements.

2. Add a button to the user interface. When clicked, the button should add a new product object to the product data list. This should then cause the user interface to update and display an updated list of product elements.

The final user interface should look and work as shown here:

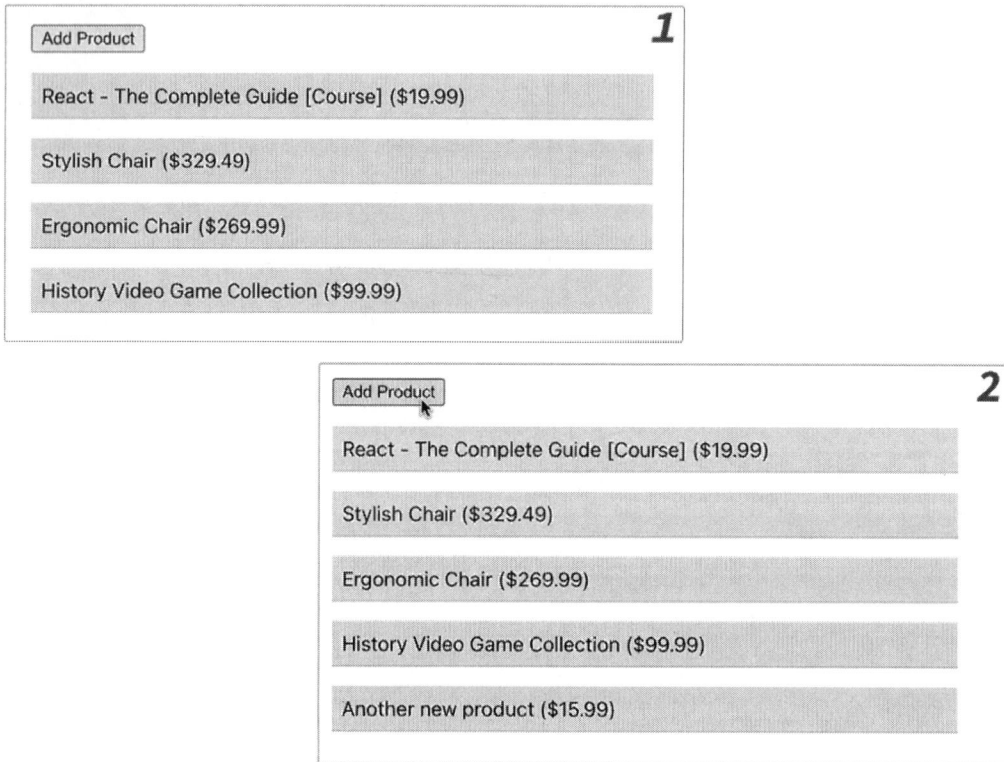

Figure 5.8: The final user interface of this activity

> **NOTE**
>
> The solution to this activity can be found on page 469.

6

STYLING REACT APPS

LEARNING OBJECTIVES

By the end of this chapter, you will be able to do the following:

- Style JSX elements via inline style assignments or with the help of CSS classes

- Set inline and class styles, both statically and dynamically or conditionally

- Build reusable components that allow for style customization

- Utilize CSS Modules to scope styles to components

- Understand the core idea behind `styled-components`, a third-party CSS-in-JS library

INTRODUCTION

React.js is a frontend JavaScript library. This means that it's all about building (web) user interfaces and handling user interaction.

Up to this point, this book has extensively explored how React may be used to add interactivity to a web app. State, event handling, and dynamic content are key concepts relating to this.

Of course, websites and web apps are not just about interactivity. You could build an amazing web app that offers interactive and engaging features, and yet it may still be unpopular if it lacks appealing visuals. Presentation is key, and the web is no exception.

Therefore, like all other apps and websites, React apps and websites need proper styling. And when working with web technologies, **Cascading Style Sheets** (**CSS**) is the language of choice.

This book is not about CSS, though. It won't explain or teach you how to use CSS as there are dedicated, better resources for that (e.g., the free CSS guides at https://developer.mozilla.org). But this chapter will teach you how to combine CSS code with JSX and React concepts such as state and props. You will learn how to add styles to your JSX elements, style custom components, and make those components' styles configurable. This chapter will also teach you how to set styles dynamically and conditionally and explore popular third-party libraries that may be used for styling.

HOW DOES STYLING WORK IN REACT APPS?

Up to this point, the apps and examples presented in this book have only had minimal styling. But they at least had some basic styling, rather than no styling at all.

But how was that styling added? How can styles be added to user interface elements (such as DOM elements) when using React?

The short answer is "just as you would to non-React apps". You can add CSS styles and classes to JSX elements just as you would to regular HTML elements. And in your CSS code, you can use all the features and selectors you know from CSS. There are no React-specific changes you have to make when writing CSS code.

The code examples used up to this point (i.e., the activities or other examples hosted on GitHub) always used regular CSS styling with the help of CSS selectors to apply some basic styles to the final user interface. Those CSS rules were defined in an **index.css** file, which is part of every newly created React project (when using **create-react-app** for project creation, as shown in *Chapter 1, React – What and Why*).

For example, here's the **index.css** file used in *Activity 5.1* of the previous chapter (*Chapter 5, Rendering Lists and Conditional Content*):

```css
body {
  margin: 2rem;
  font-family: -apple-system, BlinkMacSystemFont, 'Segoe UI', 'Roboto',
'Oxygen',
    'Ubuntu', 'Cantarell', 'Fira Sans', 'Droid Sans', 'Helvetica Neue',
    sans-serif;
  -webkit-font-smoothing: antialiased;
  -moz-osx-font-smoothing: grayscale;
}

ul {
  list-style: none;
  margin: 0;
  padding: 0;
}

li {
  background-color: #ede6f3;
  box-shadow: 0 1px rgba(0, 0, 0, 0.2);
  padding: 0.5rem;
  margin: 1rem 0;
  max-width: 30rem;
}
```

The actual CSS code and its meaning is not important (as mentioned, this book is not about CSS). What is important, though, is the fact that this code contains no JavaScript or React code at all. As mentioned, the CSS code you write is totally independent of the fact that you're using React in your app.

The more interesting question is how that code is actually applied to the rendered web page. How is it imported into that page?

Normally, you would expect style file imports (via **<link href="...">**) inside of the HTML files that are being served. Since React apps are typically about building **single-page applications** (see *Chapter 1*, *React – What and Why*), you only have one HTML file—the **index.html** file—which can be found in the **public/** folder of your React project. But if you inspect that file, you won't find any **<link href="...">** import that would point to the **index.css** file (only some other **<link>** elements that import favicons or the web page manifest file), as you can see in the following screenshot:

```
<> index.html ×
1    <!DOCTYPE html>
2    <html lang="en">
3      <head>
4        <meta charset="utf-8" />
5        <link rel="icon" href="%PUBLIC_URL%/favicon.ico" />
6        <meta name="viewport" content="width=device-width, initial-scale=1" />
7        <meta name="theme-color" content="#000000" />
8        <meta
9          name="description"
10         content="Web site created using create-react-app"
11       />
12       <link rel="apple-touch-icon" href="%PUBLIC_URL%/logo192.png" />
13       <!--
14         manifest.json provides metadata used when your web app is installed on a
15         user's mobile device or desktop. See https://developers.google.com/web/fundamentals/web-app-manifest/
16       -->
17       <link rel="manifest" href="%PUBLIC_URL%/manifest.json" />
18       <!--
19         Notice the use of %PUBLIC_URL% in the tags above.
20         It will be replaced with the URL of the `public` folder during the build.
21         Only files inside the `public` folder can be referenced from the HTML.
22
23         Unlike "/favicon.ico" or "favicon.ico", "%PUBLIC_URL%/favicon.ico" will
24         work correctly both with client-side routing and a non-root public URL.
25         Learn how to configure a non-root public URL by running `npm run build`.
26       -->
27       <title>React App</title>
28     </head>
```

Figure 6.1: The <head> section of the index.html file contains no <link> import that points to the index.css file

How are the styles defined in **index.css** imported and applied then?

You find an **import** statement in the root entry file (this is the **index.js** file in projects generated via **create-react-app**):

```
import React from 'react';
import ReactDOM from 'react-dom';

import './index.css';
import App from './App';

ReactDOM.render(
  <React.StrictMode>
    <App />
  </React.StrictMode>,
  document.getElementById('root')
);
```

The **import './index.css';** statement leads to the CSS file being imported and the defined CSS code being applied to the rendered web page.

It is worth noting that this is not standard JavaScript behavior. You can't import CSS files into JavaScript—at least not if you're just using vanilla JavaScript.

It works in React apps because the code is transpiled before it's loaded into the browser. Therefore, you won't find that **import** statement in the final JavaScript code that's executed in the browser. Instead, during the **transpilation process**, the transpiler identifies the CSS import, removes it from the JavaScript file, and injects the CSS code (or an appropriate link to the potentially bundled and optimized CSS file) into the **index.html** file. You can confirm this by inspecting the rendered **Document Object Model** (**DOM**) content of the loaded web page in the browser.

To do so, select the **Elements** tab in **developer tools** in Chrome, as shown below:

```
⌖  ⬚  |  Elements    Console    Sources    Network    Performance    »

▼ <head>
    <meta charset="utf-8">
    <link rel="icon" href="/favicon.ico">
    <meta name="viewport" content="width=device-width, initial-scale=1">
    <meta name="theme-color" content="#000000">
    <meta name="description" content="Web site created using create-react-app">
    <link rel="apple-touch-icon" href="/logo192.png">
    <link rel="manifest" href="/manifest.json">
    <title>React App</title>
    <script defer src="/static/js/bundle.js"></script>
··· ▼ <style> == $0
      * {
        box-sizing: border-box;
      }

      body {
        margin: 2rem;
        font-family: -apple-system, BlinkMacSystemFont, 'Segoe UI', 'Roboto', 'Oxygen',
          'Ubuntu', 'Cantarell', 'Fira Sans', 'Droid Sans', 'Helvetica Neue',
          sans-serif;
        -webkit-font-smoothing: antialiased;
        -moz-osx-font-smoothing: grayscale;
      }
```

Figure 6.2: The injected CSS <style> can be found in the DOM at runtime

You can define any styles you want to apply to your HTML elements (that is, to your JSX elements in your components) directly inside of the **index.css** file or in any other CSS files that are imported by the **index.css** file.

You could also add additional CSS import statements, pointing at other CSS files, to the **index.js** file or any other JavaScript files (including files that store components). However, it is important to keep in mind that CSS styles are always global. No matter whether you import a CSS file in **index.js** or in a component-specific JavaScript file, the styles defined in that CSS file will be applied globally.

That means that styles defined in a **goal-list.css** file, which may be imported in a **GoalList.js** file, could still affect JSX elements defined in a totally different component. Later in this chapter, you will learn about techniques that allow you to avoid accidental style clashes and implement style scoping.

USING INLINE STYLES

You can use CSS files to define global CSS styles and use different CSS selectors to target different JSX elements (or groups of elements).

But even though it's typically discouraged, you can also set inline styles directly on JSX elements via the **style** prop.

> **NOTE**
>
> If you're wondering why inline styles are discouraged, the following discussion on Stack Overflow provides many arguments against inline styles: https://stackoverflow.com/questions/2612483/whats-so-bad-about-inline-css.

Setting inline styles in JSX code works like this:

```
function TodoItem() {
    return <li style={{color: 'red', fontSize: '18px'}}>Learn React!</li>;
};
```

In this example, the **style** prop is added to the **<li>** element (all JSX elements support the **style** prop) and both the **color** and **size** properties of the text are set via CSS.

This approach differs from what you would use to set inline styles when working with just HTML (instead of JSX). When using plain HTML, you would set inline styles like this:

```
<li style="color: red; font-size: 18px">Learn React!</li>
```

The difference is that the **style** prop expects to receive a JavaScript object that contains the style settings—not a plain string. This is something that must be kept in mind, though, since, as mentioned previously, inline styles typically aren't used that often.

Since the **style** object is an object and not a plain string, it is passed as a value between curly braces—just as an array, a number, or any other non-string value would have to be set between curly braces (anything between double or single quotes is treated as a string value). Therefore, it's worth noting that the preceding example does not use any kind of special "double curly braces" syntax, but instead uses one pair of curly braces to surround the non-string value and another pair to surround the object data.

Inside the **style** object, any CSS style properties supported by the underlying DOM element can be set. The property names are those defined for the HTML element (i.e., the same CSS property names you could target and set with vanilla JavaScript, when mutating an HTML element).

When setting styles in JavaScript code (as with the **style** prop shown above), JavaScript CSS property names have to be used. Those names are similar to the CSS property names you would use in CSS code but not quite the same. Differences occur for property names that consist of multiple words (e.g., **font-size**). When targeting such properties in JavaScript, **camelCase** notation must be used (**fontSize** instead of **font-size**) as JavaScript properties cannot contain dashes. Alternatively, you could wrap the property name with quotes (**'font-size'**).

> **NOTE**
>
> You can find more information about the HTML element style property and JavaScript CSS property names here: https://developer.mozilla.org/en-US/docs/Web/API/HTMLElement/style.

SETTING STYLES VIA CSS CLASSES

As mentioned, using inline styles is typically discouraged, and therefore, CSS styles defined in CSS files (or between **<style>** tags in the document **<head>** section) are preferred.

In those CSS code blocks, you can write regular CSS code and use CSS selectors to apply CSS styles to certain elements. You could, for example, style all **<li>** elements on a page (no matter which component may have rendered them) like this:

```
li {
  color: red;
  font-size: 18px;
}
```

As long as this code gets added to the page (because the CSS file in which it is defined is imported in **index.js**, for instance), the styling will be applied.

Quite frequently, developers aim to target specific elements or groups of elements. Instead of applying some style to all **<li>** elements on a page, the goal could be to only target the **<li>** elements that are part of a specific list. Consider this HTML structure that's rendered to the page (it may be split across multiple components, but this doesn't matter here):

```
<nav>
  <ul>
    <li><a href="…">Home</a></li>
```

```
   <li><a href="…">New Goals</a></li>
  </ul>
  ...
  <h2>My Course Goals</h2>
  <ul>
    <li>Learn React!</li>
    <li>Master React!</li>
  </ul>
</nav>
```

In this example, the navigation list items should most likely not receive the same styling as the **course goal** list items (and vice versa).

Typically, this problem would be solved with the help of CSS classes and the class selector. You could adjust the HTML code like this:

```
<nav>
  <ul>
    <li><a href="…">Home</a></li>
    <li><a href="…">New Goals</a></li>
  </ul>
  ...
  <h2>My Course Goals</h2>
  <ul>
    <li class="goal-item">Learn React!</li>
    <li class="goal-item">Master React!</li>
  </ul>
</nav>
```

The following CSS code would then only target the **course goal** list items but not the navigation list items:

```
.goal-item {
  color: red;
  font-size: 18px;
}
```

And this approach almost works in React apps as well.

But if you try to add CSS classes to JSX elements as shown in the previous example, you will face a warning in the browser **developer tools**:

```
⊗ ▶ Warning: Invalid DOM property `class`. Did you mean          react-dom.development.js:86
  `className`?
      at input
      at div
      at form
      at Form (http://localhost:3002/main.a07d991….hot-update.js:29:90)
```

Figure 6.3: A warning output by React

As illustrated in the preceding figure, you should not add **class** as a prop but instead use **className**. Indeed, if you swap **class** for **className** as a prop name, the warning will disappear, and the class CSS styles will be applied. Hence, the proper JSX code looks like this:

```
<ul>
  <li className="goal-item">Learn React!</li>
  <li className="goal-item">>Master React!</li>
</ul>
```

But why is React suggesting you use **className** instead of **class**?

It's similar to using **htmlFor** instead of **for** when working with **<label>** objects (discussed in *Chapter 4, Working with Events and State*. Just like **for**, **class** is a keyword in JavaScript, and therefore, **className** is used as a prop name instead.

SETTING STYLES DYNAMICALLY

With inline styles and CSS classes (and global CSS styles in general), there are various ways of applying styles to elements. Thus far, all examples have shown static styles—that is, styles that will never change once the page has been loaded.

But while most page elements don't change their styles after a page is loaded, you also typically have some elements that should be styled dynamically or conditionally. Here are some examples:

- A **to-do** app where different **to-do** priorities receive different colors

- An input form where invalid form elements should be highlighted following an unsuccessful form submission

- A web-based game where players can choose colors for their avatars

In such cases, applying static styles is not enough, and dynamic styles should be used instead. Setting styles dynamically is straightforward. It's again just about applying key React concepts covered earlier (most importantly, those regarding the setting of dynamic values from *Chapter 2*, *Understanding React Components and JSX*, and *Chapter 4*, *Working with Events and State*).

Here's an example where the color of a paragraph is set dynamically to the color a user enters into an input field:

```
function ColoredText() {
  const [enteredColor, setEnteredColor] = useState('');

  function updateTextColorHandler(event) {
    setEnteredColor(event.target.value);
  };

  return (
    <>
      <input type="text" onChange={updateTextColorHandler}/>
      <p style={{color: enteredColor}}>This text's color changes
dynamically!</p>
    </>
  );
};
```

The text entered in the **<input>** field is stored in the **enteredColor** state. This state is then used to set the **color** CSS property of the **<p>** element dynamically. This is achieved by passing a **style** object with the **color** property set to the **enteredColor** value as a value to the **style** prop of the **<p>** element. The text color of the paragraph is therefore set dynamically to the value entered by the user (assuming that users enter valid CSS color values into the **<input>** field).

You're not limited to inline styles; CSS classes can also be set dynamically, as in the following snippet:

```
function TodoPriority() {
  const [chosenPriority, setChosenPriority] = useState('low-prio');

  function choosePriorityHandler(event) {
    setChosenPriority(event.target.value);
  };

  return (
```

```
    <>
      <p className={chosenPriority}>Chosen Priority: {chosenPriority}</p>
      <select onChange={choosePriorityHandler}>
        <option value="low-prio">Low</option>
        <option value="high-prio">High</option>
      </select>
    </>
  );
};
```

In this example, the **chosenPriority** state will alternate between **low-prio** and **high-prio**, depending on the drop-down selection. The state value is then output as text inside the paragraph and is also used as a dynamic CSS class name applied to the **<p>** element. For this to have any visual effect, there must, of course, be **low-prio** and **high-prio** CSS classes defined in some CSS file or **<style>** block. For example, consider the following code in **index.css**:

```
.low-prio {
  background-color: blue;
  color: white;
}


.high-prio {
  background-color: red;
  color: white;
}
```

CONDITIONAL STYLES

Closely related to **dynamic styles** are **conditional styles**. In fact, in the end, they are really just a special case of dynamic styles. In the previous examples, inline style values and class names were set equal to values chosen or entered by the user.

However, you can also derive styles or class names dynamically based on different conditions, as shown here:

```
function TextInput({isValid, isRecommended, inputConfig}) {
  let cssClass = 'input-default';

  if (isRecommended) {
    cssClass = 'input-recommended';
  }
```

```
  if (!isValid) {
    cssClass = 'input-invalid';
  }


  return <input className={cssClass} {...inputConfig} />
};
```

In this example, a wrapper component around the standard **<input>** element is built. (For more information about wrapper components see *Chapter 3, Components and Props*.) The main purpose of this wrapper component is to set some default styles for the wrapped **<input>** element. The **wrapper component** is built to provide a pre-styled input element that can be used anywhere in the app. Indeed, providing pre-styled elements is one of the most common and popular use cases for building wrapper components.

In this concrete example, the default styles are applied using CSS classes. If the **isValid** prop value is **true** and the value of the **isRecommended** prop is **false**, the **input-default** CSS class will be applied to the **<input>** element since neither of the two **if** statements become active.

If **isRecommended** is **true** (but **isValid** is **false**), the **input-recommended** CSS class would be applied. If **isValid** is **false**, the **input-invalid** class is added instead. Of course, the CSS classes must be defined in some imported CSS files (for example, in **index.css**).

Inline styles could be set in a similar way as shown in the following snippet:

```
function TextInput({isValid, isRecommended, inputConfig}) {
  let bgColor = 'black';


  if (isRecommended) {
    bgColor = 'blue';
  }


  if (!isValid) {
    bgColor = 'red';
  }


  return <input style={{backgroundColor: bgColor}} {...inputConfig} />
};
```

In this example, the background color of the **<input>** element is set conditionally, based on the values received via the **isValid** and **isRecommended** props.

COMBINING MULTIPLE DYNAMIC CSS CLASSES

In previous examples, a maximum of one CSS class was set dynamically at a time. However, it's not uncommon to encounter scenarios where multiple, dynamically derived CSS classes should be merged and added to an element.

Consider the following example:

```
function ExplanationText({children, isImportant}) {
  const defaultClasses = 'text-default text-expl';

  return <p className={defaultClasses}>{children}</p>;
}
```

Here, two CSS classes are added to **\<p\>** by simply combining them in one string. Alternatively, you could directly add a string with the two classes like this:

```
return <p className="text-default text-expl">{children}</p>;
```

This code will work, but what if the goal is to also add another class name to the list of classes, based on the **isImportant** prop value (which is ignored in the preceding example)?

Replacing the default list of classes would be easy, as you have learned:

```
function ExplanationText({children, isImportant}) {
  let cssClasses = 'text-default text-expl';

  if (isImportant) {
    cssClasses = 'text-important';
  }

  return <p className={cssClasses}>{children}</p>;
}
```

But what if the goal is not to replace the list of default classes? What if **text-important** should be added as a class to **\<p\>**, in addition to **text-default** and **text-expl**?

The **className** prop expects to receive a string value, and so passing an array of classes isn't an option. However, you can simply merge multiple classes into one string. And there are a couple of different ways of doing that:

1. String concatenation:

```
cssClasses = cssClasses + ' text-important';
```

2. Using a template literal:

```
cssClasses = `${cssClasses} text-important`;
```

3. Joining an array:

```
cssClasses = [cssClasses, 'text-important'].join(' ');
```

These examples could all be used inside the **if** statement (**if (isImportant)**) to conditionally add the **text-important** class based on the **isImportant** prop value. All three approaches, as well as variations of these approaches, will work because all these approaches produce a string. In general, any approach that yields a string can be used to generate values for **className**.

MERGING MULTIPLE INLINE STYLE OBJECTS

When working with inline styles, instead of CSS classes, you can also merge multiple style objects. The main difference is that you don't produce a string with all values, but rather an object with all combined style values.

This can be achieved by using standard JavaScript techniques for merging multiple objects into one object. The most popular technique involves using the **spread operator**, as shown in this example:

```
function ExplanationText({children, isImportant}) {
  let defaultStyle = { color: 'black' };

  if (isImportant) {
    defaultStyle = { ...defaultStyle, backgroundColor: 'red' };
  }

  return <p style={defaultStyle}>{children}</p>;
}
```

Here, you will observe that **defaultStyle** is an object with a **color** property. If **isImportant** is **true**, it's replaced with an object that contains all the properties it had before (via the spread operator, **...defaultStyle**) as well as the **backgroundColor** property.

> **NOTE**
>
> For more information on the function and use of the spread operator, see *Chapter 5, Rendering Lists and Conditional Content.*

BUILDING COMPONENTS WITH CUSTOMIZABLE STYLES

As you are aware by now, components can be reused. This is supported by the fact that they can be configured via props. The same component can be used in different places on a page with different configurations to yield a different output.

Since styles can be set both statically and dynamically, you can also make the styling of your components customizable. The preceding examples already show such customization in action; for example, the **isImportant** prop was used in the previous example to conditionally add a **red** background color to a paragraph. The **ExplanationText** component therefore already allows for indirect style customization via the **isImportant** prop.

Besides this form of customization, you could also build components that accept props already holding CSS class names or style objects. For example, the following wrapper component accepts a **className** prop that is merged with a default CSS class (**btn**):

```
function Button({children, config, className}) {
  return <button {...config} className={`btn ${className}`}>{children}</
button>;
};
```

This component could be used in another component in the following way:

```
<Button config={{onClick: doSomething}} className="btn-alert">Click me!</
Button>
```

If used like this, the final **<button>** element would receive both the **btn** as well as **btn-alert** classes.

You don't have to use **className** as a prop name; any name can be used, since it's your component. However, it's not a bad idea to use **className** because you can then keep your mental model of setting CSS classes via **className** (for built-in components, you will not have that choice).

Instead of merging prop values with default CSS class names or style objects, you can also overwrite default values. This allows you to build components that come with some styling out of the box without enforcing that styling:

```
function Button({children, config, className}) {
  let cssClasses = 'btn';
  if (className) {
    cssClasses = className;
  }
}
```

```
  return <button {...config} className={cssClasses}>{children}</button>;
};
```

You can see how all these different concepts covered throughout this book are coming together here: props allow customization, values can be set, swapped, and changed dynamically and conditionally, and therefore, highly reusable and configurable components can be built.

CUSTOMIZATION WITH FIXED CONFIGURATION OPTIONS

Besides exposing props such as **className** or **style**, which are merged with other classes or styles defined inside a component function, you can also build components that apply different styles or class names based on other prop values.

This has been shown in the previous examples where props such as **isValid** or **isImportant** were used to apply certain styles conditionally. This way of applying styles could therefore be called "indirect styling" (though this is not an official term).

Both approaches can shine in different circumstances. For wrapper components, for example, accepting **className** or **style** props (which may be merged with other styles inside the component) enables the component to be used just like a built-in component (e.g., like the component it wraps). Indirect styling, on the other hand, can be very useful if you want to build components that provide a couple of pre-defined variations.

A good example is a text box that provides two built-in themes that can be selected via a specific prop:

```
function TextBox({children, mode}) {
  let cssClasses;

  if (mode === 'alert') {
    cssClasses = 'box-alert';
  } else if (mode === 'info') {
    cssClasses = 'box-info';
  }

  return <p className={cssClasses}>{children}</p>;
};
```

This **TextBox** component always yields a paragraph element. If the **mode** prop is set to any value other than **'alert'** or **'info'**, the paragraph doesn't receive any special styling. But if **mode** is equal to **'alert'** or **'info'**, specific CSS classes are added to the paragraph.

This component therefore doesn't allow direct styling via some **className** or **style** prop that would be merged, but it does offer different variations or themes that can be set with the help of a specific prop (the **mode** prop in this case).

THE PROBLEM WITH UNSCOPED STYLES

If you consider the different examples you've so far dealt with in this chapter, there's one specific use case that occurs quite frequently: styles are relevant to a specific component only.

For example, in the **TextBox** component in the previous section, **'box-alert'** and **'box-info'** are CSS classes that are likely only relevant for this specific component and its markup. If any other JSX element in the app had a **'box-alert'** class applied to it (even though that might be unlikely), it probably shouldn't be styled the same as the **<p>** element in the **TextBox** component.

Styles from different components could clash with each other and overwrite each other because styles are not scoped (i.e., restricted) to a specific component. CSS styles are always global, unless inline styles are used (which is discouraged, as mentioned earlier).

When working with component-based libraries such as React, this lack of scoping is a common issue. It's easy to write conflicting styles as app sizes and complexities grow (or, in other words, as more and more components are added to the code base of a React app).

That's why various solutions for this problem have been developed by members of the React community. The following are two of the most popular solutions:

- CSS Modules (supported out of the box in React projects created with **create-react-app**)

- Styled components (using a third-party library called **styled-components**)

SCOPED STYLES WITH CSS MODULES

CSS Modules is the name for an approach where individual CSS files are linked to specific JavaScript files and the components defined in those files. This link is established by transforming CSS class names, such that every JavaScript file receives its own, unique CSS class names. This transformation is performed automatically as part of the code build workflow. Therefore, a given project setup must support CSS Modules by performing the described CSS class name transformation. Projects created via **create-react-app** support CSS Modules by default.

CSS Modules are enabled and used by naming CSS files in a very specific and clearly defined way: **<anything>.module.css**. **<anything>** is any value of your choosing, but the **.module** part in front of the file extension is required as it signals (to the project build workflow) that this CSS file should be transformed according to the CSS Modules approach.

Therefore, CSS files named like this must be imported into components in a specific way:

```
import classes from './file.module.css';
```

This **import** syntax is different from the **import** syntax shown at the beginning of this section for **index.css**:

```
import './index.css';
```

When importing CSS files as shown in the second snippet, the CSS code is simply merged into the **index.html** file and applied globally. When using CSS Modules instead (first code snippet), the CSS class names defined in the imported CSS file are transformed such that they are unique for the JS file that imports the CSS file.

Since the CSS class names are transformed and are therefore no longer equal to the class names you defined in the CSS file, you import an object (**classes**, in the preceding example) from the CSS file. This object exposes all transformed CSS class names under keys that match the CSS class names defined by you in the CSS file. The values of those properties are the transformed class names (as strings).

Here's a complete example, starting with a component-specific CSS file (**TextBox. module.css**):

```
.alert {
  padding: 1rem;
  border-radius: 6px;
  background-color: salmon;
  color: red;
}

.info {
  padding: 1rem;
  border-radius: 6px;
  background-color: #d6aafa;
  color: #410474;
}
```

The JavaScript file (**TextBox.js**) for the component to which the CSS code should belong looks like this:

```
import classes from './TextBox.module.css';

function TextBox({ children, mode }) {
  let cssClasses;

  if (mode === 'alert') {
    cssClasses = classes.alert;
  } else if (mode === 'info') {
    cssClasses = classes.info;
  }

  return <p className={cssClasses}>{children}</p>;
}

export default TextBox;
```

> **NOTE**
>
> The full example code can also be found at https://packt.link/13nwz.

If you inspect the rendered text element in the browser developer tools, you will note that the CSS class name applied to the **<p>** element does not match the class name specified in the **TextBox.module.css** file:

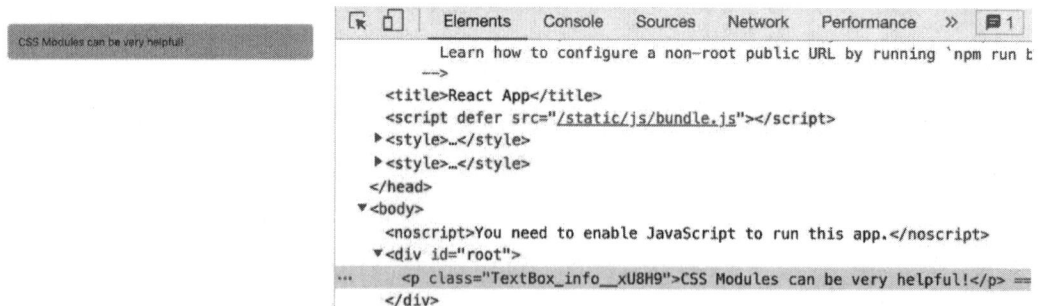

Figure 6.4: CSS class name transforms because of CSS Modules usage

This is the case because, as described previously, the class name was transformed during the build process to be unique. If any other CSS file, imported by another JavaScript file, were to define a class with the same name (**info** in this case), the styles would not clash and not overwrite each other because the interfering class names would be transformed into different class names before being applied to the DOM elements.

Indeed, in the example provided on GitHub, you can find another **info** CSS class defined in the **index.css** file:

```css
.info {
  border: 5px solid red;
}
```

That file is still imported into **index.js**, and hence its styles are applied globally to the entire document. Nonetheless, the **.info** styles clearly aren't affecting **<p>** rendered by **TextBox** (there is no red border around the text box in *Figure 6.4*). They aren't affecting that element because it doesn't have an **info** class anymore; the class was renamed to **text-box_info__vCxmZ** by the build workflow (though the name will differ as it contains a random element).

It's also worth noting that the **index.css** file is still imported into **index.js**, as shown at the beginning of this chapter. The **import** statement is not changed to **import classes from './index.css';**, nor is the CSS file called **index.module.css**.

Note, too, that you can use CSS Modules to scope styles to components and can also mix the usage of CSS Modules with regular CSS files, which are imported into JavaScript files without using CSS Modules (i.e., without scoping).

One other important aspect of using CSS Modules is that you can only use CSS class selectors (that is, in your **.module.css** files) because CSS Modules rely on CSS classes. You can write selectors that combine classes with other selectors, such as **input.invalid**, but you can't add selectors that don't use classes at all in your **.module.css** files. For example, **input { ... }** or **#some-id { ... }** selectors wouldn't work here.

CSS Modules are a very popular way of scoping styles to (React) components, and they will be used throughout many examples for the rest of this book.

THE STYLED-COMPONENTS LIBRARY

The **styled-components** library is a so-called **CSS-in-JS** solution. CSS-in-JS solutions aim to remove the separation between CSS code and JavaScript code by merging them into the same file. Component styles would be defined right next to the component logic. It comes down to personal preference whether you favor separation (as enforced by using CSS files) or keeping the two languages close to each other.

Since **styled-components** is a third-party library that's not pre-installed in newly created React projects, you have to install this library as a first step if you want to use it. This can be done via **npm** (which was automatically installed together with Node.js in *Chapter 1, React – What and Why*):

```
npm install styled-components
```

The **styled-components** library essentially provides wrapper components around all built-in core components (as in, around **p**, **a**, **button**, **input**, and so on). It exposes all these wrapper components as **tagged templates**—JavaScript functions that aren't called like regular functions, but are instead executed by adding backticks (a template literal) right after the function name, for example, **doSomething'text data'**.

> **NOTE**
>
> Tagged templates can be confusing when you see them for the first time, especially since it's a JavaScript feature that isn't used too frequently. Chances are high that you haven't worked with them too often. It's even more likely that you have never built a custom tagged template before. You can learn more about tagged templates in this excellent documentation on MDN at https://developer.mozilla.org/en-US/docs/Web/JavaScript/Reference/Template_literals#tagged_templates.

Here is a component that imports and uses **styled-components** to set and scope styling:

```
import styled from 'styled-components';

const Button = styled.button`
  background-color: #370566;
  color: white;
```

```
  border: none;
  padding: 1rem;
  border-radius: 4px;
`;

export default Button;
```

This component isn't a component function but rather a constant that stores the value returned by executing the **styled.button** tagged template. That tagged template returns a component function that yields a **<button>** element. The styles passed via the tagged template (i.e., inside the template literal) are applied to that returned button element. You can see this if you inspect the button in the browser **developer tools**:

Figure 6.5: The rendered button element receives the defined component styles

In *Figure 6.5*, you can also see how the **styled-components** library applies your styles to the element. It extracts your style definitions from the tagged template string and injects them into a **<style>** element in the **<head>** section of the document. The injected styles are then applied via a class selector that is generated (and named) by the **styled-components** library. Finally, the automatically generated CSS class name is added to the element (**<button>**, in this case) by the library.

The components exposed by the **styled-components** library spread any extra props you pass to a component onto the wrapped core component. In addition, any content inserted between the opening and closing tags is also inserted between the tags of the wrapped component.

That's why the **Button** created previously can be used like this without adding any extra logic to it:

```
import Button from './components/button';

function App() {
  function clickHandler() {
    console.log('This button was clicked!');
  }
  return <Button onClick={clickHandler}>Click me!</Button>;
}

export default App;
```

> **NOTE**
>
> The complete example code can be found on GitHub at https://packt.link/XD6IL.

You can do more with the **styled-components** library. For example, you can set styles dynamically and conditionally. This book is not primarily about that library though. It's just one of many alternatives to CSS Modules. Therefore, it is recommended that you explore the official **styled-components** documentation if you want to learn more, which you can find at https://styled-components.com/.

USING OTHER CSS OR JAVASCRIPT STYLING LIBRARIES AND FRAMEWORKS

As mentioned, there are many third-party styling libraries that can be used in React apps. There are alternatives to **styled-components** or CSS Modules that help with scoping styles. But there are also other kinds of CSS libraries:

- Utility libraries that solve very specific CSS problems—independent of the fact that you're using them in a React project (for example, **Animate.css**, which helps with adding animations)

- CSS frameworks that provide a broad variety of pre-built CSS classes that can be applied to elements to quickly achieve a certain look (e.g., **Bootstrap** or **Tailwind**)

It is important to realize that you can use any of these CSS libraries with React. You can bring your favorite CSS framework (such as Bootstrap or Tailwind) and use the CSS classes provided by that framework on the JSX elements of your React app.

Some libraries and frameworks have React-specific extensions or specifically support React, but that does not mean that you can't use libraries that don't have this.

SUMMARY AND KEY TAKEAWAYS

- Standard CSS can be used to style React components and JSX elements.

- CSS files are typically directly imported into JavaScript files, which is possible thanks to the project build process, which extracts the CSS code and injects it into the document (the HTML file).

- As an alternative to global CSS styles (with `element`, `id`, `class`, or other selectors), inline styles can be used to apply styling to JSX elements.

- When using CSS classes for styling, you must use the `className` prop (not `class`).

- Styles can be set statically and dynamically or conditionally with the same syntax that is used for injecting other dynamic or conditional values into JSX code—a pair of curly braces.

- Highly configurable custom components can be built by setting styles (or CSS classes) based on prop values or by merging received prop values with other styles or class name strings.

- When using just CSS, clashing CSS class names can be a problem.

- CSS Modules solve this problem by transforming class names into unique names (per component) as part of the build workflow.

- Alternatively, third-party libraries such as `styled-components` can be used. This library is a CSS-in-JS library that also has the advantage or disadvantage (depending on your preference) of removing the separation between JS and CSS code.

- Other CSS libraries or frameworks can be used as well; React does not impose any restrictions regarding that.

WHAT'S NEXT?

With styling covered, you're now able to build not just functional but also visually appealing user interfaces. Even if you often work with dedicated web designers or CSS experts, you still typically need to be able to set and assign styles (dynamically) that are delivered to you.

With styling being a general concept that is relatively independent of React, the next chapter will dive back into more React-specific features and topics. You will learn about **portals** and **refs**, which are two key concepts that are built into React. You will understand which problems are solved by these concepts and how the two features are used.

TEST YOUR KNOWLEDGE!

Test your knowledge of the concepts covered in this chapter by answering the following questions. You can then compare your answers to examples that can be found here: https://packt.link/vJgKl.

1. With which language are styles for React components defined?

2. Which important difference between projects with and without React has to be kept in mind when assigning classes to elements?

3. How can styles be assigned dynamically and conditionally?

4. What does "scoping" mean in the context of styling?

5. How could styles be scoped to components? Briefly explain at least one concept that helps with scoping.

APPLY WHAT YOU LEARNED

You are now not only able to build interactive user interfaces but also style those user interface elements in engaging ways. You can set and change those styles dynamically or based on conditions.

In this section, you will find two activities that allow you to apply your newly gained knowledge in combination with what you learned in previous chapters.

ACTIVITY 6.1: PROVIDING INPUT VALIDITY FEEDBACK UPON FORM SUBMISSION

In this activity, you will build a basic form that allows users to enter an email address and a password. The provided input of each input field is validated, and the validation result is stored (for each individual input field).

The aim of this activity is to add some general form styling and some conditional styling that becomes active once an invalid form has been submitted. The exact styles are up to you, but for highlighting invalid input fields, the background color of the affected input field must be changed, as well as its border color and the text color of the related label.

The steps are as follows:

1. Create a new React project and add a form component to it.

2. Output the form component in the project's root component.

3. In the form component, output a form that contains two input fields: one for entering an email address and one for entering a password.

4. Add labels to the input fields.

5. Store the entered values and check their validity upon form submission (you can be creative in forming your own validation logic).

6. Pick appropriate CSS classes from the provided **index.css** file (you can write your own classes as well).

7. Add them to the invalid input fields and their labels once invalid values have been submitted.

The final user interface should look like this:

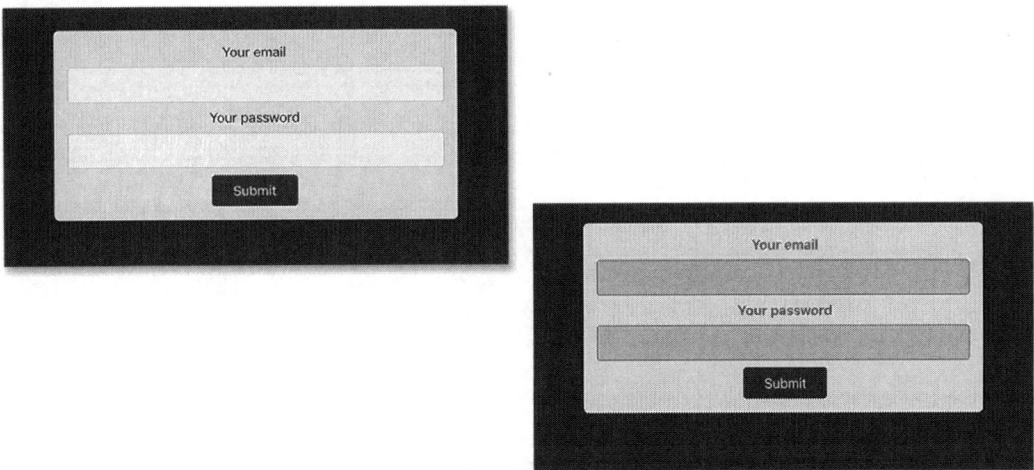

Figure 6.6: The final user interface with invalid input values highlighted in red

Since this book is not about CSS and you may not be a CSS expert, you can use the **index.css** file from the solution and focus on the React logic to apply appropriate CSS classes to JSX elements.

> **NOTE**
>
> The solution to this activity can be found on page 473.

ACTIVITY 6.2: USING CSS MODULES FOR STYLE SCOPING

In this activity, you'll take the final app built in *Activity 6.01* and adjust it to use CSS Modules. The goal is to migrate all component-specific styles into a component-specific CSS file, which uses CSS Modules for style scoping.

The final user interface therefore looks the same as it did in the previous activity. But the styles will be scoped to the **Form** component so that clashing class names won't interfere with styling.

The steps are as follows:

1. Finish the previous activity or take the finished code from GitHub.

2. Identify the styles belonging specifically to the **Form** component and move them into a new, component-specific CSS file.

3. Change CSS selectors to class name selectors and add classes to JSX elements as needed (this is because CSS Modules require class name selectors).

4. Use the component-specific CSS file as explained throughout this chapter and assign the CSS classes to the appropriate JSX elements.

> **NOTE**
>
> The solution to this activity can be found on page 478.

7

PORTALS AND REFS

LEARNING OBJECTIVES

By the end of this chapter, you will be able to do the following:

- Use direct DOM element access to interact with elements
- Expose the functions and data of your components to other components
- Control the position of rendered JSX elements in the DOM

INTRODUCTION

React.js is all about building user interfaces, and, in the context of this book, it's about building web user interfaces specifically.

Web user interfaces are ultimately all about the **Document Object Model** (**DOM**). You can use JavaScript to read or manipulate the DOM. This is what allows you to build interactive websites: you can add, remove, or edit DOM elements after a page was loaded. This can be used to add or remove overlay windows or to read values entered into input fields.

This was already discussed in *Chapter 1, React – What and Why*, and, as you learned there, React is used to simplify this process. Instead of manipulating the DOM or reading values from DOM elements manually, you can use React to describe the desired state. React then takes care of the steps needed to achieve this desired state.

However, there are scenarios and use cases wherein, despite using React, you still want to be able to directly reach out to specific DOM elements—for example, to read a value entered by a user into an input field or if you're not happy with the position of a newly inserted element in the DOM that was chosen by React.

React provides certain functionalities that help you in exactly these kinds of situations: **Portals** and **Refs**.

A WORLD WITHOUT REFS

Consider the following example: you have a website that renders an input field, requesting a user's email address. It could look something like this:

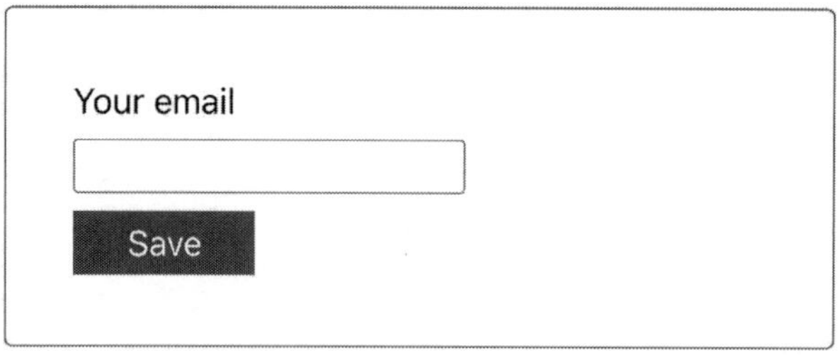

Your email

Save

Figure 7.1: An example form with an email input field

The code for the component that's responsible for rendering the form and handling the entered email address value might look like this:

```
function EmailForm() {
  const [enteredEmail, setEnteredEmail] = useState('');

  function updateEmailHandler(event) {
  setEnteredEmail(event.target.value);
  }

  function submitFormHandler(event) {
  event.preventDefault();
  // could send enteredEmail to a backend server
  }

  return (
  <form className={classes.form} onSubmit={submitFormHandler}>
    <label htmlFor="email">Your email</label>
    <input type="email" id="email" onChange={updateEmailHandler} />
    <button>Save</button>
  </form>
  );
}
```

As you can see, this example uses the **useState()** Hook, combined with the **change** event, to register keystrokes in the **email** input field and store the entered value.

This code works fine and there is nothing wrong with having this kind of code in your application. But adding the extra event listener and state, as well as adding the function to update the state whenever the **change** event is triggered, is quite a bit of boilerplate code for one simple task: getting the entered email address.

The preceding code snippet does nothing else with the email address other than submit it. In other words, the only reason for using the **enteredEmail** state in the example is to read the entered value.

In scenarios such as this, quite a bit of code could be saved if you fell back to some vanilla JavaScript logic:

```
const emailInputEl = document.getElementById('email');
const enteredEmailVal = emailInputEl.value;
```

These two lines of code (which could be merged into one line theoretically) allow you to get hold of a DOM element and read the currently stored value.

The problem with this kind of code is that it does not use React. And if you're building a React app, you should really stick to React when working with the DOM. Don't start blending your own vanilla JavaScript code *that accesses the DOM* into the React code.

This can lead to unintended behaviors or bugs, especially if you start manipulating the DOM. It could lead to bugs because React would not be aware of your changes in that case; the actual rendered UI would not be in sync with React's assumed UI. Even if you're just reading from the DOM, it's a good habit to not even start merging vanilla JavaScript DOM access methods with your React code.

To still allow you to get hold of DOM elements and read values, as shown above, React gives you a special concept that you can use: **Refs**.

Ref stands for reference, and it's a feature that allows you to reference (i.e., get hold of) elements from inside a React component. The preceding vanilla JavaScript code would do the same (it also gives you access to a rendered element), but when using refs, you can get access without mixing vanilla JavaScript code into your React code.

Refs can be created using a special React Hook called the **useRef()** Hook.

This Hook can be executed to generate a **ref** object:

```
import { useRef } from 'react';

function EmailForm() {
  const emailRef = useRef();

  // other code ...
};
```

This generated ref object, **emailRef** in the preceding example, can then be assigned to any JSX element. This assignment is done via a special prop (the **ref** prop) that is automatically supported by every JSX element:

```
return (
  <form className={classes.form} onSubmit={submitFormHandler}>
  <label htmlFor="email">Your email</label>
  <input
    ref={emailRef}
    type="email"
    id="email"
```

```
  />
  <button>Save</button>
  </form>
);
```

Just like the **key** prop introduced in *Chapter 5, Rendering Lists and Conditional Content*, the **ref** prop is provided by React. The **ref** prop wants a ref object, e.g., one that was created via **useRef()**.

With that ref object created and assigned, you can then use it to get access to the connected JSX element (to the **<input>** element in this example). There's just one important thing to note: to get hold of the connected element, you must access a special **current** prop on the created ref object. This is required because React stores the value assigned to the ref object in a nested object, accessible via the **current** property, as shown here:

```
function submitFormHandler(event) {
  event.preventDefault();
  const enteredEmail = emailRef.current.value; // .current is mandatory!
  // could send enteredEmail to a backend server
};
```

emailRef.current yields the underlying DOM object that was rendered for the connected JSX element. In this case, it therefore allows access to the input element DOM object. Since that DOM object has a **value** property, this **value** property can be accessed without issue.

> **NOTE**
>
> For further information on this topic see https://developer.mozilla.org/en-US/docs/Web/HTML/Element/input#attributes.

With this kind of code, you can read the value from the DOM element without having to use **useState()** and an event listener. The final component code therefore becomes quite a bit leaner:

```
function EmailForm() {
  const emailRef = useRef();

  function submitFormHandler(event) {
  event.preventDefault();
  const enteredEmail = emailRef.current.value;
```

```
  // could send enteredEmail to a backend server
  }


  return (
  <form className={classes.form} onSubmit={submitFormHandler}>
    <label htmlFor="email">Your email</label>
    <input
      ref={emailRef}
      type="email"
      id="email"
    />
    <button>Save</button>
  </form>
  );
}
```

REFS VERSUS STATE

Since refs can be used to get quick and easy access to DOM elements, the question that might come up is whether you should always use refs instead of state.

The clear answer to this question is "no".

Refs can be a very good alternative in use cases like the one shown above, when you need read access to an element. This is very often the case when dealing with user input. In general, refs can replace state if you're just accessing some value to read it when some function (a form submit handler function, for example) is executed. As soon as you need to change values and those changes must be reflected in the UI (for example, by rendering some conditional content), refs are out of the game.

In the example above, if, besides getting the entered value, you'd also like to reset (i.e., clear) the email input after the form was submitted, you should use state again. While you could reset the input with the help of a ref, you should not do that. You would start manipulating the DOM and only React should do that—with its own, internal methods, based on the declarative code you provide to React.

You should not reset the email input like this:

```
function EmailForm() {
  const emailRef = useRef();


  function submitFormHandler(event) {
  event.preventDefault();
```

```
const enteredEmail = emailRef.current.value;
// could send enteredEmail to a backend server

emailRef.current.value = ''; // resetting the input value
}


return (
<form className={classes.form} onSubmit={submitFormHandler}>
  <label htmlFor="email">Your email</label>
  <input
    ref={emailRef}
    type="email"
    id="email"
  />
  <button>Save</button>
</form>
);
}
```

Instead, you should reset it by using React's state concept and by following the declarative approach embraced by React:

```
function EmailForm() {
  const [enteredEmail, setEnteredEmail] = useState('');

  function updateEmailHandler(event) {
  setEnteredEmail(event.target.value);
  }


  function submitFormHandler(event) {
  event.preventDefault();
  // could send enteredEmail to a backend server


  // reset by setting the state + using the value prop below
  setEnteredEmail('');
  }


  return (
  <form className={classes.form} onSubmit={submitFormHandler}>
    <label htmlFor="email">Your email</label>
    <input
```

```
      type="email"
      id="email"
      onChange={updateEmailHandler}
      value={enteredEmail}
  />
    <button>Save</button>
  </form>
  );
}
```

> **NOTE**
>
> As a rule, you should simply try to avoid writing imperative code in React projects. Instead, tell React how the final UI should look and let React figure out how to get there.
>
> Reading values via refs is an acceptable exception and manipulating DOM elements (with or without refs) should be avoided. A rare exception would be scenarios such as calling **focus()** on an input element DOM object as methods like **focus()** don't typically cause any DOM changes that could break the React app.

USING REFS FOR MORE THAN DOM ACCESS

Accessing DOM elements (for reading values) is one of the most common use cases for using refs. As shown above, it can help you reduce code in certain situations.

But refs are more than just "element connection bridges"; they are objects that can be used to store all kinds of values—not just pointers at DOM objects. You can, for example, also store strings or numbers or any other kind of value in a ref:

```
const passwordRetries = useRef(0);
```

You can pass an initial value to **useRef()** (0 in this example) and then access or change that value at any point in time, inside of the component to which the ref belongs:

```
passwordRetries.current = 1;
```

However, you still have to use the **current** property to read and change the stored value, because, as mentioned above, this is where React will store the actual value that belongs to the Ref.

This can be useful for storing data that should "survive" component re-evaluations. As you learned in *Chapter 4, Working with Events and State*, React will execute component functions every time the state of a component changes. Since the function is executed again, any data stored in function-scoped variables would be lost. Consider the following example:

```
function Counters() {
  const [counter1, setCounter1] = useState(0);
  const counterRef = useRef(0);
  let counter2 = 0;

  function changeCountersHandler() {
  setCounter1(1);
  counter2 = 1;
  counterRef.current = 1;
  };

  return (
  <>
    <button onClick={changeCountersHandler}>Change Counters</button>
    <ul>
      <li>Counter 1: {counter1}</li>
      <li>Counter 2: {counter2}</li>
      <li>Counter 3: {counterRef.current}</li>
    </ul>
  </>
  );
};
```

In this example, counters 1 and 3 would change to 1 once the button is clicked. However, counter 2 would remain zero, even though the **counter2** variable gets changed to a value of 1 in **changeCountersHandler** as well:

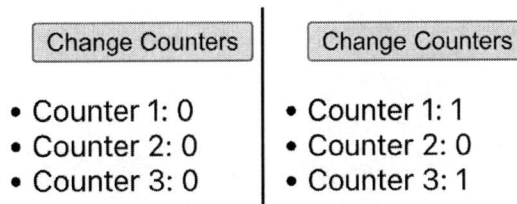

Change Counters	Change Counters
• Counter 1: 0	• Counter 1: 1
• Counter 2: 0	• Counter 2: 0
• Counter 3: 0	• Counter 3: 1

Figure 7.2: Only two of the three counter values changed

In this example, it should be expected that the state value changes, and the new value is reflected in the updated user interface. That is the whole idea behind state, after all.

The ref (**counterRef**) also keeps its updated value across component re-evaluations, though. That's the behavior described above: refs are not reset or cleared when the surrounding component function is executed again. The vanilla JavaScript variable (**counter2**) does not keep its value. Even though it is changed in **changeCountersHandler**, a new variable is initialized when the component function is executed again; thus the updated value (**1**) is lost.

In this example, it might again look like refs can replace state, but the example actually shows very well why that is **not** the case. Try replacing **counter1** with another ref (so that there is no state value left in the component) and clicking the button:

```
import { useRef } from 'react';

function Counters() {
  const counterRef1 = useRef(0);
  const counterRef2 = useRef(0);
  let counter2 = 0;

  function changeCountersHandler() {
  counterRef1.current = 1;
  counter2 = 1;
  counterRef2.current = 1;
  }

  return (
  <>
    <button onClick={changeCountersHandler}>Change Counters</button>
    <ul>
      <li>Counter 1: {counterRef1.current}</li>
      <li>Counter 2: {counter2}</li>
      <li>Counter 3: {counterRef2.current}</li>
    </ul>
  </>
  );
```

```
export default Counters;
```

Nothing will change on the page because, while the button click is registered and the **changeCountersHandler** function is executed, no state change is initiated. And state changes (initiated via the **setXYZ** state updating function calls) are the triggers that cause React to re-evaluate a component. Changes to ref values do **not** do that.

Therefore, if you have data that should survive component re-evaluations but should not be managed as state (because changes to that data should not cause the component to be re-evaluated when changed), you could use a ref:

```
const passwordRetries = useRef(0);
// later in the component ...
passwordRetries.current = 1; // changed from 0 to 1
// later ...
console.log(passwordRetries.current); // prints 1, even if the component
changed
```

This is not a feature that's used frequently, but it can be helpful from time to time. In all other cases, use normal state values.

FORWARDING REFS

Refs cannot just be used to access DOM elements. You can also use them to access React components—including your own components.

This can sometimes be useful. Consider this example: you have a **<Form>** component that contains a nested **<Preferences>** component. The latter component is responsible for displaying three checkboxes, asking the user for their newsletter preferences:

Figure 7.3: A newsletter sign-up form that shows two checkboxes to set newsletter preferences

The code of the **Preferences** component could look like this:

```
function Preferences() {
  const [wantsNewProdInfo, setWantsNewProdInfo] = useState(false);
  const [wantsProdUpdateInfo, setWantsProdUpdateInfo] = useState(false);

  function changeNewProdPrefHandler() {
    setWantsNewProdInfo((prevPref) => !prevPref);
  }

  function changeUpdateProdPrefHandler() {
    setWantsProdUpdateInfo((prevPref) => !prevPref);
  }

  return (
    <div className={classes.preferences}>
      <label>
        <input
          type="checkbox"
          id="pref-new"
          checked={wantsNewProdInfo}
          onChange={changeNewProdPrefHandler}
        />
        <span>New Products</span>
      </label>
      <label>
        <input
          type="checkbox"
          id="pref-updates"
          checked={wantsProdUpdateInfo}
          onChange={changeUpdateProdPrefHandler}
        />
        <span>Product Updates</span>
      </label>
    </div>
  );
};
```

As you can see, it's a basic component that essentially outputs the two checkboxes, adds some styling, and keeps track of the selected checkbox via state.

The **Form** component code could look like this:

```
function Form() {
  function submitHandler(event) {
    event.preventDefault();
  }

  return (
    <form className={classes.form} onSubmit={submitHandler}>
      <div className={classes.formControl}>
        <label htmlFor="email">Your email</label>
        <input type="email" id="email" />
      </div>
      <Preferences />
      <button>Submit</button>
    </form>
  );
}
```

Now imagine that upon form submission (inside of the **submitHandler** function), the **Preferences** should be reset (i.e., no checkbox is selected anymore). In addition, prior to resetting, the selected values should be read and used in the **submitHandler** function.

This would be straightforward if the checkboxes were not put into a separate component. If the entire code and JSX markup reside in the **Form** component, state could be used in that component to read and change the values. But this is not the case in this example and rewriting the code just because of this problem sounds like an unnecessary restriction.

Fortunately, Refs can help in this situation.

You can expose features (for example, functions or state values) of a component to other components by forwarding refs. Refs can essentially be used as a "communication device" between two components, just as they were used as a "communication device" with a DOM element in the previous sections.

To forward Refs, you must wrap the receiving component (**Preferences**, in this example) with a special function provided by React: **forwardRef()**.

This can be done like this:

```
const Preferences = forwardRef((props, ref) => {
  // component code ...
});


export default Preferences;
```

This looks slightly different than all the other components in this book because an arrow function is used instead of the **function** keyword. You can always use arrow functions instead of "normal functions", but here it's helpful to switch as it makes wrapping the function with **forwardRef()** very easy. Alternatively, you could stick to the **function** keyword and wrap the function like this:

```
function Preferences(props, ref) {
 // component code ...
};


export default forwardRef(Preferences);
```

It is up to you which syntax you prefer. Both work and both are commonly used in React projects.

The interesting part about this code is that the component function now receives **two** parameters instead of one. Besides receiving **props**, which component functions always do, it now also receives a special **ref** parameter. And this parameter is only received because the component function is wrapped with **forwardRef()**.

This **ref** parameter will contain any **ref** value set by the component using the **Preferences** component. For example, the **Form** component could set a **ref** parameter on **Preferences** like this:

```
function Form() {
  const preferencesRef = useRef({});

  function submitHandler(event) {
    // other code ...
  }


  return (
    <form className={classes.form} onSubmit={submitHandler}>
      <div className={classes.formControl}>
        <label htmlFor="email">Your email</label>
```

```
      <input type="email" id="email" />
   </div>
   <Preferences ref={preferencesRef} />
   <button>Submit</button>
  </form>
 );
}
```

Again, **useRef()** is used to create a **ref** object (**preferencesRef**), and that object is then passed via the special **ref** prop to the **Preferences** component. The created ref receives a default value of an empty object (**{ }**); it's this object that can then be accessed via **ref.current**. In the **Preferences** component, the **ref** value is not received as a regular prop on the **props** parameter, though. Instead, it's received via this second **ref** parameter, which exists because of **forwardRef()**.

But what's the benefit of that? How can this **preferencesRef** object now be used inside **Preferences** to enable cross-component interaction?

Since **ref** is an object that is never replaced, even if the component in which it was created via **useRef()** is re-evaluated (see previous sections above), the receiving component can assign properties and methods to that object and the creating component can then use these methods and properties. The **ref** object is therefore used as a communication vehicle.

In this example, the **Preferences** component could be changed like this to use the **ref** object:

```
const Preferences = forwardRef((props, ref) => {
  const [wantsNewProdInfo, setWantsNewProdInfo] = useState(false);
  const [wantsProdUpdateInfo, setWantsProdUpdateInfo] = useState(false);

  function changeNewProdPrefHandler() {
    setWantsNewProdInfo((prevPref) => !prevPref);
  }

  function changeUpdateProdPrefHandler() {
    setWantsProdUpdateInfo((prevPref) => !prevPref);
  }

  function reset() {
    setWantsNewProdInfo(false);
    setWantsProdUpdateInfo(false);
  }
```

```
  ref.current.reset = reset;
  ref.current.selectedPreferences = {
    newProductInfo: wantsNewProdInfo,
    productUpdateInfo: wantsProdUpdateInfo,
  };


  // also return JSX code (has not changed) ...
});
```

In **Preferences**, both the state values and a pointer at a newly added **reset** function are stored in the received **ref** object. **ref.current** is used since the object created by React (when using **useRef()**) always has such a **current** property, and that property should be used for storing the actual values in **ref**.

Since **Preferences** and **Form** operate on the same object that's stored in the **ref** object, the properties and methods assigned to the object in **Preferences** can also be used in **Form**:

```
function Form() {
  const preferencesRef = useRef({});

  function submitHandler(event) {
    event.preventDefault();


    console.log(preferencesRef.current.selectedPreferences); // reading a value
    preferencesRef.current.reset(); // executing a function stored in Preferences
  }

  return (
    <form className={classes.form} onSubmit={submitHandler}>
      <div className={classes.formControl}>
        <label htmlFor="email">Your email</label>
        <input type="email" id="email" />
      </div>
      <Preferences ref={preferencesRef} />
      <button>Submit</button>
    </form>
  );
}
```

By using forward refs like this, a parent component (**Form**, in this case) is able to use some child component (for instance, **Preferences**) in an imperative way—meaning properties can be accessed and methods called to manipulate the child component (or, to be precise, to trigger some internal functions and behavior inside the child component).

CONTROLLED VERSUS UNCONTROLLED COMPONENTS

Forwarding refs is a method that can be used to allow the **Form** and **Preferences** components to work together. But even though it might look like an elegant solution at first, it should typically not be your default solution for this kind of problem.

Using forward refs, as shown in the example above, leads to more imperative code in the end. It's imperative code because instead of defining the desired user interface state via JSX (which would be declarative), individual step-by-step instructions are added in JavaScript.

If you revisit *Chapter 1, React – What and Why* (the "*The Problem with Vanilla JavaScript*" section), you'll see that code such as **preferencesRef.current.reset()** (from the example above) looks quite similar to instructions such as **buttonElement. addEventListener(...)** (example from *Chapter 1*). Both examples use imperative code and should be avoided for the reasons mentioned in *Chapter 1* (writing step-by-step instructions leads to inefficient micro-management and often unnecessarily complex code).

Inside the **Form** component, the **reset()** function of **Preferences** is invoked. Hence the code describes the desired action that should be performed (instead of the expected outcome). Typically, when working with React you should strive for describing the desired (UI) state instead. Remember, when working with React, that you should write declarative, rather than imperative, code.

When using refs to read or manipulate data as shown in the previous sections of this chapter, you are building so-called **uncontrolled components**. The components are considered "uncontrolled" because React is not directly controlling the UI state. Instead, values are read from other components or the DOM. It's therefore the DOM that controls the state (e.g., a state such as the value entered by a user into an input field).

As a React developer, you should try to minimize the use of uncontrolled components. It's absolutely fine to use refs to save some code if you only need to gather some entered values. But as soon as your UI logic becomes more complex (for example, if you also want to clear user input), you should go for **controlled components** instead.

And doing so is quite straightforward: a component becomes controlled as soon as React manages the state. In the case of the **EmailForm** component from the beginning of this chapter, the controlled component approach was shown before refs were introduced. Using **useState()** for storing the user's input (and updating the state with every keystroke) meant that React was in full control of the entered value.

For the previous example, the **Form** and **Preferences** components, switching to a controlled component approach could look like this:

```
function Preferences({newProdInfo, prodUpdateInfo, onUpdateInfo}) {
  return (
    <div className={classes.preferences}>
      <label>
        <input
          type="checkbox"
          id="pref-new"
          checked={newProdInfo}
          onChange={onUpdateInfo.bind(null, 'pref-new')}
        />
        <span>New Products</span>
      </label>
      <label>
        <input
          type="checkbox"
          id="pref-updates"
          checked={prodUpdateInfo}
          onChange={onUpdateInfo.bind(null, 'pref-updates')}
        />
        <span>Product Updates</span>
      </label>
    </div>
  );
};
```

In this example, the **Preferences** component stops managing the checkbox state and instead receives props from its parent component (the **Form** component).

bind() is used on the **onUpdateInfo** prop (which will receive a function as a value) to "pre-configure" the function for future execution. **bind()** is a default JavaScript method that can be called on any JavaScript function to control which arguments will be passed to that function once it's invoked in the future.

> **NOTE**
>
> You can learn more about this JavaScript feature at https://academind.com/ tutorials/function-bind-event-execution.

The **Form** component now manages the checkbox states, even though it doesn't directly contain the checkbox elements. But it now begins to control the **Preferences** component and its internal state, hence turning **Preferences** into a controlled component instead of an uncontrolled one:

```
function Form() {
  const [wantsNewProdInfo, setWantsNewProdInfo] = useState(false);
  const [wantsProdUpdateInfo, setWantsProdUpdateInfo] = useState(false);

  function updateProdInfoHandler(selection) {
    // using one shared update handler function is optional
    // you could also use two separate functions (passed to Preferences)
as props
    if (selection === 'pref-new') {
      setWantsNewProdInfo((prevPref) => !prevPref);
    } else if (selection === 'pref-update') {
      setWantsProdUpdateInfo((prevPref) => !prevPref);
    }
  }

  function reset() {
    setWantsNewProdInfo(false);
    setWantsProdUpdateInfo(false);
  }

  function submitHandler(event) {
    event.preventDefault();
    // state values can be used here
    reset();
  }

  return (
    <form className={classes.form} onSubmit={submitHandler}>
      <div className={classes.formControl}>
        <label htmlFor="email">Your email</label>
```

```
        <input type="email" id="email" />
      </div>
      <Preferences
        newProdInfo={wantsNewProdInfo}
        prodUpdateInfo={wantsProdUpdateInfo}
        onUpdateInfo={updateProdInfoHandler}
      />
      <button>Submit</button>
    </form>
  );
}
```

Form manages the checkbox selection state, including resetting the state via the **reset()** function, and passes the managed state values (**wantsNewProdInfo** and **wantsProdUpdateInfo**) as well as the **updateProdInfoHandler** function, which updates the state values, to **Preferences**. The **Form** component now controls the **Preferences** component.

If you go through the two code snippets above, you'll notice that the final code is once again purely declarative. Across all components, state is managed and used to declare the expected user interface.

It is considered a good practice to go for controlled components in most cases. If you are only extracting some entered user input values, however, then using refs and creating an uncontrolled component is absolutely fine.

REACT AND WHERE THINGS END UP IN THE DOM

Leaving the topic of refs, there is one other important React feature that can help with influencing (indirect) DOM interaction: **Portals**.

When building user interfaces, you sometimes need to display elements and content conditionally. This was already covered in *Chapter 5, Rendering Lists and Conditional Content*. When rendering conditional content, React will inject that content into the place in the DOM where the overall component (in which the conditional content is defined) is located.

For example, when showing a conditional error message below an input field, that error message is right below the input in the DOM:

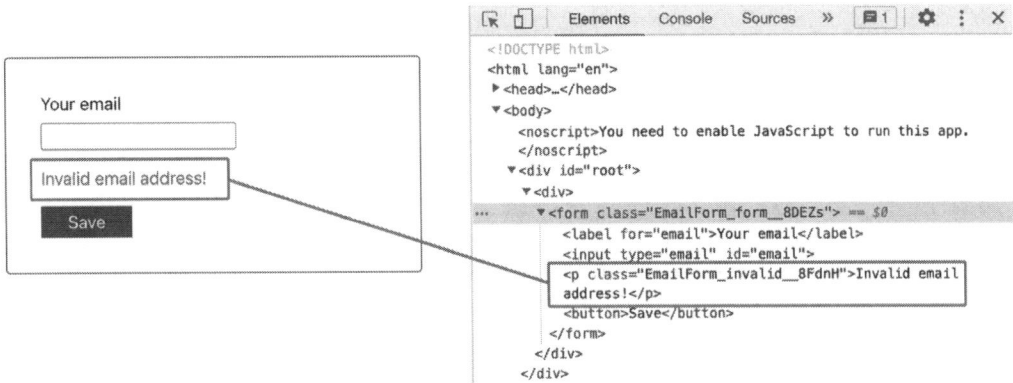

Figure 7.4: The error message DOM element sits right below the <input> it belongs to

This behavior makes sense. Indeed, it would be pretty irritating if React were to start inserting DOM elements in random places. But in some scenarios, you may prefer a (conditional) DOM element to be inserted in a different place in the DOM—for example, when working with overlay elements such as error dialogs.

In the preceding example, you could add logic to ensure that some error dialog is presented to the user if the form is submitted with an invalid email address. This could be implemented with logic similar to the **"Invalid email address!"** error message, and therefore the dialog element would, of course, also be injected dynamically into the DOM:

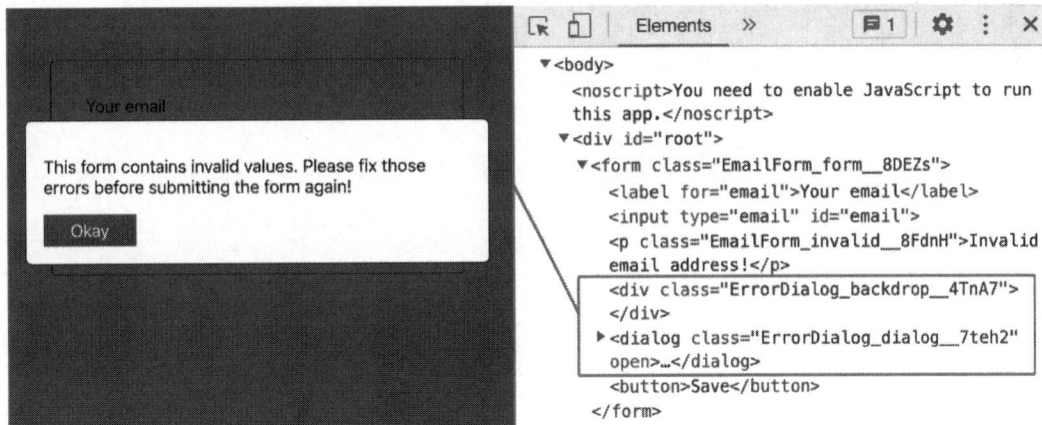

Figure 7.5: The error dialog and its backdrop are injected into the DOM

In this screenshot, the error dialog is opened as an overlay above a backdrop element, which is itself added such that it acts as an overlay to the rest of the user interface.

> **NOTE**
>
> The appearance is handled entirely by CSS, and you can take a look at the complete project (including the styling) here: https://packt.link/wFmZ7.

This example works and looks fine. However, there is room for improvement.

Semantically, it doesn't entirely make sense to have the overlay elements injected somewhere nested into the DOM next to the **<input>** element. It would make more sense for overlay elements to be closer to the root of the DOM (in other words, to be direct child elements of **<div id="root">** or even **<body>**), instead of being children of **<form>**. And it's not just a semantic problem. If the example app contains other overlay elements, those elements might clash with each other like this:

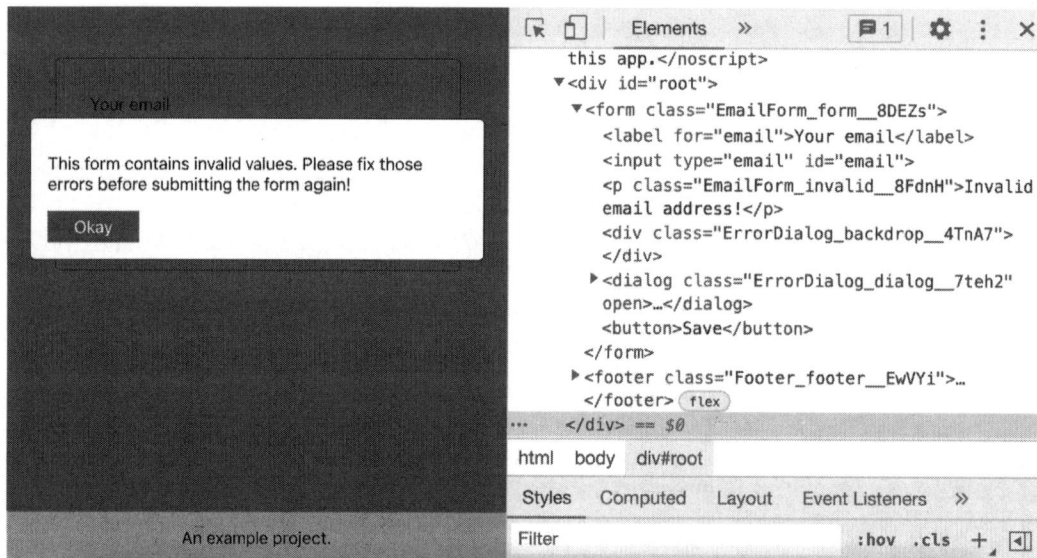

Figure 7.6: The <footer> element at the bottom is visible above the backdrop

In this example, the **<footer>** element at the bottom ("An example project") is not hidden or grayed out by the backdrop that belongs to the error dialog. The reason for that is that the footer also has some CSS styling attached that turns it into a de facto overlay (because of **position: fixed** and **left** + **bottom** being used in its CSS styles).

As a solution to this problem, you could tweak some CSS styles and, for example, use the **z-index** CSS property to control overlay levels. However, it would be a cleaner solution if the overlay elements (i.e., the **<div>** backdrop and the **<dialog>** error elements) were inserted into the DOM in a different place—for example, at the very end of the **<body>** element (but as direct children to **<body>**).

And that's exactly the kind of problem React **Portals** help you solve.

PORTALS TO THE RESCUE

A **Portal**, in React's world, is a feature that allows you to instruct React to insert a DOM element in a different place thanwhere it would normally be inserted.

Considering the example shown above, this portal feature can be used to "tell" React to not insert the **<dialog>** error and the **<div>** backdrop that belongs to the dialog inside the **<form>** element, but to instead insert those elements at the end of the **<body>** element.

To use this portal feature, you first must define a place wherein elements can be inserted (an "injection hook"). This can be done in the HTML file that belongs to the React app (i.e., **public/index.html**). There, you can add a new element (for example, a **<div>** element) somewhere in the **<body>** element:

```
<body>
  <noscript>You need to enable JavaScript to run this app.</noscript>
  <div id="root"></div>
  <div id="dialogs"></div>
</body>
```

In this case, a **<div id="dialogs">** element is added at the end of the **<body>** element to make sure that any components (and their styles) inserted in that element are evaluated last. This will ensure that their styles take a higher priority and overlay elements inserted into **<div id="dialogs">** would not be overlaid by other content coming earlier in the DOM. Adding and using multiple hooks would be possible, but for this example, only one "injection point" is needed. You can also use HTML elements other than **<div>** elements.

With the **index.html** file adjusted, React can be instructed to render certain JSX elements (i.e., components) in a specified hook via the **createPortal()** function of **react-dom**:

```
import { createPortal } from 'react-dom';

import classes from './ErrorDialog.module.css';

function ErrorDialog({ onClose }) {
  return createPortal(
    <>
      <div className={classes.backdrop}></div>
      <dialog className={classes.dialog} open>
        <p>
          This form contains invalid values. Please fix those errors
before
          submitting the form again!
        </p>
        <button onClick={onClose}>Okay</button>
      </dialog>
    </>,
    document.getElementById(,dialogs')
  );
}

export default ErrorDialog;
```

Inside this **ErrorDialog** component, which is rendered conditionally by another component (the **EmailForm** component, the example code for which is available on GitHub), the returned JSX code is wrapped by **createPortal()**. **createPortal()** takes two arguments: the JSX code that should be rendered in the DOM and a pointer at the element in **index.html** where the content should be injected.

In this example, the newly added **<div id="dialogs">** is selected via **document.getElementById('dialogs')**. Therefore, **createPortal()** ensures that the JSX code generated by **ErrorDialog** is rendered in that place in the HTML document:

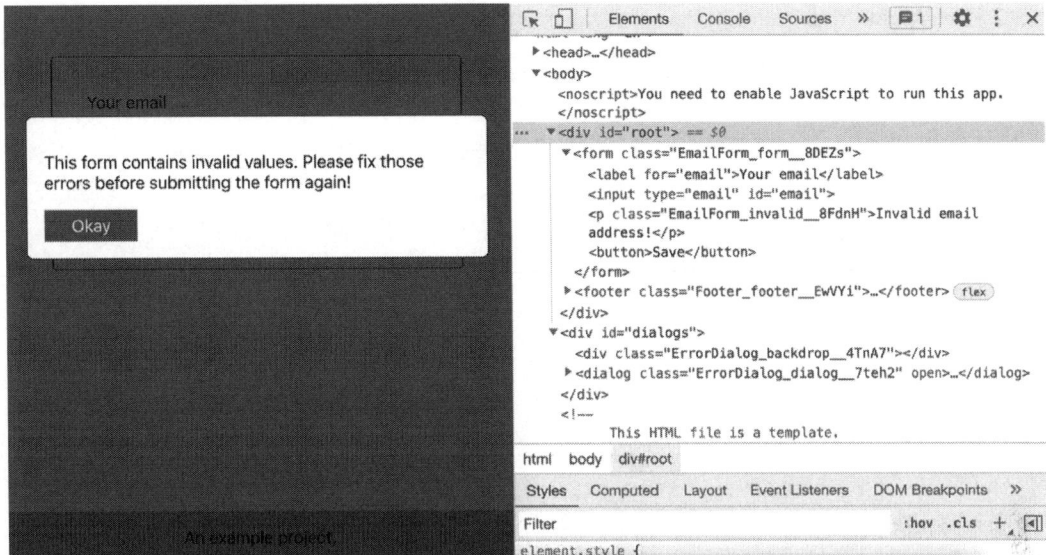

Figure 7.7: The overlay elements are inserted into <div id="dialogs">

In this screenshot, you can see that the overlay elements (**<div>** backdrop and **<dialog>** error) are indeed inserted into the **<div id="dialogs">** element, instead of the **<form>** element (as they were before).

As a result of this change, **<footer>** no longer overlays the error dialog backdrop—without any CSS code changes. Semantically, the final DOM structure also makes more sense since you would typically expect overlay elements to be closer to the root DOM node.

Still, using this portal feature is optional. The same visual result (though not the DOM structure) could have been achieved by changing some CSS styles. Nonetheless, aiming for a clean DOM structure is a worthwhile pursuit, and avoiding unnecessarily complex CSS code is also not a bad thing.

SUMMARY AND KEY TAKEAWAYS

- Refs can be used to gain direct access to DOM elements or to store values that won't be reset or changed when the surrounding component is re-evaluated.

- Only use this direct access to read values, not to manipulate DOM elements (let React do this instead).

- Components that gain DOM access via refs, instead of state and other React features, are considered uncontrolled components (because React is not in direct control).

- Prefer controlled components (using state and a strictly declarative approach) over uncontrolled components unless you're performing very simple tasks such as reading an entered input value.

- Using forward refs, you can also expose features of your own components such that they may be used imperatively.

- Portals can be used to instruct React to render JSX elements in a different place in the DOM than they normally would.

WHAT'S NEXT?

At this point in the book, you've encountered many key tools and concepts that can be used to build interactive and engaging user interfaces. But, as you will learn in the next chapter, one crucial concept is still missing: a way of handling **side effects**.

The next chapter will explore what exactly **side effects** are, why they need special handling, and how React helps you with that.

TEST YOUR KNOWLEDGE!

Test your knowledge of the concepts covered in this chapter by answering the following questions. You can then compare your answers with examples that can be found at https://packt.link/pFCSN.

1. How can refs help with handling user input in forms?

2. What is an uncontrolled component?

3. What is a controlled component?

4. When should you **not** use refs?

5. What's the main idea behind portals?

APPLY WHAT YOU HAVE LEARNED

With this newly gained knowledge about refs and portals, it's again time to practice what you have learned.

Below, you'll find two activities that allow you to practice working with refs and portals. As always, you will, of course, also need some of the concepts covered in earlier chapters (e.g., working with state).

ACTIVITY 7.1: EXTRACT USER INPUT VALUES

In this activity, you have to add logic to an existing React component to extract values from a form. The form contains an input field and a drop-down menu and you should make sure that, upon form submission, both values are read and, for the purpose of this dummy app, output to the browser console.

Use your knowledge about Refs and uncontrolled components to implement a solution without using React state.

> **NOTE**
>
> You can find the starting code for this activity at https://packt.link/PAvKn. When downloading this code, you'll always download the entire repository. Make sure to then navigate to the subfolder with the starting code (`activities/practice-1/starting-code` in this case) to use the right code snapshot.

After downloading the code and running **npm install** in the project folder (to install all the required dependencies), the solution steps are as follows:

1. Create two Refs, one for each input element that should be read (input field and drop-down menu).

2. Connect the Refs to the input elements.

3. In the submit handler function, access the connected DOM elements via the refs and read the currently entered or selected values.

4. Output the values to the browser console.

The expected result (user interface) should look like this:

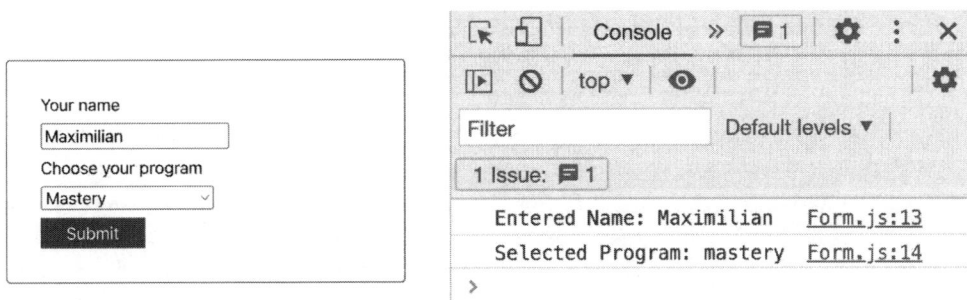

Figure 7.8: The browser developer tools console outputs the selected values

> **NOTE**
>
> The solution to this activity can be found on page 483.

ACTIVITY 7.2: ADD A SIDE-DRAWER

In this activity, you will connect an already existing **SideDrawer** component with a button in the main navigation bar to open the side drawer (i.e., display it) whenever the button is clicked. After the side drawer opens, a click on the backdrop should close the drawer again.

In addition to implementing the general logic described above, your goal will be to ensure proper positioning in the final DOM such that no other elements are overlaid on top of the **SideDrawer** (without editing any CSS code). The **SideDrawer** should also not be nested in any other components or JSX elements.

> **NOTE**
>
> This activity comes with some starting code, which can be found here:
> https://packt.link/Q4RSe.

After downloading the code and running **npm install** to install all the required dependencies, the solution steps are as follows:

1. Add logic to conditionally show or hide the **SideDrawer** component in the **MainNavigation** component.

2. Add an "injection hook" for the side drawer in the HTML document.

3. Use React's portal feature to render the JSX elements of **SideDrawer** in the newly added hook.

The final user interface should look and behave like this:

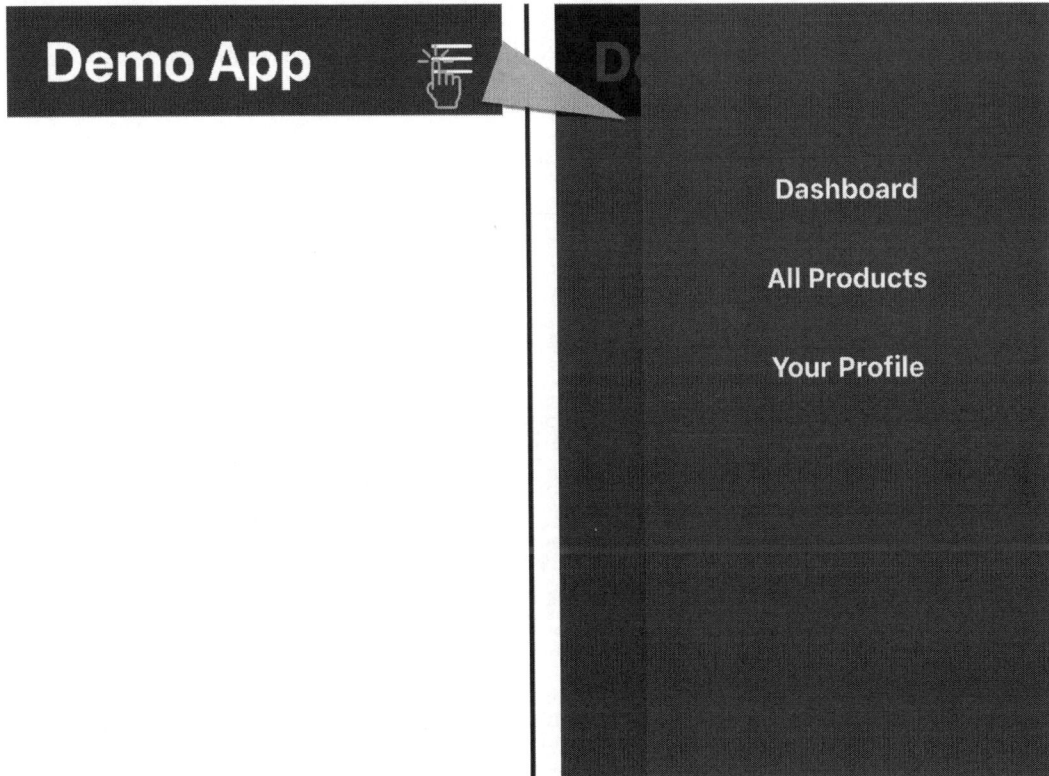

Figure 7.9: A click on the menu button opens the side drawer

Upon clicking on the menu button, the side drawer opens. If the backdrop behind the side drawer is clicked, it should close again.

The final DOM structure (with the side drawer opened) should look like this:

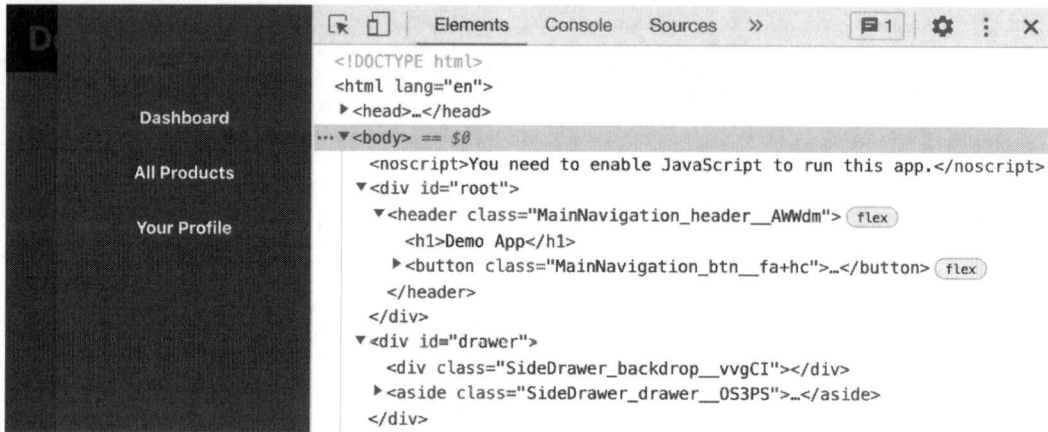

Figure 7.10: The drawer-related elements are inserted in a separate place in the DOM

The side drawer-related DOM elements (the **<div>** backdrop and **<aside>**) are inserted into a separate DOM node (**<div id="drawer">**).

> **NOTE**
>
> The solution to this activity can be found on page 485.

8

HANDLING SIDE EFFECTS

LEARNING OBJECTIVES

By the end of this chapter, you will be able to do the following:

- Identify side effects in your React apps.

- Understand and use the `useEffect()` Hook.

- Utilize the different features and concepts related to the `useEffect()` Hook to avoid bugs and optimize your code.

- Handle side effects related and unrelated to state changes.

INTRODUCTION

While all React examples previously covered in this book have been relatively straightforward, and many key React concepts were introduced, it is unlikely that many real apps could be built with those concepts alone.

Most real apps that you will build as a React developer also need to send HTTP requests, access the browser storage and log analytics data, or perform any other kind of similar task. And with components, props, events, and state alone, you'll often encounter problems when trying to add such features to your app. Detailed explanations and examples will be discussed later in this chapter, but the core problem is that tasks like this will often interfere with React's component rendering cycle, leading to unexpected bugs or even breaking the app.

This chapter will take a closer look at those kinds of actions, analyze what they have in common, and most importantly, teach you how to correctly handle such tasks in React apps.

WHAT'S THE PROBLEM?

Before exploring a solution, it's important to first understand the concrete problem.

Actions that are not directly related to producing a (new) user interface state often clash with React's component rendering cycle. They may introduce bugs or even break the entire web app.

Consider the following example code snippet:

```
import { useState } from 'react';


import classes from './BlogPosts.module.css';


async function fetchPosts() {
  const response = await fetch('https://jsonplaceholder.typicode.com/
posts');
  const blogPosts = await response.json();
  return blogPosts;
}


function BlogPosts() {
  const [loadedPosts, setLoadedPosts] = useState([]);


  fetchPosts().then((fetchedPosts) => setLoadedPosts(fetchedPosts));
```

```
  return (
    <ul className={classes.posts}>
      {loadedPosts.map((post) => (
        <li key={post.id}>{post.title}</li>
      ))}
    </ul>
  );
}


export default BlogPosts;
```

Don't execute this code as it will cause an infinite loop and send a large number of HTTP requests behind the scenes!

Next, you'll learn more about this problem, as well as a solution for it.

In this example, a React component (**BlogPosts**) is created. In addition, a non-component function (**fetchPosts()**) is defined. That function uses the built-in **fetch()** function (provided by the browser) to send an HTTP request to an external **application programming interface** (**API**) and fetch some data.

> **NOTE**
>
> The **fetch()** function is made available by the browser (all modern browsers support this function). You can learn more about **fetch()** at https://academind.com/tutorials/xhr-fetch-axios-the-fetch-api.
>
> The **fetch()** function yields a **promise**, which, in this example, is handled via **async/await**. Just like **fetch()**, promises are a key web development concept, which you can learn more about (along with **async/await**) at https://developer.mozilla.org/en-US/docs/Web/JavaScript/Reference/Statements/async_function.
>
> An API, in this context, is a site that exposes various paths to which requests can be sent—either to submit or to fetch data. jsonplaceholder.typicode.com is a dummy API, responding with dummy data. It can be used in scenarios like the preceding example, where you just need an API to send requests to. You can use it to test some concept or code without connecting or creating a real backend API. In this case, it's used to explore some React problems and concepts. Basic knowledge about sending HTTP requests with **fetch()** and APIs is expected for this chapter and the book overall. If needed, you can use pages such as MDN (https://developer.mozilla.org/) to strengthen your knowledge of such core concepts.

In the preceding code snippet, the **BlogPosts** component utilizes **useState()** to register a **loadedPosts** state value. The state is used to output a list of blog posts. Those blog posts are not defined in the app itself though. Instead, they are fetched from an external API (in this case, from a dummy backend API found at jsonplaceholder.typicode.com).

fetchPosts(), which is the utility function that contains the code for fetching blog posts data from that backend API using the built-in **fetch()** function, is called directly in the component function body. Since **fetchPosts()** is an **async** function (using **async/await**), it returns a promise. In **BlogPosts**, the code that should be executed once the promise resolves is registered via the built-in **then()** method (because React component functions shouldn't be **async** functions, **async/await** can't be used here).

Once the **fetchPosts()** promise resolves, the extracted posts data (**fetchedPosts**) is set as the new **loadedPosts** state (via **setLoadedPosts(fetchedPosts)**).

If you were to run the preceding code (which you should not do!), it would at first seem to work. But behind the scenes, it would actually start an infinite loop, hammering the API with HTTP requests. This is because, as a result of getting a response from the HTTP request, **setLoadedPosts()** is used to set a new state.

Earlier in this book (in *Chapter 4, Working with Events and State*), you learned that whenever the state of a component changes, React re-evaluates the component to which the state belongs. "Re-evaluating" simply means that the component function is executed again (by React, automatically).

Since this **BlogPosts** component calls **fetchPosts()** (which sends an HTTP request) directly inside the component function body, this HTTP request will be sent every time the component function is executed. And as the state (**loadedPosts**) is updated as a result of getting a response from that HTTP request, this process begins again, and an infinite loop is created.

The root problem, in this case, is that sending an HTTP request is a side effect—a concept that will be explored in greater detail in the next section.

UNDERSTANDING SIDE EFFECTS

Side effects are actions or processes that occur in addition to another "main process". At least, this is a concise definition that helps with understanding side effects in the context of a React app.

> **NOTE**
>
> You can also look up a more scientific definition here: https://en.wikipedia.org/wiki/Side_effect_(computer_science).

In the case of a React component, the main process would be the component render cycle in which the main task of a component is to render the user interface that is defined in the component function (the returned JSX code). The React component should return the final JSX code, which is then translated into DOM-manipulating instructions.

For this, React considers state changes as the trigger for updating the user interface. Registering event handlers such as **onClick**, adding refs, or rendering child components (possibly by using props) would be other elements that belong to this main process—because all these concepts are directly related to the main task of rendering the desired user interface.

Sending an HTTP request, as in the preceding example, is not part of this main process, though. It doesn't directly influence the user interface. While the response data might eventually be output on the screen, it definitely won't be used in the exact same component render cycle in which the request is sent (because HTTP requests are asynchronous tasks).

Since sending the HTTP request is not part of the main process (rendering the user interface) that's performed by the component function, it's considered a "side effect". It's invoked by the same function (the **BlogPosts** component function), which primarily has a different goal.

If the HTTP request were sent upon a click of a button rather than as part of the main component function body, it would not be a side effect. Consider this example:

```
import { useState } from 'react';

import classes from './BlogPosts.module.css';

async function fetchPosts() {
  const response = await fetch('https://jsonplaceholder.typicode.com/posts');
  const blogPosts = await response.json();
  return blogPosts;
}
```

```
function BlogPosts() {
  const [loadedPosts, setLoadedPosts] = useState([]);

  function fetchPostsHandler() {
    fetchPosts().then((fetchedPosts) => setLoadedPosts(fetchedPosts));
  }

  return (
    <>
      <button onClick={fetchPostsHandler}>Fetch Posts</button>
      <ul className={classes.posts}>
        {loadedPosts.map((post) => (
          <li key={post.id}>{post.title}</li>
        ))}
      </ul>
    </>
  );
}

export default BlogPosts;
```

This code is almost identical to the previous example, but it has one important difference: a **\<button\>** was added to the JSX code. And it's this button that invokes a newly added **fetchPostsHandler()** function, which then sends the HTTP request (and updates the state).

With this change made, the HTTP request is *not* sent every time the component function re-renders (that is, is executed again). Instead, it's only sent whenever the button is clicked, and therefore, this does not create an infinite loop. The HTTP request, in this case, also doesn't postulate a side effect, because the primary goal of **fetchPostsHandler()** (i.e., the main process) is to fetch new posts and update the state.

SIDE EFFECTS ARE NOT JUST ABOUT HTTP REQUESTS

In the previous example, you learned about one potential side effect that could occur in a component function: an HTTP request. You also learned that HTTP requests are not always side effects. It depends on where they are created.

In general, any action that's started upon the execution of a React component function is a side effect if that action is not directly related to the main task of rendering the component's user interface.

Here's a non-exhaustive list of examples for side effects:

- Sending an HTTP request (as shown previously)

- Storing data to or fetching data from browser storage (for example, via the built-in **localStorage** object)

- Setting timers (via **setTimeout()**) or intervals (via **setInterval()**)

- Logging data to the console via **console.log()**

- Not all side effects cause infinite loops, however. Such loops only occur if the side effect leads to a state update.

- Here's an example of a side effect that would not cause an infinite loop:

```
function ControlCenter() {
  function startHandler() {
    // do something ...
  }

  console.log('Component is rendering!'); // this is a side effect!

  return (
    <div>
      <p>Press button to start the review process</p>
      <button onClick={startHandler}>Start</button>
    </div>
  );
}
```

In this example, **console.log(...)** is a side effect because it's executed as part of every component function execution and does not influence the rendered user interface (neither for this specific render cycle nor indirectly for any future render cycles in this case, unlike the previous example with the HTTP request).

Of course, using **console.log()** like this is not causing any problems. During development, it's quite normal to log messages or data for debugging purposes. Side effects aren't necessarily a problem and, indeed, side effects like this can be used or tolerated.

But you also often need to deal with side effects such as the HTTP request from before. Sometimes, you need to fetch data when a component renders—probably not for every render cycle, but typically the first time it is executed (that is, when its generated user interface appears on the screen for the first time).

React offers a solution for this kind of problem, as well.

DEALING WITH SIDE EFFECTS WITH THE USEEFFECT() HOOK

In order to deal with side effects such as the HTTP request shown previously in a safe way (that is, without creating an infinite loop), React offers another core Hook: the **useEffect()** Hook.

The first example can be fixed and rewritten like this:

```
import { useState, useEffect } from 'react';

import classes from './BlogPosts.module.css';

async function fetchPosts() {
  const response = await fetch('https://jsonplaceholder.typicode.com/
posts');
  const blogPosts = await response.json();
  return blogPosts;
}

function BlogPosts() {
  const [loadedPosts, setLoadedPosts] = useState([]);

  useEffect(function () {
    fetchPosts().then((fetchedPosts) => setLoadedPosts(fetchedPosts));
  }, []);

  return (
    <ul className={classes.posts}>
      {loadedPosts.map((post) => (
        <li key={post.id}>{post.title}</li>
      ))}
    </ul>
  );
}

export default BlogPosts;
```

In this example, the **`useEffect()`** Hook is imported and used to control the side effect (hence the name of the Hook, **`useEffect()`**, as it deals with side effects in React components). The exact syntax and usage will be explored in the next section, but if you use this Hook, you can safely run the example and get some output like this:

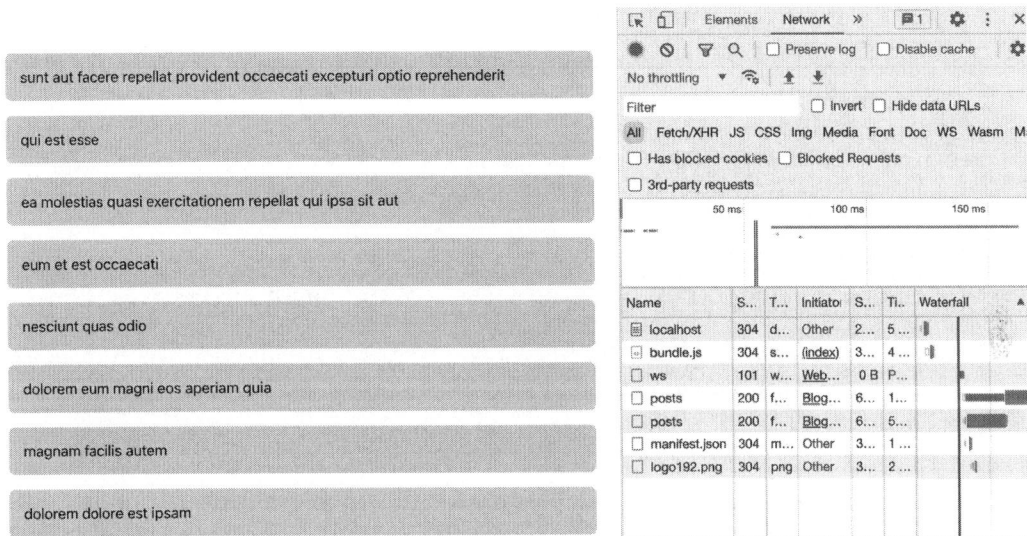

Figure 8.1: A list of dummy blog posts and no infinite loop of HTTP requests

In the preceding screenshot, you can see the list of dummy blog posts, and most importantly, when inspecting the sent network requests, you find no infinite list of requests.

`useEffect()` is therefore the solution for problems like the one outlined previously. It helps you deal with side effects so that you can avoid infinite loops and extract them from your component function's main process.

But how does **`useEffect()`** work and how is it used correctly?

HOW TO USE USEEFFECT()

As shown in the previous example code snippet, **`useEffect()`**, like all React Hooks, is executed as a function inside the component function (**`BlogPosts`**, in this case).

Though, unlike **`useState()`** or **`useRef()`**, **`useEffect()`** does not return a value, it does accept an argument (or, actually, two arguments) like those other Hooks. The first argument is *always* a function. In this case, the function passed to **`useEffect()`** is an anonymous function, created via the **`function`** keyword.

Alternatively, you could also provide an anonymous function created as an arrow function (**useEffect(() => { ... })**) or point at some named function (**useEffect(doSomething)**). The only thing that matters is that the first argument passed to **useEffect()** *must* be a function. It must not be any other kind of value.

In the preceding example, **useEffect()** also receives a second argument: an empty array (**[]**). The second argument must be an array, but providing it is *optional*. You could also omit the second argument and just pass the first argument (the function) to **useEffect()**. However, in most cases, the second argument is needed to achieve the correct behavior. Both arguments and their purpose will be explored in greater detail as follows.

The first argument is a function that will be executed by React. It will be executed *after* every component render cycle (that is, after every component function execution).

In the preceding example, if you only provide this first argument and omit the second, you will therefore still create an infinite loop. There will be an (invisible) timing difference because the HTTP request will now be sent after every component function execution (instead of as part of it), but you will still trigger a state change, which will still trigger the component function to execute again. Therefore, the effect function will run again, and an infinite loop will be created. In this case, the side effect will be extracted out of the component function technically, but the problem with the infinite loop will not be solved:

```
useEffect(function () {
    fetchPosts().then((fetchedPosts) => setLoadedPosts(fetchedPosts));
}); // this would cause an infinite loop again!
```

Extracting side effects out of React component functions is the main job of **useEffect()**, and so only the first argument (the function that contains the side effect code) is mandatory. But, as mentioned previously, you will also typically need the second argument to control the frequency with which the effect code will be executed, because that's what the second argument (an array) will do.

The second parameter received by **useEffect()** is *always* an array (unless it's omitted). This array specifies the dependencies of the effect function. Any dependency specified in this array will, once it changes, cause the effect function to execute again. If no array is specified (that is, if the second argument is omitted), the effect function will be executed again for every component function execution:

```
useEffect(function () {
   fetchPosts().then((fetchedPosts) => setLoadedPosts(fetchedPosts));
}, []);
```

In the preceding example, the second argument was not omitted, but it's an empty array. This informs React that this effect function has no dependencies. Therefore, the effect function will never be executed again. Instead, it will only be executed once, when the component is rendered for the first time. This is React's default behavior. If you set no dependencies (by providing an empty array), React will execute the effect function *once*—directly after the component function was executed for the first time.

It's important to note that specifying an empty array is very different from omitting it. If omitted, no dependency information is provided to React. Therefore, React executes the effect function after every component re-evaluation. If an empty array is provided instead, you explicitly state that this effect has no dependencies and therefore should only run once.

This brings up another important question, though: when should you add dependencies? And how exactly are dependencies added or specified?

EFFECTS AND THEIR DEPENDENCIES

Omitting the second argument to **useEffect()** causes the effect function (the first argument) to execute after every component function execution. Providing an empty array causes the effect function to run only once (after the first component function invocation). But is that all you can control?

No, it isn't.

The array passed to **useEffect()** can and should contain all variables, constants, or functions that are used inside the effect function—if those variables, constants, or functions were defined inside the component function (or in some parent component function, passed down via props).

Consider this example:

```
import { useState, useEffect } from 'react';

import classes from './BlogPosts.module.css';

const DEFAULT_URL = 'https://jsonplaceholder.typicode.com/posts';

async function fetchPosts(url) {
   const response = await fetch(url);
```

```
    const blogPosts = await response.json();
    return blogPosts;
}


function BlogPosts() {
    const [postsUrl, setPostsUrl] = useState(DEFAULT_URL);
    const [loadedPosts, setLoadedPosts] = useState([]);


    function adjustUrlHandler(event) {
        setPostsUrl(event.target.value);
    }


    useEffect(function () {
        fetchPosts().then((fetchedPosts) => setLoadedPosts(fetchedPosts));
    }, [postsUrl]);


    return (
        <>
            <input className={classes.input} type="text"
onBlur={adjustUrlHandler} />
            <ul className={classes.posts}>
                {loadedPosts.map((post) => (
                    <li key={post.id}>{post.title}</li>
                ))}
            </ul>
        </>
    );
}


export default BlogPosts;
```

This example is based on the previous example, but it was adjusted in multiple places.

The **BlogPosts** component now contains a second state value (**postsUrl**), which is updated inside **adjustUrlHandler()** whenever a newly added **<input>** field blurs (i.e., loses focus). This allows the website visitor to enter a custom URL to which the HTTP request will be sent.

By default (**DEFAULT_URL**), a dummy API (**https://jsonplaceholder. typicode.com/posts**) will be used, but the user could insert any URL of their choice. Of course, if that API doesn't return a list of blog posts, the app won't work as intended. This component therefore might be of limited practical use, but it does show the importance of effect dependencies quite well.

A new effect (and therefore a new HTTP request) should only be triggered if **postsUrl** changes. That's why **postsUrl** was added to the dependencies array of **useEffect()**. If the array had been kept empty, the effect function would only run once (as described in the previous section). Therefore, any changes to **postsUrl** wouldn't have any effect (no pun intended) on the effect function or the HTTP request executed as part of that function. No new HTTP request would be sent.

By adding **postsUrl** to the dependencies array, React registers this value (in this case, a state value, but any value can be registered) and re-executes the effect function whenever that value changes (that is, whenever a new value is set).

The most common types of effect dependencies are state values, props, and functions that might be executed inside of the effect function. The latter will be analyzed in greater depth later in this chapter.

As a rule, you should add all values (including functions) that are used inside an effect function to the effect dependencies array.

With this new knowledge in mind, if you take another look at the preceding **useEffect()** example code, you might spot some missing dependencies:

```
useEffect(function () {
  fetchPosts().then((fetchedPosts) => setLoadedPosts(fetchedPosts));
}, [postsUrl]);
```

Why are **fetchPosts**, **fetchedPosts**, and **setLoadedPosts** not added as dependencies? These are, after all, values and functions used inside of the effect function. The next section will address this in detail.

UNNECESSARY DEPENDENCIES

In the previous example, it might seem as if **fetchPosts**, **fetchedPosts**, and **setLoadedPosts** should be added as dependencies to **useEffect()**, as shown here:

```
useEffect(function () {
  fetchPosts().then((fetchedPosts) => setLoadedPosts(fetchedPosts));
}, [postsUrl, fetchPosts, fetchedPosts, setLoadedPosts]);
```

However, for **fetchPosts** and **fetchedPosts**, this would be incorrect. And for **setLoadedPosts**, it would be unnecessary.

fetchedPosts should not be added because it's not an external dependency. It's a local variable (or argument, to be precise), defined and used inside the effect function. It's not defined in the component function to which the effect belongs. If you try to add it as a dependency, you'll get an error:

```
❌ ▾Uncaught ReferenceError: fetchedPosts is not defined              BlogPosts.js:24
     at BlogPosts (BlogPosts.js:24:1)
     at renderWithHooks (react-dom.development.js:16175:1)
     at mountIndeterminateComponent (react-dom.development.js:20913:1)
     at beginWork (react-dom.development.js:22416:1)
     at HTMLUnknownElement.callCallback (react-dom.development.js:4161:1)
     at Object.invokeGuardedCallbackDev (react-dom.development.js:4210:1)
     at invokeGuardedCallback (react-dom.development.js:4274:1)
     at beginWork$1 (react-dom.development.js:27405:1)
     at performUnitOfWork (react-dom.development.js:26513:1)
     at workLoopSync (react-dom.development.js:26422:1)
```

Figure 8.2: An error occurred – fetchedPosts could not be found

fetchPosts, the function that sends the actual HTTP request, is not a function defined inside of the effect function. But it still shouldn't be added because it is defined outside the component function.

Therefore, there is no way for this function to change. It's defined once (in the **BlogPosts.js** file), and it can't change. That said, this would not be the case if it were defined inside the component function. In that case, whenever the component function executes again, the **fetchPosts** function would be recreated as well. This is a scenario that will be discussed later in this chapter (in the *"Functions as Dependencies"* section).

In this example though, **fetchPosts** can't change. Therefore, it doesn't have to be added as a dependency (and consequently should not be). The same would be true for functions, or any kind of values, provided by the browser or third-party packages. Any value that's not defined inside a component function shouldn't be added to the dependencies array.

> **NOTE**
>
> It may be confusing that a function could change—after all, the logic is hardcoded, right? But in JavaScript, functions are actually just objects and therefore may change. When the code that contains a function is executed again (e.g., a component function being executed again by React), a new function object will be created in memory.
>
> If this is not something you're familiar with, the following resource should be helpful: https://academind.com/tutorials/javascript-functions-are-objects.

So **fetchedPosts** and **fetchPosts** should both not be added (for different reasons). What about **setLoadedPosts**?

setLoadedPosts is the state updating function returned by **useState()** for the **loadedPosts** state value. Therefore, like **fetchPosts**, it's a function. Unlike **fetchPosts**, though, it's a function that's defined inside the component function (because **useState()** is called inside the component function). It's a function created by React (since it's returned by **useState()**), but it's still a function. Theoretically, it should therefore be added as a dependency. And indeed, you can add it without any negative consequences.

But state updating functions returned by **useState()** are a special case: React guarantees that those functions will never change or be recreated. When the surrounding component function (**BlogPosts**) is executed again, **useState()** also executes again. However, a new state (and a new state updating function) is only created the first time a component function is called by React. Subsequent executions don't lead to a new state value or state updating function being created.

Because of this special behavior (i.e., React guaranteeing that the function itself never changes), state updating functions may (and actually should) be omitted from the dependencies array.

For all these reasons, **fetchedPosts**, **fetchPosts**, and **setLoadedPosts** should all not be added to the dependencies array of **useEffect()**. **postsUrl** is the only dependency used by the effect function that may change (that is, when the user enters a new URL into the input field) and therefore should be listed in the array.

To sum it up, when it comes to adding values to the effect dependencies array, there are three kinds of exceptions:

- Internal values (or functions) that are defined and used inside the effect (such as **fetchedPosts**)

- External values that are not defined inside a component function (such as **fetchPosts**)

- State updating functions (such as **setLoadedPosts**)

In all other cases, if a value is used in the effect function, it *must be added* to the dependencies array! Omitting values incorrectly can lead to unexpected effect executions (that is, an effect executing too often or not often enough).

CLEANING UP AFTER EFFECTS

To perform a certain task (for example, sending an HTTP request), many effects should simply be triggered when their dependencies change. While some effects can be re-executed multiple times without issue, there are also effects that, if they execute again before the previous task has finished, are an indication that the task performed needs to be canceled. Or, maybe there is some other kind of cleanup work that should be performed when the same effect executes again.

Here's an example, where an effect sets a timer:

```
import { useState, useEffect } from 'react';

function Alert() {
  const [alertDone, setAlertDone] = useState(false);

  useEffect(function () {
    console.log('Starting Alert Timer!');
    setTimeout(function () {
      console.log('Timer expired!');
      setAlertDone(true);
    }, 2000);
  }, []);

  return (
    <>
      {!alertDone && <p>Relax, you still got some time!</p>}
      {alertDone && <p>Time to get up!</p>}
    </>
  );
}

export default Alert;
```

This **Alert** component is used in the **App** component:

```
import { useState } from 'react';

import Alert from './components/Alert';

function App() {
  const [showAlert, setShowAlert] = useState(false);
```

```
function showAlertHandler() {
    // state updating is done by passing a function to setShowAlert
    // because the new state depends on the previous state (it's the
opposite)
    setShowAlert((isShowing) => !isShowing);
}


return (
    <>
        <button onClick={showAlertHandler}>
            {showAlert ? 'Hide' : 'Show'} Alert
        </button>
        {showAlert && <Alert />}
    </>
);
}

export default App;
```

> **NOTE**
>
> You can also clone or download the full example from GitHub at
> https://packt.link/Zmkp9.

In the **App** component, the **Alert** component is shown conditionally. The
showAlert state is toggled via the **showAlertHandler** function (which is
triggered upon a button click).

In the **Alert** component, a timer is set using **useEffect()**. Without
useEffect(), an infinite loop would be created, since the timer, upon expiration,
changes some component state (the **alertDone** state via the **setAlertDone** state
updating function).

The dependency array is an empty array because this effect function does not use any
component values, variables, or functions. **console.log()** and **setTimeout()**
are functions built into the browser (and therefore external functions), and
setAlertDone() can be omitted because of the reasons mentioned in the
previous section.

If you run this app and then start toggling the alert (by clicking the button), you'll notice strange behavior. The timer is set every time the **Alert** component is rendered. But it's not clearing the existing timer. This is due to the fact that multiple timers are running simultaneously, as you can clearly see if you look at the JavaScript console in your browser's developer tools:

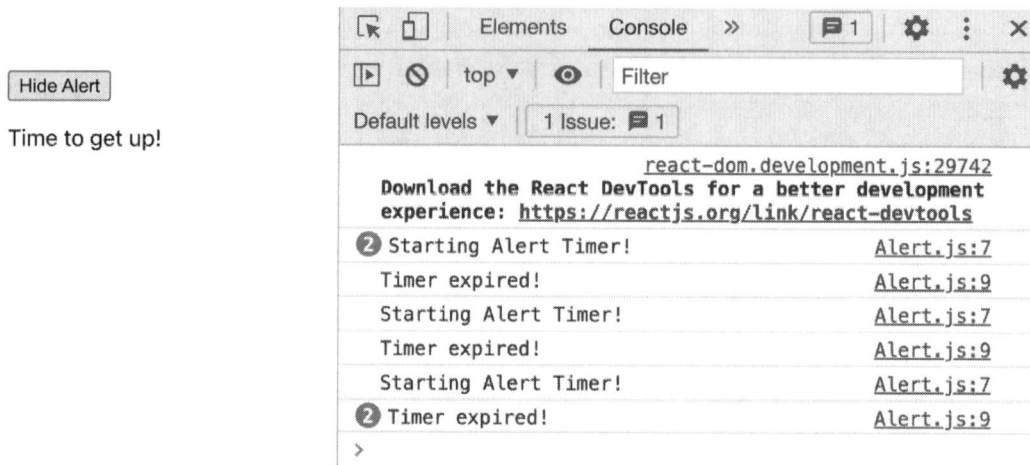

Figure 8.3: Multiple timers are started

This example is deliberately kept simple, but there are other scenarios in which you may have an ongoing HTTP request that should be aborted before a new one is sent. There are cases like that, where an effect should be cleaned up first before it runs again.

React also offers a solution for those kinds of situations: the effect function passed as a first argument to **useEffect()** can return an optional cleanup function. If you do return a function inside your effect function, React will execute that function every time *before* it runs the effect again.

Here's the **useEffect()** call of the **Alert** component with a cleanup function being returned:

```
useEffect(function () {
  let timer;

  console.log('Starting Alert Timer!');
  timer = setTimeout(function () {
    console.log('Timer expired!');
    setAlertDone(true);
  }, 2000);
```

```
  return function() {
    clearTimeout(timer);
  }
}, []);
```

In this updated example, a new **timer** variable (a local variable that is only accessible inside the effect function) is added. That variable stores a reference to the timer that's created by **setTimeout()**. This reference can then be used together with **clearTimeout()** to remove a timer.

The timer is removed in a function returned by the effect function—which is the cleanup function that will be executed automatically by React before the effect function is called the next time.

You can see the cleanup function in action if you add a **console.log()** statement to it:

```
return function() {
  console.log('Cleanup!');
  clearTimeout(timer);
}
```

In your JavaScript console, this looks as follows:

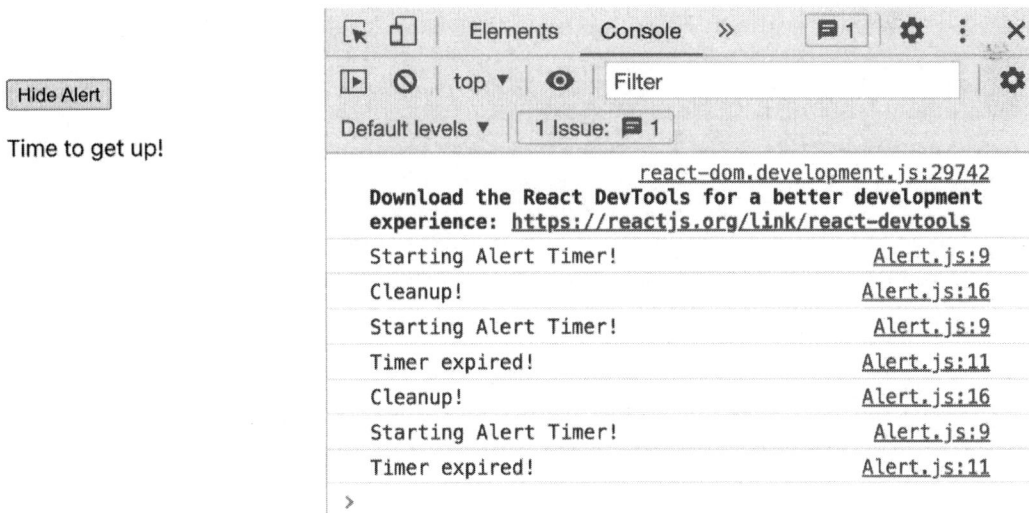

Figure 8.4: The cleanup function is executed before the effect runs again

In the preceding screenshot, you can see that the cleanup function is executed (indicated by the **Cleanup!** log) right before the effect function is executed again. You can also see that the timer is cleared successfully: the first timer never expires (there is no **Timer expired!** log for the first timer in the screenshot).

The cleanup function is not executed when the effect function is called for the first time. However, it will be called by React whenever a component that contains an effect unmounts (that is, when it's removed from the DOM).

If an effect has multiple dependencies, the effect function will be executed whenever any of the dependency values change. Therefore, the cleanup function will also be called every time some dependency changes.

DEALING WITH MULTIPLE EFFECTS

Thus far, all the examples in this chapter have dealt with only one **useEffect()** call. You are not limited to only one call per component though. You can call **useEffect()** as often as needed—and can therefore register as many effect functions as needed.

But how many effect functions do you need?

You could start putting every side effect into its own **useEffect()** wrapper. Every HTTP request, every **console.log()** statement, and every timer, you could put into separate effect functions.

That said, as you can see in some of the previous examples—specifically, the code snippet in the previous section—that's not necessary. There, you have multiple effects in one **useEffect()** call (three **console.log()** statements and one timer).

A better approach would be to split your effect functions by dependencies. If one side effect depends on state A and another side effect depends on state B, you could put them into separate effect functions (unless those two states are related), as shown here:

```
function Demo() {
  const [a, setA] = useState(0); // state updating functions aren't
called
  const [b, setB] = useState(0); // in this example

  useEffect(function() {
    console.log(a);
  }, [a]);
```

```
useEffect(function() {
  console.log(b);
}, [b]);


// return some JSX code ...
}
```

But the best approach is to split your effect functions by logic. If one effect deals with fetching data via an HTTP request and another effect is about setting a timer, it will often make sense to put them into different effect functions (that is, different **useEffect()** calls).

FUNCTIONS AS DEPENDENCIES

Different effects have different kinds of dependencies, and one common kind of dependency is functions.

As mentioned previously, functions in JavaScript are just objects. Therefore, whenever some code that contains a function definition is executed, a new function object is created and stored in memory. When calling a function, it's that specific function object in memory that is executed. In some scenarios (for example, for functions defined in component functions), it's possible that multiple objects based on the same function code exist in memory.

Because of this behavior, functions that are referenced in code are not necessarily equal, even if they are based on the same function definition.

Consider this example:

```
function Alert() {
  function setAlert() {
    setTimeout(function() {
      console.log('Alert expired!');
    }, 2000);
  }

  useEffect(function() {
    setAlert();
  }, [setAlert]);

  // return some JSX code ...
}
```

In this example, instead of creating a timer directly inside the effect function, a separate **setAlert()** function is created in the component function. That **setAlert()** function is then used in the effect function passed to **useEffect()**. Since that function is used there, and because it's defined in the component function, it should be added as a dependency to **useEffect()**.

Another reason for this is that every time the **Alert** component function is executed again (e.g., because some state or prop value changes), a new **setAlert** function object will be created. In this example, that wouldn't be problematic because **setAlert** only contains static code. A new function object created for **setAlert** would work exactly in the same way as the previous one, therefore, it would not matter.

But now consider this adjusted example

> **NOTE**
>
> The complete app can be found on GitHub at https://packt.link/pna08.

```
function Alert() {
  const [alertMsg, setAlertMsg] = useState('Expired!');

  function changeAlertMsgHandler(event) {
    setAlertMsg(event.target.value);
  }

  function setAlert() {
    setTimeout(function () {
      console.log(alertMsg);
    }, 2000);
  }

  useEffect(
    function () {
      setAlert();
    },
```

```
      []
   );


   return <input type="text" onChange={changeAlertMsgHandler} />;
}


export default Alert;
```

Now, a new **alertMsg** state is used for setting the actual alert message that's logged to the console. In addition, the **setAlert** dependency was removed from **useEffect()**.

If you run this code, you'll get the following output:

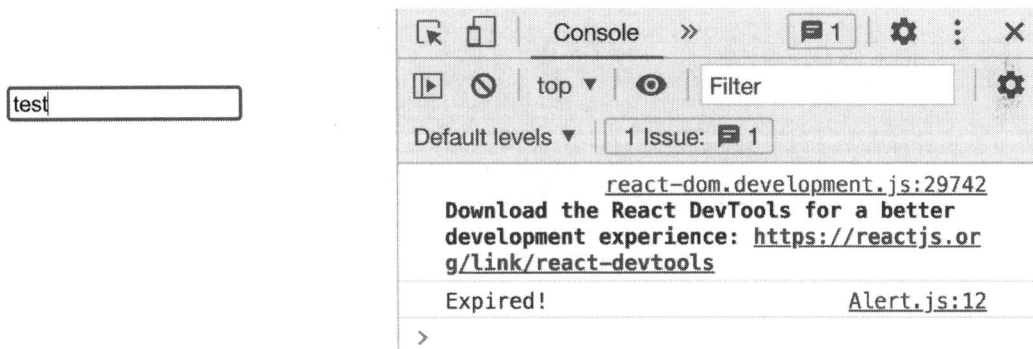

Figure 8.5: The console log does not reflect the entered value

In this screenshot, you can see that, despite a different value being entered into the input field, the original alert message is output.

The reason for this behavior is that the new alert message is not picked up. It's not used because, despite the component function being executed again (because the state changed), the effect is not executed again. And the original execution of the effect still uses the old version of the **setAlert** function—the old **setAlert** function object, which has the old alert message locked in. That's how JavaScript functions work, and that's why, in this case, the desired result is not achieved.

The solution to the problem is simple though: add **setAlert** as a dependency to **useEffect()**. You should always add all values, variables, or functions used in an effect as dependencies, and this example shows *why* you should do that. Even functions can change.

If you add **setAlert** to the effect dependency array, you'll get a different output:

```
useEffect(
  function () {
    setAlert();
  },
  [setAlert]
);
```

Please note that only a pointer to the **setAlert** function is added. You don't execute the function in the dependencies array (that would add the return value of the function as a dependency, which is typically not the goal).

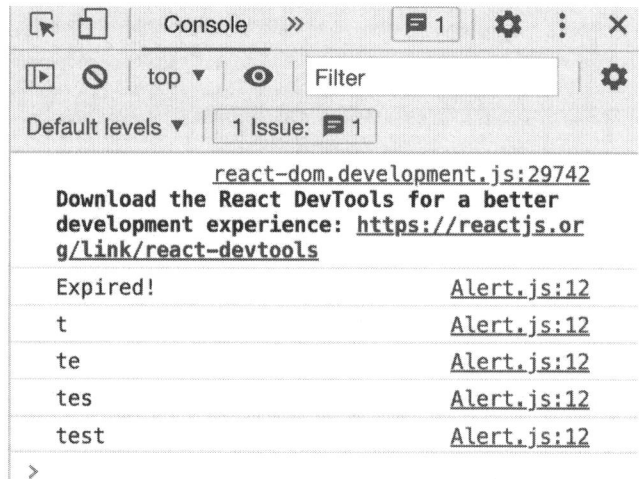

Figure 8.6: Multiple timers are started

Now, a new timer is started for every keystroke, and as a result, the entered message is output in the console.

Of course, this might also not be the desired result. You might only be interested in the final error message that was entered. This can be achieved by adding a cleanup function to the effect (and adjusting **setAlert** a little bit):

```
function setAlert() {
  return setTimeout(function () {
    console.log(alertMsg);
  }, 2000);
}

useEffect(
```

```
function () {
  const timer = setAlert();

  return function () {
    clearTimeout(timer);
  };
},
[setAlert]
);
```

As shown in the *"Cleaning Up after Effects"* section, the timer is cleared with the help of a timer reference and **clearTimeout()** in the effect's cleanup function.

After adjusting the code like this, only the final alert message that was entered will be output.

Seeing the cleanup function in action again is helpful; the main takeaway is the importance of adding all dependencies, though—including function dependencies.

An alternative to including the function as a dependency would be to move the entire function definition into the effect function because any value that's defined and used inside of an effect function must not be added as a dependency:

```
useEffect(
  function () {
    function setAlert() {
      return setTimeout(function () {
        console.log(alertMsg);
      }, 2000);
    }

    const timer = setAlert();

    return function () {
      clearTimeout(timer);
    };
  },
  []
);
```

Of course, you could also get rid of the **setAlert** function altogether then and just move the function's code into the effect function.

Either way, you will have to add a new dependency: **alertMsg**, which is now used inside of the effect function. Even though the **setAlert** function isn't a dependency anymore, you still must add any values used (and **alertMsg** is used in the effect function now):

```
useEffect(
  function () {
    function setAlert() {
      return setTimeout(function () {
        console.log(alertMsg);
      }, 2000);
    }

    const timer = setAlert();

    return function () {
      clearTimeout(timer);
    };
  },
  [alertMsg]
);
```

Hence, this alternative way of writing the code just comes down to personal preferences. It does not reduce the number of dependencies.

You would get rid of a function dependency if you were to move the function out of the component function. This is because, as mentioned in the *"Unnecessary Dependencies"* section, external dependencies (for example, built into the browser or defined outside of component functions) should not be added as dependencies.

However, in the case of the **setAlert** function, this is not possible because **setAlert** uses **alertMsg**. Since **alertMsg** is a component state value, the function that uses it must be defined inside the component function; otherwise, it won't have access to that state value.

This can all sound quite confusing, but it comes down to two simple rules:

- Always add all non-external dependencies—no matter whether they're variables or functions.

- Functions are just objects and can change if their surrounding code executes again.

AVOIDING UNNECESSARY EFFECT EXECUTIONS

Since all dependencies should be added to **useEffect()**, you sometimes end up with code that causes an effect to execute unnecessarily.

Consider the example component below.

> **NOTE**
>
> The complete example can be found on GitHub at https://packt.link/htQiK.

```
import { useState, useEffect } from 'react';

function Alert() {
  const [enteredEmail, setEnteredEmail] = useState('');
  const [enteredPassword, setEnteredPassword] = useState('');

  function updateEmailHandler(event) {
    setEnteredEmail(event.target.value);
  }

  function updatePasswordHandler(event) {
    setEnteredPassword(event.target.value);
  }

  function validateEmail() {
    if (!enteredEmail.includes('@')) {
      console.log('Invalid email!');
    }
  }

  useEffect(function () {
    validateEmail();
  }, [validateEmail]);

  return (
    <form>
      <div>
        <label>Email</label>
        <input type="email" onChange={updateEmailHandler} />
```

```
      </div>
      <div>
        <label>Password</label>
        <input type="password" onChange={updatePasswordHandler} />
      </div>
      <button>Save</button>
    </form>
  );
}

export default Alert;
```

This component contains a form with two inputs. The entered values are stored in two different state values (**enteredEmail** and **enteredPassword**). The **validateEmail()** function then performs some email validation and, if the email address is invalid, logs a message to the console. **validateEmail()** is executed with the help of **useEffect()**.

The problem with this code is that the effect function will be executed whenever **validateEmail** changes because, correctly, **validateEmail** was added as a dependency. But **validateEmail** will change whenever the component function is executed again. And that's not just the case for state changes to **enteredEmail** but also whenever **enteredPassword** changes—even though that state value is not used at all inside of **validateEmail**.

This unnecessary effect execution can be avoided with various solutions:

- You could move the code inside of **validateEmail** directly into the effect function (**enteredEmail** would then be the only dependency of the effect, avoiding effect executions when any other state changes).

- You could avoid using **useEffect()** altogether since you could perform email validation inside of **updateEmailHandler**. Having **console.log()** (a side effect) in there would be acceptable since it wouldn't cause any harm.

But in some other scenarios, you might need to use **useEffect()** (for example, to avoid an infinite loop). Fortunately, React also offers a solution for situations like this: you can wrap the function that's used as a dependency with another React Hook, the **useCallback()** Hook.

The adjusted code would look like this:

```
import { useState, useEffect, useCallback } from 'react';

function Alert() {
  const [enteredEmail, setEnteredEmail] = useState('');
  const [enteredPassword, setEnteredPassword] = useState('');

  function updateEmailHandler(event) {
    setEnteredEmail(event.target.value);
  }

  function updatePasswordHandler(event) {
    setEnteredPassword(event.target.value);
  }

  const validateEmail = useCallback(
    function () {
      if (!enteredEmail.includes('@')) {
        console.log('Invalid email!');
      }
    },
    [enteredEmail]
  );

  useEffect(
    function () {
      validateEmail();
    },
    [validateEmail]
  );

  // return JSX code ...
}

export default Alert;
```

useCallback(), like all React Hooks, is a function that's executed directly inside the component function. Like **useEffect()**, it accepts two arguments: another function (can be anonymous or a named function) and a dependencies array.

Unlike **useEffect()**, though, **useCallback()** does not execute the received function. Instead, **useCallback()** ensures that a function is only recreated if one of the specified dependencies has changed. The default JavaScript behavior of creating a new function object whenever the surrounding code executes again is (synthetically) disabled.

useCallback() returns the latest saved function object. Hence, that returned value (which is a function) is saved in a variable or constant (**validateEmail** in the previous example).

Since the function wrapped by **useCallback()** now only changes when one of the dependencies changes, the returned function can be used as a dependency for **useEffect()** without executing that effect for all kinds of state changes or component updates.

In the case of the preceding example, the effect function would then only execute when **enteredEmail** changes—because that's the only change that will lead to a new **validateEmail** function object being created.

Another common reason for unnecessary effect execution is the usage of objects as dependencies, like in this example:

```
import { useEffect } from 'react';

function Error(props) {
  useEffect(
    function () {
      // performing some error logging
      // in a real app, a HTTP request might be sent to some analytics
API
      console.log('An error occurred!');
      console.log(props.message);
    },
    [props]
  );

  return <p>{props.message}</p>;
}

export default Error;
```

This **Error** component is used in another component, the **Form** component, like this:

```
import { useState } from 'react';

import Error from './Error';

function Form() {
  const [enteredEmail, setEnteredEmail] = useState('');
  const [errorMessage, setErrorMessage] = useState('');

  function updateEmailHandler(event) {
    setEnteredEmail(event.target.value);
  }

  function submitFormHandler(event) {
    event.preventDefault();
    if (!enteredEmail.endsWith('.com')) {
      setErrorMessage('Only email addresses ending with .com are
accepted!');
    }
  }

  return (
    <form onSubmit={submitFormHandler}>
      <div>
        <label>Email</label>
        <input type="email" onChange={updateEmailHandler} />
      </div>
      {errorMessage && <Error message={errorMessage} />}
      <button>Submit</button>
    </form>
  );
}

export default Form;
```

The **Error** component receives an error message via props (**props.message**) and displays it on the screen. In addition, with the help of **useEffect()**, it does some error logging. In this example, the error is simply output to the JavaScript console. In a real app, the error might be sent to some analytics API via an HTTP request. Either way, a side effect that depends on the error message is performed.

The **Form** component contains two state values, tracking the entered email address as well as the error status of the input. If an invalid input value is submitted, **errorMessage** is set and the **Error** component is displayed.

The interesting part about this example is the dependency array of **useEffect()** inside the **Error** component. It contains the **props** object as a dependency (**props** is always an object, grouping all prop values together). When using objects (props or any other object, it does not matter) as dependencies for **useEffect()**, unnecessary effect function executions can be the result.

You can see this problem in this example. If you run the app and enter an invalid email address (e.g., **test@test.de**), you'll notice that subsequent keystrokes in the email input field will cause the error message to be logged (via the effect function) for every keystroke.

> **NOTE**
>
> The full code can be found on GitHub at https://packt.link/qqaDG.

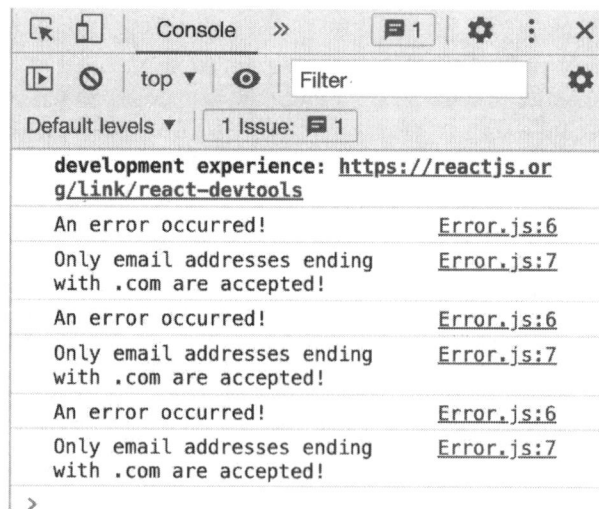

Figure 8.7: A new error message is logged for every keystroke

Those extra executions can occur because component re-evaluations (i.e., component functions being invoked again by React) will produce brand-new JavaScript objects. Even if the values of properties of those objects did not change (as in the preceding example), technically, a brand-new object in memory is created by JavaScript. Since the effect depends on the entire object, React only "sees" that there is a new version of that object and hence runs the effect again.

In the preceding example, a new props object (for the **Error** component) is created whenever the **Form** component function is called by React—even if the error message (the only prop value that's set) did not change.

In this example, that's just annoying since it clutters the JavaScript console in the developer tools. However, if you were sending an HTTP request to some analytics backend API, it could cause bandwidth problems and make the app slower. Therefore, it's best if you get into the habit of avoiding unnecessary effect executions as a general rule.

In the case of object dependencies, the best way to avoid unnecessary executions is to simply destructure the object so that you can pass only those object properties as dependencies that are needed by the effect:

```
function Error(props) {
  const { message } = props; // destructure to extract required
properties

  useEffect(
    function () {
      console.log('An error occurred!');
      console.log(props.message);
    },
    // [props] // don't use the entire props object!
    [message]
  );

  return <p>{props.message}</p>;
}
```

In the case of props, you could also destructure the object right in the component function parameter list:

```
function Error({message}) {
  // ...
}
```

Using this approach, you ensure that only the required property values are set as dependencies. Therefore, even if the object gets recreated, the property value (in this case, the value of the **message** property) is the only thing that matters. If it doesn't change, the effect function won't be executed again.

EFFECTS AND ASYNCHRONOUS CODE

Some effects deal with asynchronous code (sending HTTP requests is a typical example). When performing asynchronous tasks in effect functions, there is one important rule to keep in mind, though: the effect function itself should not be asynchronous and should not return a promise.

You might want to use **async/await** to simplify asynchronous code, but when doing so inside of an effect function, it's easy to accidentally return a promise. For example, the following code would work but does not follow best practices:

```
useEffect(async function () {
  const fetchedPosts = await fetchPosts();
  setLoadedPosts(fetchedPosts);
}, []);
```

Adding the **async** keyword in front of **function** unlocks the usage of **await** inside the function—which makes dealing with asynchronous code (that is, with promises) more convenient.

But the effect function passed to **useEffect()** should only return a normal function, if anything. It should not return a promise. Indeed, React actually issues a warning when trying to run code like the preceding:

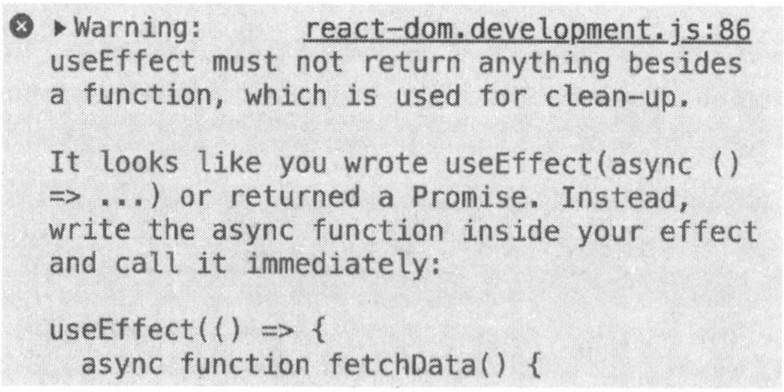

> ⊗ ▶ Warning: react-dom.development.js:86
> useEffect must not return anything besides
> a function, which is used for clean-up.
>
> It looks like you wrote useEffect(async ()
> => ...) or returned a Promise. Instead,
> write the async function inside your effect
> and call it immediately:
>
> useEffect(() => {
>   async function fetchData() {

Figure 8.8: React shows a warning about async being used in an effect function

To avoid this warning, you can use promises without **async/await**, like this:

```
useEffect(function () {
  fetchPosts().then((fetchedPosts) => setLoadedPosts(fetchedPosts));
}, []);
```

Alternatively, if you want to use **async/await**, you can create a separate wrapper function inside of the effect function, which is then executed in the effect:

```
useEffect(function () {
  async function loadData() {
    const fetchedPosts = await fetchPosts();
    setLoadedPosts(fetchedPosts);
  }

  loadData();
}, []);
```

By doing that, the effect function itself is not asynchronous (it does not return a promise), but you can still use **async/await**.

RULES OF HOOKS

In this chapter, two new Hooks were introduced: **useEffect()** and **useCallback()**. Both Hooks are very important—**useEffect()** especially, as this is a Hook you will typically use a lot. Together with **useState()** (introduced in *Chapter 4, Working with Events and State*) and **useRef()** (introduced in *Chapter 7, Portals and Refs*), you now have a solid set of key React Hooks.

When working with React Hooks, there are two rules (the so-called **rules of Hooks**) you must follow:

- Only call Hooks at the top level of component functions. Don't call them inside of if statements, loops, or nested functions.

- Only call Hooks inside of React components or custom Hooks (custom Hooks will be covered in *Chapter 11, Building Custom React Hooks*).

These rules exist because React Hooks won't work as intended if used in a non-compliant way. Fortunately, React will generate a warning message if you violate one of these rules, hence you will notice if you accidentally do so.

SUMMARY AND KEY TAKEAWAYS

- Actions that are not directly related to the main process of a function can be considered side effects.

- Side effects can be asynchronous tasks (for example, sending an HTTP request), but can also be synchronous (for example, **console.log()** or accessing browser storage).

- Side effects are often needed to achieve a certain goal, but it's a good idea to separate them from the main process of a function.

- Side effects can become problematic if they cause infinite loops (because of the update cycles between effect and state).

- **useEffect()** is a React Hook that should be used to wrap side effects and perform them in a safe way.

- **useEffect()** takes an effect function and an array of effect dependencies.

- The effect function is executed directly after the component function was invoked (not simultaneously).

- Any value, variable, or function used inside of an effect should be added to the dependencies array.

- Dependency array exceptions are external values (defined outside of a component function), state updating functions, or values defined and used inside of the effect function.

- If no dependency array is specified, the effect function executes after every component function invocation.

- If an empty dependency array is specified, the effect function runs once when the component first mounts (that is, when it is created for the first time).

- Effect functions can also return optional cleanup functions that are called right before an effect function is executed again (and right before a component is removed from the DOM).

- Effect functions must not return promises.

- For function dependencies, **useCallback()** can help reduce the number of effect executions.

- For object dependencies, destructuring can help reduce the number of effect executions.

WHAT'S NEXT?

Dealing with side effects is a common problem when building apps because most apps need some kind of side effects (for example, sending an HTTP request) to work correctly. Therefore, side effects aren't a problem themselves, but they can cause problems (for example, infinite loops) if handled incorrectly.

With the knowledge gained in this chapter, you know how to handle side effects efficiently with **useEffect()** and related key concepts.

At this point in the book, you now know all the key React concepts you need to build feature-rich web applications. The next chapter will look behind the scenes of React and explore how it works internally. You will also learn about some common optimization techniques that can make your apps more performant.

TEST YOUR KNOWLEDGE!

Test your knowledge of the concepts covered in this chapter by answering the following questions. You can then compare your answers to examples that can be found at https://packt.link/k0K8S:

1. How would you define a side effect?

2. What's a potential problem that could arise with some side effects in React components?

3. How does the **useEffect()** Hook work?

4. Which values should *not* be added to the **useEffect()** dependencies array?

5. Which value can be returned by the effect function? And which kind of value *must not* be returned?

APPLY WHAT YOU LEARNED

Now that you know about effects, you can add even more exciting features to your React apps. Fetching data via HTTP upon rendering a component is just as easy as accessing browser storage when some state changes.

In the following section, you'll find an activity that allows you to practice working with effects and **useEffect()**. As always, you will need to employ some of the concepts covered in earlier chapters (such as working with state).

ACTIVITY 8.1: BUILDING A BASIC BLOG

In this activity, you must add logic to an existing React app to render a list of blog post titles fetched from a backend web API and submit newly added blog posts to that same API. The backend API used is https://jsonplaceholder.typicode.com/, which is a dummy API that doesn't actually store any data you send to it. It will always return the same dummy data, but it's perfect for practicing sending HTTP requests.

As a bonus, you can also add logic to change the text of the submit button while the HTTP request to save the new blog post is on its way.

Use your knowledge about effects and browser-side HTTP requests to implement a solution.

> **NOTE**
>
> You can find the starting code for this activity at https://packt.link/C3bLv. When downloading this code, you'll always download the entire repository. Make sure to then navigate to the subfolder with the starting code (`activities/practice-1/starting-code`, in this case) to use the right code snapshot.
>
> For this activity, you need to know how to send HTTP requests (`GET`, `POST`, and so on) via JavaScript (for example, via the `fetch()` function or with the help of a third-party library). If you don't have that knowledge yet, this resource can get you started: http://packt.link/DJ6Hx.

After downloading the code and running `npm install` in the project folder to install all required dependencies, the solution steps are as follows:

1. Send a **GET** HTTP request to the dummy API to fetch blog posts inside the **App** component (when the component is first rendered).

2. Display the fetched dummy blog posts on the screen.

3. Handle form submissions and send a **POST** HTTP request (with some dummy data) to the dummy backend API.

4. **Bonus:** Set the button caption to "Saving..." while the request is on its way (and to "Save" when it's not).

The expected result should be a user interface that looks like this:

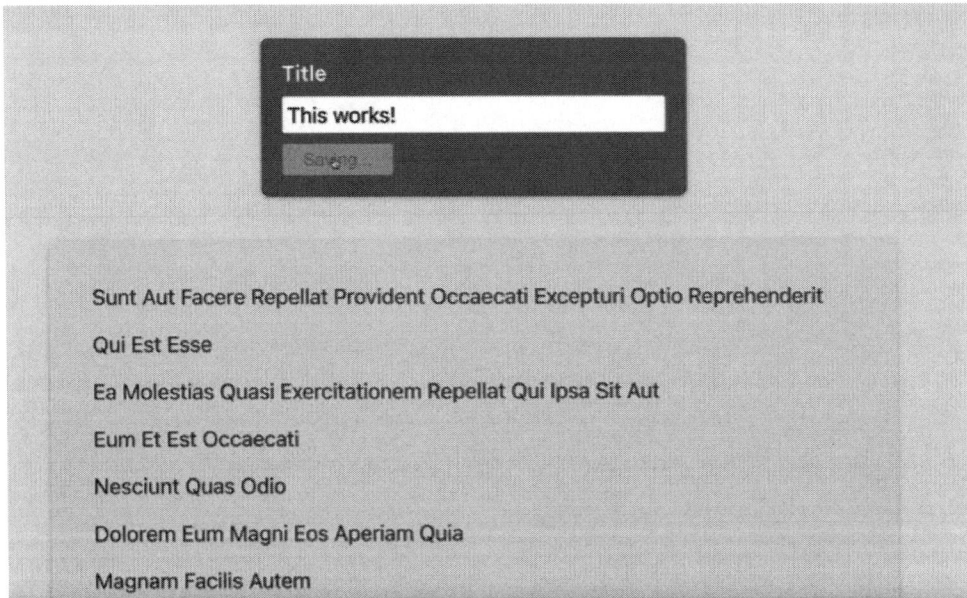

Figure 8.9: The final user interface

> **NOTE**
>
> The solution to this activity can be found on page 490.

9

BEHIND THE SCENES OF REACT AND OPTIMIZATION OPPORTUNITIES

LEARNING OBJECTIVES

By the end of this chapter, you will be able to do the following:

- Avoid unnecessary component update evaluations via React's `memo()` function.

- Avoid unnecessary code execution via the `useMemo()` and `useCallback()` Hooks.

- Load optional code lazily, only when it's needed, via React's `lazy()` function.

- Use React's developer tools to analyze your app.

INTRODUCTION

Using all the features covered up to this point, you can build non-trivial React apps and therefore highly interactive and reactive user interfaces.

This chapter, while introducing some new functions and concepts, will not provide you with tools that would enable you to build even more advanced web apps. You will not learn about groundbreaking, key concepts such as state or props (though you will learn about more advanced concepts in later chapters).

Instead, this chapter allows you to look behind the scenes of React. You will learn how React calculates required DOM updates, and how it ensures that such updates happen without impacting performance in an unacceptable way. You will also learn about some other optimization techniques employed by React—all with the goal of ensuring that your React app runs as smoothly as possible.

Besides this look behind the scenes, you will learn about various built-in functions and concepts that can be used to further optimize app performance. This chapter will not only introduce those concepts but also explain **why** they exist, **how** they should be used, and **when** to use which feature.

REVISITING COMPONENT EVALUATIONS AND UPDATES

Before exploring React's internal workings, it makes sense to briefly revisit React's logic for executing component functions.

Component functions are executed whenever their internal state changes or their parent component function is executed again. The latter happens because, if a parent component function is called, its entire JSX code (which points at the child component function) is re-evaluated. Any component functions referenced in that JSX code are therefore also invoked again.

Consider a component structure like this:

```
function NestedChild() {
  console.log('<NestedChild /> is called.');


  return <p id="nested-child">A component, deeply nested into the
component tree.</p>;
}


function Child() {
  console.log('<Child /> is called.');
```

```
  return (
    <div id="child">
      <p>
        A component, rendered inside another component, containing yet
another
        component.
      </p>
      <NestedChild />
    </div>
  );
}

function Parent() {
  console.log('<Parent /> is called.');

  const [counter, setCounter] = useState(0);

  function incCounterHandler() {
    setCounter((prevCounter) => prevCounter + 1);
  }

  return (
    <div id="parent">
      <p>A component, nested into App, containing another component
(Child).</p>
      <p>Counter: {counter}</p>
      <button onClick={incCounterHandler}>Increment</button>
      <Child />
    </div>
  );
}
```

In this example structure, the **Parent** component renders a **<div>** with two paragraphs, a button, and another component: the **Child** component. That component in turn outputs a **<div>** with a paragraph and yet another component: the **NestedChild** component (which then only outputs a paragraph).

The **Parent** component also manages some state (a dummy counter), which is changed whenever the button is clicked. All three components print a message via `console.log()`, simply to make it easy to spot when each component is called by React.

The following screenshot shows those components in action—after the button was clicked:

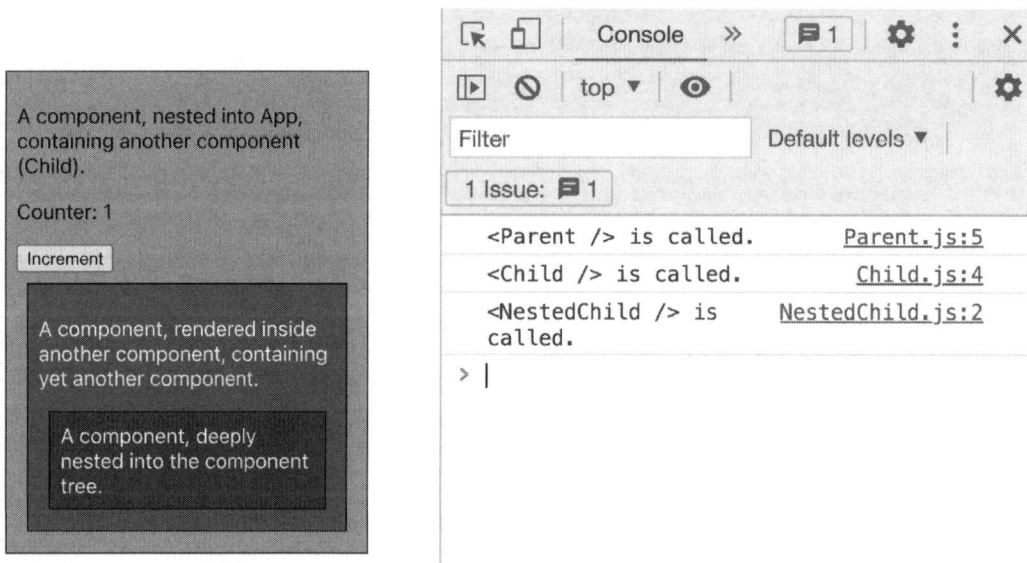

Figure 9.1: Each component function is executed

In this screenshot, you can not only see how the components are nested into each other, but also how they are all invoked by React when the **Increment** button is clicked. **Child** and **NestedChild** are invoked even though they don't manage or use any state. But since they are a child (**Child**) or descendent (**NestedChild**) of the **Parent** component, which did receive a state change, the nested component functions are called as well.

Understanding this flow of component function execution is important because this flow implies that any component function invocation also influences its descendent components. It also shows you how frequently component functions may be invoked by React and how many component functions may be affected by a single state change.

Therefore, there's one important question that should be answered: what happens to the actual page DOM (i.e., to the loaded and rendered website in the browser) when one or more component functions are invoked? Is the DOM recreated? Is the rendered UI updated?

WHAT HAPPENS WHEN A COMPONENT FUNCTION IS CALLED

Whenever a component function is executed, React evaluates whether or not the rendered user interface (i.e., the DOM of the loaded page) must be updated.

This is important: React **evaluates** whether an update is needed. It's not forcing an update automatically!

Internally, React does not take the JSX code returned by a component (or multiple components) and replace the page DOM with it.

That could be done, but it would mean that every component function execution would lead to some form of DOM manipulation—even if it's just a replacement of the old DOM content with a new, similar version. In the example shown above, the **Child** and **NestedChild** JSX code would be used to replace the currently rendered DOM every time those component functions were executed.

As you can see in the example above, those component functions are executed quite frequently. But the returned JSX code is always the same because it's static. It does not contain any dynamic values (e.g., state or props).

If the actual page DOM were replaced with the DOM elements implied by the returned JSX code, the visual result would always be the same. But there still would be some DOM manipulation behind the scenes. And that's a problem, because manipulating the DOM is quite a performance-intensive task—especially when done with a high frequency. Removing and adding or updating DOM elements should therefore only be done when needed—not unnecessarily.

Because of this, React does not throw away the current DOM and replace it with the new DOM (implied by the JSX code), just because a component function was executed. Instead, React first checks whether an update is needed. And if it's needed, only the parts of the DOM that need to change are replaced or updated.

For determining whether an update is needed (and where), React uses a concept called the **virtual DOM**.

THE VIRTUAL DOM VS THE REAL DOM

To determine whether (and where) a DOM update might be needed, React (specifically, the **react-dom** package) compares the current DOM structure to the structure implied by the JSX code returned by the executed component functions. If there's a difference, the DOM is updated accordingly; otherwise, it's left untouched.

However, just as manipulating the DOM is relatively performance-intensive, reading the DOM is as well. Even without changing anything in the DOM, reaching out to it, traversing the DOM elements, and deriving the structure from it is something you typically want to reduce to a minimum.

If multiple component functions are executed and each trigger a process where the rendered DOM elements are read and compared to the JSX structure implied by the invoked component functions, the rendered DOM will be hit with read operations multiple times within a very short time frame.

For bigger React apps that are made up of dozens, hundreds, or even thousands of components, it's highly probable that dozens of component function executions might occur within a single second. If that were to lead to the same amount of DOM read operations, there's a quite high chance that the web app would feel slow or laggy to the user.

That's why React does not use the real DOM to determine whether any user interface updates are needed. Instead, it constructs and manages a virtual DOM internally—an in-memory representation of the DOM that's rendered in the browser. The virtual DOM is not a browser feature, but a React feature. You can think of it as a deeply nested JavaScript object that reflects the components of your web app, including all the built-in HTML components such as **<div>**, **<p>**, etc. (that is, the actual HTML elements that should show up on the page in the end).

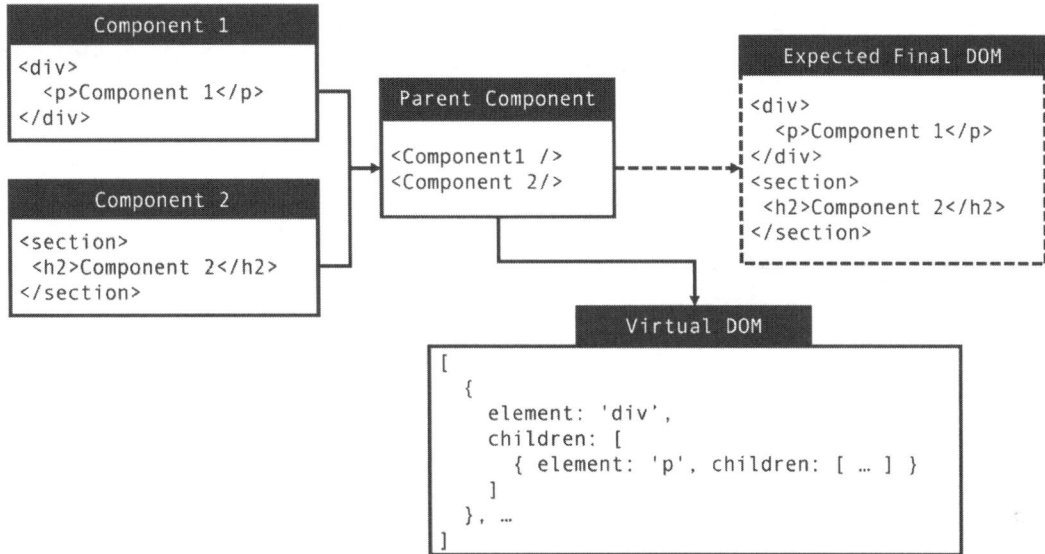

Figure 9.2: React manages a virtual representation of the expected element structure

In the figure above, you can see that the expected element structure (in other words, the expected final DOM) is actually stored as a JavaScript object (or an array with a list of objects). This is the virtual DOM, which is managed by React and used for identifying required DOM updates.

> **NOTE**
>
> Please note that the actual structure of the virtual DOM is more complex than the structure shown in the image. The chart above aims to give you an idea of what the virtual DOM is and how it might look. It's not an exact technical representation of the JavaScript data structure managed by React.

React manages this virtual DOM because comparing this virtual DOM to the expected user interface state is much less performance-intensive than reaching out to the real DOM.

Whenever a component function is called, React compares the returned JSX code to the respective virtual DOM nodes stored in the virtual DOM. If differences are detected, React will determine which changes are needed to update the DOM. Once the required adjustments are derived, these changes are applied to both the virtual and the real DOM. This ensures that the real DOM reflects the expected user interface state without having to reach out to it or update it all the time.

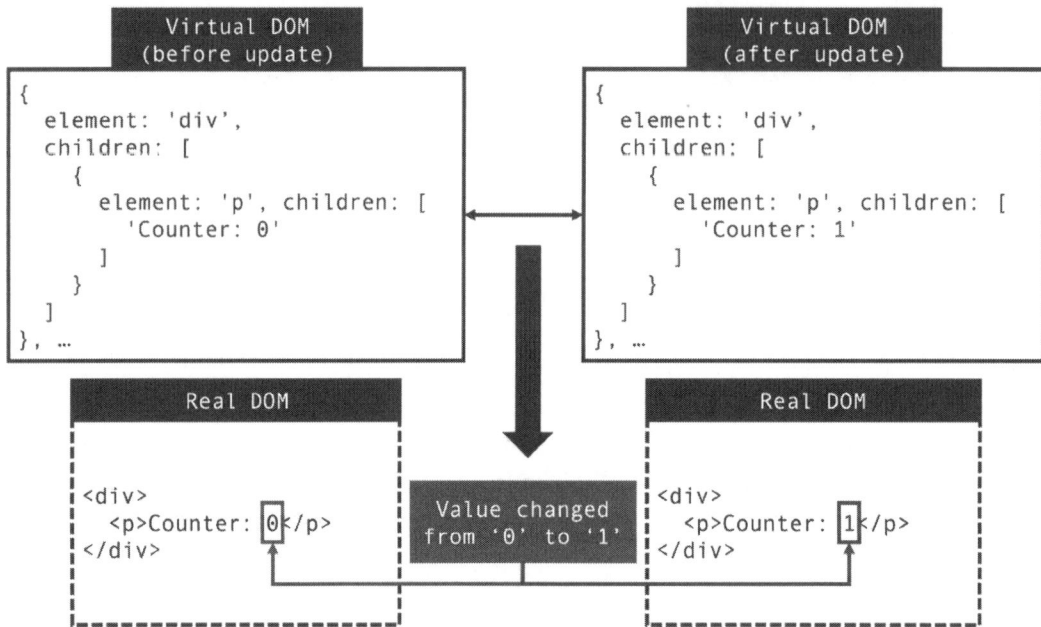

Figure 9.3: React detects required updates via the virtual DOM

In the figure above, you can see how React compares the current DOM and the expected structure with help of the virtual DOM first, before reaching out to the real DOM to manipulate it accordingly.

As a React developer, you don't need to actively interact with the virtual DOM. Technically, you don't even need to know that it exists and that React uses it internally. But it's always helpful to understand the tool (React in that case) you're working with. It's good to know that React is doing various performance optimizations for you and that you get those on top of the many other features that make your life as a developer (hopefully) easier.

STATE BATCHING

Since React uses this concept of a virtual DOM, frequent component function executions aren't a huge problem. But of course, even if comparisons are only conducted virtually, there is still some internal code that must be executed. Even with the virtual DOM, performance could degrade if lots of unnecessary (and at the same time quite complex) virtual DOM comparisons must be made.

One scenario where unnecessary comparisons are performed is in the execution of multiple sequential state updates. Since each state update causes the component function to be executed again (as well as all potential nested components), multiple state updates that are performed together (for example., in the same event handler function) will cause multiple component function invocations.

Consider this example:

```
function App() {
  const [counter, setCounter] = useState(0);
  const [showCounter, setShowCounter] = useState(false);

  function incCounterHandler() {
    setCounter((prevCounter) => prevCounter + 1);
    if (!showCounter) {
      setShowCounter(true);
    }
  }

  return (
    <>
      <p>Click to increment + show or hide the counter</p>
      <button onClick={incCounterHandler}>Increment</button>
      {showCounter && <p>Counter: {counter}</p>}
    </>
  );
}
```

This component contains two state values: **counter** and **showCounter**. When the button is clicked, the counter is incremented by 1. Now, **showCounter** is set to **true** if it was set to **false**. Therefore, the first time the button is clicked, both the **counter** and the **showCounter** states are changed (because **showCounter** is **false** initially).

Since two state values are changed, the expectation would be that the **App** component function is called twice by React—because every state update causes the connected component function to be invoked again.

However, if you add a **console.log()** statement to the **App** component function (to track how often it's executed), you will see that it's only invoked once, when the **Increment** button is clicked:

Click to increment + show or hide the counter

Increment

Counter: 1

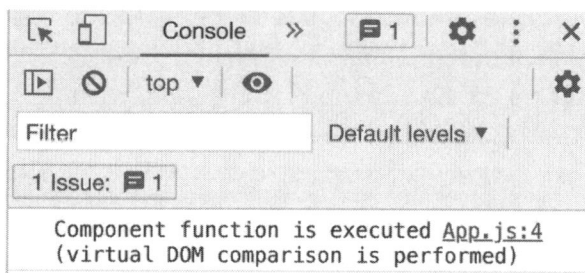

Figure 9.4: Only one console log message is displayed

> **NOTE**
>
> If you're seeing two log messages instead of one, make sure you're not using React's "Strict Mode." When running in Strict Mode during development, React executes component functions more often than it normally would.
>
> If necessary, you can disable Strict Mode by removing the **<React. StrictMode>** component from your **index.js** file. You will learn more about React's Strict Mode toward the end of this chapter.

This behavior is called **state batching**. React performs state batching when multiple state updates are initiated from the same place in your code (e.g., from inside the same event handler function).

It's a built-in functionality that ensures that your component functions are not called more often than needed. This prevents unnecessary virtual DOM comparisons.

State batching is a very useful mechanism. But there is another kind of unnecessary component evaluation that it does not prevent: child component functions that get executed when the parent component function is called.

AVOIDING UNNECESSARY CHILD COMPONENT EVALUATIONS

Whenever a component function is invoked (because its state changed, for example), any nested component functions will be called as well. See the first section of this chapter for more details.

As you saw in the example in the first section of this chapter, it is often the case that those nested components don't actually need to be evaluated again. They might not depend on the state value that changed in the parent component. They might not even depend on any values of the parent component at all.

Here's an example where the parent component function contains some state that is not used by the child component:

```
function Error({ message }) {
  if (!message) {
    return null;
  }


  return <p className={classes.error}>{message}</p>;
}



function Form() {
  const [enteredEmail, setEnteredEmail] = useState('');
  const [errorMessage, setErrorMessage] = useState();

  function updateEmailHandler(event) {
    setEnteredEmail(event.target.value);
  }

  function submitHandler(event) {
    event.preventDefault();
    if (!enteredEmail.endsWith('.com')) {
      setErrorMessage('Email must end with .com.');
    }
  }


  return (
    <form className={classes.form} onSubmit={submitHandler}>
      <div className={classes.control}>
        <label htmlFor="email">Email</label>
```

```
      <input
        id="email"
        type="email"
        value={enteredEmail}
        onChange={updateEmailHandler}
      />
    </div>
    <Error message={errorMessage} />
    <button>Sign Up</button>
  </form>
);
}
```

> **NOTE**
>
> You can find the complete example code on GitHub at https://packt.link/z3Hg2.

In this example, the **Error** component relies on the **message** prop, which is set to the value stored in the **errorMessage** state of the **Form** component. However, the **Form** component also manages an **enteredEmail** state, which is not used (not received via props) by the **Error** component. Therefore, changes to the **enteredEmail** state will cause the **Error** component to be executed again, despite the component not needing that value.

You can track the unnecessary **Error** component function invocations by adding a **console.log()** statement to that component function:

```
function Error({ message }) {
  console.log('<Error /> component function is executed.');
  if (!message) {
    return null;
  }

  return <p className={classes.error}>{message}</p>;
}
```

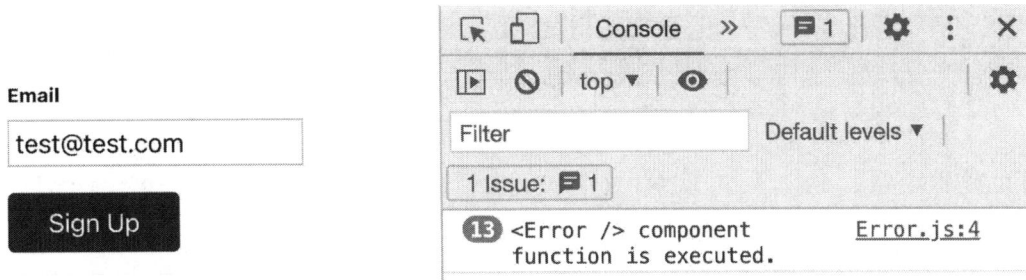

Figure 9.5: The Error component function is executed for every keystroke

In the preceding screenshot, you can see that the **Error** component function is executed for every keystroke on the input field (that is, once for every **enteredEmail** state change).

This is in line with what you have learned previously, but it is also unnecessary. The **Error** component does depend on the **errorMessage** state and should certainly be re-evaluated whenever that state changes, but executing the **Error** component function because the **enteredEmail** state value was updated is clearly not required.

That's why React offers another built-in function that you can use to control (and prevent) this behavior: the **memo()** function.

memo is imported from **react** and is used like this:

```
import { memo } from 'react';

import classes from './Error.module.css';

function Error({ message }) {
  console.log('<Error /> component function is executed.');
  if (!message) {
    return null;
  }

  return <p className={classes.error}>{message}</p>;
}

export default memo(Error);
```

You wrap the component function that should be protected from unnecessary, parent-initiated re-evaluations with **memo ()**. This causes React to check whether the component's props did change, compared to the last time the component function was called. If prop values are equal, the component function is not executed again.

By adding **memo ()**, the unnecessary component function invocations are avoided, as shown below:

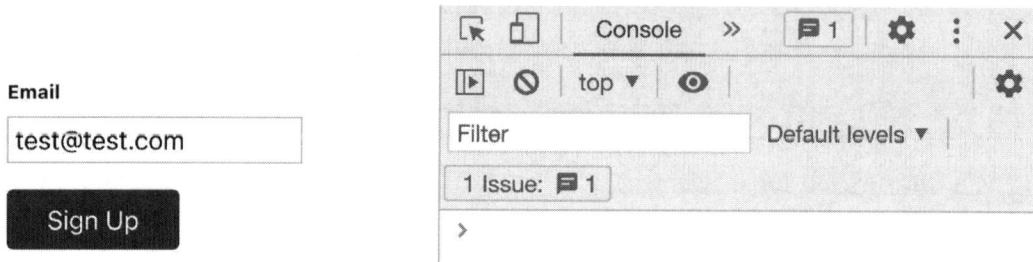

Figure 9.6: No console log messages appear

As you can see in the figure, no messages are printed to the console. This proves that unnecessary component executions are avoided (remember: before adding **memo ()**, many messages were printed to the console).

memo () also takes an optional second argument that can be used to add your own logic to determine whether prop values have changed or not. This can be useful if you're dealing with more complex prop values (e.g., objects or arrays) where custom comparison logic might be needed, as in the following example:

```
memo(SomeComponent, function(prevProps, nextProps) {
    return prevProps.user.firstName !== nextProps.user.firstName;
});
```

The (optional) second argument passed to **memo ()** must be a function that automatically receives the previous props object and the next props object. The function then must return **true** if the component (**SomeComponent**, in this example) should be re-evaluated and **false** if it should not.

Often, the second argument is not needed because the default behavior of **memo ()** (where it compares all props for inequality) is exactly what you need. But if more customization or control is needed, **memo ()** allows you to add your custom logic.

With **memo ()** in your toolbox, it's tempting to wrap every React component function with **memo ()**. Why wouldn't you do it? After all, it avoids unnecessary component function executions.

But there is a very good reason for not using **memo ()** in all your component functions. Indeed, you typically only want to use it in a few selected components.

Because avoiding unnecessary component re-evaluations with using **memo ()** comes at a cost: comparing props (old versus new) also requires some code to run. It's not "free." It's especially problematic if the result then is that the component function must be executed again (because props changed) as, in that case, you will have spent time comparing props just to then invoke the component function anyway.

Hence **memo ()** really only makes sense if you have relatively simple props (i.e., props with no deeply nested objects that you need to compare manually with a custom comparison function) and most parent component state changes don't affect those props of the child component. And even in those cases, if you have a relatively simple component function (i.e., without any complex logic in it), using **memo ()** still might not yield any measurable benefit.

The example code above (the **Error** component) is a good example: in theory, using **memo ()** makes sense here. Most state changes in the parent component won't affect **Error**, and the prop comparison will be very simple because it's just one prop (the **message** prop, which holds a string) that must be compared. But despite that, using **memo ()** to wrap **Error** will very likely not be worth it. **Error** is an extremely basic component with no complex logic in it. It simply doesn't matter if the component function gets invoked frequently. Hence, using **memo ()** in this spot would be absolutely fine—but so is not using it.

A great spot to use **memo()**, on the other hand, is a component that's relatively close to the top of the component tree (or of a deeply nested branch of components in the component tree). If you are able to avoid unnecessary executions of that one component via **memo()**, you also implicitly avoid unnecessary executions of all nested components beneath that one component. This is visually illustrated in the diagram below:

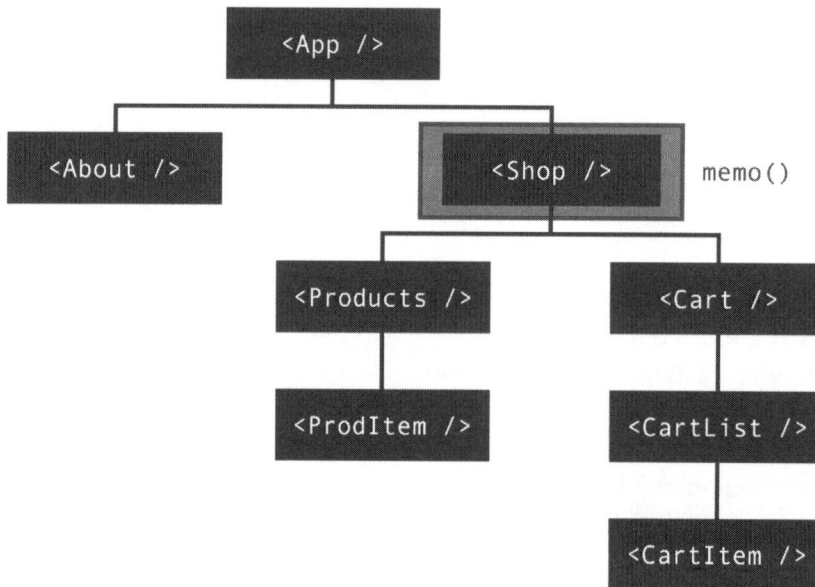

Figure 9.7: Using memo at the start of a component tree branch

In the preceding figure, **memo()** is used on the **Shop** component, which has multiple nested descendent components. Without **memo()**, whenever the **Shop** component function gets invoked, **Products, ProdItem, Cart**, etc. would also be executed. With **memo()**, assuming that it's able to avoid some unnecessary executions of the **Shop** component function, all those descendent components are no longer evaluated.

AVOIDING COSTLY COMPUTATIONS

The **memo()** function can help avoid unnecessary component function executions. As mentioned in the previous section, this is especially valuable if a component function performs a lot of work (e.g., sorting a long list).

But as a React developer, you will also encounter situations in which you have a work-intensive component that needs to be executed again because some prop value changed. In such cases, using **memo ()** won't prevent the component function from executing again. But the prop that changed might not be needed for the performance-intensive task that is performed as part of the component.

Consider the following example:

```
function sortItems(items) {
  console.log('Sorting');
  return items.sort(function (a, b) {
    if (a.id > b.id) {
      return 1;
    } else if (a.id < b.id) {
      return -1;
    }
    return 0;
  });
}


function List({ items, maxNumber }) {
  const sortedItems = sortItems(items);

  const listItems = sortedItems.slice(0, maxNumber);

  return (
    <ul>
      {listItems.map((item) => (
        <li key={item.id}>
          {item.title} (ID: {item.id})
        </li>
      ))}
    </ul>
  );
}


export default List;
```

The **List** component receives two prop values: **items** and **maxNumber**. It then calls **sortItems()** to sort the items by **id**. Thereafter, the sorted list is limited to a certain amount (**maxNumber**) of items. As a last step, the sorted and shortened list is then rendered to the screen via **map()** in the JSX code.

> **NOTE**
>
> A full example app can be found on GitHub at https://packt.link/dk9ag.

Depending on the number of items passed to the **List** component, sorting it can take a significant amount of time (for very long lists, even up to a few seconds). It's definitely not an operation you want to perform unnecessarily or too frequently. The list needs to be sorted whenever **items** change, but it should not be sorted if **maxNumber** changes—because this does not impact the items in the list (i.e., it doesn't affect the order). But with the code snippet shared above, **sortItems()** will be executed whenever either of the two prop values changes, no matter whether it's **items** or **maxNumber**.

As a result, when running the app and changing the number of displayed items, you can see multiple **"Sorting"** log messages—implying that **sortItems()** was executed every time the number of items was changed.

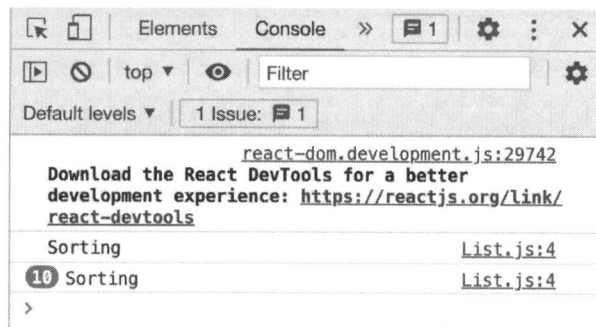

Figure 9.8: Multiple "Sorting" log messages appear in the console

The **memo()** function won't help here because the **List** component function should (and will) execute whenever **items** or **maxNumber** change. **memo()** does not help control partial code execution inside the component function.

For that, you can use another feature provided by React: the **useMemo()** Hook.

useMemo() can be used to wrap a compute-intensive operation. For it to work correctly, you also must define a list of dependencies that should cause the operation to be executed again. To some extent, it's similar to **useEffect()** (which also wraps an operation and defines a list of dependencies), but the key difference is that **useMemo()** runs at the same time as the rest of the code in the component function, whereas **useEffect()** executes the wrapped logic after the component function execution finished. **useEffect()** should not be used for optimizing compute-intensive tasks but for side effects.

useMemo(), on the other hand, exists to control the execution of performance-intensive tasks. Applied to the example mentioned above, the code can be adjusted like this:

```
import { useMemo } from 'react';

function List({ items, maxNumber }) {
  const sortedItems = useMemo(
    function () {
      console.log('Sorting');
      return items.sort(function (a, b) {
        if (a.id > b.id) {
          return 1;
        } else if (a.id < b.id) {
          return -1;
        }
        return 0;
      });
    },
    [items]
  );

  const listItems = sortedItems.slice(0, maxNumber);

  return (
    <ul>
      {listItems.map((item) => (
        <li key={item.id}>
          {item.title} (ID: {item.id})
        </li>
      ))}
    </ul>
```

```
  );
}
```

```
export default List;
```

useMemo() wraps an anonymous function (the function that previously existed as a named function, **sortItems**), which contains the entire sorting code. The second argument passed to **useMemo()** is the array of dependencies for which the function should be executed again (when a dependency value changes). In this case, **items** is the only dependency of the wrapped function, and so that value is added to the array.

With **useMemo()** used like this, the sorting logic will only execute when items change, not when **maxNumber** (or anything else) changes. As a result, you see **"Sorting"** being output in the developer tools console only once:

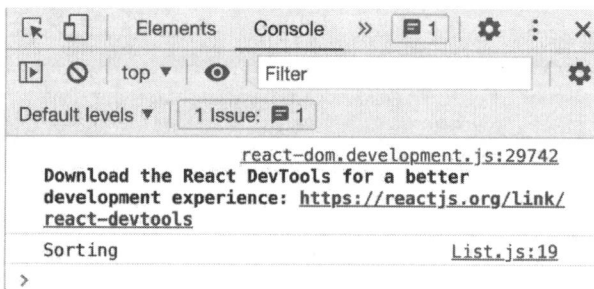

Figure 9.9: Only one "Sorting" output in the console

useMemo() can be very useful for controlling code execution inside of your component functions. It can be a great addition to **memo()** (which controls the overall component function execution). But also like **memo()**, you should not start wrapping all your logic with **useMemo()**. Only use it for very performance-intensive computations since checking for dependency changes and storing and retrieving past computation results (which **useMemo()** does internally) also comes at a performance cost.

UTILIZING USECALLBACK()

In the previous chapter, you learned about **useCallback()**. Just like **useMemo()** can be used for "expensive" calculations, **useCallback()** can be used to avoid unnecessary function re-creations. In the context of this chapter, **useCallback()** can be helpful because, in conjunction with **memo()** or **useMemo()**, it can help you avoid unnecessary code execution. It can help you in cases where a function is passed as a prop (i.e., where you might use **memo()**) or is used as a dependency in some "expensive" computation (i.e., possibly solved via **useMemo()**).

Here's an example where **useCallback()** can be combined with **memo()** to avoid unnecessary component function executions:

```
import { memo } from 'react';

import classes from './Error.module.css';

function Error({ message, onClearError }) {
  console.log('<Error /> component function is executed.');
  if (!message) {
    return null;
  }

  return (
    <div className={classes.error}>
      <p>{message}</p>
      <button className={classes.errorBtn} onClick={onClearError}>X</
button>
    </div>
  );
}

export default memo(Error);
```

The **Error** component is wrapped with the **memo()** function and so will only execute if one of the received prop values changes.

The **Error** component is used by another component, the **Form** component, like this:

```
function Form() {
  const [enteredEmail, setEnteredEmail] = useState('');
  const [errorMessage, setErrorMessage] = useState();

  function updateEmailHandler(event) {
    setEnteredEmail(event.target.value);
  }

  function submitHandler(event) {
    event.preventDefault();
    if (!enteredEmail.endsWith('.com')) {
      setErrorMessage('Email must end with .com.');
```

```
    }
  }

  function clearErrorHandler() {
    setErrorMessage(null);
  }

  return (
    <form className={classes.form} onSubmit={submitHandler}>
      <div className={classes.control}>
        <label htmlFor="email">Email</label>
        <input
          id="email"
          type="email"
          value={enteredEmail}
          onChange={updateEmailHandler}
        />
      </div>
      <Error message={errorMessage} onClearError={clearErrorHandler} />
      <button>Sign Up</button>
    </form>
  );
}
```

In this component, the **Error** component receives a pointer to the **clearErrorHandler** function (as a value for the **onClearError** prop). You might recall a very similar example from earlier in this chapter (from the *"Avoiding Unnecessary Child Component Evaluations"* section). There, **memo()** was used to ensure that the **Error** component function was not invoked when **enteredEmail** changed (because its value was not used in the **Error** component function at all).

Now with the adjusted example and the **clearErrorHandler** function pointer passed to **Error**, **memo()** unfortunately isn't preventing component function executions anymore. Why? Because functions are objects in JavaScript, and the **clearErrorHandler** function is recreated every time the **Form** component function is executed (which happens on every state change, including changes to the **enteredEmail** state).

Since a new function object is created for every state change, **clearErrorHandler** is technically a different value for every execution of the **Form** component. Therefore, the **Error** component receives a new **onClearError** prop value whenever the **Form** component function is invoked. To **memo()**, the old and new **clearErrorHandler** function objects are different from each other, and it therefore will not stop the **Error** component function from running again.

That's exactly where **useCallback()** can help:

```
const clearErrorHandler = useCallback(() => {
  setErrorMessage(null);
}, []);
```

By wrapping **clearErrorHandler** with **useCallback()**, the re-creation of the function is prevented, and so no new function object is passed to the **Error** component. Hence, **memo()** is able to detect equality between the old and new **onClearError** prop value and prevents unnecessary function component executions again.

Similarly, **useCallback()** can be used in conjunction with **useMemo()**. If the compute-intensive operation wrapped with **useMemo()** uses a function as a dependency, you can use **useCallback()** to ensure that this dependent function is not recreated unnecessarily.

AVOIDING UNNECESSARY CODE DOWNLOAD

Thus far, this chapter has mostly discussed strategies for avoiding unnecessary code execution (and that it's not always worth the effort). But it's not just the execution of code that can be an issue. It's also not great if your website visitors have to download lots of code that might never be executed at all. Because every kilobyte of JavaScript code that has to be downloaded will slow down the initial loading time of your web page—not just because of the time it takes to download the code bundle (which can be significant, if users are on a slow network and code bundles are big) but also because the browser has to parse all the downloaded code before your page becomes interactive.

For this reason, a lot of community and ecosystem effort is spent on reducing JavaScript code bundle sizes. Minification (automatic shortening of variable names and other measures to reduce the final code) and compression can help a lot and is therefore a common technique. Actually, projects created with **create-react-app** already come with a build workflow (initiated by running **npm run build**), which will produce a production-optimized code bundle that is as small as possible.

But there also are steps that can be taken by you, the developer, to reduce the overall code bundle size:

1. Try to write short and concise code.

2. Be thoughtful about including lots of third-party libraries and don't use them unless you really need to.

3. Consider using code-splitting techniques.

The first point should be fairly obvious. If you write less code, your website visitors have less code to download. Therefore, trying to be concise and write optimized code makes sense.

The second point should also make sense. For some tasks, you will actually save code by including third-party libraries that may be much more elaborate than the code solution you might come up with. But there are also situations and tasks in which you might get away with writing your own code or using some built-in function instead of including a third-party library. You should at least always think about this alternative and only include third-party libraries you absolutely need.

The last point is something React can help with.

REDUCING BUNDLE SIZES VIA CODE SPLITTING (LAZY LOADING)

React exposes a **lazy()** function that can be used to load component code conditionally—meaning, only when it's actually needed (instead of upfront).

Consider the following example, consisting of two components working together.

A **DateCalculator** component is defined like this:

```
import { useState } from 'react';
import { add, differenceInDays, format, parseISO } from 'date-fns';


import classes from './DateCalculator.module.css';


const initialStartDate = new Date();
const initialEndDate = add(initialStartDate, { days: 1 });


function DateCalculator() {
  const [startDate, setStartDate] = useState(
    format(initialStartDate, 'yyyy-MM-dd')
  );
  const [endDate, setEndDate] = useState(format(initialEndDate, 'yyyy-
```

```
MM-dd'));

  const daysDiff = differenceInDays(parseISO(endDate),
parseISO(startDate));

  function updateStartDateHandler(event) {
    setStartDate(event.target.value);
  }


  function updateEndDateHandler(event) {
    setEndDate(event.target.value);
  }


  return (
    <div className={classes.calculator}>
      <p>Calculate the difference (in days) between two dates.</p>
      <div className={classes.control}>
        <label htmlFor="start">Start Date</label>
        <input
          id="start"
          type="date"
          value={startDate}
          onChange={updateStartDateHandler}
        />
      </div>
      <div className={classes.control}>
        <label htmlFor="end">End Date</label>
        <input
          id="end"
          type="date"
          value={endDate}
          onChange={updateEndDateHandler}
        />
      </div>
      <p className={classes.difference}>Difference: {daysDiff} days</p>
    </div>
  );
}


export default DateCalculator;
```

This **DateCalculator** component is then rendered conditionally by the
App component:

```
import { useState } from 'react';


import DateCalculator from './components/DateCalculator';


function App() {
  const [showDateCalc, setShowDateCalc] = useState(false);


  function openDateCalcHandler() {
    setShowDateCalc(true);
  }


  return (
    <>
      <p>This app might be doing all kinds of things.</p>
      <p>
        But you can also open a calculator which calculates the difference
        between two dates.
      </p>
      <button onClick={openDateCalcHandler}>Open Calculator</button>
      {showDateCalc && <DateCalculator />}
    </>
  );
}


export default App;
```

In this example, the **DateCalculator** component uses a third-party library (the
date-fns library) to access various date-related utility functions (for example, a
function for calculating the difference between two dates, or **differenceInDays**).

The component then accepts two date values and calculates the difference between
those dates in days—though the actual logic of the component isn't too important
here. What is important is the fact that a third-party library and various utility
functions are used. This adds quite a bit of JavaScript code to the overall code bundle,
and all that code must be downloaded when the entire website is loaded for the first
time, even though the date calculator isn't even visible at that point in time (because
it is rendered conditionally).

You can see the overall bundle being downloaded in the following screenshot:

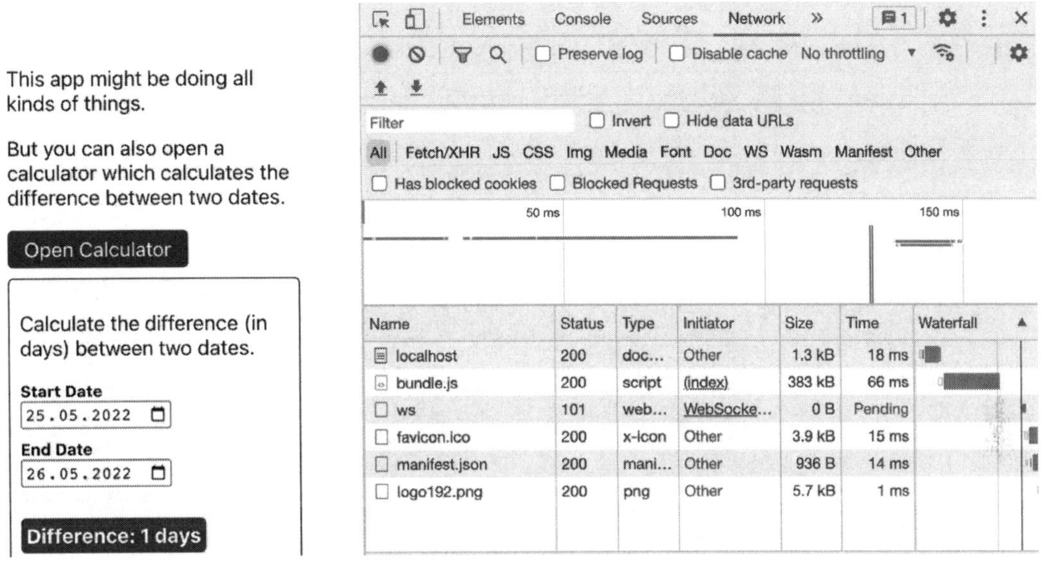

This app might be doing all kinds of things.

But you can also open a calculator which calculates the difference between two dates.

Open Calculator

Calculate the difference (in days) between two dates.

Start Date
25.05.2022

End Date
26.05.2022

Difference: 1 days

Figure 9.10: Only one bundle file is downloaded

The **Network** tab in the browser's developer tools reveals outgoing network requests. As you can see in the screenshot, a JavaScript bundle file is downloaded. You won't see any extra requests being sent when the button is clicked. This implies that all the code, including the code needed for **DateCalculator**, was downloaded upfront.

That's where code splitting with React's **lazy()** function becomes useful.

This function can be wrapped around a dynamic import to load the imported component only once it's needed.

> **NOTE**
>
> For further information on this topic, visit https://developer.mozilla.org/en-US/docs/Web/JavaScript/Reference/Statements/import#dynamic_imports.

In the preceding example, it would be used like this in the **App** component file:

```
import { lazy, useState } from 'react';

const DateCalculator = lazy(() => import('./components/DateCalculator'));

function App() {
  const [showDateCalc, setShowDateCalc] = useState(false);

  function openDateCalcHandler() {
    setShowDateCalc(true);
  }

  return (
    <>
      <p>This app might be doing all kinds of things.</p>
      <p>
        But you can also open a calculator which calculates the difference
        between two dates.
      </p>
      <button onClick={openDateCalcHandler}>Open Calculator</button>
      {showDateCalc && <DateCalculator />}
    </>
  );
}

export default App;
```

This alone won't do the trick though. You must also wrap the conditional JSX code, where the dynamically imported component is used, with another component provided by React: the **<Suspense>** component, like this:

```
import { lazy, Suspense, useState } from 'react';

const DateCalculator = lazy(() => import('./components/DateCalculator'));

function App() {
  const [showDateCalc, setShowDateCalc] = useState(false);

  function openDateCalcHandler() {
    setShowDateCalc(true);
```

```
  }

  return (
    <>
      <p>This app might be doing all kinds of things.</p>
      <p>
        But you can also open a calculator which calculates the difference
        between two dates.
      </p>
      <button onClick={openDateCalcHandler}>Open Calculator</button>
      <Suspense fallback={<p>Loading...</p>}>
        {showDateCalc && <DateCalculator />}
      </Suspense>
    </>
  );
}

export default App;
```

> **NOTE**
>
> You can find the finished example code on GitHub at https://packt.link/wj5Pi.

Suspense is a component built into React, and you must wrap it around any conditional code that uses React's **lazy()** function. **Suspense** also has one mandatory prop that must be provided, the **fallback** prop, which expects a JSX value that will be rendered as fallback content until the dynamically loaded content is available.

lazy() leads to the overall JavaScript code being split up into multiple bundles. And the bundle that contains the **DateCalculator** component (and its dependencies, such as the **date-fns** library code) is only downloaded when it's needed—that is, when the button in the **App** component is clicked. If that download were to take a bit longer, the **fallback** content of **Suspense** would be shown on the screen in the meantime.

> **NOTE**
>
> React's **Suspense** component is not limited to being used in conjunction with the `lazy()` function. In the past it was, but starting with React 18, it can also be used to show some fallback content while other data (i.e., data from a database) is being fetched.
>
> Right now, capabilities are nonetheless quite limited. However, in future React versions, this should become more useful.

After adding `lazy()` and the **Suspense** component as described, a smaller bundle is initially downloaded. In addition, if the button is clicked, more code files are downloaded:

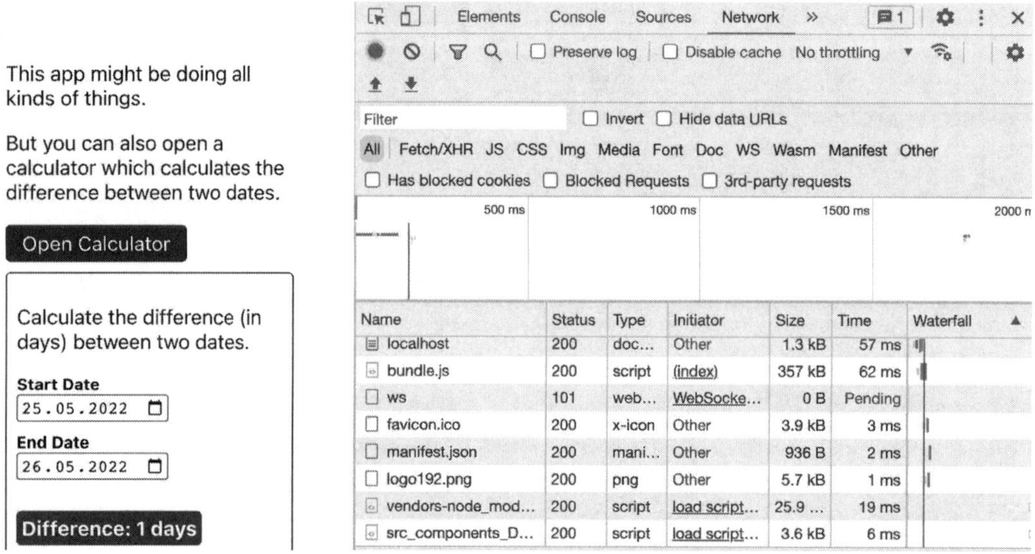

Figure 9.11: Multiple bundles are downloaded

Just as with all the other optimization techniques described thus far, the `lazy()` function is not a function you should start wrapping around all your imports. If an imported component is very small and simple (and doesn't use any third-party code), splitting the code isn't really worth it, especially since you have to consider that the additional HTTP request required for downloading the extra bundle also comes with some overhead.

It also doesn't make sense to use `lazy()` on components that will be loaded initially anyways. Only consider using it on conditionally loaded components.

STRICT MODE

Throughout this chapter, you have learned a lot about React's internals and various optimization techniques. Not really an optimization technique, but still related, is another feature offered by React called **Strict Mode**.

You may have stumbled across code like this before:

```
import React from 'react';

// ... other code ...
root.render(<React.StrictMode><App /></React.StrictMode >);
```

`<React.StrictMode>` is another built-in component provided by React. It doesn't render any visual element, but it will enable some extra checks that are performed behind the scenes by React.

Most checks are related to identifying the use of unsafe or legacy code (i.e., features that will be removed in the future). But there are also some checks that aim to help you identify potential problems with your code.

For example, when using strict mode, React will execute component functions twice and also unmount and remount every component whenever it mounts for the first time. This is done to ensure that you're managing your state and side effects in a consistent and correct way (for example, that you do have cleanup functions in your effect functions).

> **NOTE**
>
> Strict Mode only affects your app and its behavior during development. It does not influence your app once you build it for production. Extra checks of effects such as double component function execution will not be performed in production.

Building React apps with Strict Mode enabled can sometimes lead to confusion or annoying error messages. You might, for example, wonder why your component effects are executing too often.

Therefore, it's your personal decision whether you want to use Strict Mode or not. You could also enable it (by wrapping it around your **`<App />`** component) occasionally only.

DEBUGGING CODE AND THE REACT DEVELOPER TOOLS

Earlier in this chapter, you learned that component functions may execute quite frequently and that you can prevent unnecessary executions using **memo()** and **useMemo()** (and that you shouldn't always prevent it).

Identifying component executions by adding **console.log()** inside the component functions is one way of gaining insight into a component. It's the approach used throughout this chapter. However, for large React apps with dozens, hundreds, or even thousands of components, using **console.log()** can get tedious.

That's why the React team also built an official tool to help with gaining app insights. The React developer tools are an extension that can be installed into all major browsers (Chrome, Firefox, and Edge). You can find and install the extension by simply searching the web for **"<your browser> react developer tools"** (e.g., "chrome react developer tools").

Once you have installed the extension, you can access it directly from inside the browser. For example, when using Chrome, you can access the React developer tools extensions directly from inside Chrome's developer tools (which can be opened via the menu in Chrome). Explore the specific extension documentation (in your browser's extensions store) for details on how to access it.

The React developer tools extension offers two areas: a **Components** page and a **Profile** page:

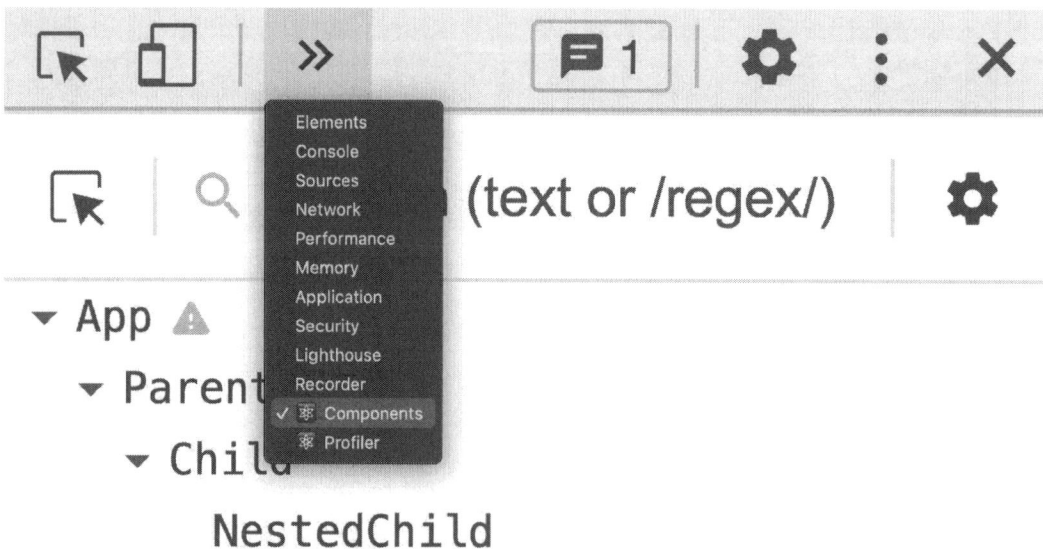

Figure 9.12: The React developer tools can be accessed via browser developer tools

The **Components** page can be used to analyze the component structure of the currently rendered page. You can use this page to understand the structure of your components (i.e., the "tree of components"), how components are nested into each other, and even the configuration (props, state) of components.

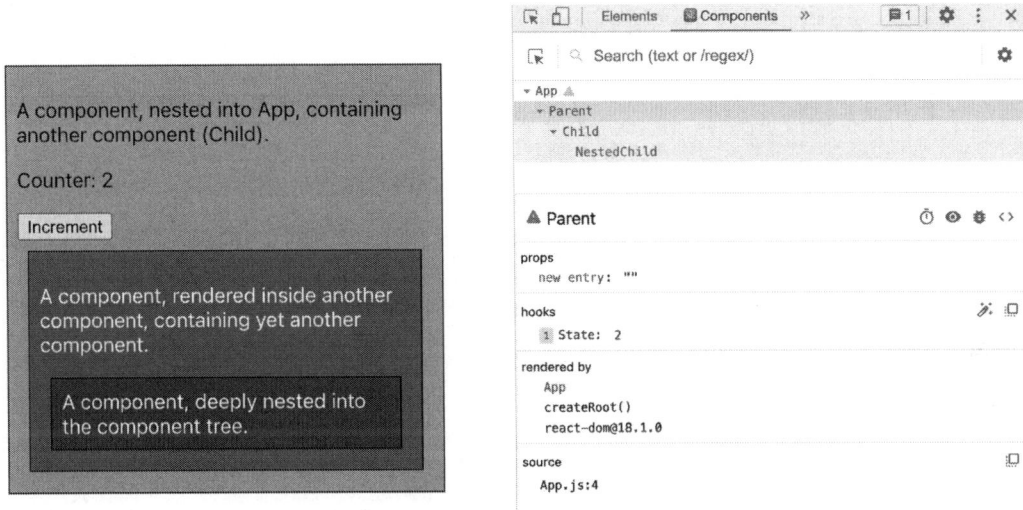

Figure 9.13: Component relations and data are shown

This page can be very useful when attempting to understand the current state of a component, how a component is related to other components, and which other components may therefore influence a component (e.g., cause it to be re-evaluated).

However, in the context of this chapter, the more useful page is the **Profiler** page:

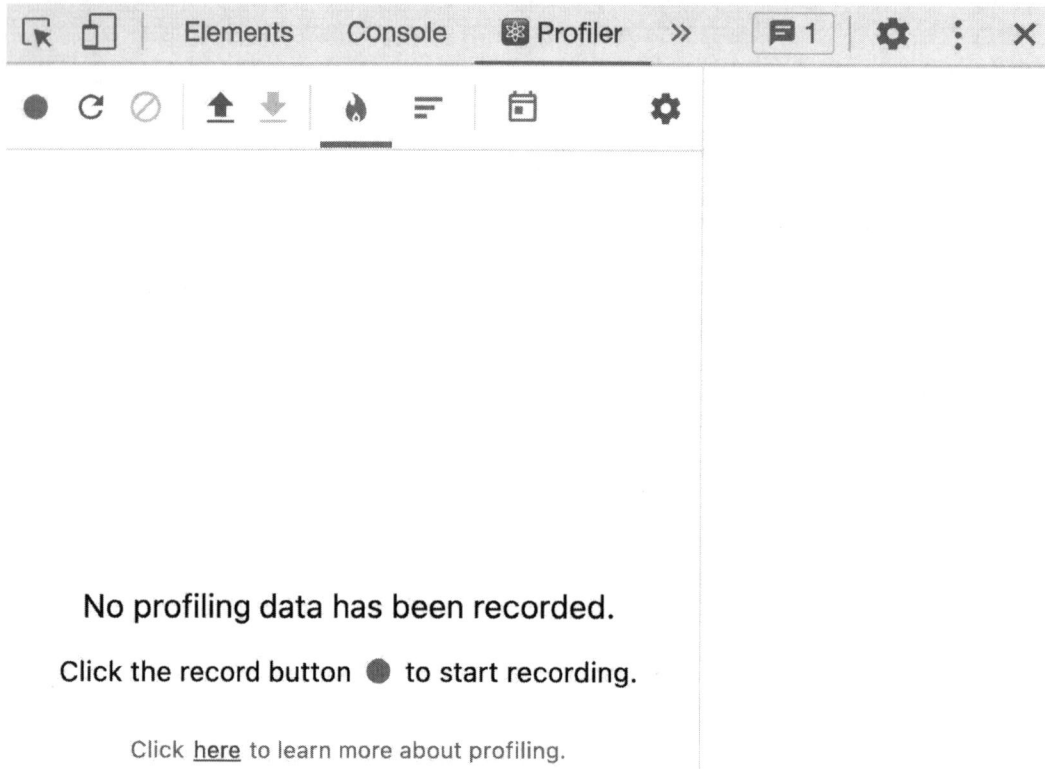

Figure 9.14: The Profiler page (without any data gathered)

On this page, you can begin recording component evaluations (i.e., component function executions). You can do this by simply pressing the **Record** button in the top-left corner (the blue circle). This button will then be replaced by a **Stop** button, which you can press to end the recording.

After recording the React app for a couple of seconds (and interacting with it during that period), an example result could look like this:

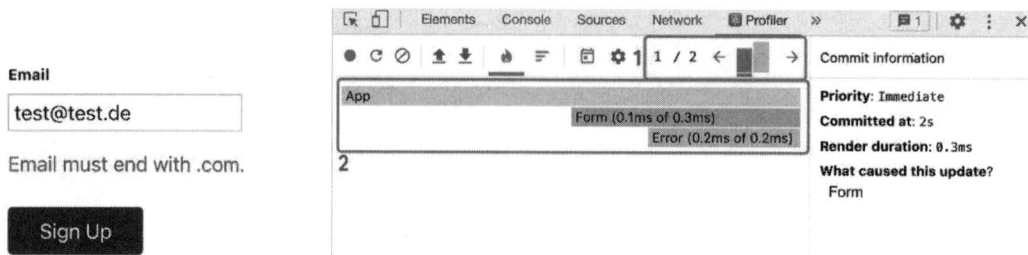

Figure 9.15: The Profiler page shows various bars after recording finished

This result consists of two main areas:

- A list of bars, indicating the number of component re-evaluations (every bar reflects one re-evaluation cycle that affected one or more components). You can click these bars to explore more details about a specific cycle.

- For the selected evaluation cycle, a list of the affected components is presented. You can identify affected components easily as their bars are colored and timing information is displayed for them.

You can select any render cycle from 1 (in this case, there are two for this recording session) to view which components were affected. The bottom part of the window (2) shows all affected components by highlighting them with some color and outputting the overall amount of time taken by this component to be re-evaluated (for example, **0.1ms of 0.3ms**).

> **NOTE**
>
> It's worth noting that this tool also proves that component evaluation is extremely fast—**0.1ms** for re-evaluating a component is way too fast for any human to realize that something happened behind the scenes.

On the right side of the window, you also learn more about this component evaluation cycle. For example, you learn where it was triggered. In this case, it was triggered by the **Form** component (it's the same example as discussed earlier in this chapter, in the *"Avoiding Unnecessary Child Component Evaluations"* section).

The **Profiler** page can therefore also help you to identify component evaluation cycles and determine which components are affected. In this example, you can see a difference if the **memo()** function is wrapped around the **Error** component:

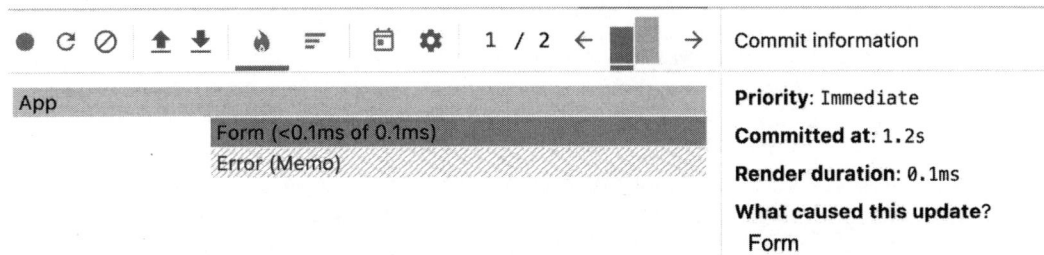

Figure 9.16: Only the Form component is affected, not the Error component

After re-adding the **memo()** function as a wrapper around the **Error** component (as explained earlier in this chapter), you can use the **Profiler** page of the React developer tools to confirm that the **Error** component is no longer unnecessarily evaluated. To do this, you should start a new recording session and reproduce the situation, where previously, without **memo()**, the **Error** component would've been called again.

The diagonal grayed-out lines across the **Error** component in the **Profiler** window signal that this component was not affected by some other component function invocation.

The React developer tools can therefore be used to gain deeper insights into your React app and your components. You can use them in addition or instead of calling **console.log()** in a component function.

SUMMARY AND KEY TAKEAWAYS

- React components are re-evaluated (executed) whenever their state changes or the parent component is evaluated.

- React optimizes component evaluation by calculating required user interface changes with help of a virtual DOM first.

- Multiple state updates that occur at the same time and in the same place are batched together by React. This ensures that unnecessary component evaluations are avoided.

- The **memo()** function can be used to control component function executions.

- **memo()** looks for prop value differences (old props versus new props) to determine whether a component function must be executed again.

- **useMemo()** can be used to wrap performance-intensive computations and only perform them if key dependencies changed.

- Both **memo()** and **useMemo()** should be used carefully since they also come at a cost (the comparisons performed).

- The initial code download size can be reduced with help of code splitting via the **lazy()** function (in conjunction with the built-in **Suspense** component)

- React's Strict Mode can be enabled (via the built-in **`<React.StrictMode>`** component) to perform various extra checks and detect potential bugs in your application.

- The React developer tools can be used to gain deeper insights into your React app (for example, component structure and re-evaluation cycles).

WHAT'S NEXT?

As a developer, you should always know and understand the tool you're working with—in this case, React.

This chapter allowed you to get a better idea of how React works under the hood and which optimizations are implemented automatically. In addition, you also learned about various optimization techniques that can be implemented by you.

The next chapter will go back to solving actual problems you might face when trying to build React apps. Instead of optimizing React apps, you will learn more about techniques and features that can be used to solve more complex problems related to component and application state management.

TEST YOUR KNOWLEDGE!

Test your knowledge of the concepts covered in this chapter by answering the following questions. You can then compare your answers to examples that can be found at https://packt.link/hPDal:

1. Why does React use a virtual DOM to detect required DOM updates?

2. How is the real DOM affected when a component function is executed?

3. Which components are great candidates for the **`memo()`** function? Which components are bad candidates?

4. How is **`useMemo()`** different from **`memo()`**?

5. What's the idea behind code splitting and the **`lazy()`** function?

APPLY WHAT YOU LEARNED

With your newly gained knowledge about React's internals and some of the optimization techniques you can employ in order to improve your apps, you can now apply this knowledge in the following activity.

ACTIVITY 9.1: OPTIMIZE AN EXISTING APP

In this activity, you're handed an existing React app that can be optimized in various places. Your task is to identify optimization opportunities and implement appropriate solutions. Keep in mind that too much optimization can actually lead to a worse result.

> **NOTE**
>
> You can find the starting code for this activity at https://packt.link/cYqyu. When downloading this code, you'll always download the entire repository. Make sure to then navigate to the subfolder with the starting code (`activities/practice-1/starting-code` in this case) to use the right code snapshot.
>
> The provided project also uses many features covered in earlier chapters. Take the time to analyze it and understand the provided code. This is a great practice and allows you to see many key concepts in action.

Once you have downloaded the code and run **npm install** in the project folder (to install all required dependencies), you can start the development server via **npm start**. As a result, upon visiting **localhost:3000**, you should see the following user interface:

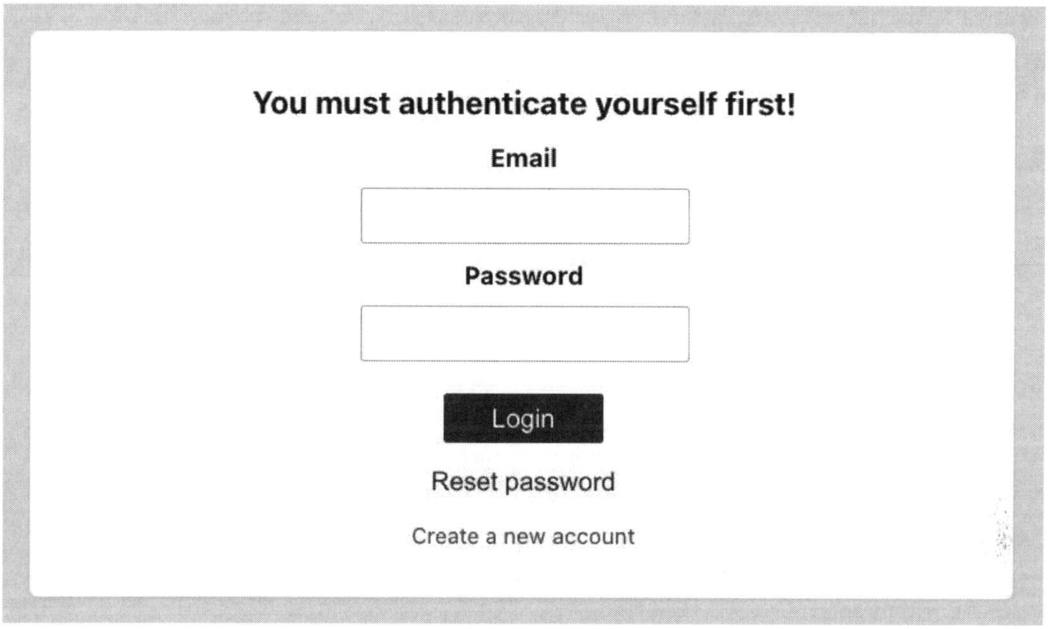

Figure 9.17: The running starting project

Take your time to get acquainted with the provided project. Experiment with the different buttons in the user interface, fill in some dummy data into the form input fields, and analyze the provided code. Please note that this dummy project does not send any HTTP requests to any server. All entered data is discarded the moment it is entered.

To complete the activity, the solution steps are as follows:

1. Find optimization opportunities by looking for unnecessary component function executions.

2. Also identify unnecessary code execution inside of component functions (where the overall component function invocation can't be prevented).

3. Determine which code could be loaded lazily instead of eagerly.

4. Use the `memo()` function, the `useMemo()` Hook, and React's `lazy()` function to improve the code.

You can tell that you came up with a good solution and sensible adjustments if you can see extra code fetching network requests (in the **Network** tab of your browser developer tools) for clicking on the `Reset password` or `Create a new account` buttons:

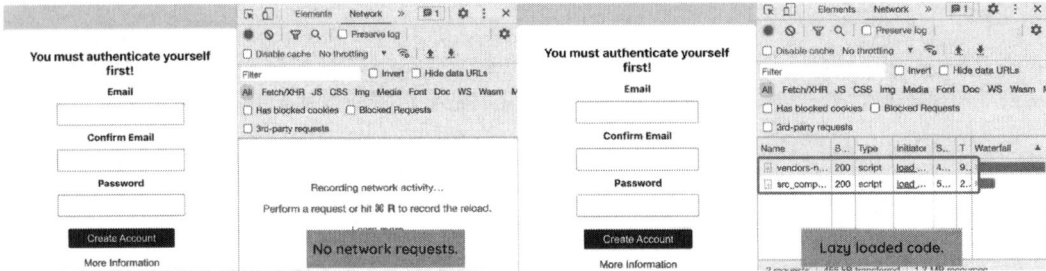

Figure 9.18: In the final solution, some code is lazy loaded

In addition, you should see no `Validated password.` console message when typing into the email input fields (`Email` and `Confirm Email`) of the signup form (that is, the form you switch to when clicking `Create a new account`):

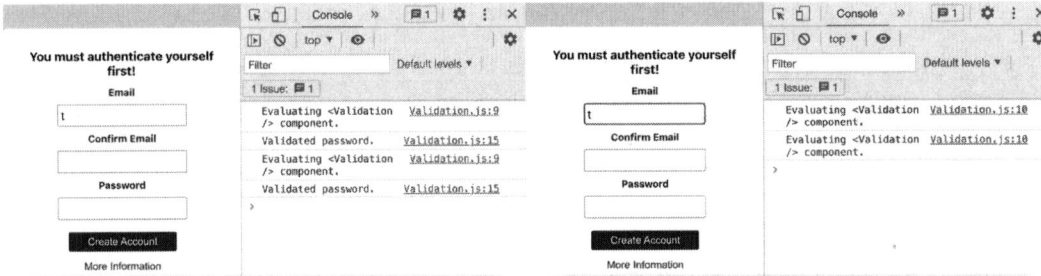

Figure 9.19: No "Validated password." output in the console

You also shouldn't get any console outputs when clicking the **More Information** button:

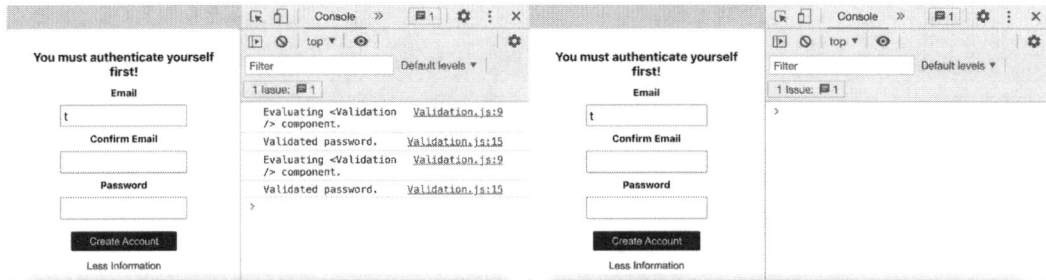

Figure 9.20: No console messages when clicking "More Information"

> **NOTE**
>
> The solution to this activity can be found on page 496.

10

WORKING WITH COMPLEX STATE

LEARNING OBJECTIVES

By the end of this chapter, you will be able to do the following:

- Manage cross-component or even app-wide state (instead of just component-specific state).

- Distribute data across multiple components.

- Handle complex state values and changes.

INTRODUCTION

State is one of the core concepts you must understand (and work with) to use React effectively. Basically, every React app utilizes (many) state values across many components to present a dynamic, reactive user interface.

From simple state values that contain a changing counter or values entered by users, all the way up to more complex state values such as the combination of multiple form inputs or user authentication information, state is everywhere. And in React apps, it's typically managed with the help of the **useState()** Hook.

However, once you start building more complex React applications (e.g., online shops, admin dashboards, and similar sites), it is likely that you'll face various challenges related to state. State values might be used in component A but changed in component B or be made up of multiple dynamic values that may change for a broad variety of reasons (e.g., a cart in an online shop, which is a combination of products, where every product has a quantity, a price, and possibly other traits that may be changed individually).

You can handle all these problems with **useState()**, props, and the other concepts covered by this book thus far. But you will notice that solutions based on **useState()** alone gain a complexity that can be difficult to understand and maintain. That's why React has more tools to offer—tools created for these kinds of problems, which this chapter will highlight and discuss.

A PROBLEM WITH CROSS-COMPONENT STATE

You don't even need to build a highly sophisticated React app to encounter a common problem: state that spans multiple components.

For example, you might be building a news app where users can bookmark certain articles. The user interface could look like this:

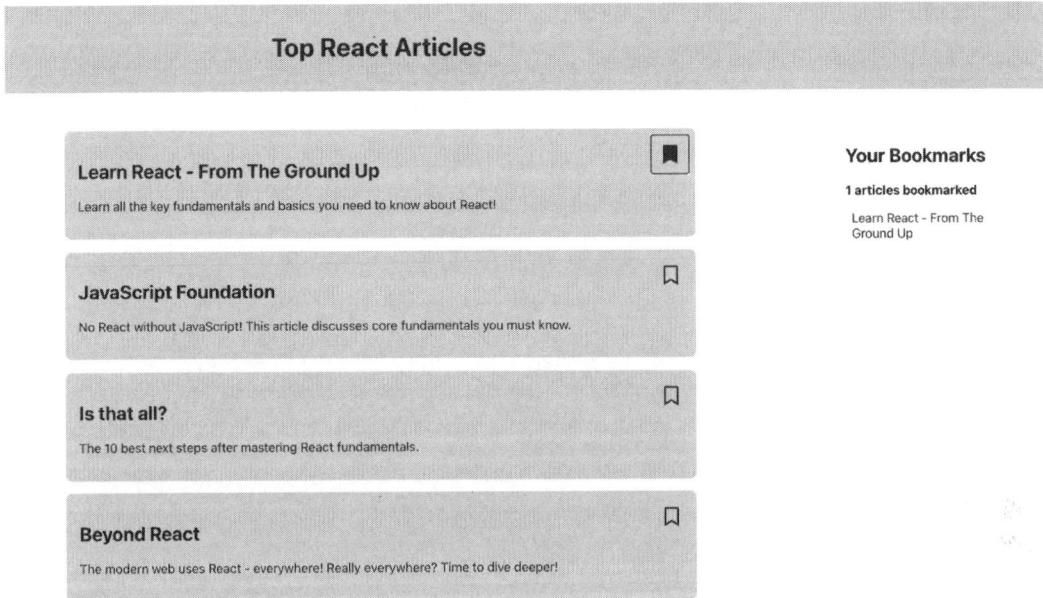

Figure 10.1: An example user interface

As you can see in the preceding figure, the list of articles is on the left, and a summary of the bookmarked articles can be found in a sidebar on the right.

A common solution is to split this user interface into multiple components. The list of articles, specifically, would probably be in its own component—just like the bookmark summary sidebar.

However, in that scenario, both components would need to access the same shared state—that is, the list of bookmarked articles. The article list component would require access in order to add (or remove) articles. The bookmark summary sidebar component would require it as it needs to display the bookmarked articles.

The component tree and state usage for this kind of app could look like this:

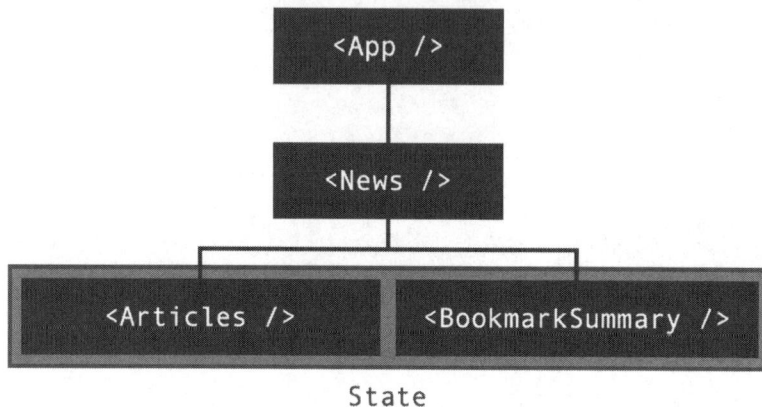

Figure 10.2: Two sibling components share the same state

In this figure, you can see that the state is shared across these two components. You also see that the two components have a shared parent component (the **News** component, in this example).

Since the state is used by two components, you would not manage it in either of those components. Instead, it's *lifted up*, as described in *Chapter 4, Working with Events and State* (in the "*Lifting State Up*" section). When lifting state up, the state values and pointers to the functions that manipulate the state values are passed down to the actual components that need access via props.

This works and is a common pattern. You can (and should) keep on using it. But what if a component that needs access to some shared state is deeply nested in other components? What if the app component tree from the preceding example looked like this?

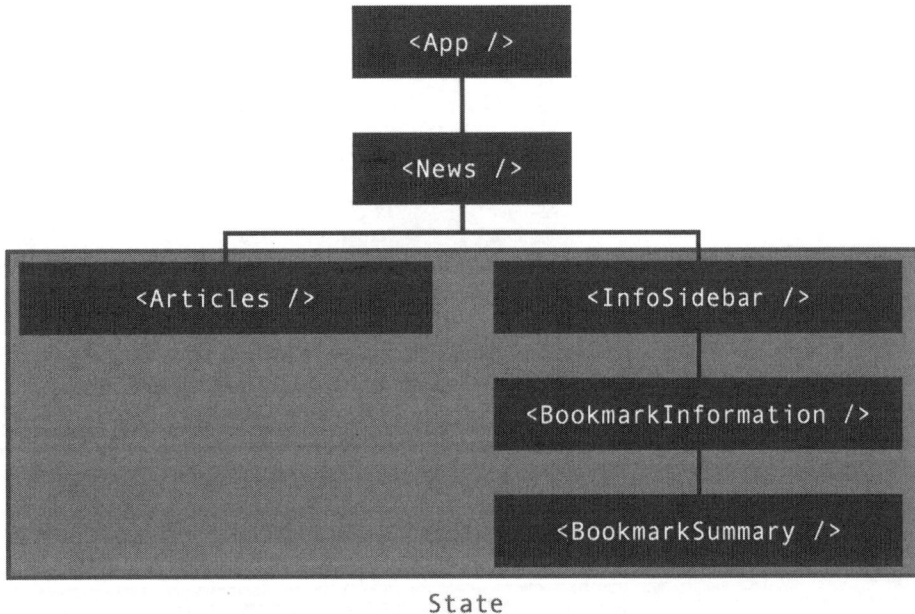

Figure 10.3: A component tree with multiple layers of state-dependent components

In this figure, you can see that the **BookmarkSummary** component is a deeply nested component. Between it and the **News** component (which manages the shared state), you have two other components: the **InfoSidebar** component and the **BookmarkInformation** component. In more complex React apps, having multiple levels of component nesting, as in this example, is very common.

Of course, even with those extra components, state values can still be passed down via props. You just need to add props to **all** components between the component that holds the state and the component that needs the state. For example, you must pass the **bookmarkedArticles** state value to the **InfoSidebar** component (via props) so that that component can forward it to **BookmarkInformation**:

```
import BookmarkInformation from '../BookmarkSummary/BookmarkInformation';
import classes from './InfoSidebar.module.css';


function InfoSidebar({ bookmarkedArticles }) {
  return (
    <aside className={classes.sidebar}>
```

```
        <BookmarkInformation bookmarkedArticles={bookmarkedArticles} />
    </aside>
  );
}

export default InfoSidebar;
```

The same procedure is repeated inside of the **BookmarkInformation** component.

> **NOTE**
>
> You can find the complete example on GitHub at https://packt.link/Ft8AM.

This kind of pattern is called **prop drilling**. Prop drilling means that a state value is passed through multiple components via props. And it's passed through components that don't need the state themselves at all—except for forwarding it to a child component (as the **InfoSidebar** and **BookmarkInformation** components are doing in the preceding example).

As a developer, you will typically want to avoid this pattern because prop drilling has a few weaknesses:

- Components that are part of prop drilling (such as **InfoSidebar** or **BookmarkInformation**) are not really reusable anymore because any component that wants to use them has to provide a value for the forwarded state prop.

- Prop drilling also leads to a lot of overhead code that has to be written (the code to accept props and forward props).

- Refactoring components becomes more work because state props have to be added or removed.

For these reasons, prop drilling is only acceptable if all components involved are only used in this specific part of the overall React app, and the probability of reusing or refactoring them is low.

Since prop drilling should be avoided (in most situations), React offers an alternative: the **context** API.

USING CONTEXT TO HANDLE MULTI-COMPONENT STATE

React's context feature is one that allows you to create a value that can easily be shared across as many components as needed, without using props.

Using the context API is a multi-step process, the steps for which are described here:

1. You must create a context value that should be shared.

2. The context must be provided in a parent component of the components that need access to the context object.

3. Components that need access (for reading or writing) must subscribe to the context.

React manages the context value (and its changes) internally and automatically distributes it to all components that have subscribed to the context.

Before any component may subscribe, however, the first step is to create a context object. This is done via React's **createContext()** function:

```
import { createContext } from 'react';

createContext('Hello Context'); // a context with an initial string value
createContext({}); // a context with an initial (empty) object as a value
```

This function takes an initial value that should be shared. It can be any kind of value (e.g., a string or a number), but typically, it's an object. This is because most shared values are a combination of the actual values and functions that should manipulate those values. All these things are then grouped together into a single context object.

Of course, the initial context value can also be an empty value (e.g., **null**, **undefined**, an empty string, etc.) if needed.

createContext() also returns a value: a context object that should be stored in a capitalized variable (or constant) because it contains a nested property that is a React component (and React components should start with capital characters).

Here's how the **createContext()** function can be used for the example discussed earlier in this chapter:

```
import { createContext } from 'react';

const BookmarkContext = createContext({
  bookmarkedArticles: []
});

export default BookmarkContext; // making it available outside of its file
```

Here, the initial value is an object that contains the **bookmarkedArticles** property, which holds an (empty) array. You could also store just the array as an initial value (i.e., **createContext([])**) but an object is better since more will be added to it later in the chapter.

This code is typically placed in a separate context code file that's often stored in a folder named **store** (because this context feature can be used as a central state store) or **context**. However, this is just a convention and is not technically required. You can put this code anywhere in your React app.

Of course, this initial value is not a replacement for state; it's a static value that never changes. But this was just the first of three steps related to context. The next step is to provide the context.

PROVIDING AND MANAGING CONTEXT VALUES

In order to use context values in other components, you must first provide the value. This is done using the value returned by **createContext()**. That function yields an object that contains a nested **Provider** property. And that property contains a React component that should be wrapped around all other components that need access to the context value.

In the preceding example, the **BookmarkContext.Provider** component could be used in the **News** component to wrap it around both the **Articles** and **InfoSidebar** components:

```
import Articles from '../Articles/Articles';
import InfoSidebar from '../InfoSidebar/InfoSidebar';
import BookmarkContext from '../../store/bookmark-context';

function News() {
  return (
```

```
    <BookmarkContext.Provider>
      <Articles />
      <InfoSidebar />
    </BookmarkContext.Provider>
  );
}
```

However, this code does not work because one important thing is missing: the **Provider** component expects a **value** prop, which should contain the current context value that should be distributed to interested components. While you do provide an initial context value (which could have been empty), you also need to inform React about the current context value because, very often, context values change (they are often used as a replacement for the cross-component state, after all).

Hence, the code could be altered like this:

```
import Articles from '../Articles/Articles';
import InfoSidebar from '../InfoSidebar/InfoSidebar';
import BookmarkContext from '../../store/bookmark-context';

function News() {
  const bookmarkCtxValue = {
    bookmarkedArticles: []
  }; // for now, it's the same value as used before, for the initial
context

  return (
    <BookmarkContext.Provider value={bookmarkCtxValue}>
      <Articles />
      <InfoSidebar />
    </BookmarkContext.Provider>
  );
}
```

With this code, an object with a list of bookmarked articles is distributed to interested descendent components.

The list is still static though. But that can be changed with a tool you already know about: the **useState()** Hook. Inside the **News** component, you can use the **useState()** Hook to manage the list of bookmarked articles, like this:

```
import { useState } from 'react';

import Articles from '../Articles/Articles';
import InfoSidebar from '../InfoSidebar/InfoSidebar';
import BookmarkContext from '../../store/bookmark-context';

function News() {
  const [savedArticles, setSavedArticles] = useState([]);

  const bookmarkCtxValue = {
    bookmarkedArticles: savedArticles // using the state as a value now!
  };

  return (
    <BookmarkContext.Provider value={bookmarkCtxValue}>
      <Articles />
      <InfoSidebar />
    </BookmarkContext.Provider>
  );
}
```

With this change, the context changes from static to dynamic. Whenever the **savedArticles** state changes, the context value will change.

Therefore, that's the missing piece when it comes to providing the context. If the context should be dynamic (and changeable from inside some nested child component), the context value should also include a pointer to the function that triggers a state update.

For the preceding example, the code is therefore adjusted like this:

```
import { useState } from 'react';

import Articles from '../Articles/Articles';
import InfoSidebar from '../InfoSidebar/InfoSidebar';
import BookmarkContext from '../../store/bookmark-context';

function News() {
```

```
  const [savedArticles, setSavedArticles] = useState([]);

  function addArticle(article) {
    setSavedArticles((prevSavedArticles) => [...prevSavedArticles,
article]);
  }

  function removeArticle(articleId) {
    setSavedArticles((prevSavedArticles) => prevSavedArticles.filter(
      (article) => article.id !== articleId)
    );
  }

  const bookmarkCtxValue = {
    bookmarkedArticles: savedArticles,
    bookmarkArticle: addArticle,
    unbookmarkArticle: removeArticle
  };

  return (
    <BookmarkContext.Provider value={bookmarkCtxValue}>
      <Articles />
      <InfoSidebar />
    </BookmarkContext.Provider>
  );
}
```

The following are two important things changed in this code snippet:

- Two new functions were added: **addArticle** and **removeArticle**.

- Properties that point at these functions were added to **bookmarkCtxValue**:
  the **bookmarkArticle** and **unbookmarkArticle** methods.

The **addArticle** function adds a new article (which should be bookmarked) to the
savedArticles state. The function form of updating the state value is used since
the new state value depends on the previous state value (the bookmarked article is
added to the list of already bookmarked articles).

Similarly, the **removeArticle** function removes an article from the
savedArticles list by filtering the existing list such that all items, except for
the one that has a matching **id** value, are kept.

If the **News** component did not use the new context feature, it would be a component that uses state just as you saw many times before in this book. But now, by using React's context API, those existing capabilities are combined with a new feature (the context) to create a dynamic, distributable value.

Any components nested in the **Articles** or **InfoSidebar** components (or their descendent components) will be able to access this dynamic context value, and the **bookmarkArticle** and **unbookmarkArticle** methods in the context object, without any prop drilling.

> ### NOTE
>
> You don't have to create dynamic context values. You could also distribute a static value to nested components. This is possible but a rare scenario, since most React apps do typically need dynamic state values that can change across components.

USING CONTEXT IN NESTED COMPONENTS

With the context created and provided, it's ready to be used by components that need to access or change the context value.

To make the context value accessible by components nested inside the context's **Provider** component (**BookmarkContext.Provider**, in the preceding example), React offers a **useContext()** Hook that can be used.

useContext() requires one argument: the context object that was created via **createContext()**, i.e., the value returned by that function. **useContext()** then returns the value passed to the **Provider** component (via its **value** prop).

For the preceding example, the context value can be used in the **BookmarkSummary** component like this:

```
import { useContext } from 'react';

import BookmarkContext from '../../store/bookmark-context';
import classes from './BookmarkSummary.module.css';

function BookmarkSummary() {
  const bookmarkCtx = useContext(BookmarkContext);
```

```
    const numberOfArticles = bookmarkCtx.bookmarkedArticles.length;

    return (
        <>
            <p className={classes.summary}>{numberOfArticles} articles
bookmarked</p>
            <ul className={classes.list}>
                {bookmarkCtx.bookmarkedArticles.map((article) => (
                    <li key={article.id}>{article.title}</li>
                ))}
            </ul>
        </>
    );
}

export default BookmarkSummary;
```

In this code, **useContext()** receives the **BookmarkContext** value, which is imported from the **store/bookmark-context.js** file. It then returns the value stored in the context, which is the **bookmarkCtxValue** found in the previous code example. As you can see in that snippet, **bookmarkCtxValue** is an object with three properties: **bookmarkedArticles**, **bookmarkArticle** (a method), and **unbookmarkArticle** (also a method).

This returned object is stored in a **bookmarkCtx** constant. Whenever the context value changes (because the **setSavedArticles** state-updating function in the **News** component is executed), this **BookmarkSummary** component will also be executed again by React, and thus **bookmarkCtx** will hold the latest state value.

Finally, in the **BookmarkSummary** component, the **bookmarkedArticles** property is accessed on the **bookmarkCtx** object. This list of articles is then used to calculate the number of bookmarked articles, output a short summary, and display the list on the screen.

Similarly, **BookmarkContext** can be used via **useContext()** in the **Articles** component:

```
import { useContext } from 'react';
import { FaBookmark, FaRegBookmark } from 'react-icons/fa';

import dummyArticles from '../../data/dummy-articles';
import BookmarkContext from '../../store/bookmark-context';
```

```
import classes from './Articles.module.css';

function Articles() {
  const bookmarkCtx = useContext(BookmarkContext);

  return (
    <ul className={classes.list}>
      {dummyArticles.map((article) => {
        // will be true if this article item is also
        // included in the bookmarkedArticles array
        const isBookmarked = bookmarkCtx.bookmarkedArticles.some(
          (bArticle) => bArticle.id === article.id
        );

        let buttonAction = () => {}; // dummy value, will be finished
later!
        // default button icon: Empty bookmark icon, because not
bookmarked
        let buttonIcon = <FaRegBookmark />;

        if (isBookmarked) {
          buttonAction = () => {}; // dummy value, will be finished later!
          buttonIcon = <FaBookmark />;
        }

        return (
          <li key={article.id}>
            <h2>{article.title}</h2>
            <p>{article.description}</p>
            <button onClick={buttonAction}>{buttonIcon}</button>
          </li>
        );
      })}
    </ul>
  );
}
export default Articles;
```

In this component, the context is used to determine whether or not a given article is currently bookmarked (this information is required in order to change the icon and functionality of the button).

That's how context values (whether static or dynamic) can be read in components. Of course, they can also be changed, as discussed in the next section.

CHANGING CONTEXT FROM NESTED COMPONENTS

React's context feature is often used to share data across multiple components without using props. It's therefore also quite common that some components must manipulate that data. For example, the context value for a shopping cart must be adjustable from inside the component that displays product items (because those probably have an **"Add to cart"** button).

However, to change context values from inside a nested component, you cannot simply overwrite the stored context value. The following code would not work as intended:

```
const bookmarkCtx = useContext(BookmarkContext);


// Note: This does NOT work
bookmarkCtx.bookmarkedArticles = []; // setting the articles to an empty
array
```

This code does not work. Just as you should not try to update state by simply assigning a new value, you can't update context values by assigning a new value. That's why two methods (**bookmarkArticle** and **unbookmarkArticle**) were added to the context value in the "*Providing and Managing Context Values*" section. These two methods point at functions that trigger state updates (via the state-updating function provided by **useState()**).

Therefore, in the **Articles** component, where articles can be bookmarked or unbookmarked via button clicks, these methods should be called:

```
// This code is part of the Article component function
// default button action => bookmark article, because not bookmarked yet
let buttonAction = () => bookmarkCtx.bookmarkArticle(article);
// default button icon: Empty bookmark icon, because not bookmarked
let buttonIcon = <FaRegBookmark />;

if (isBookmarked) {
  buttonAction = () => bookmarkCtx.unbookmarkArticle(article.id);
  buttonIcon = <FaBookmark />;
}
```

The **bookmarkArticle** and **unbookmarkArticle** methods are called inside of anonymous functions that are stored in a **buttonAction** variable. That variable is assigned to the **onClick** prop of the **<button>** (see the previous code snippet).

With this code, the context value can be changed successfully. Thanks to the steps taken in the previous section (*"Using Context in Nested Components"*), whenever the context value is updated, it is then also automatically reflected in the user interface.

> **NOTE**
>
> The finished example code can be found on GitHub at https://packt.link/ ocLLR.

GETTING BETTER CODE COMPLETION

In the section *"Using Context to Handle Multi-Component State"*, a context object was created via **createContext()**. That function received an initial context value—an object that contains a **bookmarkedArticles** property, in the preceding example.

In this example, the initial context value isn't too important. It's not often used because it's overwritten with a new value inside the **News** component regardless. However, depending on which **Integrated Development Environment (IDE)** you're using, you can get better code auto-completion when defining an initial context value that has the same shape and structure as the final context value that will be managed in other React components.

Therefore, since two methods were added to the context value in the section *"Providing and Managing Context Values"*, those methods should also be added to the initial context value in **store/bookmark-context.js**:

```
const BookmarkContext = createContext({
  bookmarkedArticles: [],
  bookmarkArticle: () => {},
  unbookmarkArticle: () => {}
});


export default BookmarkContext;
```

The two methods are added as empty functions that do nothing because the actual logic is set in the **News** component. The methods are only added to this initial context value to provide better IDE auto-completion. This step is therefore optional.

CONTEXT OR "LIFTING STATE UP"?

At this point, you now have two tools for managing cross-component state:

- You can lift state up, as described earlier in the book (in *Chapter 4, Working with Events and State*, in section "*Lifting State Up*").

- Alternatively, you can use React's context API as explained in this chapter.

Which of the two approaches should you use in each scenario?

Ultimately, it is up to you how you manage this, but there are some straightforward rules you can follow:

- Lift the state up if you only need to share state across one or two levels of component nesting.

- Use the context API if you have long chains of components (i.e., deep nesting of components) with shared state. Once you start to use a lot of prop drilling, it's time to consider React's context feature.

- Also use the context API if you have a relatively flat component tree but want to reuse components (i.e., you don't want to use props for passing state to components).

OUTSOURCING CONTEXT LOGIC INTO SEPARATE COMPONENTS

With the previously explained steps, you have everything you need to manage cross-component state via context.

But there is one pattern you can consider for managing your dynamic context value and state: creating a separate component for providing (and managing) the context value.

In the preceding example, the **News** component was used to provide the context and manage its (dynamic, state-based) value. While this works, your components can get unnecessarily complex if they have to deal with context management. Creating a separate, dedicated component for that can therefore lead to code that's easier to understand and maintain.

For the preceding example, that means that, inside of the **store/bookmark-context.js** file, you could create a **BookmarkContextProvider** component that looks like this:

```
export function BookmarkContextProvider({ children }) {
  const [savedArticles, setSavedArticles] = useState([]);

  function addArticle(article) {
    setSavedArticles((prevSavedArticles) => [...prevSavedArticles,
article]);
  }

  function removeArticle(articleId) {
    setSavedArticles((prevSavedArticles) =>
      prevSavedArticles.filter((article) => article.id !== articleId)
    );
  }

  const bookmarkCtxValue = {
    bookmarkedArticles: savedArticles,
    bookmarkArticle: addArticle,
    unbookmarkArticle: removeArticle,
  };

  return (
    <BookmarkContext.Provider value={bookmarkCtxValue}>
      {children}
    </BookmarkContext.Provider>
  );
}
```

This component contains all the logic related to managing a list of bookmarked articles via state. It creates the same context value as before (a value that contains the list of articles as well as two methods for updating that list).

The **BookmarkContextProvider** component does one additional thing though. It uses the special **children** prop (covered in *Chapter 3, Components and Props*, in section *"The Special 'children' Prop"*) to wrap whatever is passed between the **BookmarkContextProvider**'s component tags with **BookmarkContext. Provider**.

This allows for the use of the **BookmarkContextProvider** component in the **News** component, like so:

```
import Articles from '../Articles/Articles';
import InfoSidebar from '../InfoSidebar/InfoSidebar';
import { BookmarkContextProvider } from '../../store/bookmark-context';

function News() {
  return (
    <BookmarkContextProvider>
      <Articles />
      <InfoSidebar />
    </BookmarkContextProvider>
  );
}

export default News;
```

Instead of managing the entire context value, the **News** component now simply imports the **BookmarkContextProvider** component and wraps that component around **Articles** and **BookmarkSummary**. The **News** component, therefore, is leaner.

> **NOTE**
>
> This pattern is entirely optional. It's neither an official best practice nor does it yield any performance benefits.

COMBINING MULTIPLE CONTEXTS

Especially in bigger and more feature-rich React applications, it is possible (and quite probable), that you will need to work with multiple context values that are likely unrelated to each other. For example, an online shop could use one context for managing the shopping cart, another context for the user authentication status, and yet another context value for tracking page analytics.

React fully supports use cases like this. You can create, manage, provide, and use as many context values as needed. You can manage multiple (related or unrelated) values in a single context or use multiple contexts. You can provide multiple contexts in the same component or in different components. It is totally up to you and your app's requirements.

You can also use multiple contexts in the same component (meaning that you can call **`useContext()`** multiple times, with different context values).

LIMITATIONS OF USESTATE()

Thus far in this chapter, the complexity of cross-component state has been explored. But state management can also get challenging in scenarios where some state is only used inside a single component.

`useState()` is a great tool for state management in most scenarios (of course, right now, it's also the only tool that's been covered). Therefore, **`useState()`** should be your default choice for managing state. But **`useState()`** can reach its limits if you need to derive a new state value that's based on the value of another state variable, as in this example:

```
setIsLoading(fetchedPosts ? false : true);
```

This short snippet is taken from a component where an HTTP request is sent to fetch some blog posts.

> **NOTE**
>
> You'll find the complete example code on GitHub at https://packt.link/FiOCM. You will also see more excerpts from the code later in this chapter.

When initiating the request, an **`isLoading`** state value (responsible for showing a loading indicator on the screen) should be set to **`true`** only if no data was fetched before. If data was fetched before (i.e., **`fetchedPosts`** is not **`null`**), that data should still be shown on the screen, instead of some loading indicator.

At first sight, this code might not look problematic. But it actually violates an important rule related to **`useState()`**: you should not reference the current state for setting a new state value. If you need to do so, you should instead use the function form of the state updating function (see *Chapter 4, Working with Events and State*, section "*Updating State Based on Previous State Correctly*").

However, in the preceding example, this solution won't work. If you switch to the functional state-updating form, you only get access to the current value of the state you're trying to update. You don't get (safe) access to the current value of some other state. And in the preceding example, another state (**`fetchedPosts`** instead of **`isLoading`**) is referenced. Therefore, you must violate the mentioned rule.

This violation also has real consequences (in this example). The following code snippet is part of a function called **fetchPosts**, which is wrapped with **useCallback()**:

```
const fetchPosts = useCallback(async function fetchPosts() {
  setIsLoading(fetchedPosts ? false : true);
  setError(null);

  try {
    const response = await fetch(
      'https://jsonplaceholder.typicode.com/posts'
    );

    if (!response.ok) {
      throw new Error('Failed to fetch posts.');
    }

    const posts = await response.json();

    setIsLoading(false);
    setError(null);
    setFetchedPosts(posts);
  } catch (error) {
    setIsLoading(false);
    setError(error.message);
    setFetchedPosts(null);
  }
}, []);
```

This function sends an HTTP request and changes multiple state values based on the state of the request.

useCallback() is used to avoid an infinite loop related to **useEffect()** (see *Chapter 8, Handling Side Effects* to learn more about **useEffect()**, infinite loops, and **useCallback()** as a remedy). Normally, **fetchedPosts** should be added as a dependency to the **dependencies** array passed as a second argument to the **useCallback()** function. However, in this example, this can't be done because **fetchedPosts** is changed inside the function wrapped by **useCallback()**, and the state value is therefore not just a dependency but also actively changed. This causes an infinite loop.

As a result, a warning is shown in the terminal and the intended behavior of not showing the loading indicator if data was fetched before is not achieved:

```
WARNING in [eslint]
src/App.js
  Line 34:6:  React Hook useCallback has a missing dependency: 'fetchedPosts'. Either include it or remove the dependency array. You can
  also replace multiple useState variables with useReducer if 'setIsLoading' needs the current value of 'fetchedPosts'  react-hooks/exhau
stive-deps
```

Figure 10.4: A warning about the missing dependency is output in the terminal

Problems like the one just described are common if you have multiple related state values that depend on each other.

One possible solution would be to move from multiple, individual state slices (**fetchedPosts**, **isLoading**, and **error**) to a single, combined state value (i.e., to an object). That would ensure that all state values are grouped together and can thereby be accessed safely when using the functional state-updating form. The state-updating code then could look like this:

```
setHttpState(prevState => ({
  fetchedPosts: prevState.fetchedPosts,
  isLoading: prevState.fetchedPosts ? false : true,
  error: null
}));
```

This solution would work. However, ending up with ever more complex (and nested) state objects is not typically desirable as it can make state management a bit harder and bloat your component code.

That's why React offers an alternative to **useState()**: the **useReducer()** Hook.

MANAGING STATE WITH USEREDUCER()

Just like **useState()**, **useReducer()** is a React Hook. And just like **useState()**, it is a Hook that can trigger component function re-evaluations. But, of course, it works slightly differently; otherwise, it would be a redundant Hook.

useReducer() is a Hook meant to be used for managing complex state objects. You will rarely (probably never) use it to manage simple string or number values.

This Hook takes two main arguments:

- A reducer function
- An initial state value

This brings up an important question: what is a reducer function?

UNDERSTANDING REDUCER FUNCTIONS

In the context of **useReducer ()**, a reducer function is a function that itself receives two parameters:

* The current state value

* An action that was dispatched

Besides receiving arguments, a reducer function must also return a value: the new state. It's called a reducer function because it reduces the old state (combined with an action) to a new state.

To make this all a bit easier to grasp and reason through, the following code snippet shows how **useReducer ()** is used in conjunction with such a reducer function:

```
const initialHttpState = {
  data: null,
  isLoading: false,
  error: null,
};

function httpReducer(state, action) {
  if (action.type === 'FETCH_START') {
    return {
      ...state, // copying the existing state
      isLoading: state.data ? false : true,
      error: null,
    };
  }

  if (action.type === 'FETCH_ERROR') {
    return {
      data: null,
      isLoading: false,
      error: action.payload,
    };
  }

  if (action.type === 'FETCH_SUCCESS') {
    return {
      data: action.payload,
      isLoading: false,
```

```
      error: null,
    };
  }


  return initialHttpState; // default value for unknown actions
}


function App() {
  useReducer(httpReducer, initialHttpState);


  // more component code, not relevant for this snippet / explanation
}
```

At the bottom of this snippet, you can see that **useReducer()** is called inside of the **App** component function. Like all React Hooks, it must be called inside of component functions or other Hooks. You can also see the two arguments that were mentioned previously (the reducer function and initial state value) being passed to **useReducer()**.

httpReducer is the reducer function. The function takes two arguments (**state**, which is the old state, and **action**, which is the dispatched action) and returns different state objects for different action types.

This reducer function takes care of all possible state updates. The entire state-updating logic is therefore outsourced from the component (note that **httpReducer** is defined outside of the component function).

But the component function must, of course, be able to trigger the defined state updates. That's where actions become important.

> **NOTE**
>
> In this example, the reducer function is created outside of the component function. You could also create it inside the component function, but that is not recommended. If you create the reducer function inside the component function, it will technically be recreated every time the component function is executed. This impacts performance unnecessarily since the reducer function does not need access to any component function values.

DISPATCHING ACTIONS

The code shown previously is incomplete. When calling **useReducer()** in a component function, it does not just take two arguments. Instead, the Hook also returns a value—an array with exactly two elements (just like **useState()**, though the elements are different).

useReducer() should therefore be used like this (in the **App** component):

```
const [httpState, dispatch] = useReducer(httpReducer, initialHttpState);
```

In this snippet, array destructuring is used to store the two elements (and it is always exactly two!) in two different constants: **httpState** and **dispatch**.

The first element in the returned array (**httpState**, in this case) is the state value returned by the reducer function. It's updated (meaning that the component function is called by React) whenever the reducer function is executed again. The element is called **httpState** in this example because it contains the state value, which is related to an HTTP request in this instance. That said, how you name the element in your own case is up to you.

The second element (**dispatch**, in the example) is a function. It's a function that can be called to trigger a state update (i.e., to execute the reducer function again). When executed, the **dispatch** function must receive one argument—that is, the action value that will be available inside of the reducer function (via the reducer function's second argument). Here's how **dispatch** can be used in a component:

```
dispatch({ type: 'FETCH_START' });
```

The element is called **dispatch** in the example because it's a function used for dispatching actions to the reducer function. Just as before, the name is up to you, but **dispatch** is a commonly chosen name.

The shape and structure of that action value are also entirely up to you, but it's often set to an object that contains a **type** property. The **type** property is used in the reducer function to perform different actions for different types of actions. **type** therefore acts as an action identifier. You can see the **type** property being used inside the **httpReducer** function:

```
function httpReducer(state, action) {
  if (action.type === 'FETCH_START') {
    return {
      ...state, // copying the existing state
      isLoading: state.data ? false : true,
      error: null,
```

```
    };
  }

  if (action.type === 'FETCH_ERROR') {
    return {
      data: null,
      isLoading: false,
      error: action.payload,
    };
  }

  if (action.type === 'FETCH_SUCCESS') {
    return {
      data: action.payload,
      isLoading: false,
      error: null,
    };
  }

  return initialHttpState; // default value for unknown actions
}
```

You can add as many properties to the action object as needed. In the preceding example, some state updates access **action.payload** to extract some extra data from the action object. Inside a component, you would pass data along with the action like this:

```
dispatch({ type: 'FETCH_SUCCESS', payload: posts });
```

Again, the property name (**payload**) is up to you, but passing extra data along with the action allows you to perform state updates that rely on data generated by the component function.

Here's the complete, final code for the entire **App** component function:

```
// code for httpReducer etc. did not change

function App() {
  const [httpState, dispatch] = useReducer(httpReducer,
initialHttpState);

  // Using useCallback() to prevent an infinite loop in useEffect() below
  const fetchPosts = useCallback(async function fetchPosts() {
```

```
    dispatch({ type: 'FETCH_START' });

    try {
      const response = await fetch(
        'https://jsonplaceholder.typicode.com/posts'
      );

      if (!response.ok) {
        throw new Error('Failed to fetch posts.');
      }

      const posts = await response.json();

      dispatch({ type: 'FETCH_SUCCESS', payload: posts });
    } catch (error) {
      dispatch({ type: 'FETCH_ERROR', payload: error.message });
    }
  }, []);

  useEffect(
    function () {
      fetchPosts();
    },
    [fetchPosts]
  );

  return (
    <>
      <header>
        <h1>Complex State Blog</h1>
        <button onClick={fetchPosts}>Load Posts</button>
      </header>
      {httpState.isLoading && <p>Loading...</p>}
      {httpState.error && <p>{httpState.error}</p>}
      {httpState.data && <BlogPosts posts={httpState.data} />}
    </>
  );
}
```

In this code snippet, you can see how different actions (with different **type** and sometimes **payload** properties) are dispatched. You can also see that the **httpState** value is used to show different user interface elements based on the state (e.g., **<p>Loading...</p>** is shown if **httpState.isLoading** is **true**).

SUMMARY AND KEY TAKEAWAYS

- State management can have its challenges—especially when dealing with cross-component (or app-wide) state or complex state values.

- Cross-component state can be managed by lifting state up or by using React's Context API.

- The Context API is typically preferable if you do a lot of prop drilling (forwarding state values via props across multiple component layers).

- When using the context API, you use **createContext()** to create a new context object.

- The created context object yields a **Provider** component that must be wrapped around the part of the component tree that should get access to the context.

- Components can access the context value via the **useContext()** Hook.

- For managing complex state values, **useReducer()** can be a good alternative to **useState()**.

- **useReducer()** utilizes a reducer function that converts the current state and a dispatched action to a new state value.

- **useReducer()** returns an array with exactly two elements: the state value and a dispatch function, which is used for dispatching actions

WHAT'S NEXT?

Being able to manage both simple and complex state values efficiently is important. This chapter introduced two crucial tools that help with the task.

With the context API's **useContext()** and **useReducer()** Hooks, two new React Hooks were introduced. Combined with all the other Hooks covered thus far in the book, these mark the last of the React Hooks you will need in your everyday work as a React developer.

As a React developer, you're not limited to the built-in Hooks though. You can also build your own Hooks. The next chapter will finally explore how that works and why you might want to build custom Hooks in the first place.

TEST YOUR KNOWLEDGE!

Test your knowledge of the concepts covered in this chapter by answering the following questions. You can then compare your answers to the examples that can be found at https://packt.link/wc8xd:

1. What problem can be solved with React's context API?

2. Which three main steps have to be taken when using the context API?

3. When might **useReducer()** be preferred over **useState()**?

4. When working with **useReducer()**, what's the role of actions?

APPLY WHAT YOU LEARNED

Apply your knowledge about the context API and the **useReducer()** Hook to some real problems.

ACTIVITY 10.1: MIGRATING AN APP TO THE CONTEXT API

In this activity, your task is to improve an existing React project. Currently, the app is built without the context API and so cross-component state is managed by lifting the state up. In this project, prop drilling is the consequence in some components. Therefore, the goal is to adjust the app such that the context API is used for cross-component state management.

> **NOTE**
>
> You can find the starting code for this activity at https://packt.link/93LSa. When downloading this code, you'll always download the entire repository. Make sure to then navigate to the subfolder with the starting code (`activities/practice-1/starting-code` in this case) to use the right code snapshot.
>
> The provided project also uses many features covered in earlier chapters. Take your time to analyze it and understand the provided code. This is a great practice and allows you to see many key concepts in action.

Once you have downloaded the code and run **npm install** in the project folder (to install all required dependencies), you can start the development server via **npm start**. As a result, upon visiting **localhost:3000**, you should see the following user interface:

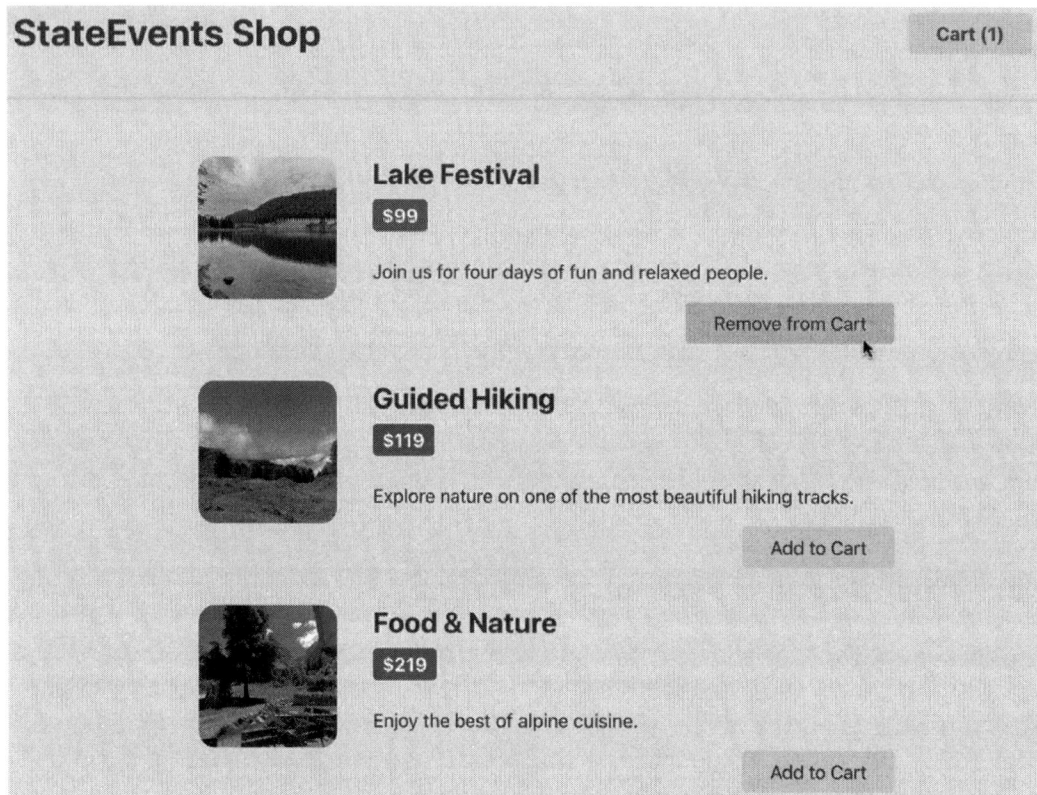

Figure 10.5: The running starting project

To complete the activity, the steps are as follows:

1. Create a new context for the cart items.

2. Create a **Provider** component for the context and handle all context-related state changes there.

3. Provide the context (with the help of the **Provider** component) and make sure all components that need access to the context have access.

4. Remove the old logic (where state was lifted up).

5. Use the context in all the components that need access to it.

The user interface should be the same as that shown in *Figure 10.5* once you have completed the activity. Make sure that the user interface works exactly as it did before you implemented React's context features.

> **NOTE**
>
> The solution to this activity can be found on page 503.

ACTIVITY 10.2: REPLACING USESTATE() WITH USEREDUCER()

In this activity, your task is to replace the **useState()** Hooks in the **Form** component with **useReducer()**. Use only one single reducer function (and thus only one **useReducer()** call) and merge all relevant state values into one state object.

> **NOTE**
>
> You can find the starting code for this activity at https://packt.link/wUDJu. When downloading this code, you'll always download the entire repository. Make sure to then navigate to the subfolder with the starting code (**activities/practice-1/starting-code** in this case) to use the right code snapshot.
>
> The provided project also uses many features covered in earlier chapters. Take your time to analyze it and understand the provided code. This is a great practice and allows you to see many key concepts in action.

Once you have downloaded the code and run **npm install** in the project folder (to install all required dependencies), you can start the development server via **npm start**. As a result, upon visiting **localhost:3000**, you should see the following user interface:

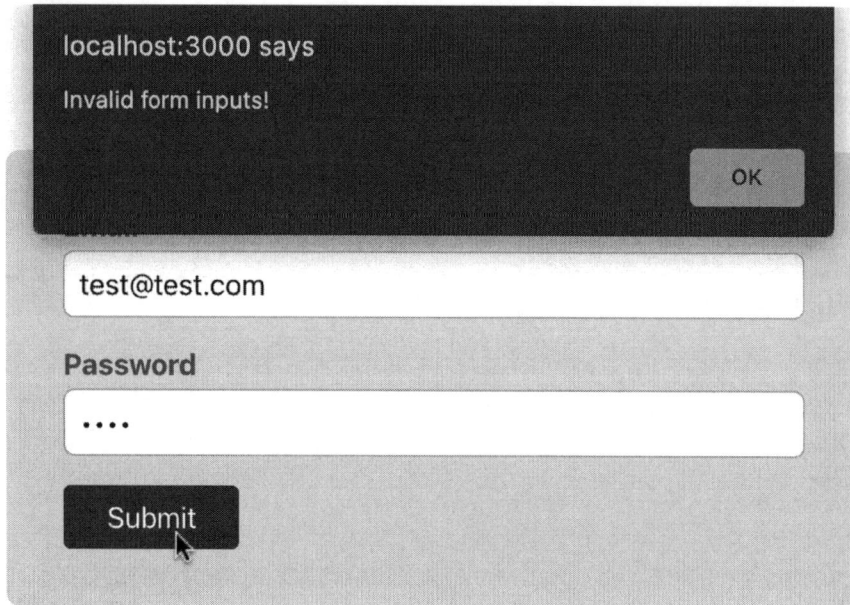

localhost:3000 says

Invalid form inputs!

OK

test@test.com

Password

....

Submit

Figure 10.6: The running starting project

To complete the activity, the solution steps are as follows:

1. Remove (or comment out) the existing logic in the Form component that uses the **useState()** Hook for state management.

2. Add a reducer function that handles two actions (email changed and password changed) and also returns a default value.

3. Update the state object based on the dispatched action type (and payload, if needed).

4. Use the reducer function with the **useReducer()** Hook.

5. Dispatch the appropriate actions (with the appropriate data) in the **Form** component.

6. Use the state value where needed.

The user interface should be the same as that shown in *Figure 10.6* once you've finished the activity. Make sure that the user interface works exactly as it did before you implemented React's context features.

> **NOTE**
>
> The solution to this activity can be found on page 510.

11

BUILDING CUSTOM REACT HOOKS

LEARNING OBJECTIVES

By the end of this chapter, you will be able to do the following:

- Build your own React Hooks.
- Use custom and default React Hooks in your components.

INTRODUCTION

Throughout this book, one key React feature has been referenced repeatedly in many different variations. That feature is React Hooks.

Hooks power almost all core functionalities and concepts offered by React—from state management in a single component to accessing cross-component state (context) in multiple components. They enable you to access JSX elements via refs and allow you to handle side effects inside of component functions.

Without Hooks, modern React would not work, and building feature-rich applications would be impossible.

Thus far, only built-in Hooks have been introduced and used. However, you can build your own custom Hooks as well. In this chapter, you will learn why you might want to do this and how it works.

WHY WOULD YOU BUILD CUSTOM HOOKS?

In the previous chapter (*Chapter 10, Working with Complex State*), when the **useReducer()** Hook was introduced, an example was provided in which the Hook was utilized in sending an HTTP request. Here's the relevant, final code again:

```
const initialHttpState = {
  data: null,
  isLoading: false,
  error: null,
};

function httpReducer(state, action) {
  if (action.type === 'FETCH_START') {
    return {
      ...state, // copying the existing state
      isLoading: state.data ? false : true,
      error: null,
    };
  }

  if (action.type === 'FETCH_ERROR') {
    return {
      data: null,
      isLoading: false,
      error: action.payload,
```

```
    };
  }

  if (action.type === 'FETCH_SUCCESS') {
    return {
      data: action.payload,
      isLoading: false,
      error: null,
    };
  }

  return initialHttpState; // default value for unknown actions
}

function App() {
  const [httpState, dispatch] = useReducer(httpReducer,
initialHttpState);

  // Using useCallback() to prevent an infinite loop in useEffect() below
  const fetchPosts = useCallback(async function fetchPosts() {
    dispatch({ type: 'FETCH_START' });

    try {
      const response = await fetch(
        'https://jsonplaceholder.typicode.com/posts'
      );

      if (!response.ok) {
        throw new Error('Failed to fetch posts.');
      }

      const posts = await response.json();

      dispatch({ type: 'FETCH_SUCCESS', payload: posts });
    } catch (error) {
      dispatch({ type: 'FETCH_ERROR', payload: error.message });
    }
  }, []);

  useEffect(
    function () {
```

```
      fetchPosts();
    },
    [fetchPosts]
  );


  return (
    <>
      <header>
        <h1>Complex State Blog</h1>
        <button onClick={fetchPosts}>Load Posts</button>
      </header>
      {httpState.isLoading && <p>Loading...</p>}
      {httpState.error && <p>{httpState.error}</p>}
      {httpState.data && <BlogPosts posts={httpState.data} />}
    </>
  );
};
```

In this code example, an HTTP request is sent whenever the **App** component is rendered for the first time. The HTTP request fetches a list of (dummy) posts. Until the request finishes, a loading message (**<p>Loading...</p>**) is displayed to the user. In the case of an error, an error message is displayed.

As you can see, quite a lot of code must be written to handle this relatively basic use case. And, especially in bigger React apps, it is quite likely that multiple components will need to send HTTP requests. They probably won't need to send the exact same request to the same URL (**https://jsonplaceholder.typicode.com/posts**, in this example), but it's definitely possible that different components will fetch different data from different URLs.

Therefore, almost the exact same code must be written over and over again in multiple components. And it's not just the code for sending the HTTP request (i.e., the function wrapped by **useCallback()**). Instead, the HTTP-related state management (done via **useReducer()**, in this example), as well as the request initialization via **useEffect()**, must be repeated in all those components.

And that is where custom Hooks come in to save the day. Custom Hooks help you avoid this repetition by allowing you to build reusable, potentially stateful "logic snippets" that can be shared across components.

WHAT ARE CUSTOM HOOKS?

Before starting to build custom Hooks, it's very important to understand what exactly custom Hooks are.

In React apps, custom Hooks are regular JavaScript functions that satisfy the following conditions:

- The function name starts with "use" (just as all built-in Hooks start with "use": `useState()`, `useReducer()`, etc.).

- The function does not just return JSX code (otherwise, it would essentially be a React component with a strange function name), though it could return some JSX code—as long as that's not the only value returned.

And that's it. If a function simply meets these two conditions, it can (and should) be called a custom (React) Hook.

Custom Hooks are special because you can call other built-in and custom React Hooks inside of their function bodies. Normally, this would not be allowed. React Hooks (both built-in and custom) can only be called inside of component functions. If you try to call a Hook in some other place (e.g., in a regular, non-Hook function), you will get an error, as shown below:

```
❌ ▸Warning: Invalid hook call. Hooks can only be called inside of the body of  react.development.js:209
   a function component. This could happen for one of the following reasons:
   1. You might have mismatching versions of React and the renderer (such as React DOM)
   2. You might be breaking the Rules of Hooks
   3. You might have more than one copy of React in the same app
   See https://reactjs.org/link/invalid-hook-call for tips about how to debug and fix this problem.
```

Figure 11.1: React complains if you call a Hook function in the wrong place

Hooks, whether custom or built-in, must only be called inside of component functions. And, even though the error message doesn't explicitly mention it, they may be called inside of custom Hooks.

This is an extremely important feature because it means that you can build reusable non-component functions that can contain state logic (via `useState()` or `useReducer()`), handle side effects in your reusable custom Hook functions (via `useEffect()`), or use any other React Hook. With normal, non-Hook functions, none of these would be possible, and you would therefore be unable to outsource any logic that involves a React Hook into such functions.

In this way, custom Hooks complement the concept of React components. While React components are reusable UI building blocks (which may contain stateful logic), custom Hooks are reusable logic snippets that can be used in your component functions. Thus, custom Hooks help you reuse shared logic across components.

Applied to the problem discussed previously (regarding the HTTP request logic), custom Hooks enable you to outsource the logic for sending an HTTP request and handling the related states (loading, error, etc.).

A FIRST CUSTOM HOOK

Before exploring advanced scenarios and solving the HTTP request problem mentioned previously, here's a more basic example for a first, custom Hook:

```
import { useState } from 'react';

function useCounter() {
  const [counter, setCounter] = useState(0);

  function increment() {
    setCounter(oldCounter => oldCounter + 1);
  };

  function decrement() {
    setCounter(oldCounter => oldCounter - 1);
  };

  return { counter, increment, decrement };
};

export default useCounter;
```

As you can see, **useCounter** is a regular JavaScript function. The name of the function starts with **use**, and React therefore treats this function as a custom Hook (meaning you won't get any error messages when using other Hooks inside of it).

Inside **useCounter()**, a **counter** state is managed via **useState()**. The state is changed via two nested functions (**increment** and **decrement**), and the state, as well as the functions, is returned by **useCounter** (grouped together in a JavaScript object).

> **NOTE**
>
> The syntax used to group **counter**, **increment**, and **decrement** together uses a regular JavaScript feature: shorthand property names.
>
> If a property name in an object literally matches the name of the variable whose value is assigned to the property, you can use this shorter notation.
>
> Instead of writing **{ counter: counter, increment: increment, decrement: decrement }**, you can use the shorthand notation shown in the snippet above.

This custom Hook can be stored in a separate file (e.g., in a **hooks** folder inside the React project, such as **src/hooks/use-counter.js**). Thereafter, it can be used in any React component, and you can use it in as many React components as needed.

For example, the following two components (**Demo1** and **Demo2**) could use this **useCounter** Hook as follows:

```
import useCounter from './hooks/use-counter';

function Demo1() {
  const { counter, increment, decrement } = useCounter();

  return (
    <>
      <p>{counter}</p>
      <button onClick={increment}>Inc</button>
      <button onClick={decrement}>Dec</button>

    </>
  );
};


function Demo2() {
  const { counter, increment, decrement } = useCounter();
```

```
    return (
      <>
        <p>{counter}</p>
        <button onClick={increment}>Inc</button>
        <button onClick={decrement}>Dec</button>
      </>
    );
};

function App() {
  return (
    <main>
      <Demo1 />
      <Demo2 />
    </main>
  );
};

export default App;
```

> **NOTE**
>
> You will find the full example code at https://packt.link/e8zRK.

The **Demo1** and **Demo2** components both execute **useCounter()** inside of their component functions. The **useCounter()** function is called a normal function because it **is** a regular JavaScript function.

Since the **useCounter** Hook returns an object with three properties (**counter**, **increment**, and **decrement**), **Demo1** and **Demo2** use object destructuring to store the property values in local constants. These values are then used in the JSX code to output the **counter** value and connect the two **<button>** elements to the **increment** and **decrement** functions.

After pressing the buttons a couple of times each, the resulting user interface might look like this:

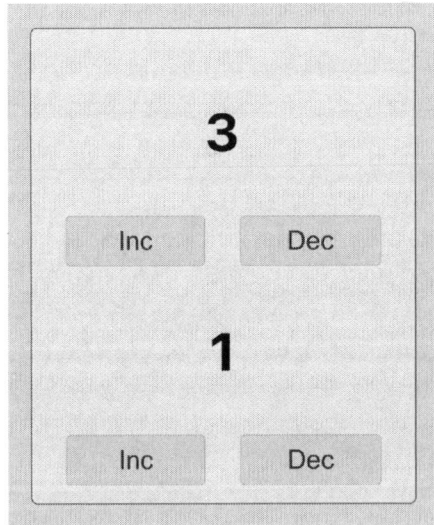

Figure 11.2: Two independent counters

In this screenshot, you can also see a very interesting and important behavior of custom Hooks. That is, if the same stateful custom Hook is used in multiple components, every component gets its own state. The **counter** state is not shared. The **Demo1** component manages its own **counter** state (through the **useCounter()** custom Hook), and so does the **Demo2** component.

CUSTOM HOOKS: A FLEXIBLE FEATURE

The two independent states of **Demo1** and **Demo2** show a very important feature of custom Hooks: you use them to share logic, not to share state. If you needed to share state across components, you would do so with React context (see the previous chapter).

When using Hooks, every component uses its own "instance" (or "version") of that Hook. It's always the same logic, but any state or side effects handled by a Hook are handled on a per-component basis.

It's also worth noting that custom Hooks **can** be stateful but **don't have to be**. They can manage state via **useState()** or **useReducer()**, but you could also build custom Hooks that only handle side effects (without any state management).

There's only one thing you implicitly have to do in custom Hooks: you must use some other React Hook (custom or built-in). This is because, if you didn't include any other Hook, there would be no need to build a custom Hook in the first place. A custom Hook is just a regular JavaScript function (with a name starting with **use**) with which you are allowed to use other Hooks. If you don't need to use any other Hooks, you can simply build a normal JavaScript function with a name that does not start with **use**.

You also have a lot of flexibility regarding the logic inside the Hook, its parameters, and the value it returns. Regarding the Hook logic, you can add as much logic as needed. You can manage no state or multiple state values. You can include other custom Hooks or only use built-in Hooks. You can manage multiple side effects, work with refs, or perform complex calculations. There are no restrictions regarding what can be done in a custom Hook.

CUSTOM HOOKS AND PARAMETERS

You can also accept and use parameters in your custom Hook functions. For example, the **useCounter** Hook from the "*A First Custom Hook*" section above can be adjusted to take an initial counter value and separate values by which the counter should be increased or decreased, as shown in the following snippet:

```
import { useState } from 'react';

function useCounter(initialValue, incVal, decVal) {
  const [counter, setCounter] = useState(initialValue);

  function increment() {
    setCounter(oldCounter => oldCounter + incVal);
  };

  function decrement() {
    setCounter(oldCounter => oldCounter - decVal);
  };

  return { counter, increment, decrement };
};

export default useCounter;
```

In this adjusted example, the **initialValue** parameter is used to set the initial state via **useState(initialValue)**. The **incVal** and **decVal** parameters are used in the **increment** and **decrement** functions to change the **counter** state with different values.

Of course, once parameters are used in a custom Hook, fitting parameter values must be provided when the custom Hook is called in a component function (or in another custom Hook). Therefore, the code for the **Demo1** and **Demo2** components must also be adjusted—for example, like this:

```
function Demo1() {
  const { counter, increment, decrement } = useCounter(1, 2, 1);

  return (
    <>
      <p>{counter}</p>
      <button onClick={increment}>Inc</button>
      <button onClick={decrement}>Dec</button>

    </>
  );
};


function Demo2() {
  const { counter, increment, decrement } = useCounter(0, 1, 2);

  return (
    <>
      <p>{counter}</p>
      <button onClick={increment}>Inc</button>
      <button onClick={decrement}>Dec</button>
    </>
  );
};
```

> **NOTE**
>
> You can also find this code on GitHub at https://packt.link/bMony.

Now, both components pass different parameter values to the **useCounter** Hook function. Therefore, they can reuse the same Hook and its internal logic dynamically.

CUSTOM HOOKS AND RETURN VALUES

As shown with **useCounter**, custom Hooks may return values. And this is important: they **may** return values, but they don't have to. If you build a custom Hook that only handles some side effects (via **useEffect()**), you don't have to return any value (because there probably isn't any value that should be returned).

But if you do need to return a value, you decide which type of value you want to return. You could return a single number or string. If your Hook must return multiple values (like **useCounter** does), you can group these values into an array or object. You can also return arrays that contain objects or vice versa. In short, you can return anything. It is a normal JavaScript function, after all.

Some built-in Hooks such as **useState()** and **useReducer()** return arrays (with a fixed number of elements). **useRef()**, on the other hand, returns an object (which always has a **current** property). **useEffect()** returns nothing. Your Hooks can therefore return whatever you want.

For example, the **useCounter** Hook from prevously could be rewritten to return an array instead:

```
import { useState } from 'react';

function useCounter(initialValue, incVal, decVal) {
  const [counter, setCounter] = useState(initialValue);

  function increment() {
    setCounter((oldCounter) => oldCounter + incVal);
  }

  function decrement() {
    setCounter((oldCounter) => oldCounter - decVal);
  }

  return [counter, increment, decrement];
}

export default useCounter;
```

To use the returned values, then, the **Demo1** and **Demo2** components need to switch from object destructuring to array destructuring, as follows:

```
function Demo1() {
  const [counter, increment, decrement] = useCounter(1, 2, 1);

  return (
    <>
      <p>{counter}</p>
      <button onClick={increment}>Inc</button>
      <button onClick={decrement}>Dec</button>
    </>
  );
}

function Demo2() {
  const [counter, increment, decrement] = useCounter(0, 1, 2);

  return (
    <>
      <p>{counter}</p>
      <button onClick={increment}>Inc</button>
      <button onClick={decrement}>Dec</button>
    </>
  );
}
```

The two components behave like before, so you can decide which return value you prefer.

> **NOTE**
>
> This finished code can also be found on GitHub at https://packt.link/adTM2.

A MORE COMPLEX EXAMPLE

The previous examples were deliberately rather simple. Now that the basics of custom Hooks are clear, it makes sense to dive into a slightly more advanced and realistic example.

Consider the HTTP request example from the beginning of this chapter:

```
const initialHttpState = {
  data: null,
  isLoading: false,
  error: null,
};

function httpReducer(state, action) {
  if (action.type === 'FETCH_START') {
    return {
      ...state, // copying the existing state
      isLoading: state.data ? false : true,
      error: null,
    };
  }

  if (action.type === 'FETCH_ERROR') {
    return {
      data: null,
      isLoading: false,
      error: action.payload,
    };
  }

  if (action.type === 'FETCH_SUCCESS') {
    return {
      data: action.payload,
      isLoading: false,
      error: null,
    };
  }

  return initialHttpState; // default value for unknown actions
}
```

```
function App() {
  const [httpState, dispatch] = useReducer(httpReducer,
initialHttpState);

  // Using useCallback() to prevent an infinite loop in useEffect() below
  const fetchPosts = useCallback(async function fetchPosts() {
    dispatch({ type: 'FETCH_START' });

    try {
      const response = await fetch(
        'https://jsonplaceholder.typicode.com/posts'
      );

      if (!response.ok) {
        throw new Error('Failed to fetch posts.');
      }

      const posts = await response.json();

      dispatch({ type: 'FETCH_SUCCESS', payload: posts });
    } catch (error) {
      dispatch({ type: 'FETCH_ERROR', payload: error.message });
    }
  }, []);

  useEffect(
    function () {
      fetchPosts();
    },
    [fetchPosts]
  );

  return (
    <>
      <header>
        <h1>Complex State Blog</h1>
        <button onClick={fetchPosts}>Load Posts</button>
      </header>
      {httpState.isLoading && <p>Loading...</p>}
      {httpState.error && <p>{httpState.error}</p>}
```

```
      {httpState.data && <BlogPosts posts={httpState.data} />}
    </>
  );
};
```

In that example, the entire **useReducer()** logic (including the reducer function, **httpReducer**) and the **useEffect()** call can be outsourced into a custom Hook. The result would be a very lean **App** component and a reusable Hook that could be used in other components as well.

This custom Hook could be named **useFetch** (since it fetches data), and it could be stored in **hooks/use-fetch.js**. Of course, both the Hook name as well as the file storage path are up to you. Here's how the first version of **useFetch** might look:

```
import { useCallback, useEffect, useReducer } from 'react';

const initialHttpState = {
  data: null,
  isLoading: false,
  error: null,
};

function httpReducer(state, action) {
  if (action.type === 'FETCH_START') {
    return {
      ...state,
      isLoading: state.data ? false : true,
      error: null,
    };
  }

  if (action.type === 'FETCH_ERROR') {
    return {
      data: null,
      isLoading: false,
      error: action.payload,
    };
  }

  if (action.type === 'FETCH_SUCCESS') {
    return {
      data: action.payload,
```

```
      isLoading: false,
      error: null,
    };
  }

  return initialHttpState;
}

function useFetch() {
  const [httpState, dispatch] = useReducer(httpReducer,
initialHttpState);

  const fetchPosts = useCallback(async function fetchPosts() {
    dispatch({ type: 'FETCH_START' });

    try {
      const response = await fetch(
        'https://jsonplaceholder.typicode.com/posts'
      );

      if (!response.ok) {
        throw new Error('Failed to fetch posts.');
      }

      const posts = await response.json();

      dispatch({ type: 'FETCH_SUCCESS', payload: posts });
    } catch (error) {
      dispatch({ type: 'FETCH_ERROR', payload: error.message });
    }
  }, []);

  useEffect(
    function () {
      fetchPosts();
    },
    [fetchPosts]
  );
}

export default useFetch;
```

Please note that this is not the final version.

In this first version, the **useFetch** Hook contains the **useReducer()** and **useEffect()** logic. It's worth noting that the **httpReducer** function is created outside of **useFetch**. This ensures that the function is not recreated unnecessarily when **useFetch()** is re-executed (which will happen often as it is called every time the component that uses this Hook is re-evaluated). The **httpReducer** function will therefore only be created once (for the entire application lifetime), and that same function instance will be shared by all components that use **useFetch**.

Since **httpReducer** is a pure function (that is, it always produces new return values that are based purely on the parameter values), sharing this function instance is fine and won't cause any unexpected bugs. If **httpReducer** were to store or manipulate any values that are not based on function inputs, it should be created inside of **useFetch** instead. This way, you avoid having multiple components accidentally manipulate and use shared values.

However, this version of the **useFetch** Hook has two big issues:

- Currently, no value is returned. Therefore, components that use this Hook won't get access to the fetched data or the loading state.

- The HTTP request URL is hardcoded into **useFetch**. As a result, all components that use this Hook will send the same kind of request to the same URL.

The first issue can be solved by returning the fetched data (or **undefined**, if no data was fetched yet), the loading state value, and the error value. Since these values are exactly the values that make up the **httpState** object returned by **useReducer()**, **useFetch** can simply return that entire **httpState** object, as shown here:

```
// httpReducer function and initial state did not change, hence omitted
here
function useFetch() {
  const [httpState, dispatch] = useReducer(httpReducer,
initialHttpState);

  const fetchPosts = useCallback(async function fetchPosts() {
    dispatch({ type: 'FETCH_START' });

    try {
      const response = await fetch(
        'https://jsonplaceholder.typicode.com/posts'
      );
```

```
      if (!response.ok) {
        throw new Error('Failed to fetch posts.');
      }


      const posts = await response.json();


      dispatch({ type: 'FETCH_SUCCESS', payload: posts });
    } catch (error) {
      dispatch({ type: 'FETCH_ERROR', payload: error.message });

    }
  }, []);

  useEffect(
    function () {
      fetchPosts();
    },
    [fetchPosts]
  );


  return httpState;
}
```

The only thing that changed in this code snippet is the last line of the **useFetch** function. With **return httpState**, the state managed by **useReducer()** (and therefore by the **httpReducer** function) is returned by the custom Hook.

To fix the second problem (i.e., the hardcoded URL), a parameter should be added to **useFetch**:

```
// httpReducer function and initial state did not change, hence omitted
here
function useFetch(url) {
  const [httpState, dispatch] = useReducer(httpReducer,
initialHttpState);

  const fetchPosts = useCallback(async function fetchPosts() {
    dispatch({ type: 'FETCH_START' });

    try {
      const response = await fetch(url);

      if (!response.ok) {
        throw new Error('Failed to fetch posts.');
```

```
      }

      const posts = await response.json();

      dispatch({ type: 'FETCH_SUCCESS', payload: posts });
    } catch (error) {
      dispatch({ type: 'FETCH_ERROR', payload: error.message });
    }
  }, [url]);

  useEffect(
    function () {
      fetchPosts();
    },
    [fetchPosts]
  );

  return httpState;
}
```

In this snippet, the **url** parameter was added to **useFetch**. This parameter value is then used inside the **try** block when calling **fetch(url)**. Please note that **url** was also added as a dependency to the **useCallback()** dependencies array.

Since **useCallback()** is wrapped around the fetching function (to prevent infinite loops by **useEffect()**), any external values used inside of **useCallback()** must be added to its dependencies array. Since **url** is an external value (meaning it's not defined inside of the wrapped function), it must be added. This also makes sense logically: if the **url** parameter were to change (i.e., if the component that uses **useFetch** changes it), a new HTTP request should be sent.

This final version of the **useFetch** Hook can now be used in all components to send HTTP requests to different URLs and use the HTTP state values as needed by the components.

For example, the **App** component can use **useFetch** like this:

```
import BlogPosts from './components/BlogPosts';
import useFetch from './hooks/use-fetch';

function App() {
  const { data, isLoading, error } = useFetch(
    'https://jsonplaceholder.typicode.com/posts'
```

```
  );

  return (
    <>
      <header>
        <h1>Complex State Blog</h1>
      </header>
      {isLoading && <p>Loading...</p>}
      {error && <p>{error}</p>}
      {data && <BlogPosts posts={data} />}
    </>
  );
}


export default App;
```

The component imports and calls **useFetch()** (with the appropriate URL as an argument) and uses object destructuring to get the **data**, **isLoading**, and **error** properties from the **httpState** object. These values are then used in the JSX code.

Of course, the **useFetch** Hook could also return a pointer to the **fetchPosts** function (in addition to **httpState**) to allow components such as the **App** component to manually trigger a new request, as shown here:

```
// httpReducer function and initial state did not change, hence omitted
here
function useFetch(url) {
  const [httpState, dispatch] = useReducer(httpReducer,
initialHttpState);

  const fetchPosts = useCallback(async function fetchPosts() {
    dispatch({ type: 'FETCH_START' });

    try {
      const response = await fetch(url);

      if (!response.ok) {
        throw new Error('Failed to fetch posts.');
      }

      const posts = await response.json();

      dispatch({ type: 'FETCH_SUCCESS', payload: posts });
```

```
    } catch (error) {
      dispatch({ type: 'FETCH_ERROR', payload: error.message });
    }
  }, []);


  useEffect(
    function () {
      fetchPosts();
    },
    [fetchPosts]
  );


  return [ httpState, fetchPosts ];
}
```

In this example, the **return** statement was changed. Instead of returning just **httpState**, **useFetch** now returns an array that contains the **httpState** object and a pointer to the **fetchPosts** function. Alternatively, **httpState** and **fetchPosts** could have been merged into an object (instead of an array).

In the **App** component, **useFetch** could now be used like this:

```
import BlogPosts from './components/BlogPosts';
import useFetch from './hooks/use-fetch';


function App() {
  const [{ data, isLoading, error }, fetchPosts] = useFetch(
    'https://jsonplaceholder.typicode.com/posts'
  );


  return (
    <>
      <header>
        <h1>Complex State Blog</h1>
        <button onClick={fetchPosts}>Load Posts</button>
      </header>
      {isLoading && <p>Loading...</p>}
      {error && <p>{error}</p>}
      {data && <BlogPosts posts={data} />}
    </>
```

```
  );
}

export default App;
```

The **App** component uses array and object destructuring combined to extract the returned values (and the values nested in the **httpState** object). A newly added **<button>** element is then used to trigger the **fetchPosts** function.

This example effectively shows how custom Hooks can lead to much leaner component functions by allowing for easy logic reuse, with or without state or side effects.

SUMMARY AND KEY TAKEAWAYS

- You can create custom Hooks to outsource and reuse logic that relies on other built-in or custom Hooks.

- Custom Hooks are regular JavaScript functions with names that start with **use**.

- Custom Hooks can call any other Hooks.

- Therefore, custom Hooks can, for example, manage state or perform side effects.

- All components can use custom Hooks by simply calling them like any other (built-in) Hooks.

- When multiple components use the same custom Hook, every component receives its own "instance" (i.e., its own state value, etc.).

- Inside of custom Hooks, you can accept any parameter values and return any values of your choice.

WHAT'S NEXT?

Custom Hooks are a key React feature since they help you to write leaner components and reuse (stateful) logic across them. Especially when building more complex React apps (consisting of dozens or even hundreds of components), custom Hooks can lead to tremendously more manageable code.

Custom Hooks are the last key React feature you must know about. Combined with components, props, state (via **useState()** or **useReducer()**), side effects, and all the other concepts covered in this and previous chapters, you now have everything you need to build production-ready React apps—or, to be precise, almost everything.

Most React apps don't just consist of one single page. Instead, at least on most websites, users should be able to switch between multiple pages. For example, an online shop has a list of products, product detail pages, a shopping cart page, and many other pages.

The next chapter will therefore explore how you can build such multipage apps with React.

TEST YOUR KNOWLEDGE!

Test your knowledge of the concepts covered in this chapter by answering the following questions. You can then compare your answers to examples that can be found at https://packt.link/sRKeZ:

1. What is the definition of a custom Hook?

2. Which special feature can be used inside a custom Hook?

3. What happens when multiple components use the same custom Hook?

4. How can custom Hooks be made more reusable?

APPLY WHAT YOU LEARNED

Apply your knowledge about custom Hooks.

ACTIVITY 11.1: BUILD A CUSTOM KEYBOARD INPUT HOOK

In this activity, your task is to refactor a provided component such that it's leaner and no longer contains any state or side-effect logic. Instead, you should create a custom Hook that contains that logic. This Hook could then potentially be used in other areas of the React application as well.

> **NOTE**
>
> You can find the starting code for this activity at https://packt.link/rdwd9. When downloading this code, you'll always download the entire repository. Make sure to then navigate to the subfolder with the starting code (`activities/practice-1/starting-code`, in this case) to use the right code snapshot.
>
> The provided project also uses many features covered in earlier chapters. Take your time to analyze it and understand the provided code. This is a great practice and allows you to see many key concepts in action.

Once you have downloaded the code and run **npm install** in the project folder to install all required dependencies, you can start the development server via **npm start**. As a result, upon visiting **localhost:3000**, you should see the following user interface:

Press a key!

Supported keys: s, c, p

Figure 11.3: The running starting project

To complete the activity, the solution steps are as follows:

1. Create a new custom Hook file (e.g., in the **src/hooks** folder) and create a Hook function in that file.

2. Move the side effect and state management logic into that new Hook function.

3. Make the custom Hook more reusable by accepting and using a parameter that controls which keys are allowed.

4. Return the state managed by the custom Hook.

5. Use the custom Hook and its returned value in the **App** component.

The user interface should be the same once you have completed the activity, but the code of the **App** component should change. After finishing the activity, **App** should contain only this code:

```
function App() {
  const pressedKey = useKeyEvent(['s', 'c', 'p']); // this is your Hook!

  let output = '';

  if (pressedKey === 's') {
    output = '😊';
  } else if (pressedKey === 'c') {
    output = '😎';
  } else if (pressedKey === 'p') {
    output = '🎉';
  }


  return (
```

```
  <main>
    <h1>Press a key!</h1>
    <p>
      Supported keys: <kbd>s</kbd>, <kbd>c</kbd>, <kbd>p</kbd>
    </p>
    <p id="output">{output}</p>
  </main>
 );
}
```

NOTE

The solution to this activity can be found on page 516.

12

MULTIPAGE APPS WITH REACT ROUTER

LEARNING OBJECTIVES

By the end of this chapter, you will be able to do the following:

- Build multipage single-page applications (and understand why this is not an oxymoron).

- Use the React Router package to load different React components for different URL paths.

- Create static and dynamic routes (and understand what routes are in the first place).

- Navigate the website user via both links and programmatic commands.

- Build nested page layouts.

INTRODUCTION

Having worked through the first eleven chapters of this book, you should now know how to build React components and web apps, as well as how to manage components and app-wide state, and how to share data between components (via props or context).

But even though you know how to compose a React website from multiple components, all these components are on the same single website page. Sure, you can display components and content conditionally, but users will never switch to a different page. This means that the URL path will never change; users will always stay on **your-domain.com**. Also, at this point in time, your React apps don't support any paths such as **your-domain.com/products** or **your-domain.com/blog/latest**.

> **NOTE**
>
> **Uniform Resource Locators** (**URLs**) are references to web resources. For example, https://academind.com/courses is a URL that points to a specific page of the author's website. In this example, **academind.com** is the **domain name** of the website and **/courses** is the **path** to a specific website page.

For React apps, it might make sense that the path of the loaded website never changes. After all, in *Chapter 1*, *React – What and Why*, you learned that you build **single-page applications** (**SPAs**) with React.

But even though it might make sense, it's also quite a serious limitation.

ONE PAGE IS NOT ENOUGH

Having just a single page means that complex websites that would typically consist of multiple pages (e.g., an online shop with pages for products, orders, and more) become quite difficult to build with React. Without multiple pages, you have to fall back to state and conditional values to display different content on the screen.

But without changing URL paths, your website visitors can't share links to anything but the starting page of your website. Also, any conditionally loaded content will be lost when a new visitor visits that starting page. That will also be the case if users simply reload the page they're currently on. A reload fetches a new version of the page, and so any state (and therefore user interface) changes are lost.

For these reasons, you absolutely need a way of including multiple pages (with different URL paths) in a single React app for most React websites. Thanks to modern browser features and a highly popular third-party package, that is indeed possible (and the default for most React apps).

Via the **React Router** package, your React app can listen to URL path changes and display different components for different paths. For example, you could define the following path-component mappings:

- **<domain>/** => **<Home />** component is loaded.
- **<domain>/products** => **<ProductList />** component is loaded.
- **<domain>/products/p1** => **<ProductDetail />** component is loaded.
- **<domain>/about** => **<AboutUs />** component is loaded.
- Technically, it's still an SPA because there's still only one HTML page being sent to website users. But in that single-page React app, different components are rendered conditionally by the React Router package based on the specific URL paths that are being visited. As the developer of the app, you don't have to manually manage this kind of state or render content conditionally. In addition, your website is able to handle different URL paths, and therefore, individual pages can be shared or reloaded.

GETTING STARTED WITH REACT ROUTER AND DEFINING ROUTES

React Router is a third-party React library that can be installed in any React project. Once installed, you can use various components in your code to enable the aforementioned features.

Inside your React project, the package is installed via this command:

```
npm install react-router-dom
```

Once installed, you can import and use various components (and Hooks) from that library.

To start supporting multiple pages in your React app, you need to set up **routing** by going through the following steps:

1. Create different components for your different pages (e.g., **Dashboard** and **Orders** components).

2. Use the **BrowserRouter**, **Routes**, and **Route** components from the React Router library to enable routing and define the **routes** that should be supported by the React app.

In this context, the term **routing** refers to the React app being able to load different components for different URL paths (e.g., different components for the **/** and **/orders** paths). A route is a definition that's added to the React app that defines the URL path for which a predefined JSX snippet should be rendered (e.g., the **Orders** component should be loaded for the **/orders** path).

In an example React app that contains **Dashboard** and **Orders** components, and wherein the React Router library was installed via **npm install**, you can enable routing and navigation between these two components by editing the **App** component (in **src/App.js**) like this:

```
import { BrowserRouter, Routes, Route } from 'react-router-dom';

import Dashboard from './routes/Dashboard';
import Orders from './routes/Orders';

function App() {
  return (
    <BrowserRouter>
      <Routes>
        <Route path="/" element={<Dashboard />} />
        <Route path="/orders" element={<Orders />} />
      </Routes>
    </BrowserRouter>
  );
}

export default App;
```

> **NOTE**
>
> You can find the complete example code on GitHub at https://packt.link/uX1mb.

In the preceding code snippet, three components are used from the **react-router-dom** package:

- **BrowserRouter**, which enables all routing-related features (e.g., it sets up a listener that detects and analyzes URL changes). This component must only be used once in the entire application (typically in your root component, such as the **App** component).

- **Routes**, which contains your route definitions. You can use this component multiple times to define multiple, independent groups of routes. Whenever the URL path changes, **Routes** checks whether any of its route definitions (via **Route**) matches that URL path and should therefore be activated.

- **Route**, which is used to define an individual route. The **path** prop is used to define the URL path that should activate this route. Only one route can be active per **Routes** group. Once activated, the content defined via the **elements** prop is rendered.

The placement of the **Routes** and **Route** components also defines where the conditional page content should be displayed. You can think of the **<Route />** element being replaced with the content defined via the **element** prop once the route becomes active. Therefore, the positioning of the **Route** components matter.

If you run the provided example React app (via **npm start**), you'll see the following output on the screen:

Figure 12.1: The Dashboard component content is loaded for localhost:3000

The content of the **Dashboard** component is displayed on the screen. Please note that this content is not defined in the **App** component (in the code snippet shared previously). Instead, there, only two route definitions were added: one for the **/** path (i.e., for `localhost.3000/`) and one for the **/orders** path (`localhost:3000/orders`).

> **NOTE**
>
> `localhost` is a local address that's typically used for development. When you deploy your React app (i.e., you upload it to a web server), you will receive a different domain—or assign a custom domain. Either way, it will not be `localhost` after deployment.
>
> The part after `localhost` (`:3000`) defines the network port to which the request will be sent. Without the additional port information, ports **80** or **443** (as the default HTTP(S) ports) are used automatically. During development, however, these are not the ports you want. Instead, you would typically use ports such as **3000**, **8000**, or **8080** as these are normally unoccupied by any other system processes and hence can be used safely. Projects created via **create-react-app** use port **3000**.

Since `localhost:3000` is loaded by default (when running **npm start**), the first route definition (`<Route path="/" element={<Dashboard />} />`) becomes active. This route is active because its path (`"/"`) matches the path of `localhost:3000` (since this is the same as `localhost:3000/`).

As a result, the JSX code defined via **element** is rendered on the screen. In this case, this means that the content of the **Dashboard** component is displayed because the **element** prop value of this route definition is `<Dashboard />`. It is quite common to use single components (such as `<Dashboard />`, in this example), but you could render any JSX content.

In the preceding example, no complex page is displayed. Instead, only some text shows up on the screen. This will change later in this chapter, though.

But it gets interesting if you manually change the URL from just `localhost:3000` to `localhost:3000/orders` in the browser address bar. In any of the previous chapters, this would not have changed the page content. But now, with routing enabled and the appropriate routes being defined, the page content does change, as shown:

The "Orders" component.

Figure 12.2: For /orders, the content of the Orders component is displayed

Once the URL changes, the content of the **Orders** component is displayed on the screen. It's again just some basic text in this first example, but it shows that different code is rendered for different URL paths.

However, this basic example has a major flaw (besides the quite boring page content). Right now, users must enter URLs manually. But, of course, that's not how you typically use websites.

ADDING PAGE NAVIGATION

To allow users to switch between different website pages without editing the browser address bar manually, websites normally contain links. A link is typically added via the **<a>** HTML element (the anchor element), like this:

```
<a href="/orders">All Orders</a>
```

For the previous example, on-page navigation could therefore be added by modifying the **App** component code like this:

```
import { BrowserRouter, Routes, Route } from 'react-router-dom';

import Dashboard from './routes/Dashboard';
import Orders from './routes/Orders';

function App() {
  return (
    <BrowserRouter>
    <nav>
     <ul>
       <li><a href="/">Home</a></li>
       <li><a href="/orders">All Orders</a></li>
   </ul>
    </nav>
      <Routes>
        <Route path="/" element={<Dashboard />} />
```

```
            <Route path="/orders" element={<Orders />} />
        </Routes>
    </BrowserRouter>
  );
}


export default App;
```

The **<nav>**, **<ul>**, and **<li>** elements are optional. It's just an approach for structuring the main navigation of a page in a semantically correct way. But with the two **<a>** elements added, website visitors see two navigation options that they can click to switch between pages:

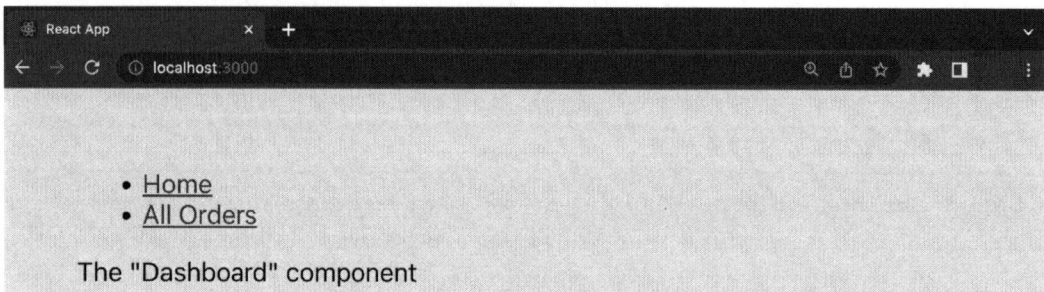

Figure 12.3: Two navigation links are presented to the user

Of course, you would typically add more CSS styling, but these two links allow users to navigate to either the **Dashboard** or **Orders** page (i.e., render the respective component).

> **NOTE**
>
> The code for this example can be found at https://packt.link/8H5yl.

This approach works but has a major flaw: the website is reloaded every time a user clicks one of those links. You can tell that it's reloaded because the browser's refresh icon changes to a cross (briefly) whenever you click a link.

This happens because the browser sends a new HTTP request to the server whenever a link is clicked. Even though the server always returns the same single HTML page, the page is reloaded during that process (because of the new HTTP request that was sent).

While that's not a problem on this simple demo page, it would be an issue if you had a state (e.g., an app-wide state managed via context) that should not be reset during a page change.

The following, slightly adjusted, example app illustrates this problem:

```
function App() {
  const [counter, setCounter] = useState(0);

  function incCounterHandler() {
    setCounter((prevCounter) => prevCounter + 1);
  }

  return (
    <BrowserRouter>
      <nav>
        <ul>
          <li>
            <a href="/">Home</a>
          </li>
          <li>
            <a href="/orders">All Orders</a>
          </li>
        </ul>
      </nav>
      <p>
        {counter} - <button onClick={incCounterHandler}>Increase</button>
      </p>
      <Routes>
        <Route path="/" element={<Dashboard />} />
        <Route path="/orders" element={<Orders />} />
      </Routes>
    </BrowserRouter>
  );
}
```

> **NOTE**
>
> The code for this example can be found at https://packt.link/ZZgPu.

In this example, a simple counter was added to the **App** component. Since the two route definitions (the **<Route />** elements) are inside the **App** component, that component should not be replaced when a user visits a different page.

At least, that's the theory. As you can see in the following screenshot, the **counter** state is lost whenever any link is clicked:

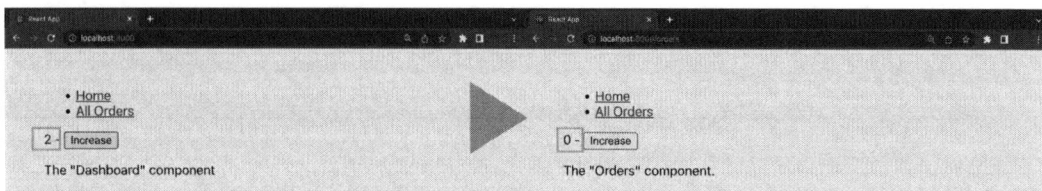

Figure 12.4: The counter state is reset when switching the page

In the screenshot, you can see that the counter is initially set to **2** (because the button was clicked twice). After navigating from **Dashboard** to the **Orders** page (via the appropriate navigation link), the counter changes to **0**.

That happens because the page is reloaded due to the HTTP request that's sent by the browser.

To work around this issue and avoid this unintended page reload, you must prevent the browser's default behavior. Instead of sending a new HTTP request, the browser should simply update the URL (from **localhost:3000** to **localhost:3000/orders**). The React Router library can then react to this URL change and update the screen as needed. Therefore, to the website user, it seems as if a different page was loaded. But behind the scenes, it's just the page document (the DOM) that was updated.

Thankfully, you don't have to implement the logic for this on your own. Instead, the React Router library exposes a special **Link** component that should be used for rendering links that behave as described previously.

To use this new component, the code in **src/App.js** must be adjusted like this:

```
import { useState } from 'react';
import { BrowserRouter, Routes, Route, Link } from 'react-router-dom';
```

```
import Dashboard from './routes/Dashboard';
import Orders from './routes/Orders';

function App() {
  const [counter, setCounter] = useState(0);

  function incCounterHandler() {
    setCounter((prevCounter) => prevCounter + 1);
  }

  return (
    <BrowserRouter>
      <nav>
        <ul>
          <li>
            <Link to="/">Home</Link>
          </li>
          <li>
            <Link to="/orders">All Orders</Link>
          </li>
        </ul>
      </nav>
      <p>
        {counter} - <button onClick={incCounterHandler}>Increase</button>
      </p>
      <Routes>
        <Route path="/" element={<Dashboard />} />
        <Route path="/orders" element={<Orders />} />
      </Routes>
    </BrowserRouter>
  );
}

export default App;
```

NOTE

The code for this example can be found at https://packt.link/kPXCL.

Inside the **\<li\>** elements, the new **Link** component is used. That component requires the **to** prop, which is used to define the URL path that should be loaded.

By using this component in place of the **\<a\>** anchor element, the counter state is no longer reset. This is because React Router now prevents the browser's default behavior (i.e., the unintended page reload described above) and displays the correct page content.

The **Link** component is therefore the default component that should be used for adding links to React websites. However, there are the following two exceptions:

- **External links**: Links that lead to external resources and websites

- **Navigation links**: Links that should (possibly) change their appearance upon route changes

External links are links that lead to any resource that's not one of your React app routes. For example, you could have a link that leads to a Wikipedia page. Since that's not part of your React app, the **Link** component is not the correct choice. Instead, you should use the **\<a\>** element for those kinds of links:

```
<a href="https://wikipedia.org">Look it up!</a>
```

But the second exception, navigation links, is worth a closer look.

FROM LINK TO NAVLINK

You can, in theory, always use the **Link** component for internal links. But you will sometimes have links on your page that should change their appearance (e.g., their color) when they lead to the currently active route. Links placed in the main navigation bar often need that behavior in order to reflect which page is active at the moment.

On many websites, the main navigation bar signals to the user which page they are currently on—simply by highlighting the navigation item that leads to the current page in the navigation bar.

Consider this code snippet, which is the example from previously without the state but with some extra styling and a **\<header\>** element (also only added for styling and semantic purposes):

```
import { BrowserRouter, Routes, Route, Link } from 'react-router-dom';


import Dashboard from './routes/Dashboard';
import Orders from './routes/Orders';
```

```
function App() {
  return (
    <BrowserRouter>
      <header>
        <nav>
          <ul>
            <li>
              <Link to="/">Dashboard</Link>
            </li>
            <li>
              <Link to="/orders">All Orders</Link>
            </li>
          </ul>
        </nav>
      </header>
      <Routes>
        <Route path="/" element={<Dashboard />} />
        <Route path="/orders" element={<Orders />} />
      </Routes>
    </BrowserRouter>
  );
}

export default App;
```

This code snippet does not yet have any new functionality or behavior. It just adds a more realistic-looking main navigation bar:

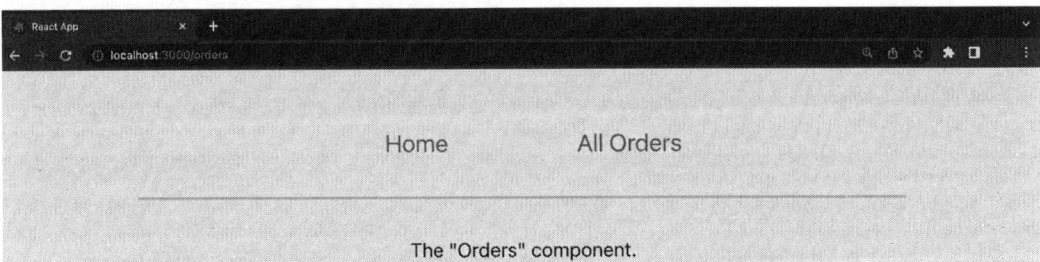

Figure 12.5: The styled navigation bar is above the main route content

In this screenshot, the navigation bar received some styling. It now looks more like a proper website.

But you might notice that it's not always immediately obvious which page the user is currently on. Sure, the dummy page content currently displays the page name (**"Orders"** or **"Dashboard"**), and the URL path also is **/orders** or **/**. But, when navigating a website, the most obvious clue users are accustomed to is a highlighted element in the main navigation bar.

To prove this point, compare the previous screenshot to the following one:

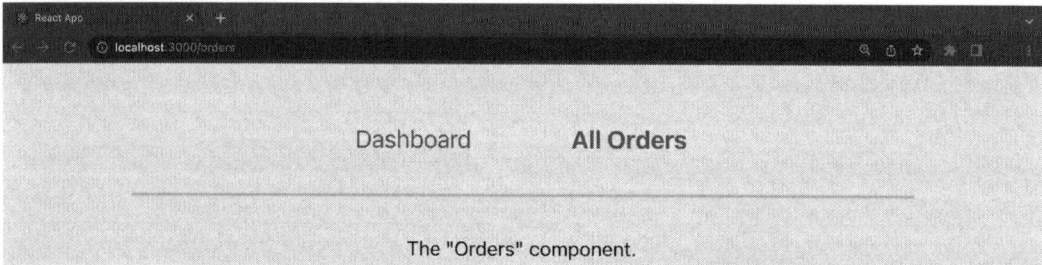

The "Orders" component.

Figure 12.6: The highlighted All Orders navigation link appears bold

In this version of the website, it's immediately clear that the user is on the **"Orders"** page since the **All Orders** navigation link is highlighted (in this case by making it bold). It's subtle things such as this that make websites more usable and can ultimately lead to higher user engagement.

But how can this be achieved?

To do this, you would not use the **Link** component but instead, a special alternative component, offered by **react-router-dom**: the **NavLink** component.

The **NavLink** component is used pretty much like the **Link** component. You wrap it around some text (the link's caption), and you define the target path via the **to** prop. But the **NavLink** component offers two special props:

- The **style** prop

- The **className** prop

To be precise, the **Link** component also supports **style** and **className**, which are standard HTML element props, after all. **Link** supports these props to allow developers to style the link elements.

But when using **NavLink**, **style** and **className** work slightly differently. Instead of requiring the standard **style** and **className** prop values (see *Chapter 6, Styling React Apps*), the two props now accept functions.

The function passed to either **style** or **className** automatically receives an argument (provided by the React Router library). This will be an object with a Boolean **isActive** property that indicates whether this link is leading to the currently active route.

This **isActive** value can then be used to conditionally return different **style** or **className** values based on the current state of the navigation link.

The adjusted **App.js** code that leads to the user interface shown in the previous screenshot looks like this:

```
import { BrowserRouter, Routes, Route, NavLink } from 'react-router-dom';

import Dashboard from './routes/Dashboard';
import Orders from './routes/Orders';

function App() {
  return (
    <BrowserRouter>
      <header>
        <nav>
          <ul>
            <li>
              <NavLink
                to="/"
                style={({ isActive }) =>
                  isActive ? { fontWeight: 'bold' } : undefined
                }
              >
                Dashboard
              </NavLink>
            </li>
            <li>
              <NavLink
                to="/orders"
                style={({ isActive }) =>
                  isActive ? { fontWeight: 'bold' } : undefined
                }
```

```
            >
                All Orders
            </NavLink>
          </li>
        </ul>
      </nav>
    </header>
    <Routes>
      <Route path="/" element={<Dashboard />} />
      <Route path="/orders" element={<Orders />} />
    </Routes>
  </BrowserRouter>
  );
}

export default App;
```

In this code snippet, the **NavLink** component replaces the **Link** component. The **style** prop is added to both **NavLink** components, and for both links, an arrow function is passed to **style** (though you can also use a normal function). The **isActive** property is extracted from the received object via object destructuring. In the function body, a ternary expression is used to either return a style value of **{ fontWeight: 'bold' }** or **undefined** (in which case no special styling is added).

> **NOTE**
>
> You can find the finished code for this example on GitHub at https://packt. link/FcM7A.

One important note is that **NavLink** will consider a route to be active if its path matches the current URL path *or* if its path starts with the current URL path. For example, if you had a **/blog/all-posts** route, a **NavLink** component that points at just **/blog** would be considered active if the current route is **/blog/all-posts** (because that route path starts with **/blog**). If you don't want this behavior, you can add the special **end** prop to the **NavLink** component, as follows:

```
<NavLink
  to="/blog"
  style={({ isActive }) => isActive ? { color: 'red' } : undefined}
```

```
  end>
    Blog
</NavLink>
```

With this special prop added, this NavLink would only be considered active if the current route is exactly **/blog—for /blog/all-posts**, the link would not be active.

NavLink is always the preferred choice when the styling of a link depends on the currently active route. For all other internal links, use **Link**. For external links, **<a>** is the element of choice.

ROUTE COMPONENTS VERSUS "NORMAL" COMPONENTS

It's worth mentioning and noting that, in the previous examples, the **Dashboard** and **Orders** components were regular React components. You could use these components anywhere in your React app—not just as values for the **element** prop of the **Route** component.

The two components are special in that both are stored in the **src/routes** folder in the project directory. They are not stored in the **src/components** folder, which was used for components throughout this book.

That's not something you have to do, though. Indeed, the folder names are entirely up to you. These two components could be stored in **src/components**. You could also store them in an **src/elements** folder. It really is up to you. But using **src/routes** is quite common for components that are exclusively used for routing. Popular alternatives are **src/screens**, **src/views**, and **src/pages** (again, it is up to you).

If your app includes any other components that are not used as routing elements, you would still store those in **src/components** (i.e., in a different path). This is not a hard rule or a technical requirement, but it does help with keeping your React projects manageable. Splitting your components across multiple folders makes it easier to quickly understand which components fulfill which purpose in the project.

In the example project mentioned previously, you can, for example, refactor the code such that the navigation code is stored in a separate component (e.g., a **MainNavigation** component, stored in **src/components/shared/MainNavigation.js**). The component code looks like this:

```
import { NavLink } from 'react-router-dom';

import classes from './MainNavigation.module.css';

function MainNavigation() {
  return (
    <header className={classes.header}>
      <nav>
        <ul className={classes.links}>
          <li>
            <NavLink
              to="/"
              className={({ isActive }) =>
                isActive ? classes.active : undefined
              }
              end
            >
              Dashboard
            </NavLink>
          </li>
          <li>
            <NavLink
              to="/orders"
              className={({ isActive }) =>
                isActive ? classes.active : undefined
              }
            >
              All Orders
            </NavLink>
          </li>
        </ul>
      </nav>
    </header>
```

```
  );
}
```

```
export default MainNavigation;
```

In this code snippet, the **NavLink** component is adjusted to assign a CSS class named **active** to any link that belongs to the currently active route. In general, CSS classes are added to various elements (with the help of CSS Modules, as discussed in *Chapter 6, Styling React Apps*). Besides that, it's essentially the same navigation menu code as that used earlier in this chapter.

This **MainNavigation** component can then be imported and used in the **App.js** file like this:

```
import { BrowserRouter, Routes, Route } from 'react-router-dom';

import MainNavigation from './components/shared/MainNavigation';
import Dashboard from './routes/Dashboard';
import Orders from './routes/Orders';

function App() {
  return (
    <BrowserRouter>
      <MainNavigation />
      <Routes>
        <Route path="/" element={<Dashboard />} />
        <Route path="/orders" element={<Orders />} />
      </Routes>
    </BrowserRouter>
  );
}
```

```
export default App;
```

Importing and using the **MainNavigation** component leads to a leaner **App** component and yet preserves the same functionality as before.

These changes show how you can combine routing, components that are only used for routing (**Dashboard** and **Orders**), and components that are used outside of routing (**MainNavigation**).

But you can also take it a step further. Semantically, it makes sense to wrap your route component content (i.e., the JSX code returned by **Dashboard** and **Orders**) with the **\<main\>** element. This default HTML element is commonly used to wrap the main content of the page.

Since both components would therefore wrap their returned values with **\<main\>**, you can create a separate **Layout** component that's wrapped around the entire block of route definitions (i.e., around the **Routes** component) and looks like this:

```
import MainNavigation from './MainNavigation';

function Layout({ children }) {
  return (
    <>
      <MainNavigation />
      <main>{children}</main>
    </>
  );
}

export default Layout;
```

This component uses the special **children** prop (see *Chapter 3, Components and Props*) to wrap the **\<main\>** element around whatever JSX content is placed between the **\<Layout\>** tags. In addition, it renders the **MainNavigation** component above the **\<main\>** element.

The **Layout** component (which could be stored in **src/components/shared/Layout.js**) can then be imported and used in **App.js**, as follows:

```
import { BrowserRouter, Routes, Route } from 'react-router-dom';

import Layout from './components/shared/Layout';
import Dashboard from './routes/Dashboard';
import Orders from './routes/Orders';

function App() {
  return (
    <BrowserRouter>
      <Layout>
        <Routes>
          <Route path="/" element={<Dashboard />} />
```

```
            <Route path="/orders" element={<Orders />} />
        </Routes>
    </Layout>
  </BrowserRouter>
  );
}

export default App;
```

<Layout> is wrapped around the **<Routes>** element, which contains the various route definitions. Therefore, no matter which route is active, its content is wrapped with the **<main>** element and **MainNavigation** is placed above it.

As a result, with some additional CSS styling added, the website looks like this:

Figure 12.7: Both route components share the same layout

It's essentially the same look as before, but it's now achieved via a leaner **App** component and by splitting application responsibilities (such as providing navigation, managing routes, etc.) into different components.

> **NOTE**
>
> You can find the finished code for this example on GitHub at https://packt.link/TkNsc.

But even with this split into multiple components, the demo application still suffers from an important problem: it only supports static, predefined routes. But, for most websites, those kinds of routes are not enough.

FROM STATIC TO DYNAMIC ROUTES

Thus far, all examples have had two routes: **/** for the **Dashboard** component and **/orders** for the **Orders** component. But you can, of course, add as many routes as needed. If your website consists of 20 different pages, you can (and should) add 20 route definitions (i.e., 20 **Route** components) to your **App** component.

On most websites, however, you will also have some routes that can't be defined manually—because not all routes are known in advance.

Consider the example from before, enriched with additional components and some realistic dummy data:

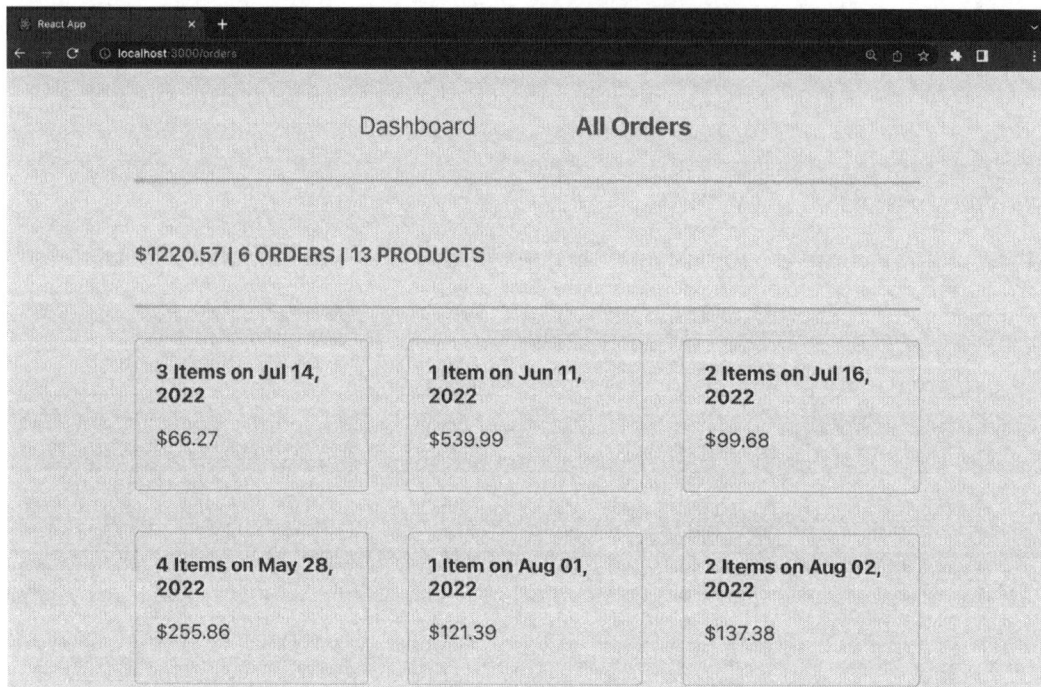

Figure 12.8: A list of order items

> **NOTE**
>
> You can find the code for this example on GitHub at https://packt.link/KcDA6. In the code, you'll notice that many new components and style files were added. The code does not use any new features, though. It's just used to display a more realistic user interface and output some dummy data.

In the preceding screenshot, *Figure 12.8*, you can see a list of order items being output on the **All Orders** page (i.e., by the **Orders** component).

In the underlying code, every order item is wrapped with a **Link** component so that a separate page with more details will be loaded for each item:

```
function OrdersList() {
  return (
    <ul className={classes.list}>
      {orders.map((order) => (
        <li key={order.id}>
          <Link to='/orders'><OrderItem order={order} /></Link>
        </li>
      ))}
    </ul>
  );
}
```

In this code snippet, the path for the **Link** component is set to **/orders**. However, that's not the final value that should be assigned. Instead, this example highlights an important problem: while it's the same component that should be loaded for every order item (i.e., some component that displays detailed data about the selected order), the exact content of the component depends on which order item was selected. It's the same component with different data.

Outside of routing, you would use props to reuse the same component with different data. But with routing, it's not just about the component. You also must support different paths—because the detailed data for different orders should be loaded via different paths. Otherwise, you would again end up with URLs that are not shareable or reloadable.

Therefore, the path must include not only some static identifier (such as **/orders**) but also a dynamic value that's different for every order item. For three order items with **id** values **o1**, **o2**, and **o3**, the goal could be to support the **/orders/o1**, **/orders/o2**, and **/order/o3** paths.

For this reason, the following three route definitions could be added:

```
<Route path="/orders/o1" element={ <OrderDetail id="o1" /> } />
<Route path="/orders/o2" element={ <OrderDetail id="o2" /> } />
<Route path="/orders/o3" element={ <OrderDetail id="o3" /> } />
```

But this solution has a major flaw. Adding all these routes manually is a huge amount of work. And that's not even the biggest problem. You typically don't even know all values in advance. In this example, when a new order is placed, a new route would have to be added. But you can't adjust the source code of your website every time a visitor places an order.

Clearly, then, a better solution is needed. React Router offers that better solution as it supports *dynamic routes*.

Dynamic routes are defined just like other routes, except that, when defining their **path** values, you will need to include one or more placeholder values with identifiers of your choice.

The **OrderDetail** route definition therefore looks like this:

```
<Route path="/orders/:id" element={ <OrderDetail /> } />
```

The following three key things have changed:

- It's just one route definition instead of a (possibly) infinite list of definitions.
- **path** contains a dynamic route segment (**:id**).
- **OrderDetail** no longer receives an **id** prop.

The **:id** syntax is a special syntax supported by React Router. Whenever a segment of a path starts with a colon, React Router treats it as a dynamic segment. That means that it will be replaced with a different value in the actual URL path. For the **/orders/:id** route path, the **/orders/o1**, **/orders/o2**, and **/orders/abc** paths would all match and therefore activate the route.

Of course, you don't have to use **:id**. You can use any identifier of your choice. For the preceding example, **:orderId**, **:order**, or **:oid** could also make sense.

The identifier will help your app to load the correct data inside the page component (inside **OrderDetail** in this case). That's why the **id** prop was removed from **OrderDetail**. Since only one route is defined, only one specific **id** value can be passed via props. That won't help. Therefore, a different way of loading order-specific data must be used.

EXTRACTING ROUTE PARAMETERS

In the previous example, when a website user visits **/orders/o1** or **/orders/o2** (or the same path for any other order ID), the **OrderDetail** component is loaded. This component should then output more information about the specific order that was selected (i.e., the order whose **id** is encoded in the URL path).

By the way, that's not just the case for this example; you can think of many other types of websites as well. You could also have, for example, an online shop with routes for products (**/products/p1**, **/products/p2**, etc.), or a travel blog where users can visit individual blog posts (**/blog/post1**, **/blog/post2**, etc.).

In all these cases, the question is, how do you get access to the data that should be loaded for the specific identifier (e.g., the ID) that's included in the URL path? Since it's always the same component that's loaded, you need a way of dynamically identifying the order, product, or blog post for which the detail data should be fetched.

One possible solution would be the usage of props. Whenever you build a component that should be reusable yet configurable and dynamic, you can use props to accept different values. For example, the **OrderDetail** component could accept an **id** prop and then, inside the component function body, load the data for that specific order ID.

However, as mentioned in the previous section, this is not a possible solution when loading the component via routing. Keep in mind that the **OrderDetail** component is created when defining the route:

```
<Route path="/orders/:id" element={ <OrderDetail />} />
```

Since the component is created when defining the route in the **App** component, you can't pass in any dynamic, ID-specific prop values.

Fortunately, though, that's not necessary. React Router gives you a solution that allows you to extract the data encoded in the URL path from inside the component that's displayed on the screen (when the route becomes active): the **useParams()** Hook.

This Hook can be used to get access to the route parameters of the currently active route. Route parameters are simply the dynamic values encoded in the URL path—**id**, in the case of this **OrderDetail** example.

Inside the **OrderDetail** component, **useParams()** can therefore be used to extract the specific order **id** and load the appropriate order data, as follows:

```
import { useParams } from 'react-router-dom';

import Details from '../components/orders/Details';
import { getOrderById } from '../data/orders';

function OrderDetail() {
  const params = useParams();
```

```
  const orderId = params.id; // in this example, orderId is "o1" or "o2"
etc.
  const order = getOrderById(orderId);


  return <Details order={order} />;
}


export default OrderDetail;
```

As you can see in this snippet, **useParams()** returns an object that contains all route parameters of the currently active route as properties. Since the route path was defined as **/orders/:id**, the **params** object contains an **id** property. The value of that property is then the actual value encoded in the URL path (e.g., **o1**). If you choose a different identifier name in the route definition (e.g., **/orders/:orderId** instead of **/orders/:id**), that property name must be used to access the value in the **params** object (i.e., access **params.orderId**).

> **NOTE**
>
> You find the complete code on GitHub at https://packt.link/YKmjL.

By using route parameters, you can thus easily create dynamic routes that lead to different data being loaded. But, of course, defining routes and handling route activation are not that helpful if you do not have links leading to the dynamic routes.

CREATING DYNAMIC LINKS

As mentioned earlier in this chapter (in the *Adding Page Navigation* section), website visitors should be able to click on links that should then take them to the different pages that make up the overall website—meaning, those links should activate the various routes defined with the help of React Router.

As explained in the *Adding Page Navigation* and *From Link to NavLink* sections, for internal links (i.e., links leading to routes defined inside the React app), the **Link** or **NavLink** components are used.

So, for static routes such as **/orders**, links are created like this:

```
<Link to="/orders">All Orders</Link> // or use <NavLink> instead
```

When building a link to a dynamic route such as **/orders/:id**, you can therefore simply create a link like this:

```
<Link to="/orders/o1">All Orders</Link>
```

This specific link loads the **OrderDetails** component for the order with the ID **o1**.

Building the link as follows would be incorrect:

```
<Link to="/orders/:id">All Orders</Link>
```

The dynamic path segment (**:id**) is only used when defining the route—not when creating a link. The link has to lead to a specific resource (a specific order, in this case).

But creating links to specific orders, as shown previously, is not very practical. Just as it wouldn't make sense to define all dynamic routes individually (see the *From Static to Dynamic Routes* section), it doesn't make sense to create the respective links manually.

Sticking to the orders example, there is also no need to create links like that as you already have a list of orders that's output on one page (the **Orders** component, in this case). Similarly, you could have a list of products in an online shop. In all these cases, the individual items (orders, products, etc.) should be clickable and lead to details pages with more information.

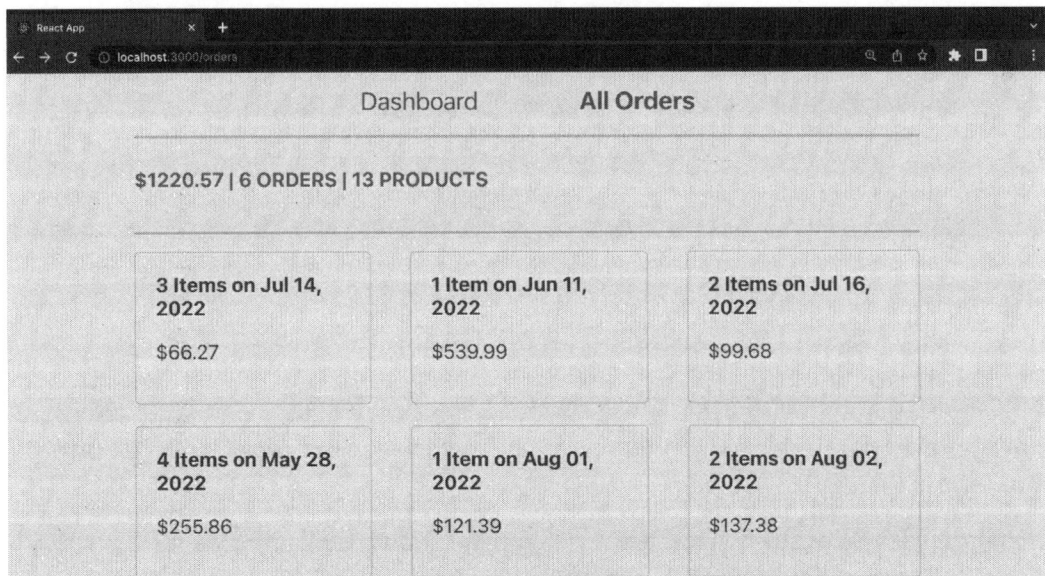

Figure 12.9: A list of clickable order items

Therefore, the links can be generated dynamically when rendering the list of JSX elements. In the case of the orders example, the code looks like this:

```
function OrdersList() {
  return (
    <ul className={classes.list}>
      {orders.map((order) => (
        <li key={order.id}>
          <Link to={`/orders/${order.id}`}><OrderItem order={order} /></Link>
        </li>
      ))}
    </ul>
  );
}
```

In this code example, the value of the **to** prop is set equal to a string that includes the dynamic **order.id** value. Therefore, every list item receives a unique link that leads to a different details page. Or, to be precise, the link always leads to the same component but with a different order **id** value, hence loading different order data.

> **NOTE**
>
> In this code snippet (which can be found at https://packt.link/iDObH, the string is created as a **template literal**. That's a default JavaScript feature that simplifies the creation of strings that include dynamic values.
>
> You can learn more about template literals on MDN at https://developer.mozilla.org/en-US/docs/Web/JavaScript/Reference/Template_literals.

NAVIGATING PROGRAMMATICALLY

In the previous section, as well as earlier in this chapter, user navigation was enabled by adding links to the website. Indeed, links are the default way of adding navigation to a website. But there are scenarios where programmatic navigation is required instead.

Programmatic navigation means that a new page should be loaded via JavaScript code (rather than using a link). This kind of navigation is typically required if the active page changes in response to some action—e.g., upon form submission.

If you take the example of form submission, you will normally want to extract and save the submitted data. But thereafter, the user will sometimes need to be redirected to a different page. For example, it makes no sense to keep the user on a **Checkout** page after processing the entered credit card details. You might want to redirect the user to a **Success** page instead.

In the example discussed throughout this chapter, the **All Orders** page could include an input field that allows users to directly enter an order **id** and load the respective orders data after clicking the **Find** button.

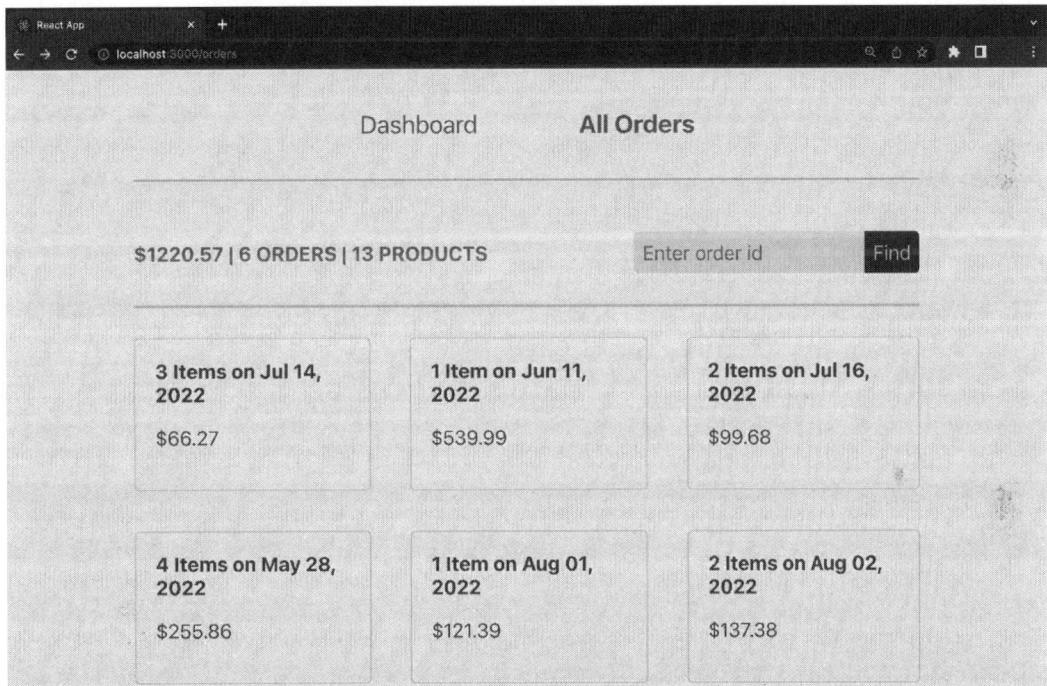

Figure 12.10: An input field that can be used to quickly load a specific order

In this example, the entered order **id** is first processed and validated before the user is sent to the respective details page. If the provided **id** is invalid, an error message is shown instead. The code looks like this:

```
function OrdersSummary() {
  const orderIdInputRef = useRef();


  const { quantity, total } = getOrdersSummaryData();


  function findOrderHandler(event) {
    event.preventDefault();
```

```
      const orderId = orderIdInputRef.current.value;
      const orderExists = orders.some((order) => order.id === orderId);

      if (!orderExists) {
        alert('Could not find an order for the entered id.');
        return;
      }
      // should navigate the user here
    }

    return (
      <div className={classes.row}>
        <p className={classes.summary}>
          ${total.toFixed(2)} | {orders.length} Orders | {quantity}
Products
        </p>
        <form className={classes.form} onSubmit={findOrderHandler}>
          <input
            type="text"
            placeholder="Enter order id"
            aria-label="Find an order by id."
            ref={orderIdInputRef}
          />
          <button>Find</button>
        </form>
      </div>
    );
  }
```

The code snippet does not yet include the code that will actually trigger the page change, but it does show how the user input is read and validated.

Therefore, this is a perfect scenario for the use of programmatic navigation. A link can't be used here since it would immediately trigger a page change—without allowing you to validate the user input first (at least not after the link was clicked).

The React Router library also supports programmatic navigation for cases like this. You can import and use the special **useNavigate()** Hook to gain access to a navigation function that can be used to trigger a navigation action (i.e., a page change):

```
import { useNavigate } from 'react-router-dom';


const navigate = useNavigate();
navigate('/orders'); // programmatic alternative to <Link to="/orders">
```

Hence, the **OrdersSummary** component from previously can be adjusted like this to use this new Hook:

```
function OrdersSummary() {
  const orderIdInputRef = useRef();
  const navigate = useNavigate();

  const { quantity, total } = getOrdersSummaryData();

  function findOrderHandler(event) {
    event.preventDefault();
    const orderId = orderIdInputRef.current.value;
    const orderExists = orders.some((order) => order.id === orderId);

    if (!orderExists) {
      alert('Could not find an order for the entered id.');
      return;
    }

    navigate(`/orders/${orderId}`);
  }

  // returned JSX code did not change, hence omitted
}
```

It's worth noting that the value passed to **navigate()** is a dynamically constructed string. Programmatic navigation supports both static and dynamic paths.

> **NOTE**
>
> The code for this example can be found at https://packt.link/9cdSZ.

No matter whether you need link-based or programmatic navigation, the two approaches also support another important feature: redirecting users.

REDIRECTING

Thus far, all the explored navigation options (links and programmatic navigation) forward a user to a specific page.

In most cases, that's the intended behavior. But in some cases, the goal is to redirect a user instead of forwarding them.

The difference is subtle but important. When a user is forwarded, they can use the browser's navigation buttons (**Back** and **Forward**) to go back to the previous page or forward to the page they came from. For redirects, that's not possible. Whenever a user is redirected to a specific page (rather than forwarded), they can't use the **Back** button to return to the previous page.

Redirecting users can, for example, be useful for ensuring that users can't go back to a login page after authenticating successfully.

When using React Router, the default behavior is to forward users. But you can easily switch to redirecting by adding the special **replace** prop to the **Link** (or **NavLink**) components, as follows:

```
<Link to="/success" replace>Confirm Checkout</Link>
```

When using programmatic navigation, you can pass a second, optional argument to the **navigate()** function. That second parameter value must be an object that can contain a **replace** property that should be set to **true**, if you want to redirect users:

```
navigate('/dashboard', { replace: true });
```

Being able to redirect or forward users allows you to build highly user-friendly web applications that offer the best possible user experience for different scenarios.

NESTED ROUTES

Another core feature offered by React Router that has not yet been covered is its support for nested routes.

Nested routes are routes that are descendants of other routes. Just as you can build a tree of components, you can also build a tree of route definitions. Though, typically, you don't need very deep levels of route nesting.

This feature can be tricky to understand at first, however, so consider the following example **App** component:

```
function App() {
  return (
    <BrowserRouter>
      <Layout>
        <Routes>
          <Route path="/" element={<Dashboard />} />
          <Route path="/orders" element={<OrdersRoot />}>
            <Route element={<Orders />} index />
            <Route path=":id" element={<OrderDetail />} />
          </Route>
        </Routes>
      </Layout>
    </BrowserRouter>
  );
}
```

> **NOTE**
>
> You can find the complete code on GitHub at https://packt.link/PKFAv.

As you can see in this example, the route definition for the **/orders** route contains two child route definitions:

- **<Route element={<Orders />} index />**

- **<Route path=":id" element={<OrderDetail />} />**

The first interesting thing about these two route definitions is that they are children of another route definition (that is, another **Route** component). Thus far, all route definitions were only direct children of **Routes** (and therefore siblings to each other).

Besides being nested inside another route definition, these two route definitions also have some strange props. The second nested route has a path of **":id"** instead of **"/:id"**, and the first nested route has no path at all but a special **index** prop instead.

The **index** prop will be explained further shortly.

Regarding the paths, paths starting with a slash (/) are absolute paths. They're always appended directly after the domain name. On the other hand, paths that do not start with a slash are relative paths; they are appended after the currently active path. Hence, the nested :id path yields an overall path of /orders/:id if activated, while the /orders route is active. This switch from absolute to relative paths is needed when building nested routes because the inner routes will actually be connected to the outer route.

But what's the idea behind nested routes?

You might notice that the parent route of the two nested routes will render an <OrdersRoot /> element when activated (due to its **element** prop value). So, whenever a user visits /orders, that component gets rendered.

But it's actually not just that component that will be rendered. The first nested component (which displays <Orders />) will also be displayed because of its **index** prop. The **index** prop "tells" React Router that this route should also be active if its parent route is displayed and no other nested route was activated.

The idea of nested routes is that multiple routes can be active simultaneously to render a hierarchical component structure. In the preceding example, when a user visits /orders, both the **OrdersRoot** and **Orders** components would be rendered. For /orders/o1, **OrdersRoot** and **OrderDetail** would be shown on the screen.

But these components would not only show up on the screen at the same time (as they would were they simply rendered as siblings), but are also nested into each other. The final structure for /orders/o1 would be similar to the following component composition:

```
<App>
  <OrdersRoot>
    <OrderDetail />
  </OrdersRoot>
</App>
```

But this still doesn't explain why you might want to use nested routes. What's the advantage of producing such nested component structures via routing?

It can be helpful if multiple routes have some shared user interface.

For example, both the **OrderDetail** and **Orders** components might need to display the order search input field like this:

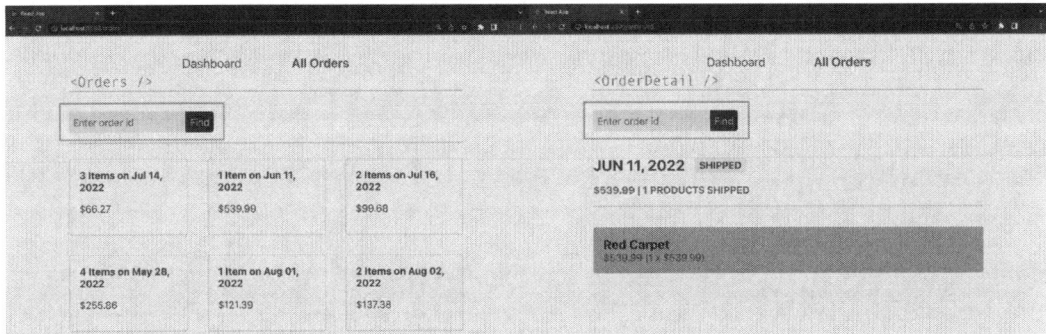

Figure 12.11: Both components have a shared order-specific user interface element

In this screenshot, the **Orders** and **OrderDetail** components share the order search input. But this input is not part of the overall layout (that is, the one stored in the **Layout** component, which is wrapped around the entire set of route definitions). It's not included in the general page layout because it should not affect all routes— only the order-specific ones. For example, the **/** route (the dashboard route) should not display this order ID search field.

Thanks to nested routes, this can be achieved. This piece of the user interface can be shared by including it in the **OrdersRoot** component. Since that's the component loaded for the parent route of the two nested routes, it and its content will be included for both child routes.

The code for the **OrdersRoot** component looks like this:

```
import { Outlet } from 'react-router-dom';
import OrderSearch from '../components/orders/OrderSearch';

function OrdersRoot() {
  return (
    <>
      <OrderSearch />
      <Outlet />
    </>
  );
}
```

It's quite a simple component, but it does include that shared **OrderSearch** component (which renders and controls the search input field you see in the preceding screenshot).

However, the **OrdersRoot** component also renders another interesting component: the **Outlet** component.

Outlet is a special component provided by React Router. After importing it from **react-router-dom**, it can be used to denote the location where child route components should be rendered.

React Router does not guess where to render any child routes you might have defined. Instead, you have to "tell" it by adding the **<Outlet />** element in exactly that location where React Router should create and display the child route elements. For the preceding example, **Orders** and **OrderDetail** (which are the child route components) are therefore rendered into this place.

Nested routes are a feature that's not necessarily needed all the time. But they can be very useful for building more complex user interfaces where certain elements should be shared among different routes. Especially if components must be shared across some but not all routes, nested routes can be a great solution that's easy to implement. On the other hand, if some component is needed on all pages (e.g., the main navigation bar), creating a **Layout** component that wraps all route definitions might be more feasible. That said, if you prefer to, you could also use nested routes in that case.

HANDLING UNDEFINED ROUTES

Previous sections in this chapter have all assumed that you have predefined routes that should be reachable by website visitors. But what if a visitor enters a URL that's simply not supported?

For example, the demo website used throughout this chapter supports the **/**, **/orders**, and **/orders/<some-id>** paths. But it does not support **/home**, **/products/p1**, **/abc**, or any other path that's not one of the defined route paths.

To show a custom *"Not Found"* page, you can define a **"Catch All"** route with a special path—the ***** path:

```
<Route path="*" element={ <NotFound /> } />
```

When adding this route to the list of route definitions in the **App** component, the **NotFound** component will be displayed on the screen when no other route matches the entered or generated URL path.

LAZY LOADING

In *Chapter 9, Behind the Scenes of React and Optimization Opportunities*, you learned about lazy loading—a technique that can be used to load certain pieces of the React application code only when needed.

Code splitting makes a lot of sense if some components will be loaded conditionally and may not be needed at all. Hence, routing is a perfect scenario for lazy loading. When applications have multiple routes, some routes may never be visited by a user. Even if all routes are visited, not all the code for all app routes (i.e., for their components) must be downloaded right at the start of the application. Instead, it makes sense to only download code for individual routes when they actually become active.

Thankfully, lazy loading with routing works just as explained in *Chapter 9*; you use React's **lazy()** function, the dynamic **import()** function, and React's **Suspense** component to split your code into multiple bundles.

Since the goal is to split code by route, all these features are used in the place where your route definitions are. In most cases, that will be the **App** component.

For the example application discussed throughout this chapter, lazy loading is implemented like this:

```
import { lazy, Suspense } from 'react';
import { BrowserRouter, Routes, Route } from 'react-router-dom';


import Layout from './components/shared/Layout';
import Dashboard from './routes/Dashboard';

const OrdersRoot = lazy(() => import('./routes/OrdersRoot'));
const Orders = lazy(() => import('./routes/Orders'));
const OrderDetail = lazy(() => import('./routes/OrderDetail'));

function App() {
  return (
    <BrowserRouter>
      <Layout>
        <Suspense fallback={<p>Loading...</p>}>
          <Routes>
            <Route path="/" element={<Dashboard />} />
            <Route path="/orders" element={<OrdersRoot />}>
              <Route element={<Orders />} index />
```

```
                <Route path=":id" element={<OrderDetail />} />
            </Route>
        </Routes>
    </Suspense>
    </Layout>
  </BrowserRouter>
 );
}

export default App;
```

In this code example, **lazy** and **Suspense** are imported from React. The **OrdersRoot**, **Orders**, and **OrderDetail** components are no longer directly imported but are instead created via the **lazy()** function, which uses the dynamic **import()** function to dynamically load the component code when needed.

> **NOTE**
>
> The code for this example can be found at https://packt.link/NIfVW.

Finally, the route definitions are wrapped with the **Suspense** component so that React can show some fallback content (**<p>Loading...</p>**, in this case) if downloading the code takes a bit longer.

As explained in *Chapter 9*, *Behind the Scenes of React and Optimization Opportunities*, adding lazy loading can improve your React application's performance considerably. You should always consider using lazy loading, but you should not use it for every route. It would be especially illogical for routes that are guaranteed to be loaded early, for instance. In the previous example, it would not make too much sense to lazy load the **Dashboard** component since that's the default route (with a path of **/**).

But routes that are not guaranteed to be visited at all (or at least not immediately after the website is loaded) are great candidates for lazy loading.

SUMMARY AND KEY TAKEAWAYS

- Routing is a key feature for many React apps.

- With routing, users can visit multiple pages despite being on an **SPA**.

- The most common package that helps with routing is the React Router library (**react-router-dom**).

- Routes are defined with the help of the **Routes** and **Route** components (typically in the **App** component, but you can do it anywhere).

- The **Route** component takes a **path** (for which the route should become active) and an **element** (the content that should be displayed) prop.

- Users can navigate between routes by manually changing the URL path, by clicking links or because of programmatic navigation.

- Internal links (i.e., links leading to application routes defined by you) should be created via the **Link** or **NavLink** components, while links to external resources use the standard **<a>** element.

- Programmatic navigation is triggered via the **navigate()** function, which is yielded by the **useNavigate()** Hook.

- You can define static and dynamic routes: static routes are the default, while dynamic routes are routes where the path (in the route definition) contains a dynamic segment (denoted by a colon, e.g., **:id**).

- The actual values for dynamic path segments can be extracted via the **useParams()** Hook.

- React Router also supports nested routes, which helps with sharing user interface elements between routes.

- You can use lazy loading to load route-specific code only when the route is actually visited by the user.

WHAT'S NEXT?

Routing is a feature that's not supported by React out of the box but still matters for most React applications. That's why it's included in this book and why the React Router library exists. Routing is a crucial concept that completes your knowledge about the most essential React ideas and concepts, allowing you to build both simple and complex React applications.

This chapter also concludes the list of core React features you must know as a React developer. Of course, you can always dive deeper to explore more patterns and third-party libraries. The next (and last) chapter will share some resources and possible next steps you could dive into after finishing this book.

TEST YOUR KNOWLEDGE!

Test your knowledge of the concepts covered in this chapter by answering the following questions. You can then compare your answers to the examples that can be found at https://packt.link/xQKlJ:

1. How is routing different from loading content conditionally?

2. What's the purpose of the **Routes** and **Route** components?

3. How should you add links to different routes to your pages?

4. How can dynamic routes (e.g., details for one of many products) be added to your app?

5. How can dynamic route parameter values be extracted (e.g., to load product data)?

6. What's the purpose of nested routes?

APPLY WHAT YOU LEARNED

Apply your knowledge about routing to the following activities.

ACTIVITY 12.1: CREATING A BASIC THREE-PAGE WEBSITE

In this activity, your task is to create a basic first version for a brand-new online shop website. The website must support three main pages:

- A welcome page

- A products overview page that shows a list of available products

- A product details page, which allows users to explore product details

Final website styling, content, and data will be added by other teams, but you should provide some dummy data and default styling. You must also add a main navigation bar at the top of each website page.

The finished pages should look like this:

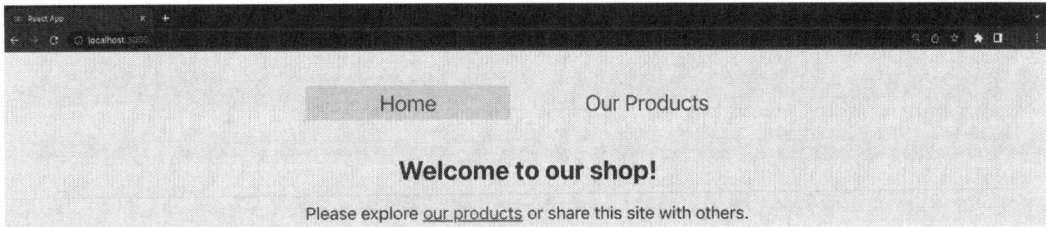

Figure 12.12: The final welcome page

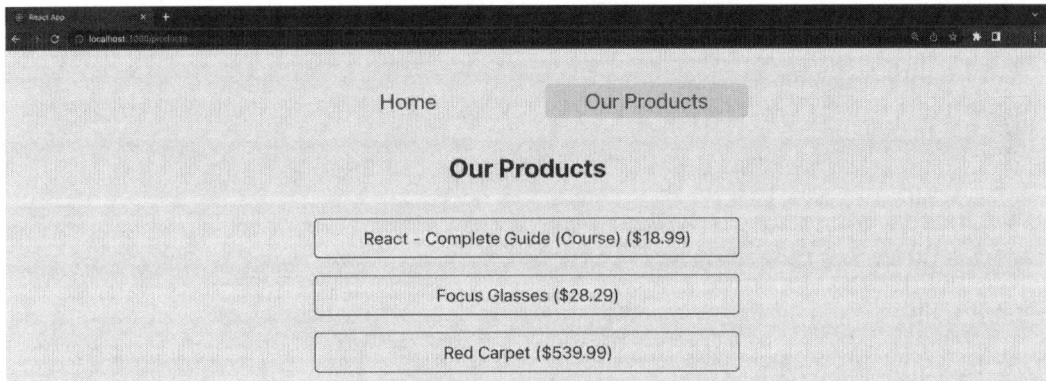

Figure 12.13: The final products page

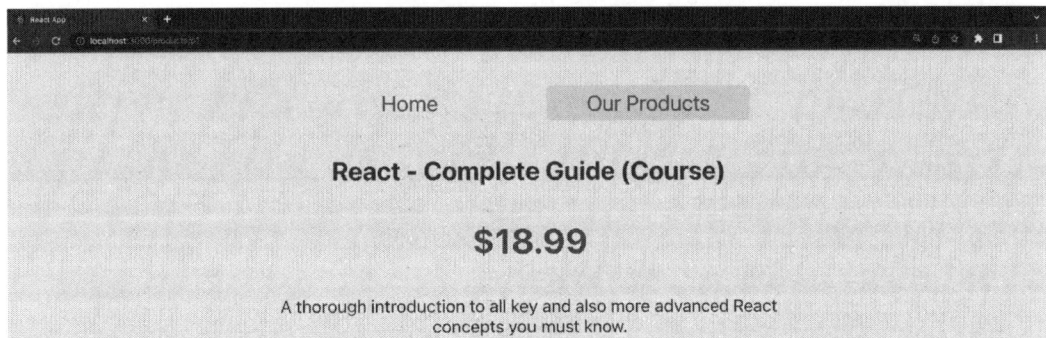

Figure 12.14: The final product details page

> **NOTE**
>
> For this activity, you can, of course, write all CSS styles on your own. But if you want to focus on the React and JavaScript logic, you can also use the finished CSS file from the solution at https://packt.link/Am59v.
>
> If you use that file, explore it carefully to ensure you understand which IDs or CSS classes might need to be added to certain JSX elements of your solution. You can also use the solution's dummy data instead of creating your own dummy product data. You will find the data for this at https://packt.link/xLCx1.

To complete the activity, the solution steps are as follows:

1. Create a new React project and install the React Router package.

2. Create components (with the content shown in the preceding screenshot) that will be loaded for the three required pages.

3. Enable routing and add the route definitions for the three pages.

4. Add a main navigation bar that's visible for all pages.

5. Add all required links and ensure that the navigation bar links reflect whether or not a page is active.

> **NOTE**
>
> The solution to this activity can be found on page 520.

ACTIVITY 12.2: ENHANCING THE BASIC WEBSITE

In this activity, your task is to enhance the basic website you built in the previous activity. In addition to all the features added there, this website should also use a main layout that wraps all pages. Your job is to implement this layout with the help of a feature provided by React Router.

You must also improve the initial loading time of the website by conditionally loading code that's not needed immediately once it is required.

Last but not least, you have been asked to implement a *"Not Found"* page that should be displayed for all URL paths that are not supported by the website.

> **NOTE**
>
> If you skipped the previous activity or need a refresher, you can use the solution provided for it as a starting point for this activity. You will find this in the GitHub repository at http://packt.link/wPcgN.

The *"Not Found"* page should look like this:

Figure 12.15: The final "Not Found" page

To complete the activity, the solution steps are as follows:

1. Create a new layout component (which includes the main navigation) and use it with the help of React Router's nested routes feature.

2. Add code splitting to the website and load all routes, for which it makes sense, lazily.

3. Add a new Not Found page component to the website. Also, add the respective route definition and consider loading it lazily.

> **NOTE**
>
> The solution to this activity can be found on page 528.

13

MANAGING DATA WITH REACT ROUTER

LEARNING OBJECTIVES

By the end of this chapter, you will be able to do the following:

- Use React Router to fetch or send data without using `useEffect()` or `useState()`

- Share data between different routes without using React's context feature

- Update the UI based on the current data submission status

- Create page and action routes

- Improve the user experience by deferring the loading of non-critical data

INTRODUCTION

In the preceding chapter, you learned how to use React Router to load different components for different URL paths. This is an important feature as it allows you to build multipage websites while still using React.

Routing is a crucial feature for many web applications, and React Router is therefore a very important package. But just as most websites need routing, almost all websites need to fetch and manipulate data. For example, HTTP requests in most websites are sent to load data (such as a list of products or blog posts) or to mutate data (for example, to create a product or a blog post).

In *Chapter 8*, *Handling Side Effects*, you learned that you can use the `useEffect()` Hook and various other React features to send HTTP requests from inside a React application. But if you're using React Router (specifically, version 6.4. or higher), you get some new, even more powerful tools for working with data.

This chapter will explore which new features are added by React Router 6.4 and how they may be used to simplify the process of fetching or sending data.

DATA FETCHING AND ROUTING ARE TIGHTLY COUPLED

As mentioned previously, most websites do need to fetch (or send) data and most websites do need more than one page. But it's important to realize that these two concepts are typically closely related.

Whenever a user visits a new page (such as `/posts`), it's likely that some data will need to be fetched. In the case of a `/posts` page, the required data is probably a list of blog posts that is retrieved from a backend server. The rendered React component (such as `Posts`) must therefore send an HTTP request to the backend server, wait for the response, handle the response (as well as potential errors) and, ultimately, display the fetched data.

Of course, not all pages need to fetch data. Landing pages, "About Us" pages, or "Terms & Use" pages probably don't need to fetch data when a user visits them. Instead, data on those pages is likely to be static. It might even be included in the source code as it doesn't change frequently.

But many pages do need to get data from a backend every time they're loaded—for instance, "Products", "News", "Events" pages, or other infrequently updated pages like the "User Profile".

And data fetching isn't everything. Most websites also contain features that require data submission—be it a blog post that can be created or updated, product data that's administered, or a user comment that can be added. Hence, sending data to a backend is also a very common use case.

And beyond requests, components might also need to interact with other browser APIs, such as `localStorage`. For example, user settings might need to be fetched from storage as a certain page loads.

Naturally, all these interactions happen on pages. But it might not be immediately obvious how tightly data fetching and submission are coupled to routing.

Most of the time, data is fetched when a route becomes active, i.e., when a component (the page component) is rendered for the first time. Sure, users might also be able to click a button to refresh the data, but while this is optional, data fetching upon initial page load is almost always required.

And when it comes to sending data, there is also a close connection to routing. At first sight, it's not clear how it's related because, while it makes sense to fetch data upon page load, it's less likely that you will need to send some data immediately (except perhaps tracking or analytics data).

But it's very likely that *after* sending data, you will want to navigate to a different page, meaning that it's actually the other way around and instead of initiating data fetching as a page loads, you want to load a different page after sending some data. For example, after an administrator entered some product data and submitted the form, they should typically be redirected to a different page (for example, from **/products/new** to the **/products** page).

The connection between data fetching, submission, and routing can therefore be summarized by the following points:

- **Data fetching** often should be initiated when a route becomes active (if that page needs data)
- After **submitting data** the user should often be redirected to another route

Because these concepts are tightly coupled, React Router (since version 6.4) provides extra features that vastly simplify the process of working with data.

SENDING HTTP REQUESTS WITHOUT REACT ROUTER

Working with data is not just about sending HTTP requests. As mentioned in the previous section, you may also need to store or retrieve data via **localStorage** or perform some other operation as a page gets loaded. But sending HTTP requests is an especially common scenario and will therefore be the main use case considered for the majority of this chapter. Nonetheless, it's vital to keep in mind that what you learn in this chapter is not limited to sending HTTP requests.

As you will learn in this chapter, React Router (6.4 or higher) provides various features that help with sending HTTP requests (or using other data fetching and manipulation APIs) and routing, but you can also send HTTP requests (or interact with **localStorage** or other APIs) without these features. Indeed, *Chapter 8, Handling Side Effects*, already taught you how HTTP requests can be sent from inside React components.

The following snippet exemplifies how a given list of blog posts could be fetched and displayed:

```
import { useState, useEffect } from 'react';

function Posts() {
  const [loadedPosts, setLoadedPosts] = useState();
  const [isLoading, setIsLoading] = useState(false);
  const [error, setError] = useState();

  useEffect(() => {
    async function fetchPosts() {
      setIsLoading(true);

      try {
        const response = await fetch(
          'https://jsonplaceholder.typicode.com/posts'
        );

        if (!response.ok) {
          throw new Error('Fetching posts failed.');
        }

        const resData = await response.json();
        setLoadedPosts(resData);
      } catch (error) {
```

```
        setError(error.message);
      }

      setIsLoading(false);
    }

  fetchPosts();
}, []);

let content = <p>No posts found.</p>;

if (isLoading) {
  content = <p>Loading...</p>;
}

if (error) {
  content = <p>{error}</p>;
}

if (loadedPosts) {
  content = (
    <ul className="posts">
      {loadedPosts.map((post) => (
        <li key={post.id}>{post.title}</li>
      ))}
    </ul>
  );
}

return (
  <main>
    <h1>Your Posts</h1>
    {content}
  </main>
);
}
```

This example component uses the same dummy backend server (returning dummy data) that was used in *Chapter 8, Handling Side Effects*: `https://jsonplaceholder.typicode.com`.

> **NOTE**
>
> You can find the complete code on GitHub at https://packt.link/hlXz6.

This backend returns a list of blog posts, which are then displayed as list items by the **Posts** component. However, these items are only displayed If the following statements are **true**:

- The HTTP request is done (i.e., **isLoading** is **false**)

- There is no error (i.e., **error** is **undefined** or **null**)

The request is sent via **useEffect()**. The **fetchPosts()** function defined in **useEffect()** is called when the component renders for the first time. That's the case because **useEffect()** has an empty list of dependencies. It therefore only executes once.

This example contains no new concepts. Instead, all these topics (and a very similar example) were covered in *Chapter 8, Handling Side Effects*. But even though it's a relatively basic example, where only one request is sent and the response data can be used without any further transformations, quite a bit of code is required to implement this functionality.

And that's where React Router (6.4. or higher) comes in.

LOADING DATA WITH REACT ROUTER

With React Router, the example from the previous chapter can be simplified down to this code snippet:

```
import { useLoaderData } from 'react-router-dom';

function Posts() {
  const loadedPosts = useLoaderData();

  return (
    <main>
      <h1>Your Posts</h1>
```

```
    <ul className="posts">
      {loadedPosts.map((post) => (
        <li key={post.id}>{post.title}</li>
      ))}
    </ul>
  </main>
  );
}


export default Posts;


export async function loader() {
  const response = await fetch('https://jsonplaceholder.typicode.com/
posts');
  if (!response.ok) {
    throw new Error('Could not fetch posts');
  }
  return response;
}
```

Believe it or not, it really *is* that much less code than in the previous example. Though, to be fair, the content that should be displayed in case of an error is missing here. It's in a separate file (which will be shown later), but it would only add three extra lines of code.

> **NOTE**
>
> Don't try pasting the preceding example into an existing React app—even if that app has React Router 6.4 installed. A special route definition syntax (introduced later in this chapter) is required to enable these new React Router features.

In the preceding code snippet, you see a couple of new features that haven't been covered yet in the book. The **loader()** function and the **useLoaderData()** Hook are added by React Router. These features, along with many others that will be explored throughout this chapter, have been available since version 6.4 of the React Router package.

With that version (or a more recent one) installed, you can set an extra **loader** prop on your route definitions. This prop accepts a function that will be executed by React Router whenever this route is activated:

```
<Route path="/posts" element={<Posts />} loader={() => {...}} />
```

This function can be used to perform any data fetching or other tasks required to successfully display the page component. The logic for getting that required data can therefore be extracted from the component and moved into a separate function.

Since many websites have dozens or even hundreds of routes, adding these loader functions inline on the **<Route />** element can quickly lead to complex and confusing route definitions. For this reason, you will typically add (and export) the **loader()** function in the same file that contains the component that needs the data.

When setting up the route definitions, you can then import the component and its loader function and use it like this:

```
import Posts, { loader as postsLoader } from './components/Posts';

// ... other code ...

<Route path="/posts" element={<Posts />} loader={postsLoader} />
```

Assigning an alias (**postsLoader**, in this example) to the imported loader function is optional but recommended since you most likely have multiple loader functions from different components, which would otherwise lead to name clashes.

With this **loader** defined, React Router will execute the **loader()** function whenever a route is activated. To be precise, the **loader()** function is called **before** the component function is executed (that is, before the component is rendered).

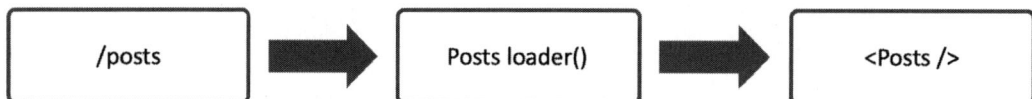

Figure 13.1: The Posts component is rendered after the loader is executed

This also explains why the **Posts** component example at the beginning of this section contained no code that handled any loading state. This is simply because there *was* no loading state since a component function is only executed after its loader has finished (and the data is available). React Router won't finish the page transition until the **loader()** function has finished its job (though, as you will learn towards the end of this chapter, there is a way of changing this behavior).

The **loader()** function can perform any operation of your choice (such as sending an HTTP request, or reaching out to browser storage via the **localStorage** API). Inside that function, you should return the data that should be exposed to the component function. It's also worth noting that the **loader()** function can return any kind of data. It may also return a **Promise** object that then resolves to any kind of data. In that case, React Router will automatically wait for the **Promise** to be fulfilled before executing the related route component function. The **loader()** function can thus perform both asynchronous and synchronous tasks.

> **NOTE**
>
> It's important to understand that the **loader()** function, like all the other code that makes up your React app, executes on the client side (that is, in the browser of a website visitor). Therefore, you may perform any action that could be performed anywhere else (for example, inside **useEffect()**) in your React app as well.
>
> You must not try to run code that belongs to the server side. Directly reaching out to a database, writing to the file system, or performing any other server-side tasks will fail or introduce security risks, meaning that you might accidentally expose database credentials on the client side.

Of course, the component that belongs to a **loader** (that is, the component that's part of the same **<Route />** definition) needs the data returned by the **loader**. This is why React Router offers a new Hook for accessing that data: the **useLoaderData()** Hook.

When called inside a component function, this Hook yields the data returned by the **loader** that belongs to the component. If that returned data is a **Promise**, React Router (as mentioned earlier) will automatically wait for that **Promise** to resolve and provide the resolved data when **useLoaderData()** is called.

The **loader()** function may also return an HTTP response object (or a **Promise** resolving to a response). This is the case in the preceding example because the **fetch()** function yields a **Promise** that resolves to a response. In that instance, **useLoaderData()** automatically extracts the response body and provides direct access to the data that was attached to the response.

> **NOTE**
>
> If a response should be returned, the returned object must adhere to the standard **Response** interface, as defined here: https://developer.mozilla.org/en-US/docs/Web/API/Response.
>
> Returning responses might be strange at first. After all, the **loader()** code is still executed inside the browser (not on a server). Therefore, technically, no request was sent, and no response should be required (since the entire code is executed in the same environment, that is, the browser).
>
> For that reason, you don't have to return a response; you may return any kind of value. But Remix supports the usage of a response object (as a "data vehicle") as an alternative.

useLoaderData() can be called in any component rendered by the currently active route component. That may be the route component itself (**Posts**, in the preceding example), but it may also be any nested component.

For example, **useLoaderData()** can also be used in a **PostsList** component that's included in the **Posts** component (which has a **loader** added to its route definition):

```
import { useLoaderData } from 'react-router-dom';

function PostsList() {
  const loadedPosts = useLoaderData();

  return (
    <main>
      <h1>Your Posts</h1>
      <ul className="posts">
        {loadedPosts.map((post) => (
          <li key={post.id}>{post.title}</li>
        ))}
```

```
        </ul>
      </main>
    );
  }
export default PostsList;
```

For this example, the **Posts** component file looks like this:

```
import PostsList from '../components/PostsList';

function Posts() {
  return (
    <main>
      <h1>Your Posts</h1>
      <PostsList />
    </main>
  );
}

export default Posts;

export async function loader() {
  const response = await fetch('https://jsonplaceholder.typicode.com/
posts');
  if (!response.ok) {
    throw new Error('Could not fetch posts');
  }
  return response;
}
```

This means that **useLoaderData()** can be used in exactly the place where you need the data. The **loader()** function can also be defined wherever you want but it must be added to the route where the data is required.

You can't use **useLoaderData()** in components where no loader is defined for the currently active route.

ENABLING THESE EXTRA ROUTER FEATURES

If you want to use these data-related React Router features, it's not enough to have version 6.4 or higher installed. This is an important prerequisite, but you also must tweak your route definition code a little bit.

In *Chapter 12, Multipage Apps with React Router*, you learned that routes can be defined as follows:

```
import { BrowserRouter, Routes, Route } from 'react-router-dom';

import Posts from './pages/Posts';
import Welcome from './pages/Welcome';

function App() {
  return (
    <BrowserRouter>
      <Routes>
          <Route index element={<Welcome />} />
          <Route path="/posts" element={<Posts />} />
      </Routes>
    </BrowserRouter>
  );
}
```

You can still do that with version 6.4, but you won't be able to use React Router's new data-related features. Instead, to enable these features, the preceding route definition code must be changed to look like this:

```
import {
  createBrowserRouter,
  createRoutesFromElements,
  Route,
  RouterProvider,
} from 'react-router-dom';

import Posts, { loader as postsLoader } from './pages/Posts';
import Welcome from './pages/Welcome';

const router = createBrowserRouter(
  createRoutesFromElements(
    <>
      <Route path="/" element={<Welcome />} />
      <Route path="/posts" element={<Posts />} loader={postsLoader} />
    </>
  )
);
```

```
function App() {
  return <RouterProvider router={router} />;
}
```

Instead of returning **`<BrowserRouter>`** (which includes the route definitions, wrapped by **`<Routes>`**), you must now create a **router** object by calling **`createBrowserRouter()`**.

This function then accepts an array of route definition objects. You can create this array on your own (shown later) or get a valid list of objects by executing **`createRoutesFromElements()`** and passing your route definition JSX code to that function.

Note that **`createRoutesFromElements()`** only takes a single element, such as a fragment (see *Chapter 2, Understanding React Components and JSX*), as used in this example, or a **`<Route>`** element. This single element is wrapped around all other **`<Route>`** elements.

The created **router** object is then passed as a value for the **router** prop to the **`<RouterProvider>`** component.

As an alternative to **`createRoutesFromElements()`**, you can also define your route objects manually, like this:

```
const router = createBrowserRouter([
  { path: '/', element: <Welcome /> },
  { path: '/posts', element: <Posts />, loader: postsLoader },
]);
```

This approach is a bit more concise, though it may be unfamiliar. Essentially, instead of using React components (such as **`<Route>`**) to define routes, you would use plain JavaScript objects (grouped into an array) for this method.

You can use whichever approach you prefer. Conceptually and feature-wise there is no difference between the two.

LOADING DATA FOR DYNAMIC ROUTES

For most websites, it's unlikely that static, pre-defined routes alone will be sufficient to meet your needs. For instance, if you created a blogging site with exclusively static routes, you would be limited to a simple list of blog posts on **/posts**. To add more details about a selected blog post on routes such as **/posts/1** or **/posts/2** (for posts with different **id** values) you would need to include dynamic routes.

As you learned in the previous chapter, dynamic routes can be defined like this:

```
<Route path="/posts/:id" element={<PostDetails />} />
```

This code still works (when using **createRoutesFromElements()**), though you can also use the alternative approach of defining route objects, as mentioned earlier, and define a dynamic route (via **createBrowserRouter()**), as shown here:

```
const router = createBrowserRouter([
  // … other routes
  { path: '/posts/:id', element: <PostDetails /> }
]);
```

Of course, React Router also supports data fetching with help of the **loader()** function for dynamic routes.

The **PostDetails** component can be implemented like this:

```
import { useLoaderData } from 'react-router-dom';

function PostDetails() {
  const post = useLoaderData();
  return (
    <main id="post-details">
      <h1>{post.title}</h1>
      <p>{post.body}</p>
    </main>
  );
}

export default PostDetails;

export async function loader({ params }) {
  const response = await fetch(
    'https://jsonplaceholder.typicode.com/posts/' + params.id
  );
  if (!response.ok) {
    throw new Error('Could not fetch post for id ' + params.id);
  }
  return response;
}
```

If it looks very similar to the **Posts** component in the *"Loading Data with React Router"* section, that's no coincidence. Because the **loader()** function works in exactly the same way, there is just one extra feature being used to get hold of the dynamic path segment value: a **params** object that's made available by React Router.

When adding a **loader()** function to a route definition, React Router calls that function whenever the route becomes active, right before the component is rendered. When executing that function, React Router passes an object that contains extra information as an argument to **loader()**.

This object passed to **loader()** includes two main properties:

- A **request** property that contains an object with more details about the request that led to the route activation

- A **params** property that yields an object containing a key-value map of all dynamic route parameters for the active route

The **request** object doesn't matter for this example and will be discussed in the next section. But the **params** object contains an **id** property that carries the **id** value of the post for which the route is loaded. The property is named **id** because, in the route definition, **/posts/:id** was chosen as a path. If a different placeholder name had been chosen, a property with that name would have been available on **params** (for example, for **/posts/:postId**, this would be **params.postId**). This behavior is similar to the **params** object yielded by **useParams()**, as explained in *Chapter 12, Multipage Apps with React Router*.

With help of the **params** object and the post **id**, the appropriate post **id** can be included in the outgoing request URL (for the **fetch()** request), and hence the correct post data can be loaded from the backend API. Once the data arrives, React Router will render the **PostDetails** component and expose the loaded post via the **useLoaderData()** Hook.

LOADERS, REQUESTS, AND CLIENT-SIDE CODE

In the preceding section, you learned about a **request** object being provided to the **loader()** function. Getting such a **request** object might be confusing because React Router is a client-side library—all the code executes in the browser, not on a server. Therefore, no request should reach the React app (as HTTP requests are sent from the client to the server, not between JavaScript functions on the client side).

And, indeed, there is no request being sent via HTTP. Instead, React Router creates a request object via the browser's built-in **Request** interface to use it as a "data vehicle." This request is not sent via HTTP, but it's used as a value for the **request** property on the data object that is passed to your **loader()** function.

> **NOTE**
>
> For more information on the built-in **Request** interface, visit https://developer.mozilla.org/en-US/docs/Web/API/Request.

This **request** object will be unnecessary in many **loader** functions, but there are occasional scenarios in which you can extract useful information from that object—information that might be needed in the **loader** to fetch the right data.

For example, you can use the **request** object and its **url** property to get access to any search parameters (query parameters) that may be included in the currently active page's URL:

```
export async function loader({ request }) {
  // e.g. for localhost:3000/posts?sort=desc
  const sortDirection = new URL(request.url).searchParams.get('sort');

  // Example: Fetch sorted posts, based on local 'sort' query param value
  const response = await fetch(
    'https://example.com/posts?sorting=' + sortDirection
  );
  return response;
}
```

In this code snippet, the **request** value is used to get hold of a query parameter value that's used in the React app URL. That value is then used in an outgoing request.

However, it is vital that you keep in mind that the code inside your **loader()** function, just like all your other React code, always executes on the client side (at least, as long as you don't combine React with any other frameworks like NextJS or Remix).

> **NOTE**
>
> These frameworks are beyond the scope of this book. Both NextJS and Remix build up on top of React and, for example, add server-side rendering of React components. Visit https://nextjs.org or https://remix.run for more information. In addition, the author also offers courses for both frameworks. For NextJS, visit https://acad.link/nextjs and, for Remix, visit https://acad.link/remix.

LAYOUTS REVISITED

React Router supports the concept of layout routes. These are routes that contain other routes and render those other routes as nested children, and as you may recall, this concept was introduced in *Chapter 12, Multipage Apps with React Router*.

With React Router 6.4, a layout route can be defined like this:

```
const router = createBrowserRouter([
  {
    path: '/',
    element: <Root />,
    children: [
      { index: true, element: <Welcome /> },
    ]
  }
]);
```

The **index** route is a child route of the **/** route, which in turn is the layout route in this example. The **Root** component could look like this:

```
function Root() {
  return (
    <>
      <header>
        <MainNavigation />
      </header>
```

```
      <Outlet />
   </>
  );
}
```

As mentioned, layout routes were introduced in the previous chapter. But when using the extra data capabilities offered by React Router, there are two noteworthy changes:

- Unlike with **<BrowserRouter />**, if you need some shared layout, you can't wrap a React component around your route definitions. **createBrowserRouter()** only accepts React fragments and **<Route />** elements—no other components. For that reason, you must use a layout route as shown in the previous example instead.

- Layout routes can also be used to share data across routes without using React's context feature.

Because of the first point, you'll typically use more layout routes than you did prior to the release of React Router 6.4. Before that version, you could simply wrap any component you wanted around your route definitions. For example, the following code works without issue:

```
import { BrowserRouter, Routes, Route } from 'react-router-dom';

import Layout from './components/shared/Layout';
import Dashboard from './routes/Dashboard';
import Orders from './routes/Orders';

function App() {
  return (
    <BrowserRouter>
      <Layout>
        <Routes>
          <Route path="/" element={<Dashboard />} />
          <Route path="/orders" element={<Orders />} />
        </Routes>
      </Layout>
    </BrowserRouter>
  );
}

export default App;
```

Since **BrowserRouter** does not support the extra data capabilities (such as the **loader()** function) you must use **createBrowserRouter()** instead. But **createBrowserRouter()** does not accept anything but route definitions. That's why shared layouts must be implemented via layout routes instead of wrapper components.

The second point is the more interesting one, though. Layout routes can be used for sharing data across routes.

Consider this example website:

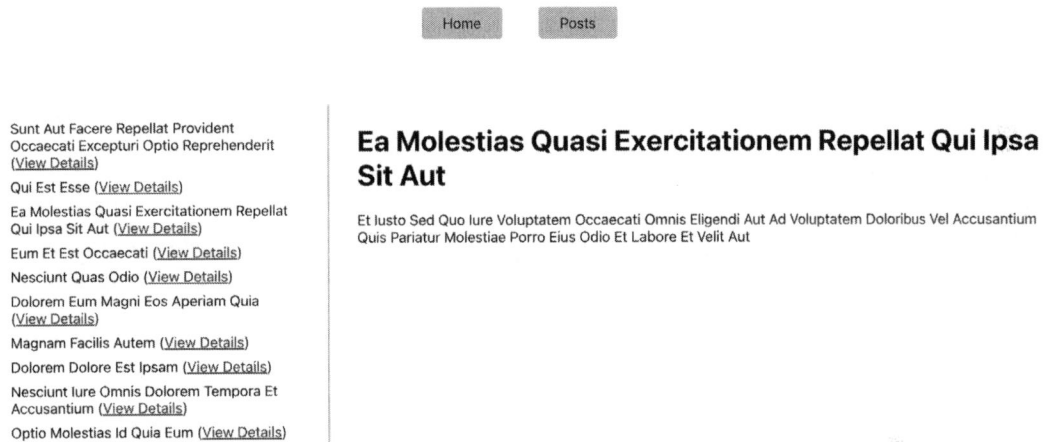

Figure 13.2: A website with a header, a sidebar, and some main content

This website has a header with a navigation bar, a sidebar showing a list of available posts, and a main area that displays the currently selected blog post.

> **NOTE**
>
> The dummy data shown in *Figure 13.2* is fetched from https://jsonplaceholder.typicode.com/posts. You will find the complete source code for this example at https://packt.link/Ef8LS.

This example includes two layout routes:

- The root layout route, which includes the top navigation bar that is shared across all pages

- A posts layout route, which includes the sidebar and the main content of its child routes (for example, the details for a selected post)

The route definitions code looks like this:

```
const router = createBrowserRouter([
  {
    path: '/',
    element: <Root />, // main layout, adds navigation bar
    children: [
      { index: true, element: <Welcome /> },
      {
        path: '/posts',
        element: <PostsLayout />, // posts layout, adds posts sidebar
        loader: postsLoader,
        children: [
          { index: true, element: <Posts /> },
          { path: ':id', element: <PostDetails />, loader:
postDetailLoader },
        ],
      },
    ],
  },
]);
```

With this setup, both the **<Posts />** and the **<PostDetails />** components are rendered next to the sidebar (since the sidebar is part of the **<PostsLayout />** element).

The interesting part is that the **/posts** route (i.e., the layout route) loads the post data, as it has the **postsLoader** assigned to it, and so the **PostsLayout** component file looks like this:

```
import { Outlet, useLoaderData } from 'react-router-dom';

import PostsList from '../components/PostsList';

function PostsLayout() {
  const loadedPosts = useLoaderData();
  return (
    <div id="posts-layout">
      <nav>
        <PostsList posts={loadedPosts} />
      </nav>
      <main>
        <Outlet />
      </main>
    </div>
  );
}

export default PostsLayout;

export async function loader() {
  const response = await fetch('https://jsonplaceholder.typicode.com/
posts');
  if (!response.ok) {
    throw new Error('Could not fetch posts');
  }
  return response;
}
```

Since layout routes are also regular routes, you can add **loader()** functions and **useLoaderData()** just as you could in any other route. But because layout routes are activated for multiple child routes, their data is also displayed for different routes. In the preceding example, the list of blog posts is always displayed on the left side of the screen, no matter if a user visits **/posts** or **/posts/10**:

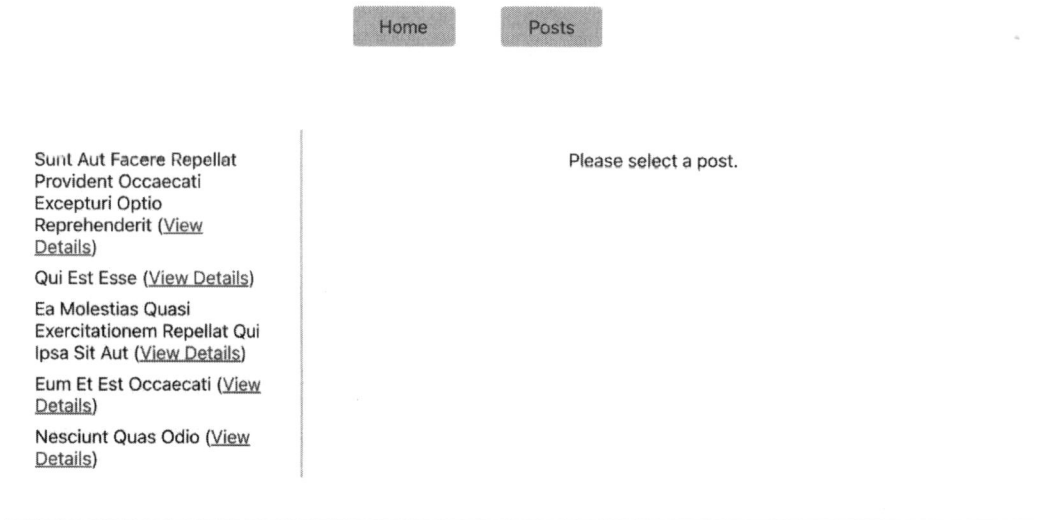

Home   Posts

Sunt Aut Facere Repellat Provident Occaecati Excepturi Optio Reprehenderit (View Details)

Qui Est Esse (View Details)

Ea Molestias Quasi Exercitationem Repellat Qui Ipsa Sit Aut (View Details)

Eum Et Est Occaecati (View Details)

Nesciunt Quas Odio (View Details)

Please select a post.

Home   Posts

Sunt Aut Facere Repellat Provident Occaecati Excepturi Optio Reprehenderit (View Details)

Qui Est Esse (View Details)

Ea Molestias Quasi Exercitationem Repellat Qui Ipsa Sit Aut (View Details)

Eum Et Est Occaecati (View Details)

Nesciunt Quas Odio (View Details)

Ea Molestias Quasi Exercitationem Repellat Qui Ipsa Sit Aut

Et Iusto Sed Quo Iure Voluptatem Occaecati Omnis Eligendi Aut Ad Voluptatem Doloribus Vel Accusantium Quis Pariatur Molestiae Porro Eius Odio Et Labore Et Velit Aut

Figure 13.3: The same layout and data are used for different child routes

In this screenshot, the layout and data used do not change as different child routes are activated. React Router also avoids unnecessary data refetching (for the blog posts list data) as you switch between child routes. It's smart enough to realize that the surrounding layout hasn't changed.

REUSING DATA ACROSS ROUTES

Layouts do not just help you share data by sharing components that use data (such as the sidebar in the previous example). They also allow you to load data in a layout route and use it in a child route.

For example, the **PostDetails** component (that is, the component that's rendered for the **/posts/:id** route) needs the data for a single post, and that data can be retrieved via a **loader** attached to the **/posts/:id** route:

```
export async function loader({ params }) {
  const response = await fetch(
    'https://jsonplaceholder.typicode.com/posts/' + params.id
  );
  if (!response.ok) {
    throw new Error('Could not fetch post for id ' + params.id);
  }
  return response;
}
```

This example was discussed earlier in this chapter in the *Loading Data for Dynamic Routes* section. This approach is fine, but in some situations, this extra HTTP request can be avoided.

In the example from the previous section, the **PostsLayout** route already fetched a list of all posts. That layout component is also active for the **PostDetails** route. In such a scenario, fetching a single post is unnecessary, since all the data has already been fetched for the list of posts. Of course, refetching would be required if the request for the list of posts didn't yield all the data required by **PostDetails**.

But if all the data is available, React Router allows you to tap into the loader data of a parent route component via the **useRouteLoaderData()** Hook.

This Hook can be used like this:

```
const posts = useRouteLoaderData('posts');
```

useRouteLoaderData() requires a route identifier as an argument. It requires an identifier assigned to the ancestor route that contains the data that should be reused. You can assign such an identifier via the **id** property to your routes as part of the route definitions code:

```
const router = createBrowserRouter([
  {
    path: '/',
    element: <Root />, // main layout, adds navigation bar
    children: [
      { index: true, element: <Welcome /> },
      {
        path: '/posts',
        id: 'posts', // the id value is up to you
        element: <PostsLayout />, // posts layout, adds posts sidebar
        loader: postsLoader,
        children: [
          { index: true, element: <Posts /> },
          { path: ':id', element: <PostDetails />, loader:
postDetailLoader },
        ],
      },
    ],
  },
]);
```

The **useRouteLoaderData()** Hook then returns the same data **useLoaderData()** yields in that route to which you added the **id**. In this example, it would provide a list of blog posts.

In **PostDetails**, this list can be used like this:

```
import { useParams, useRouteLoaderData } from 'react-router-dom';

function PostDetails() {
  const params = useParams();
  const posts = useRouteLoaderData('posts');
  const post = posts.find((post) => post.id.toString() === params.id);
  return (
    <main id="post-details">
      <h1>{post.title}</h1>
      <p>{post.body}</p>
```

```
    </main>
  );
}


export default PostDetails;
```

The **useParams()** Hook is used to get access to the dynamic route parameter value, and the **find()** method is used on the list of posts to identify a single post with a fitting **id** property. In this example, you would thus avoid sending an unnecessary HTTP request by reusing data that's already available.

HANDLING ERRORS

In the first example at the very beginning of this chapter (where the HTTP request was sent with help of **useEffect()**), the code did not just handle the success case but also possible errors. In all the React Router-based examples since then, error handling was omitted. Error handling was not discussed up to this point because while React Router plays an important role in error handling, it's vital to first gain a solid understanding of how React Router 6.4 works in general and how it helps with data fetching. But, of course, errors can't always be avoided and definitely should not be ignored.

Thankfully, handling errors is also very straightforward and easy when using React Router's data capabilities. You can set an **errorElement** property on your route definitions and define the element that should be rendered when an error occurs:

```
// ... other imports
import Error from './components/Error';

const router = createBrowserRouter([
  {
    path: '/',
    element: <Root />,
    errorElement: <Error />,
    children: [
      { index: true, element: <Welcome /> },
      {
        path: '/posts',
        id: 'posts',
        element: <PostsLayout />,
        loader: postsLoader,
        children: [
```

```
            { index: true, element: <Posts /> },
            { path: ':id', element: <PostDetails /> },
          ],
        },
      ],
    },
  ]);
```

This **errorElement** property can be set on any route definition of your choice, or even multiple route definitions simultaneously. React Router will render the **errorElement** of the route closest to the place where the error was thrown.

In the preceding snippet, no matter which route produced an error, it would always be the root route's **errorElement** that was displayed (since that's the only route definition with an **errorElement**). But if you also added an **errorElement** to the **/posts** route, and the **:id** route produced an error, it would be the **errorElement** of the **/posts** route that was shown on the screen, as follows:

```
const router = createBrowserRouter([
  {
    path: '/',
    element: <Root />,
    errorElement: <Error />, // used for any errors not handled by nested
routes
    children: [
      { index: true, element: <Welcome /> },
      {
        path: '/posts',
        id: 'posts',
        element: <PostsLayout />,
        // used if /posts or /posts/:id throws an error
        errorElement: <PostsError />,
        loader: postsLoader,
        children: [
          { index: true, element: <Posts /> },
          { path: ':id', element: <PostDetails /> },
        ],
      },
    ],
  },
]);
```

This allows you, the developer, to set up fine-grained error handling.

Inside the component used as a value for the **errorElement**, you can get access to the error that was thrown via the **useRouteError()** Hook:

```
import { useRouteError } from 'react-router-dom';

function Error() {
  const error = useRouteError();

  return (
    <>
      <h1>Oh no!</h1>
      <p>An error occurred</p>
      <p>{error.message}</p>
    </>
  );
}

export default Error;
```

With this simple yet effective error-handling solution, React Router allows you to avoid managing error states yourself. Instead, you simply define a standard React element (via the **element** prop) that should be displayed when things go right and an **errorElement** to be displayed if things go wrong.

ONWARD TO DATA SUBMISSION

Thus far, you've learned a lot about data fetching. But as mentioned earlier in this chapter, React Router also helps with data submission.

Consider the following example component:

```
function NewPost() {
  return (
    <form id="post-form">
      <p>
        <label htmlFor="title">Title</label>
        <input type="text" id="title" name="title" />
      </p>
      <p>
        <label htmlFor="text">Text</label>
        <textarea id="text" name="text" rows={3} />
```

```
      </p>
      <button>Save Post</button>
    </form>
  );
}


export default NewPost;
```

This component renders a **<form>** element that allows users to enter the details for a new post. Due to the following route configuration, the component is displayed whenever the **/posts/new** route becomes active:

```
const router = createBrowserRouter([
  {
    path: '/',
    element: <Root />,
    errorElement: <Error />,
    children: [
      { index: true, element: <Welcome /> },
      {
        path: '/posts',
        id: 'posts',
        element: <PostsLayout />,
        loader: postsLoader,
        children: [
          { index: true, element: <Posts /> },
          { path: ':id', element: <PostDetails /> },
          { path: 'new', element: <NewPost /> },
        ],
      },
    ],
  },
]);
```

Without React Router's data-related features, you would typically handle form submission like this:

```
function NewPost() {
  const titleInput = useRef();
  const textInput = useRef();
  const navigate = useNavigate();
```

```
async function submitHandler(event) {
    event.preventDefault(); // prevent the browser from sending a HTTP
request
    const enteredTitle = titleInput.current.value;
    const enteredText = textInput.current.value;
    const postData = {
      title: enteredTitle,
      text: enteredText
    };

    await fetch('https://jsonplaceholder.typicode.com/posts', {
      method: 'POST',
      body: JSON.stringify(postData),
      headers: {'Content-Type': 'application/json'}
    });
    navigate('/posts');
  }

  return (
    <form onSubmit={submitHandler}>
      <p>
        <label htmlFor="title">Title</label>
        <input type="text" id="title" ref={titleInput} />
      </p>
      <p>
        <label htmlFor="text">Text</label>
        <textarea id="text" rows={3} ref={textInput} />
      </p>
      <button>Save Post</button>

    </form>
  );
}
```

Just as before when fetching data, this requires a lot of code and logic added to the component. You must manually handle the form submission, input data extraction, sending the HTTP request, and transitioning to a different page after sending the HTTP request. All these things happen inside the component. In addition, you might also need to manage loading state and potential errors (excluded in the preceding example).

Again, React Router offers some help. Where a **loader()** function can be added to handle data loading, an **action()** function can be defined to handle data submission.

When using the new **action()** function, the preceding example component looks like this:

```
import { Form, redirect } from 'react-router-dom';

function NewPost() {
  return (
    <Form method="post" id="post-form">
      <p>
        <label htmlFor="title">Title</label>
        <input type="text" id="title" name="title" />
      </p>
      <p>
        <label htmlFor="text">Text</label>
        <textarea id="text" rows={3} name="text" />
      </p>
      <button>Save Post</button>
    </Form>
  );
}

export default NewPost;

export async function action({ request }) {
  const formData = await request.formData();
  const postData = Object.fromEntries(formData);
  await fetch('https://jsonplaceholder.typicode.com/posts', {
    method: 'POST',
    body: JSON.stringify(postData),
    headers: { 'Content-Type': 'application/json' },
  });
  return redirect('/posts');
}
```

This code is shorter and, most importantly, simpler (even though it might not look simpler yet, since it includes a couple of new features).

Besides the addition of the **action()** function, the example code snippet includes the following important changes and features:

- A **<Form>** component that's used instead of **<form>**.

- The **method** prop is set on the **<Form>** (to **"post"**), and the **onSubmit** event handler was removed.

- The form input elements have names assigned to them (via the **name** prop), and the refs were removed.

- In the action, the entered data is extracted via a **formData()** method (combined with **Object.fromEntries()**).

- The user is redirected via a newly added **redirect()** function (instead of **useNavigate()** and **navigate()**).

But what are these elements about?

WORKING WITH ACTION() AND FORM DATA

Just like **loader()**, **action()** is a special function that can be added to route definitions, as follows:

```
import NewPost, { action as newPostAction } from './components/NewPost';

// ...

{ path: 'new', element: <NewPost />, action: newPostAction },
```

With the **action** prop set on a route definition, the assigned function is automatically called whenever a **<Form>** targeting this route is submitted. **Form** is a component provided by React Router that should be used instead of the default **<form>** element.

Internally, **Form** uses the default **<form>** element but prevents the browser default of creating and sending an HTTP request upon form submission. Instead, React Router creates a **FormData** object and calls the **action()** function defined for the route that's targeted by the **<Form>**, passing a request object, based on the built-in **Request** interface, to it. The passed request object contains the form data generated by React Router.

> **NOTE**
>
> For further reading on React Router's **FormData** object, visit https://
> developer.mozilla.org/en-US/docs/Web/API/FormData.

The form data object that is created by React Router includes all form input values entered into the submitted form. To be registered, an input element such as **<input>**, **<select>**, or **<textarea>** must have the **name** attribute assigned to it. The values set for those **name** attributes can later be used to extract the entered data.

The **Form** component also sets the HTTP method of the request object to the value assigned to the **method** prop. It's important to understand that the request is not sent via HTTP since **action()**, just like **loader()** or the component function, still executes in the browser rather than the server. React Router simply uses this request object as a "data vehicle" for passing information (such as the form data or chosen method) to the **action()** function.

The **action()** function then receives an object with a **request** property that contains the created request object with the included form data:

```
export function action({ request }) {
  // do something with 'request' (e.g., extract data)
}
```

The **method** property could be used inside the **action()** function to perform different actions for different forms. For example, one form could generate and pass a **POST** request via **<Form method="post">**, whereas another form might yield a **DELETE** request via **<Form method="delete">**. The same action could handle both form submissions and perform different tasks based on the value of the **method** property:

```
export function action({ request }) {
  if (request.method === 'DELETE') {
```

```
      // do something, e.g., send a "delete post" request to backend API
   }


   if (request.method === 'POST') {
      // do something, e.g., send a "create new post" request to backend
API
   }
}
```

But while using the **method** for performing different tasks for different forms can be very useful, the form data that's attached to the **request** object is often even more important. The **request** object can be used to extract the values entered into the form input fields like this:

```
export async function action({ request }) {
  const formData = await request.formData();
  const postData = Object.fromEntries(formData);

  // ...
}
```

The built-in **formData()** method yields a **Promise** that resolves to an object that offers a **get()** method that could be used to get an entered value by its identifier (that is, by the **name** attribute value set on the input element). For example, the value entered into **<input name="title">** could be retrieved via **formData.get('title')**.

Alternatively, you can follow the approach chosen in the preceding code snippet and convert the **formData** object to a simple key-value object via **Object.fromEntries(formData)**. This object (**postData**, in the preceding example) contains the names set on the form input elements as properties and the entered values as values for those properties (meaning that **postData.title** would yield the value entered in **<input name="title">**).

The extracted data can then be used for any operations of your choice. That could be an extra validation step or an HTTP request sent to some backend API, where the data may get stored in a database or file:

```
export async function action({ request }) {
  const formData = await request.formData();
  const postData = Object.fromEntries(formData);
  await fetch('https://jsonplaceholder.typicode.com/posts', {
    method: 'POST',
    body: JSON.stringify(postData),
```

```
    headers: { 'Content-Type': 'application/json' },
  });
  return redirect('/posts');
}
```

Finally, once all intended steps were performed, the **action()** function should return a value—any value of any type. Though, as with the **loader()** function, you may also return a response.

Indeed, for actions, it's highly likely that you will want to navigate to a different page once the action has been performed (that is, once the HTTP request to an API has been sent). This may be required to navigate the user away from the data input page to a page that displays all available data entries (for example, from **/posts/new** to **/posts**).

To simplify this common pattern, React Router provides a **redirect()** function that yields a response object that causes React Router to switch to a different route. You can therefore return the result of calling **redirect()** in your **action()** function to ensure that the user is navigated to a different page. It's the equivalent of calling **navigate()** (via **useNavigate()**) when manually handling form submissions.

RETURNING DATA INSTEAD OF REDIRECTING

As mentioned, your **action()** functions may return anything. You don't have to return a response object. And while it is quite common to return a redirect response, you may occasionally want to return some raw data instead.

One scenario in which you might **not** want to redirect the user is after validating the user's input. Inside the **action()** function, before sending the entered data to some API, you may wish to validate the provided values first. If an invalid value (such as an empty title) is detected, a great user experience is typically achieved by keeping the user on the route with the **<Form>**. The values entered by the user shouldn't be cleared and lost; instead, the form should be updated to present useful validation error information to the user. This information can be passed from the **action()** to the component function so that it can be displayed there (for example, next to the form input fields).

In situations like this, you can return a "normal" value (that is, not a redirect response) from your **action()** function:

```
export async function action({ request }) {
  const formData = await request.formData();
  const postData = Object.fromEntries(formData);
```

```
  let validationErrors = [];

  if (postData.title.trim().length === 0) {
    validationErrors.push('Invalid post title provided.')
  }
  if (postData.text.trim().length === 0) {
    validationErrors.push('Invalid post text provided.')
  }

  if (validationErrors.length > 0) {
    return validationErrors;
  }

  await fetch('https://jsonplaceholder.typicode.com/posts', {
    method: 'POST',
    body: JSON.stringify(postData),
    headers: { 'Content-Type': 'application/json' },
  });
  return redirect('/posts');
}
```

In this example, a **validationErrors** array is returned if the entered **title** or **text** values are empty.

Data returned by an **action()** function can be used in the route component (or any other nested component) via the **useActionData()** Hook:

```
import { Form, redirect, useActionData } from 'react-router-dom';

function NewPost() {
  const validationErrors = useActionData();

  return (
    <Form method="post" id="post-form">
      <p>
        <label htmlFor="title">Title</label>
        <input type="text" id="title" name="title" />
      </p>
      <p>
        <label htmlFor="text">Text</label>
        <textarea id="text" name="text" rows={3} />
      </p>
```

```
    <ul>
      {validationErrors &&
        validationErrors.map((err) => <li key={err}>{err}</li>)}
    </ul>
    <button>Save Post</button>
  </Form>
);
}
```

useActionData() works a lot like **useLoaderData()**, but unlike **useLoaderData()**, it's not guaranteed to yield any data. This is because while **loader()** functions always get called before the route component is rendered, the **action()** function only gets called once the **<Form>** is submitted.

In this example, **useActionData()** is used to get access to the **validationErrors** returned by **action()**. If **validationErrors** is truthy (that is, is not **undefined**), the array will be mapped to a list of error items that are displayed to the user:

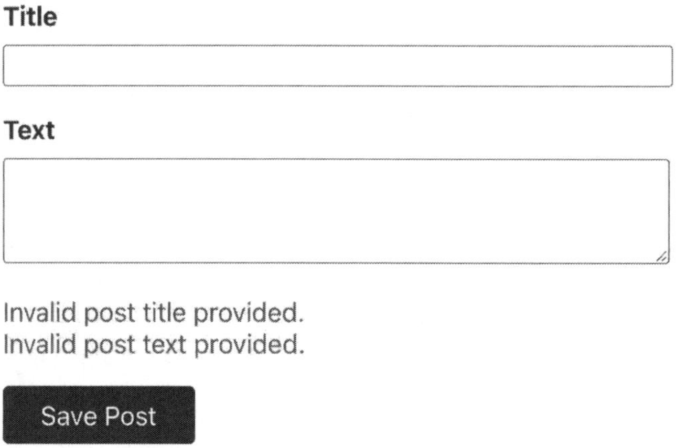

Title

[   ]

Text

[   ]
[   ]
[   ]

Invalid post title provided.
Invalid post text provided.

[Save Post]

Figure 13.4: Validation errors are output below the input fields

The **action()** function is therefore quite versatile in that you can use it to perform an action and redirect away as well as to conduct more than one operation and return different values for different use cases.

CONTROLLING WHICH <FORM> TRIGGERS WHICH ACTION

In *Chapter 12, Multipage Apps with React Router*, you learned that when **<Form>** is used instead of **<form>**, React Router will execute the targeted **action()** function. But which **action()** function is targeted by **<Form>**?

By default, it's the **action()** function assigned to the route that also renders the form. Consider this route definition:

```
{ path: '/posts/new', element: <NewPost />, action: newPostAction }
```

With this definition, the **newPostAction()** function would be triggered whenever any **<Form>** inside of the **NewPost** component (or any nested component) is submitted.

In many cases, this default behavior is exactly what you want. But you can also target **action()** functions defined on other routes, and these can be triggered by setting the **action** prop on **<Form>** to the path of the route that contains the **action()** that should be executed:

```
// form rendered in a component that belongs to /posts
<Form method="post" action="/save-data">

  ...

</Form>
```

This form would lead to the **action** belonging to the **/save-data** route to be executed—even though the **<Form>** component is rendered as part of a component that belongs to a different route (e.g., **/posts**).

It is worth noting, though, that targeting a different route will lead to a page transition to that route's path, even if your action does not return a redirect response. In a later section of this chapter, entitled *"Behind-the-Scenes Data Fetching and Submission"*, you will learn how that behavior could be avoided.

REFLECTING THE CURRENT NAVIGATION STATUS

After submitting a form, the **action()** function that's triggered may need some time to perform all intended operations. Sending HTTP requests to APIs in particular can take up to a few seconds.

Of course, it's not a great user experience if the user doesn't get any feedback about the current data submission status. It's not immediately clear if anything happened at all after the submit button was clicked.

For that reason, you might want to show a loading spinner or update the button caption while the **action()** function is running. Indeed, one common way of providing user feedback is to disable the submit button and change its caption like this:

Title

First Post

Text

Some text

Saving...

Figure 13.5: The submit button is grayed out

You can get the current React Router status (that is, whether it's currently transitioning to another route or executing an **action()** function) via the **useNavigation()** Hook. This Hook provides a navigation object that contains various pieces of routing-related information.

Most importantly, this object has a **state** property that yields a string describing the current navigation status. This property is set to one of the following three possible values:

- **submitting**: If an **action()** function is currently executing
- **loading**: If a **loader()** function is currently executing (for example, because of a **redirect()** response)
- **idle**: If no **action()** or **loader()** functions are currently being executed

You can therefore use this **state** property to find out whether React Router is currently navigating to a different page or executing an **action()**. Hence, the submit button can be updated as shown in the preceding screenshot via this code:

```
import { Form, redirect, useActionData, useNavigation } from 'react-router-dom';

function NewPost() {
  const validationErrors = useActionData();

  const navigation = useNavigation();
```

```
    const isSubmitting = navigation.state !== 'idle';

  return (
    <Form method="post" id="post-form">
      <p>
        <label htmlFor="title">Title</label>
        <input type="text" id="title" name="title" />
      </p>
      <p>
        <label htmlFor="text">Text</label>
        <textarea id="text" name="text" rows={3} />
      </p>
      <ul>
        {validationErrors &&
          validationErrors.map((err) => <li key={err}>{err}</li>)}
      </ul>
      <button disabled={isSubmitting}>
        {isSubmitting ? 'Saving...' : 'Save Post'}
      </button>
    </Form>
  );
}
```

In this example, the **isSubmitting** constant is **true** if the current navigation state is anything but **'idle'**. This constant is then used to disable the submit button (via the **disabled** attribute) and adjust the button's caption.

SUBMITTING FORMS PROGRAMMATICALLY

In some cases, you won't want to instantly trigger an **action()** when a form is submitted—for example, if you need to ask the user for confirmation first such as when triggering actions that delete or update data.

For such scenarios, React Router allows you to submit a form (and therefore trigger an **action()** function) programmatically. Instead of using the **Form** component provided by React Router, you handle the form submission manually using the default **<form>** element. As part of your code, you can then use a **submit()** function provided by React Router's **useSubmit()** Hook to trigger the **action()** manually once you're ready for it.

Consider this example:

```
import {
  redirect,
  useParams,
  useRouteLoaderData,
  useSubmit,
} from 'react-router-dom';

function PostDetails() {
  const params = useParams();
  const posts = useRouteLoaderData('posts');
  const post = posts.find((post) => post.id.toString() === params.id);

  const submit = useSubmit();

  function submitHandler(event) {
    event.preventDefault();

    const proceed = window.confirm('Are you sure?');

    if (proceed) {
      submit(
        { message: 'Your data, if needed' },
        {
          method: 'delete',
        }
      );
    }
  }

  return (
    <main id="post-details">
      <h1>{post.title}</h1>
      <p>{post.body}</p>
```

```
      <form onSubmit={submitHandler}>
        <button>Delete</button>
      </form>
    </main>
  );
}

export default PostDetails;

// action must be added to route definition!
export async function action({ request }) {
  const formData = await request.formData();
  console.log(formData.get('message'));
  console.log(request.method);
  return redirect('/posts');
}
```

In this example, the **action()** is manually triggered by programmatically submitting data via the **submit()** function provided by **useSubmit()**. This approach is required as it would otherwise be impossible to ask the user for confirmation (via the browser's **window.confirm()** method).

Because data is submitted programmatically, the default **<form>** element should be used and the **submit** event handled manually. As part of this process, the browser's default behavior of sending an HTTP request must also be prevented manually.

Typically, using **<Form>** instead of programmatic submission is preferable. But in certain situations, such as the preceding example, being able to control form submission manually can be useful.

BEHIND-THE-SCENES DATA FETCHING AND SUBMISSION

There also are situations in which you may need to trigger an action or load data without causing a page transition.

A "Like" button would be an example. When it's clicked, a process should be triggered in the background (such as storing information about the user and the liked post), but the user should not be directed to a different page:

Sunt Aut Facere Repellat Provident Occaecati Excepturi Optio Reprehenderit

Quia Et Suscipit Suscipit Recusandae
Consequuntur Expedita Et Cum Reprehenderit
Molestiae Ut Ut Quas Totam Nostrum Rerum Est
Autem Sunt Rem Eveniet Architecto

♥ Like this post

Figure 13.6: A like button below a post

To achieve this behavior, you could wrap the button into a **`<Form>`** and, at the end of the **`action()`** function, simply redirect back to the page that is already active.

But technically, this would still lead to an extra navigation action. Therefore, **`loader()`** functions would be executed and other possible side-effects might occur (the current scroll position could be lost, for example). For that reason, you might want to avoid this kind of behavior.

Thankfully, React Router offers a solution: the **`useFetcher()`** Hook, which yields an object that contains a **`submit()`** method. Unlike the **`submit()`** function provided by **`useSubmit()`**, the **`submit()`** method yielded by **`useFetcher()`** is meant for triggering actions (or **`loader()`** functions) without starting a page transition.

A "Like" button, as described previously, can be implemented like this (with help of **`useFetcher()`**):

```
import {
  // ... other imports
  useFetcher,
} from 'react-router-dom';
```

```
import { FaHeart } from 'react-icons/fa';

function PostDetails() {
  // ... other code & logic

  const fetcher = useFetcher();

  function likePostHandler() {
    fetcher.submit(null, {
      method: 'post',
      action: `/posts/${post.id}/like`, // targeting an action on another
route
    });
  }

  return (
    <main id="post-details">
      <h1>{post.title}</h1>
      <p>{post.body}</p>
      <p>
        <button className="icon-btn" onClick={likePostHandler}>
          <FaHeart />
          <span>Like this post</span>
        </button>
      </p>
      <form onSubmit={submitHandler}>
        <button>Delete</button>
      </form>
    </main>
  );
}
```

The **fetcher** object returned by **useFetcher()** has various properties. For example, it also contains properties that provide information about the current status of the triggered action or loader (including any data that may have been returned).

But this object also includes two important methods:

- **load()**: To trigger the **loader()** function of a route (e.g., **fetcher.load('/route-path')**)

- **submit()**: To trigger an **action()** function with the provided data and configuration

In the code snippet above, the **submit()** method is called to trigger the action defined on the **/posts/<post-id>/like** route. Without **useFetcher()** (i.e., when using **useSubmit()** or **<Form>**), React Router would switch to the selected route path when triggering its action. With **useFetcher()**, this is avoided, and the action of that route can be called from inside another route (meaning the action defined for **/posts/<post-id>/like** is called while the **/posts/<post-id>** route is active).

This also allows you to define routes that don't render any element (that is, in which there is no page component) and instead only contain a **loader()** or **action()** function. For example, the **/posts/<post-id>/like** route file looks like this:

```
export function action({ params }) {
  console.log('Triggered like action.');
  console.log(`Liking post with id ${params.id}.`);
  // Do anything else
  // May return data or response, including redirect() if needed
}
```

It's registered as a route as follows:

```
import { action as likeAction } from './pages/like';
// ...
{ path: ':id/like', action: likeAction },
```

This works because this **action()** is only triggered via the **submit()** method provided by **useFetcher()**. **<Form>** and the **submit()** function yielded by **useSubmit()** would instead initiate a route transition to **/posts/<post-id>/like**. Without the **element** property being set on the route definition, this transition would lead to an empty page, as shown here:

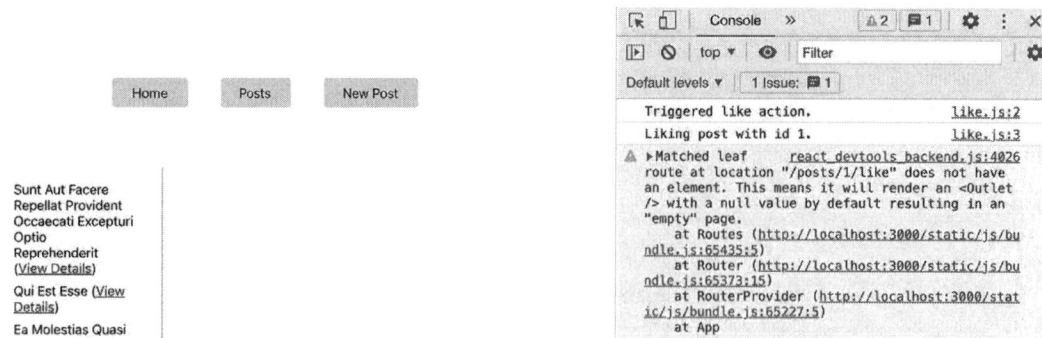

Figure 13.7: An empty (nested) page is displayed, along with a warning message

Because of the extra flexibility it offers, **useFetcher()** can be very useful when building highly interactive user interfaces. It's not meant as a replacement for **useSubmit()** or **\<Form\>** but rather as an additional tool for situations where no route transition is required or wanted.

DEFERRING DATA LOADING

Up to this point in the chapter, all data-fetching examples have assumed that a page should only be displayed once all its data has been fetched. That's why there was never any loading state that would have been managed (and hence no loading spinner that would have been displayed).

In many situations, this is exactly the behavior you want as it does not often make sense to show a loading spinner for a fraction of a second just to then replace it with the actual page data.

But there are also situations in which the opposite behavior might be desirable— for example, if you know that a certain page will take quite a while to load its data (possibly due to a complex database query that must be executed on the backend) or if you have a page that loads different pieces of data and some pieces are much slower than others.

In such scenarios, it may make sense to render the page component even though some data is still missing. React Router also supports this use case by allowing you to defer data loading, which in turn enables the page component to be rendered before the data is available.

Deferring data loading is as simple as using the **defer()** function provided by React Router like this:

```
import { defer } from 'react-router-dom';
// ... other imports
export async function loader() {
  return defer({
    posts: getPosts(),
  });
}
```

In this example, **getPosts()** is a function that returns a (slow) **Promise**:

```
async function getPosts() {
  const response = await fetch('https://jsonplaceholder.typicode.com/
posts');
  await wait(3); // utility function, simulating a slow response
  if (!response.ok) {
    throw new Error('Could not fetch posts');
  }
  const data = await response.json();
  return data;
}
```

React Router's **defer()** function takes an object as an argument. This object contains one key-value pair for every data fetching operation that's part of the **loader()** function. The values in this object are of type **Promise**; otherwise, there wouldn't be anything to defer.

Inside the component function where **useLoaderData()** is used, you must also use a new component provided by React Router: the **Await** component. It's used like this:

```
import { Suspense } from 'react';
import { Await } from 'react-router-dom';
// ... other imports

function PostsLayout() {
  const data = useLoaderData();

  return (
    <div id="posts-layout">
      <nav>
        <Suspense fallback={<p>Loading posts...</p>}>
          <Await resolve={data.posts}>
            {(loadedPosts) => <PostsList posts={loadedPosts} />}
          </Await>
        </Suspense>
      </nav>
      <main>
        <Outlet />
      </main>
    </div>
```

```
  ) ;
}
```

The **<Await>** element takes a **resolve** prop that receives a value from the loader data. It's wrapped by the **< Suspense>** component provided by React.

The value passed to resolve is a **Promise**. It's one of the values stored in the object that was passed to **defer()**. For that reason, you use the key names defined in the object that was passed to **defer()** to access the data in the component function (meaning that **data.posts** is used because of **defer({posts: getPosts()})**).

Await automatically waits for the **Promise** to resolve before then calling the function that's passed to **<Await>** as a child (that is, the function passed between the **<Await>** opening and closing tags). This function is executed by React Router once the data of the deferred operation is available. Therefore, inside that function, **loadedPosts** is received as a parameter, and the final user interface elements can be rendered.

The **Suspense** component that's used as a wrapper around **<Await>** defines some fallback content that is rendered as long as the deferred data is not yet available. In the *"Lazy Loading"* section of the previous chapter, the **Suspense** component was used to show some fallback content until the missing code was downloaded. Now, it's used to bridge the time until the required data is available.

When using **defer()** (and **<Await>**) like this, you would still load other parts of the website while waiting for the posts data:

Home   Posts   New Post

Loading posts...

Sunt Aut Facere Repellat Provident Occaecati Excepturi Optio Reprehenderit

Quia Et Suscipit Suscipit Recusandae Consequuntur Expedita Et Cum Reprehenderit Molestiae Ut Ut Quas Totam Nostrum Rerum Est Autem Sunt Rem Eveniet Architecto

Figure 13.8: Post details are already visible while the list of posts is loading

Another big advantage of **defer()** is that you can easily combine multiple fetching processes and control which processes should be deferred and which ones should not. For example, a route might be fetching different pieces of data. If only one process tends to be slow, you could defer only the slow one like this:

```
export async function loader() {
  return defer(
    {
      posts: getPosts(), // slow operation => deferred
      userData: await getUserData() // fast operation => NOT deferred
    }
  );
}
```

In this example, **getUserData()** is not deferred because the **await** keyword is added in front of it. Therefore, JavaScript waits for that **Promise** (the **Promise** returned by **getUserData()**) to resolve before returning from **loader()**. Hence, the route component is rendered once **getUserData()** finishes but before **getPosts()** is done.

SUMMARY AND KEY TAKEAWAYS

- React Router can help you with data fetching and submission.

- You can register **loader()** functions for your routes, causing data fetching to be initialized as a route becomes active.

- **loader()** functions return data (or responses, wrapping data) that can be accessed via **useLoaderData()** in your component functions.

- **loader()** data can be used across components via **useRouteLoaderData()**.

- You can also register **action()** functions on your routes that are triggered upon form submissions.

- To trigger **action()** functions, you must use React Router's **<Form>** component or submit data programmatically via **useSubmit()** or **useFetcher()**.

- **useFetcher()** can be used to load or submit data without initiating a route transition.

- When fetching slow data, you can use **defer()** to defer loading some or all of a route's data.

WHAT'S NEXT?

Fetching and submitting data are extremely common tasks, especially when building more complex React applications.

Typically, those tasks are closely connected to route transitions, and React Router is the perfect tool for handling this kind of operation. With the release of version 6.4, the React Router package offers powerful data management capabilities that vastly simplify these processes.

In this chapter, you learned how React Router assists you with fetching or submitting data and which advanced features help you handle both basic and more complex data manipulation scenarios.

This chapter also concludes the list of core React features you must know as a React developer. Of course, you can always dive deeper to explore more patterns and third-party libraries. The next (and last) chapter will share some resources and possible next steps you could dive into after finishing this book.

TEST YOUR KNOWLEDGE!

Test your knowledge of the concepts covered in this chapter by answering the following questions. You can then compare your answers to the examples found at https://packt.link/cbDjn:

1. How are data fetching and submission related to routing?

2. What is the purpose of **loader()** functions?

3. What is the purpose of **action()** functions?

4. What is the difference between **<Form>** and **<form>**?

5. What is the difference between **useSubmit()** and **useFetcher()**?

6. What is the idea behind **defer()**?

APPLY WHAT YOU LEARNED

Apply your knowledge about routing, combined with data manipulation, to the following activity.

ACTIVITY 13.1: A TO-DOS APP

In this activity, your task is to create a basic to-do list web app that allows users to manage their daily to-do tasks. The finished page must allow users to add to-do items, update to-do items, delete to-do items and view a list of to-do items.

The following paths must be supported:

- `/`: The main page, responsible for loading and displaying a list of to-do items

- `/new`: A page, opened as a modal above the main page, allowing users to add a new to-do item

- `/:id`: A page, also opened as a modal above the main page, allowing users to update or delete a selected to-do item

If no to-do items exist yet, a fitting info message should be shown on the `/` page. If users try to visit `/:id` with an invalid to-do ID, an error modal should be displayed.

> ### NOTE
>
> For this activity, there is no backend API you could use. Instead, use `localStorage` to manage the to-dos data. Keep in mind that the `loader()` and `action()` functions are executed on the client side and can therefore use any browser APIs, including `localStorage`.
>
> You will find example implementations for adding, updating, deleting, and getting to-do items from `localStorage` at https://packt.link/XCbu0.
>
> Also, don't be confused by the pages that open as modals above other pages. Ultimately, these are simply nested pages, styled as modal overlays. In case you get stuck, you can use the example `Modal` wrapper component found at https://packt.link/qPlvp.
>
> For this activity, you can write all CSS styles on your own if you so choose. But if you want to focus on the React and JavaScript logic, you can also use the finished CSS file from the solution at https://packt.link/G0IKW.
>
> If you use that file, explore it carefully to ensure you understand which IDs or CSS classes might need to be added to certain JSX elements of your solution.

To complete the activity, perform the following steps:

1. Create a new React project and install the React Router package (make sure it's version 6.4 or later).

2. Create components (with the content shown in the preceding screenshots) that will be loaded for the three required pages. Also add links (or programmatic navigation) between these pages.

3. Enable routing and add the route definitions for the three pages.

4. Create **loader()** functions to load (and use) all the data needed by the individual pages.

5. Add **action()** functions for adding, updating, and deleting to-dos.

6. Add error handling in case data loading or saving fails.

The finished pages should look like this:

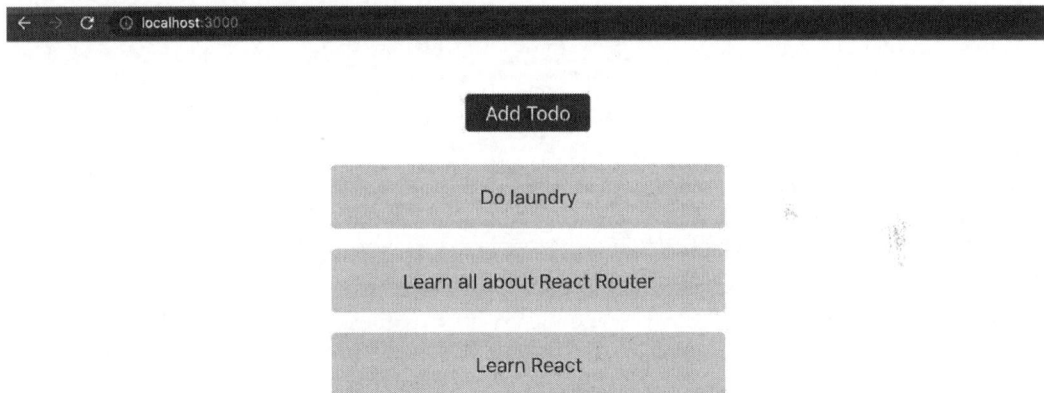

Figure 13.9: The main page displaying a list of to-dos

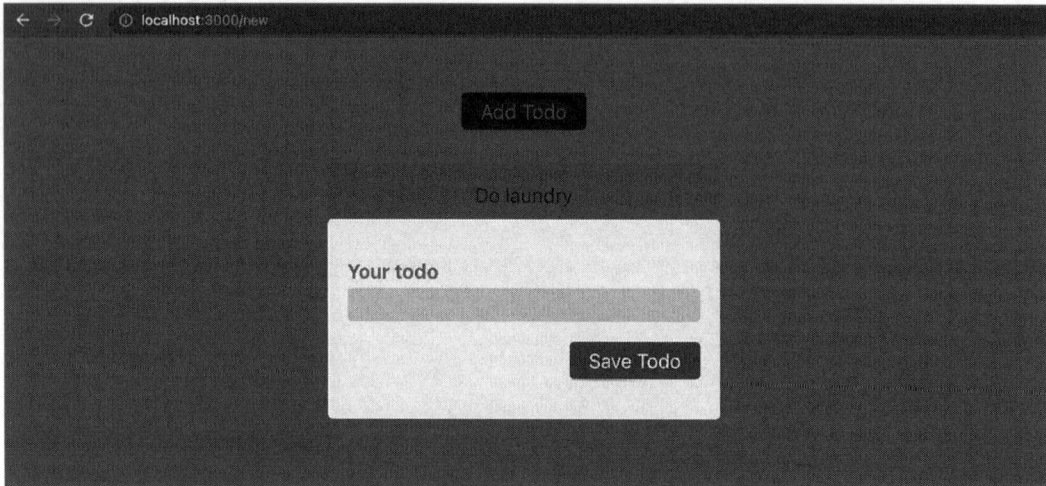

Figure 13.10: The /new page, opened as a modal, allowing users to add a new to-do

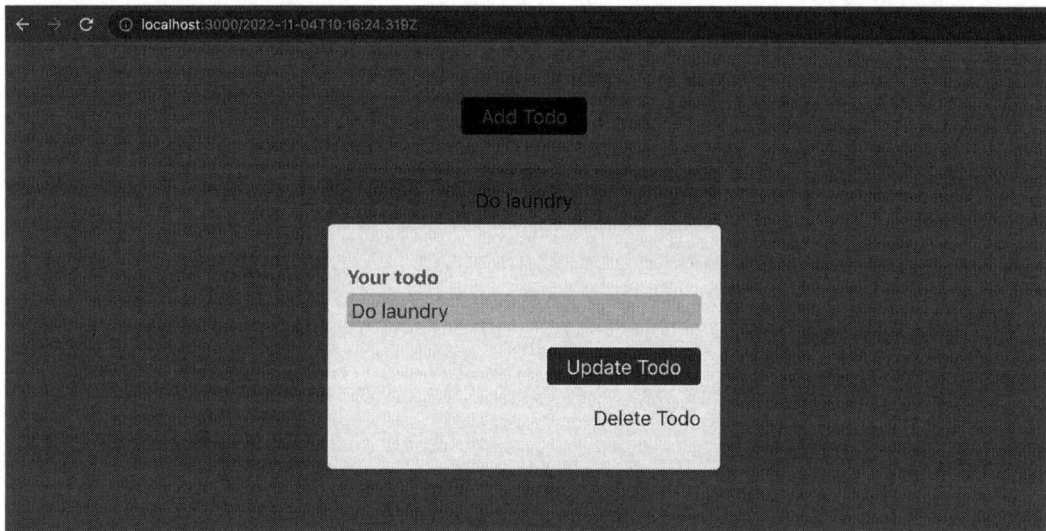

Figure 13.11: The /:id page, also opened as a modal, allowing users to edit or delete a to-do

No todos found

Start adding some!

Add Todo

Figure 13.12: An info message, displayed if no to-dos were found

> **NOTE**
>
> The solution to this activity can be found on page 533.

14

NEXT STEPS AND FURTHER RESOURCES

LEARNING OBJECTIVES

By the end of this chapter, you will know the following:

- How to best practice what you've learned throughout this book
- Which React topics you can explore next
- Which popular third-party React packages might be worth a closer look

INTRODUCTION

With this book, you've gotten a thorough (re-)introduction to the key React concepts you must know in order to work with React successfully, providing both theoretical and practical guidance for components, props, state, context, React Hooks, routing, and many other crucial concepts.

But React is more than just a collection of concepts and ideas. It powers an entire ecosystem of third-party libraries that help with many common React-specific problems. There is also a huge React community that shares solutions for common problems or popular patterns.

In this last, brief chapter, you'll learn about some of the most important and popular third-party libraries you might want to explore. You will also be introduced to other great resources that help with learning React. In addition, this chapter will share some recommendations on how best to proceed and continue to grow as a React developer after finishing this book.

HOW SHOULD YOU PROCEED?

In working through this book, you've learned a lot about React. But it's always challenging to then proceed and apply that knowledge to real projects.

So, how should you proceed? How do you best apply your knowledge and, hence, continue to grow as a React developer?

The most important factor is that you use your knowledge. Don't just read a book. Instead, use your newly gained skills to build some demo projects.

You don't have to build the next Amazon or TikTok. There's a reason why applications like these are built by huge teams. But you should build small demo projects that focus on a couple of core problems. You could, for example, build a very basic website that allows users to store and view their daily goals, or build a basic meetups page where visitors can organize and join meetup events.

To put it simply: practice is king. You must apply what you've learned and build stuff. Because by building demo projects, you'll automatically encounter problems that you'll have to solve without a solution at hand. You'll have to try out different approaches and search the internet for possible (partial) solutions. Ultimately, this is how you learn the most and how you develop your problem-solving skills.

You won't find a solution for all problems in this book, but this book does give you the basic tools and building blocks that will help you with those problems. Solutions are then built by combining these building blocks and by building upon the knowledge gathered throughout this book.

INTERESTING PROBLEMS TO EXPLORE

So, which problems and demo apps could you explore and try to build?

In general, you can try to build (simplified) clones of popular web apps (such as a highly simplified version of Amazon). Ultimately, your imagination is the limit, but in the following sections, you will find details and advice for three project ideas and the challenges that come with them.

BUILD A SHOPPING CART

A very common type of website is an online shop. You can find online shops for all kinds of products—ranging from physical goods such as books, clothing, or furniture to digital products such as video games or movies—and building such an online shop would be an interesting project idea and challenge.

Online shops do come with many features that can't be built with React. For example, the whole payment process is mostly a backend task where requests must be handled by servers. Inventory management would be another feature that takes place in databases and on servers, and not in the browsers of your website visitors. But there are also features that require interactive user interfaces (and that therefore benefit from using React), such as different pages that show lists of available products, product details, or the current status of an order, as you learned in *Chapter 12, Multipage Apps with React Router*. You also typically have shopping carts on websites. Building such a cart, combined with the functionality of adding and removing items, would similarly utilize several React features—for example, state management, as explained in *Chapter 4, Working with Events and State*.

It all starts with having a couple of pages (routes) for dummy products, product details, and the shopping cart itself. The shopping cart displays items that need to be managed via app-wide state (e.g., via context as covered in *Chapter 10, Working with Complex State*), as website visitors must be able to add items to the cart from the product detail page. You will also need a broad variety of React components—many of which must be reusable (e.g., the individual shopping cart items that are displayed). Your knowledge of React components and props from *Chapter 2, Understanding React Components and JSX*, and *Chapter 3, Components and Props*, will help with that.

The shopping cart state is also a non-trivial state. A simple list of products typically won't do the trick—though you can, of course, at least apply your knowledge from *Chapter 5, Rendering Lists and Conditional Content*. Instead, you must check whether an item is already part of the cart or if it's added for the first time. If it's part of the cart already, you must update the quantity of the cart item. Of course, you'll also need to ensure users are able to remove items from the cart or reduce the quantity of an item. And if you want to get even fancier, you can even simulate price changes that must be factored in when updating the shopping cart state.

As you can see, this extremely simple dummy online shop already offers quite a bit of complexity. Of course, you could also add backend functionality and store dummy products in a database. This can be done but is not required to practice working with React. Instead, you can use dummy data that's stored in variables or constants in your React code.

BUILD AN APPLICATION'S AUTHENTICATION SYSTEM (USER SIGNUP AND LOGIN)

A lot of websites allow users to sign up or log in. For many websites, user authentication is required before performing certain tasks. For example, you must create a Google account before uploading videos to YouTube or using Gmail (and many other Google services). Similarly, an account is typically needed before taking paid online courses or buying (digital) video games online. You also can't perform online banking without being logged in. And that's just a short list; many more examples could be added, but you get the idea. User authentication is required for a broad variety of reasons on many websites.

And on even more websites, it's optionally available. For example, you might be able to order products as a guest, but you benefit from extra advantages when creating an account (e.g., you may track your order history or collect reward points).

Of course, building your own version of YouTube is much too challenging to be a good practice project. There's a reason why Google has thousands of developers on its payroll. But you can identify and clone individual features—such as user authentication.

Build your own user authentication system with React. Make sure that users can sign up and log in. Add a few example pages (routes) to your website and find a way of making some pages only available to logged-in users. These targets might not sound like much, but you will actually face quite a lot of challenges along the way— challenges that force you to find solutions for brand-new problems.

In addition, you can get even more advanced and dive into backend development as well (in addition to the frontend development done with React). While you could just use some dummy logic in your React app code to simulate HTTP requests that are sent to your servers behind the scenes, you could also add a real demo backend instead. That backend would need to store user accounts in a database, validate login requests, and send back authentication tokens that inform the React frontend about the current authentication status of a user. In your React app, these HTTP requests would be treated as side effects, as covered in *Chapter 8, Handling Side Effects*.

The backend would be built with a different technology than React though (such as with Node.js and the Express library) and is therefore quite a bit more advanced. Alternatively, you can keep things simple by instead having some app-wide "user is authenticated" state in your React app. In that case, you could still get a bit more advanced by storing that state in the browser (e.g., via `localStorage`) to restore it after page reloads.

As you can tell, this "simple" project idea (or, rather, feature idea) presents a lot of challenges and will require you to build on your React knowledge and find solutions for a broad variety of problems.

BUILD AN EVENT MANAGEMENT WEBSITE

If you first were to build your own shopping cart system and get started with user authentication, you could then take it a step further and build a more complex website that combines these features (and offers new, additional features).

One such project idea would be an event management site. This is a website on which users can create accounts and, once they're logged in, events. All visitors can then browse these events and register for them. It would be up to you whether registration as guests (without creating an account first) is possible or not.

It's also your choice whether you want to add backend logic (that is, a server that handles requests and stores users and events in a database) or you will simply store all data in your React application (via app-wide state). If you don't add a backend, all data will be lost whenever the page is reloaded, and you can't see the events created by other users on other machines, but you can still practice all these key React features.

And there are many React features that are needed for this kind of dummy website: reusable components, pages (routes), component-specific and app-wide state, handling and validating user input, displaying conditional and list data, and much more.

Again, this is clearly not an exhaustive list of examples. You can build whatever you want. Be creative and experiment, because you'll only master React if you use it to solve problems.

COMMON AND POPULAR REACT LIBRARIES

No matter which kind of React app you're building, you'll encounter many problems and challenges along the way. From handling and validating user input to sending HTTP requests, complex applications come with many challenges.

You can solve all challenges on your own and even write all the (React) code that's needed on your own. And for practicing, this might indeed be a good idea. But as you're building more and more complex apps, it might make sense to outsource certain problems.

Thankfully, React features a rich and vibrant ecosystem that offers third-party packages that solve all kinds of common problems. Here's a brief, non-exhaustive list of popular third-party libraries that might be helpful:

- **React Hook Form**: A library that simplifies the process of handling and validating user input (https://react-hook-form.com/).

- **Formik**: Another popular library that helps with form input handling and validation (https://formik.org/).

- **Axios**: A general JavaScript library that simplifies the process of sending HTTP requests and handling responses (https://axios-http.com/).

- **SWR**: A React-specific alternative to Axios, also aiming to simplify the process of sending HTTP requests and using response data (https://swr.vercel.app/).

- **Redux**: In the past, this was an essential React library. Nowadays, it can still be important as it can greatly simplify the management of (complex) cross-component or app-wide state (https://redux.js.org/).

This is just a short list of some helpful and popular libraries. Since there's an endless number of potential challenges, you could also compile an infinite list of libraries. Search engines and Stack Overflow (a message board for developers) are your friends when it comes to finding more libraries that solve other problems.

OTHER RESOURCES

As mentioned, React does have a highly vibrant ecosystem—and not just when it comes to third-party libraries. You'll also find hundreds of thousands of blog posts, discussing all kinds of best practices, patterns, ideas, and solutions to possible problems. Searching for the right keywords (such as "React form validation with Hooks") will almost always yield interesting articles or helpful libraries.

You'll also find plenty of paid online courses, such as the "React – The Complete Guide" course at https://www.udemy.com/course/react-the-complete-guide-incl-redux/?couponCode=D_0922, and free tutorials on YouTube.

The official documentation is another great place to explore as it contains deep dives into core topics as well as more tutorial articles: https://reactjs.org/.

BEYOND REACT FOR WEB APPLICATIONS

This book focused on using React to build websites. This was for a couple of reasons. The first is that React, historically, was created to simplify the process of building complex web user interfaces, and React is powering more and more websites every day. It's one of the most widely used client-side web development libraries and more popular than ever before.

But it also makes sense to learn how to use React for web development because you need no extra tools—only a text editor and a browser.

That said, React can be used to build user interfaces outside the browser and websites as well. With React Native and Ionic for React, you have two very popular projects and libraries that use React to build native mobile apps for iOS and Android.

Therefore, after learning all these React essentials, it makes a lot of sense to also explore these projects. Pick up some React Native or Ionic courses (or use the official documentation) to learn how you can use all the React concepts covered in this book to build real native mobile apps that can be distributed through the platform app stores.

React can be used to build all kinds of interactive user interfaces for various platforms. Now that you've finished this book, you have the tools you need to build your next project with React—no matter which platform it targets.

FINAL WORDS

With all the concepts discussed throughout this book, as well as the extra resources and starting points to dive deeper, you are well prepared to build feature-rich and highly user-friendly web applications with React.

No matter if it's a simple blog or a complex Software-as-a-Service solution, you now know the key React concepts you need in order to build a React-driven web app your users will love.

I hope you got a lot out of this book. Definitely share any feedback you have, for example, via Twitter (@maxedapps) or by sending an email to customercare@packt.com.

APPENDIX

CHAPTER 2: UNDERSTANDING REACT COMPONENTS & JSX

ACTIVITY 2.1: CREATING A REACT APP TO PRESENT YOURSELF

Solution:

Perform the following steps to complete this activity:

1. Create a new React project by running npx create-react-app my-app. You can replace my-app with any name of your choice, and you can run this command in any fitting place on your system (e.g., on your desktop). Start the development web server by running npm start inside the created project folder.

2. Open the project with any code editor of your choice—for example, with Visual Studio Code (https://code.visualstudio.com/).

3. Open the App.js file and replace the existing JSX code that is returned with JSX code that structures and contains the information about yourself that you want to output.

```
function App() {
  return (
    <>
      <h2>Hi, this is me - Max!</h2>
      <p>Right now, I am 32 years old and I live in Munich.</p>
      <p>
        My full name is Maximilian Schwarzmüller and I am a web
developer as
        well as top-rated, bestselling online course instructor.
      </p>
    </>
  );
}
```

4. The final output should look like the following:

Hi, this is me - Max!

Right now, I am 32 years old and I live in Munich.

My full name is Maximilian Schwarzmüller and I am a web developer as well as top-rated, bestselling online course instructor.

Figure 2.5: The final activity result—some user information being output on the screen.

> **NOTE**
>
> You will find all code files for this solution at https://packt.link/DJh7X.

ACTIVITY 2.2: CREATING A REACT APP TO LOG YOUR GOALS FOR THIS BOOK

Solution:

Perform the following steps to complete this activity:

1. Create a new React project by running npx create-react-app my-app. You can replace my-app with any name of your choice, and you can run this command in any fitting place on your system (e.g., on your desktop). Start the development web server by running npm start inside the created project folder.

2. Create a new /src/components folder in the project

3. In the /src/components folder, create multiple component files—for example, FirstGoal.js, SecondGoal.js, ThirdGoal.js, GoalList.js and Header.js

   Your project folder should now look something like this:

```
> node_modules
> public
∨ src
  ∨ components
    JS FirstGoal.js
    JS GoalList.js
    JS Header.js
    JS SecondGoal.js
    JS ThirdGoal.js
  JS App.js
  # index.css
  JS index.js
◆ .gitignore
{} package-lock.json
{} package.json
```

Figure 2.6: React project with a "components" folder and multiple component files added.

4. Edit the individual goal component files (FirstGoal.js, etc.) and define and export component functions inside of them. Every component function should return a list item with any JSX markup of your choice and the goal title and text as main content. Here's an example for the first goal:

```
function FirstGoal() {
  return (
    <li>
      <article>
        <h2>Teach React in a highly-understandable way</h2>
        <p>
          I want to ensure, that you get the most out of this book
and you
          learn all about React!
        </p>
      </article>
    </li>
  );
}


export default FirstGoal;
```

5. In the GoalList.js file, define and export a GoalList component function and import the individual components. Thereafter, return JSX code that renders an unordered list (<ul>) with the custom goal components as list items:

```
import FirstGoal from './FirstGoal';
import SecondGoal from './SecondGoal';
import ThirdGoal from './ThirdGoal';


function GoalList() {
  return (
    <ul>
      <FirstGoal />
      <SecondGoal />
      <ThirdGoal />
```

```
      </ul>
    );
  }


  export default GoalList;
```

6. In the Header.js file, define and export a Header component and return some header JSX markup:

```
function Header() {
  return (
    <header>
      <h1>My Goals For This Book</h1>
    </header>
  );
}


export default Header;
```

7. Import the GoalList and Header components into the App.js file and replace the default JSX code with your own JSX code that renders these two components:

```
import GoalList from './components/GoalList';
import Header from './components/Header';


function App() {
  return (
    <>
      <Header />
      <GoalList />
    </>
  );
}


export default App;
```

The final output should look like the following:

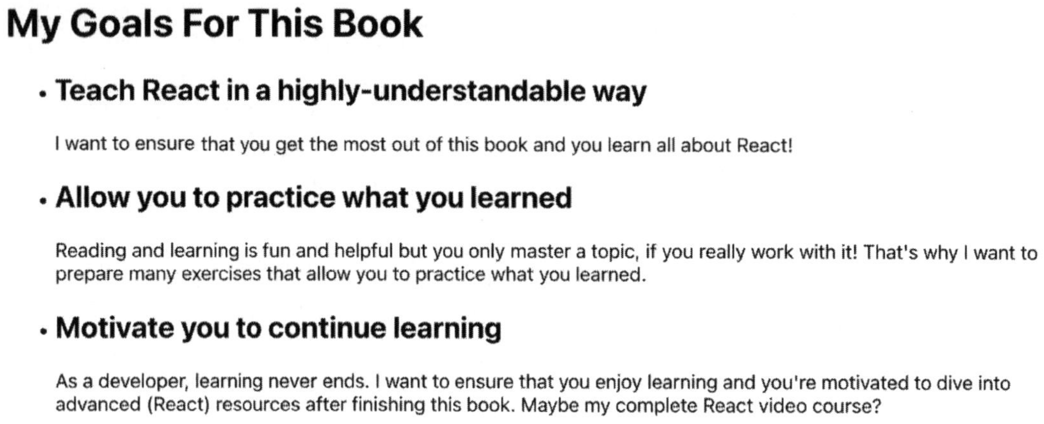

My Goals For This Book

- ### Teach React in a highly-understandable way

  I want to ensure that you get the most out of this book and you learn all about React!

- ### Allow you to practice what you learned

  Reading and learning is fun and helpful but you only master a topic, if you really work with it! That's why I want to prepare many exercises that allow you to practice what you learned.

- ### Motivate you to continue learning

  As a developer, learning never ends. I want to ensure that you enjoy learning and you're motivated to dive into advanced (React) resources after finishing this book. Maybe my complete React video course?

Figure 2.7: The final page output, showing a list of goals.

> **NOTE**
>
> You will find all code files for this solution at https://packt.link/8tvm6.

CHAPTER 3: COMPONENTS & PROPS

ACTIVITY 3.1: CREATING AN APP TO OUTPUT YOUR GOALS FOR THIS BOOK

Solution:

1. Finish *Activity 2.2* from the previous chapter.

2. Add a new component to the **src/components** folder, a component function named **GoalItem**, in a new **GoalItem.js** file.

3. Copy the component function (including the returned JSX code) from **FirstGoal.js** and add a new **props** parameter to the function. Remove the title and description text from the JSX code:

```
function GoalItem(props) {
  return (
    <li>
      <article>
        <h2></h2>
        <p>

        </p>
      </article>
    </li>
  );
}


export default GoalItem;
```

4. Output the title and description in the **GoalItem** component via props—for example, by using **props.title** and **props.children** (in the fitting places in the JSX code, in other words, between the **<h2>** and **<p>** tags).

5. In the **GoalList** component, remove the **FirstGoal**, **SecondGoal**, and so on components (imports and JSX code) and import and use the new **GoalItem** component instead. Output **<GoalItem>** once for every goal that should be displayed, and pass the **title** prop and a value for the **children** prop to these components:

```
import GoalItem from './GoalItem';


function GoalList() {
  return (
```

```
        <ul>
          <GoalItem title="Teach React in a highly-understandable way">
            Some goal text…
          </GoalItem>
          <GoalItem title="Allow you to practice what you learned">
            Some goal text…
          </GoalItem>
          <GoalItem title="Motivate you to continue learning">
            Some goal text…
          </GoalItem>
        </ul>
      );
    }


    export default GoalList;
```

6. Delete the redundant **FirstGoal.js**, **SecondGoal.js**, etc. files.

The final user interface could look like this:

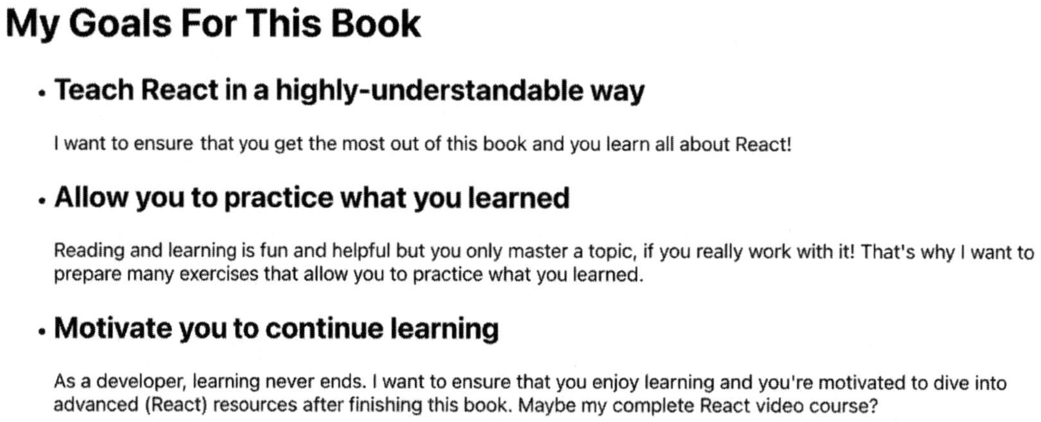

My Goals For This Book

• Teach React in a highly-understandable way

I want to ensure that you get the most out of this book and you learn all about React!

• Allow you to practice what you learned

Reading and learning is fun and helpful but you only master a topic, if you really work with it! That's why I want to prepare many exercises that allow you to practice what you learned.

• Motivate you to continue learning

As a developer, learning never ends. I want to ensure that you enjoy learning and you're motivated to dive into advanced (React) resources after finishing this book. Maybe my complete React video course?

Figure 3.2: The final result: Multiple goals output below each other

> **NOTE**
>
> You will all code files for this solution at https://packt.link/2R4Xo.

CHAPTER 4: WORKING WITH EVENTS & STATE

ACTIVITY 4.1: BUILDING A SIMPLE CALCULATOR

Solution:

Perform the following steps to complete this activity:

1. Add four new components into an **src/components** folder in a new React project: **Add.js**, **Subtract.js**, **Divide.js**, and **Multiply.js** (also add appropriately named component functions inside the component files).

2. Add the following code to **Add.js**:

```
function Add() {

  function changeFirstNumberHandler(event) {

  }

  function changeSecondNumberHandler(event) {

  }

  return (
    <p>
      <input type="number" onChange={changeFirstNumberHandler} /> +
      <input type="number" onChange={changeSecondNumberHandler} /> =
...
    </p>
  );
}

export default Add;
```

This component outputs a paragraph that contains two input elements (for the two numbers) and the result of the calculation. The input elements use the **onChange** prop to listen to the change event. Upon this event, the **changeFirstNumberHandler** and **changeSecondNumberHandler** functions are executed.

3. In order to make the component dynamic and derive the result based on the actual user input, state must be added. Import the **useState** Hook from React and initialize an object that contains a property for each of the two numbers. Alternatively, you could also use two individual state slices. Update the state(s) inside the two functions that are connected to the **change** event and set the state to the entered user value.

Make sure you convert the entered value to a number by adding a **+** in front of the value. Otherwise, string values will be stored, which will lead to incorrect results when adding the numbers.

The updated **Add.js** component should look like this:

```
import { useState } from 'react';

function Add() {
  const [enteredNumbers, setEnteredNumbers] = useState({
    first: 0, second: 0
  });

  function changeFirstNumberHandler(event) {
    setEnteredNumbers((prevNumbers) => ({
      first: +event.target.value, // "+" converts strings to numbers!
      second: prevNumbers.second,
    }));
  }

  function changeSecondNumberHandler(event) {
    setEnteredNumbers((prevNumbers) => ({
      first: prevNumbers.first,
      second: +event.target.value,
    }));
  }


  return (
    <p>
      <input type="number" onChange={changeFirstNumberHandler} /> +
      <input type="number" onChange={changeSecondNumberHandler} /> =
...
    </p>
  );
```

```
}

export default Add;
```

4. Next, derive the actual result of the mathematical operation. For this, a new **result** variable or constant can be added. Set it to the result of adding the two numbers that are stored in state.

The finished **Add.js** file looks like this:

```
import { useState } from 'react';

function Add() {
  const [enteredNumbers, setEnteredNumbers] = useState({
    first: 0, second: 0
  });

  function changeFirstNumberHandler(event) {
    setEnteredNumbers((prevNumbers) => ({
      first: +event.target.value,
      second: prevNumbers.second,
    }));
  }

  function changeSecondNumberHandler(event) {
    setEnteredNumbers((prevNumbers) => ({
      first: prevNumbers.first,
      second: +event.target.value,
    }));
  }

  const result = enteredNumbers.first + enteredNumbers.second;

  return (
    <p>
      <input type="number" onChange={changeFirstNumberHandler} /> +{'
'}
      <input type="number" onChange={changeSecondNumberHandler} /> =
{result}
    </p>
  );
```

```
    }

    export default Add;
```

5. Finally, copy the same code into the three other component files (**Subtract. js**, **Multiply.js**, and **Divide.js**). Just make sure to replace the component function name (also in the **export** statement) and to update the mathematical operation.

The final result and UI of the calculator should look like this:

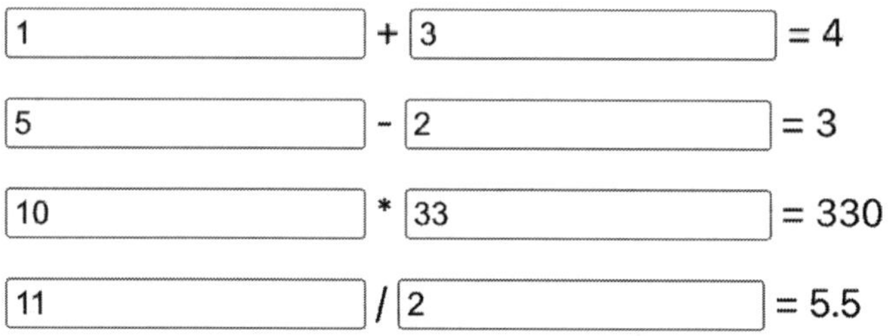

Figure 4.5: Calculator user interface

> **NOTE**
>
> You'll find all code files for this solution at https://packt.link/kARx8.

ACTIVITY 4.2: ENHANCING THE CALCULATOR

Solution:

Perform the following steps to complete this activity:

1. Remove three of the four components from the previous activity and rename the remaining one to **Calculation.js** (also rename the function in the component file).

2. Add a **<select>** drop-down (between the two inputs) to the **Calculation** component and add the four math operations as options (**<option>** elements) to it. You might want to give each option a clear identifier (such as **'add'**, **'subtract'**, and so on) via the built-in **value** prop. Remove the result.

The finished JSX code of the **Calculation** component should look like this:

```
return (
  <p>
    <input type="number" onChange={changeFirstNumberHandler} />
    <select>
      <option value="add">+</option>
      <option value="subtract">-</option>
      <option value="multiply">*</option>
      <option value="divide">/</option>
    </select>
    <input type="number" onChange={changeSecondNumberHandler} />
  </p>
```

3. Next, add a **Result.js** file with a **Result** component in the **src/components** folder. In that component, output the result of the calculation (for the moment, output some dummy number):

```
function Result() {
  return <p>Result: 5000</p>;
}


export default Result;
```

4. The problem now is that the inputs are in a different component than the result. The solution is to *lift the state up* to a common ancestor component. In this simple app, that would again be the **App** component. That component should manage the entered numbers and the chosen math operation states. It should also derive the result—dynamically, based on the chosen operation and the entered numbers. For this, an if statement can be used in the **component** function:

```
import { useState } from 'react';

import Calculation from './components/Calculation';
import Result from './components/Result';

function App() {
  const [enteredNumbers, setEnteredNumbers] = useState({
    first: 0, second: 0
  });
  const [chosenOperation, setChosenOperation] = useState('add');
```

```
// valid state values: 'add', 'subtract', 'multiply', 'divide'

function changeFirstNumberHandler(event) {
  setEnteredNumbers((prevNumbers) => ({
    first: +event.target.value,
    second: prevNumbers.second,
  }));
}

function changeSecondNumberHandler(event) {
  setEnteredNumbers((prevNumbers) => ({
    first: prevNumbers.first,
    second: +event.target.value,
  }));
}

function updateOperationHandler(event) {
  setChosenOperation(event.target.value);
}

let result;

if (chosenOperation === 'add') {
  result = enteredNumbers.first + enteredNumbers.second;
} else if (chosenOperation === 'subtract') {
  result = enteredNumbers.first - enteredNumbers.second;
} else if (chosenOperation === 'multiply') {
  result = enteredNumbers.first * enteredNumbers.second;
} else {
  result = enteredNumbers.first / enteredNumbers.second;
}

// return statement omitted, will be defined in the next step
}

export default App;
```

Since the component function will be re-executed by React whenever some state changes, **result** will be recalculated upon every state change.

5. Finally, include the two other components (**Calculation** and **Result**) in the returned JSX code of the **App** component. Use props to pass the event handler functions (**changeFirstNumberHandler**, **changeSecondNumberHandler**, and **updateOperationHandler**) to the **Calculation** component. Similarly, pass the derived **result** to the **Result** component. For the event handler functions, the props can be named **onXYZ** to indicate that functions are provided as values and that those functions will be used as event handler functions.

Therefore, the returned JSX code of the **App** component should look like this:

```
return (
  <>
    <Calculation
      onFirstNumberChanged={changeFirstNumberHandler}
      onSecondNumberChanged={changeSecondNumberHandler}
      onOperationChanged={updateOperationHandler}
    />
    <Result calculationResult={result} />
  </>
);
```

The **Calculation** component receives and uses the three **onXYZ** props like this:

```
function Calculation({
  onFirstNumberChanged,
  onSecondNumberChanged,
  onOperationChanged,
}) {
  return (
    <p>
      <input type="number" onChange={onFirstNumberChanged} />
      <select onChange={onOperationChanged}>
        <option value="add">+</option>
        <option value="subtract">-</option>
        <option value="multiply">*</option>
        <option value="divide">/</option>
      </select>
      <input type="number" onChange={onSecondNumberChanged} />
    </p>
  );
```

```
}

export default Calculation;
```

The **Result** component receives **calculationResult** and uses it like this:

```
function Result({ calculationResult }) {
    return <p>Result: {calculationResult}</p>;
}

export default Result;
```

The final result and UI of the calculator should look like this:

Figure 4.6: User interface of the enhanced calculator

> **NOTE**
>
> You'll find all code files for this solution at https://packt.link/0tdpg.

CHAPTER 5: RENDERING LISTS & CONDITIONAL CONTENT

ACTIVITY 5.1: SHOWING A CONDITIONAL ERROR MESSAGE

Solution:

Perform the following steps to complete this activity:

1. Create a new React project and remove the default JSX code returned by the **App** component. Instead, return a **<form>** element that contains an **<input>** of **type="text"** (for the purpose of this activity, it should not be **type="email"** to make entering incorrect email addresses easier). Also add a **<label>** for the **<input>** and a **<button>** that submits the form. The final JSX code returned by **App** should look something like this:

```
function App() {
  return (
      <form>
          <label htmlFor="email">Your email</label>
          <input type="text" id="email"/>
          <button>Submit</button>
      </form>
  );
}


export default App;
```

2. Register **change** events on the **<input>** element to store and update the entered email address via state:

```
import { useState } from 'react';


function App() {
  const [enteredEmail, setEnteredEmail] = useState();


  function emailChangeHandler(event) {
    setEnteredEmail(event.target.value);
    // enteredEmail is then not used hered, hence you could get a
    // warning related to this. You can ignore it for this example
  }


  return (
      <form>
```

```
            <label htmlFor="email">Your email</label>
            <input type="text" id="email" onChange={emailChangeHandler}
      />
            <button>Submit</button>
          </form>
      );
    }


    export default App;
```

3. Add a **submit** event handler function that is triggered every time the form is submitted. Prevent the browser default (of sending an HTTP request) by calling **event.preventDefault()** inside the **submit** event handler function. Also add logic to determine whether an email address is valid (contains an @ sign) or not (no @ sign):

```
    import { useState } from 'react';


    function App() {
      const [enteredEmail, setEnteredEmail] = useState();

      function emailChangeHandler(event) {
        setEnteredEmail(event.target.value);
      }


      function submitFormHandler(event) {
        event.preventDefault();
        const emailIsValid = enteredEmail.includes('@');
        // emailIsValid is then not used hered, hence you could get a
        // warning related to this. You can ignore it for this example
      }


      return (
          <form onSubmit={submitFormHandler}>
            <label htmlFor="email">Your email</label>
            <input type="text" id="email" onChange={emailChangeHandler}
      />
            <button>Submit</button>
          </form>
      );
```

```
}


export default App;
```

4. Add a new state slice (the following example has been named
    inputIsInvalid and set to **false** as a default) that stores the email
    validity information. Update the **inputIsInvalid** state based on the
    emailIsValid constant defined in **submitFormHandler**. Use the state to
    show an error message (inside a **<p>**) conditionally:

```
import { useState } from 'react';


function App() {
  const [enteredEmail, setEnteredEmail] = useState();
  const [inputIsInvalid, setInputIsInvalid] = useState(false);


  function emailChangeHandler(event) {
    setEnteredEmail(event.target.value);
  }


  function submitFormHandler(event) {
    event.preventDefault();
    const emailIsValid = enteredEmail.includes('@');
    setInputIsInvalid(!emailIsValid);
  }


  return (
    <section>
      <form onSubmit={submitFormHandler}>
        <label htmlFor="email">Your email</label>
        <input type="text" id="email" onChange={emailChangeHandler}
/>
        <button>Submit</button>
      </form>
      {inputIsInvalid && <p>Invalid email address entered!</p>}
    </section>
  );


}


export default App;
```

5. The **&&** operator is used in this example, but you could also use **if** statements, ternary expressions, or any other possible approach. It's also up to you whether you prefer to create and output conditional JSX elements *inline* (that is, directly inside of the returned JSX code) or with the help of a separate variable or constant.

The final user interface should look and work as shown here:

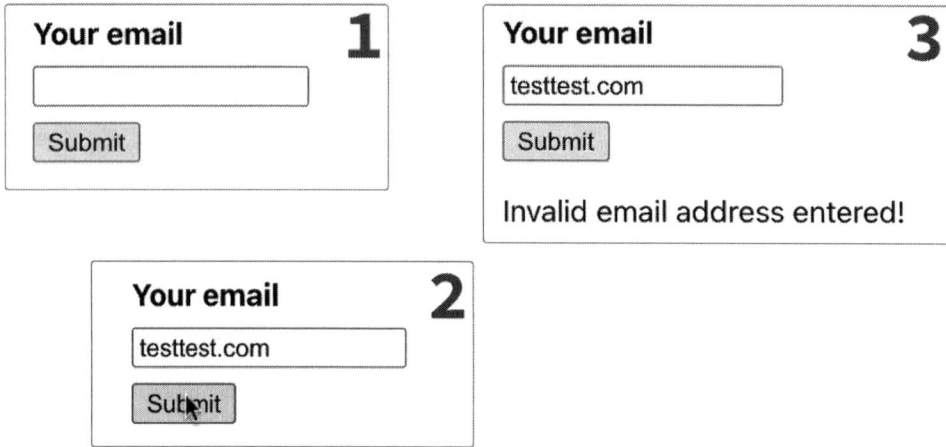

Figure 5.9: The final user interface of this activity

> **NOTE**
>
> You can find all code files for this solution at https://packt.link/GgEPO.

ACTIVITY 5.2: OUTPUTTING A LIST OF PRODUCTS

Solution:

Perform the following steps to complete this activity:

1. Create a new React project and remove the default JSX code returned by the **App** component. Instead, return a **<section>** that contains both a **<button>** (which will later be used to add a new product) and an (empty) **<ul>** element:

```
import { useState } from 'react';


function App() {
  return (
    <section>
      <button>Add Product</button>
      <ul></ul>
    </section>
  );
}


export default App;
```

2. Add an array of initial dummy products to the **App** component. Use this array as the initial value for the **products** state that must be added to the **App** component:

```
import { useState } from 'react';


const INITIAL_PRODUCTS = [
  { id: 'p1', title: 'React - The Complete Guide [Course]', price:
19.99 },
  { id: 'p2', title: 'Stylish Chair', price: 329.49 },
  { id: 'p3', title: 'Ergonomic Chair', price: 269.99 },
  { id: 'p4', title: 'History Video Game Collection', price: 99.99 },
];


function App() {
  const [products, setProducts] = useState(INITIAL_PRODUCTS);


  return (
    <section>
      <button>Add Product</button>
```

```
      <ul></ul>
    </section>
  );
}


export default App;
```

3. Output the list of products as part of the returned JSX code:

```
import { useState } from 'react';

const INITIAL_PRODUCTS = [
  { id: 'p1', title: 'React - The Complete Guide [Course]', price:
19.99 },
  { id: 'p2', title: 'Stylish Chair', price: 329.49 },
  { id: 'p3', title: 'Ergonomic Chair', price: 269.99 },
  { id: 'p4', title: 'History Video Game Collection', price: 99.99 },
];


function App() {
  const [products, setProducts] = useState(INITIAL_PRODUCTS);

  return (
    <section>
      <button>Add Product</button>
      <ul>
        {products.map((product) => (
          <li key={product.id}>
            {product.title} (${product.price})
          </li>
        ))}
      </ul>
    </section>
  );
}


export default App;
```

4. This example uses the **map()** method, but you could also use a **for** loop to populate an array with JSX elements, and then output that array as part of the JSX code. It's also up to you whether you create and output the list of JSX elements *inline* (that is, directly inside of the returned JSX code) or with the help of a separate variable or constant.

5. Add a **click** event handler to the **<button>**. Also, add a new function that is triggered upon **click** events on the button. Inside the function, update the **products** state such that a new (dummy) product is added. For the **id** value of that product, you can generate a pseudo-unique **id** by using a new **Date().toString()**:

```
import { useState } from 'react';

const INITIAL_PRODUCTS = [
  { id: 'p1', title: 'React - The Complete Guide [Course]', price:
19.99 },
  { id: 'p2', title: 'Stylish Chair', price: 329.49 },
  { id: 'p3', title: 'Ergonomic Chair', price: 269.99 },
  { id: 'p4', title: 'History Video Game Collection', price: 99.99 },
];

function App() {
  const [products, setProducts] = useState(INITIAL_PRODUCTS);

  function addProductHandler() {
    setProducts((curProducts) =>
      curProducts.concat({
        id: new Date().toString(),
        title: 'Another new product',
        price: 15.99,
      })
    );
  }

  return (
    <section>
      <button onClick={addProductHandler}>Add Product</button>
      <ul>
        {products.map((product) => (
          <li key={product.id}>
```

```
                {product.title} (${product.price})
            </li>
        ))}
      </ul>
    </section>
  );
}

export default App;
```

The final user interface should look and work as shown here:

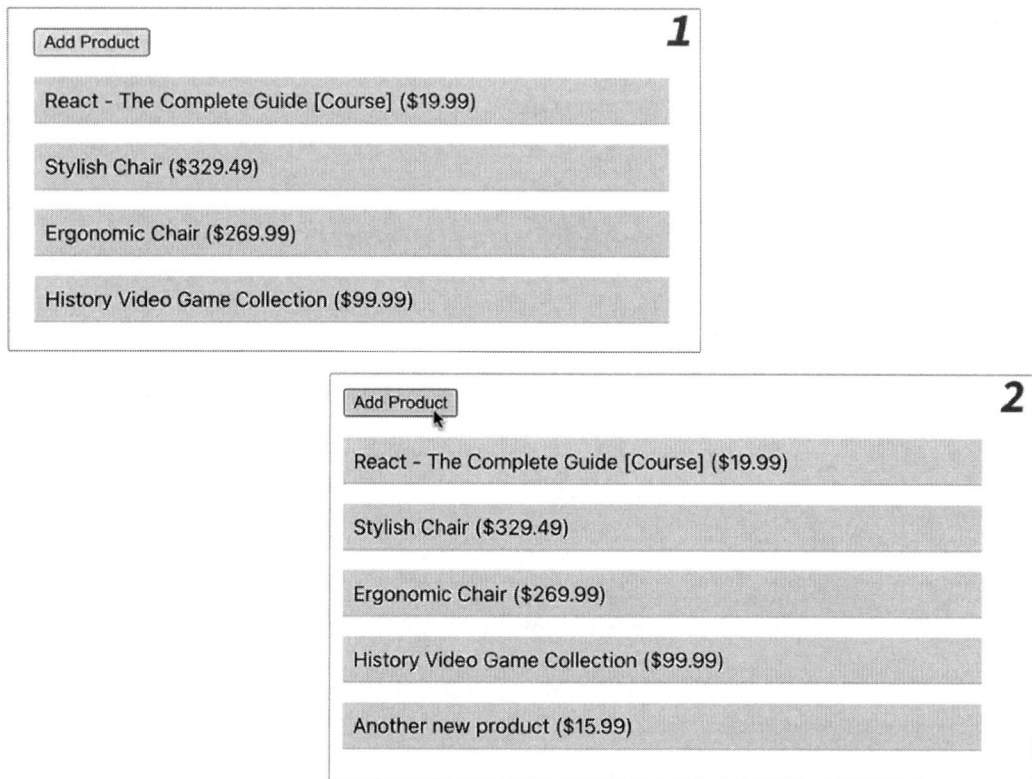

Figure 5.10: The final user interface of this activity

CHAPTER 6: STYLING REACT APPS

ACTIVITY 6.1: PROVIDING INPUT VALIDITY FEEDBACK UPON FORM SUBMISSION

Solution:

Perform the following steps to complete this activity:

1. Create a new React project and add a **Form** component function in a **components/Form.js** file in the project.

2. Export the component and import it into **App.js**.

3. Output the **<Form />** component as part of App's JSX code.

4. In the component, output a **<form>** that contains two **<input>** elements as well as **<label>** elements that belong to those input elements—one input for entering an email address and another input for entering a password.

5. Add a **<button>** element that submits the form:

```
function Form() {
  return (
    <form>
      <div>
        <label htmlFor="email">
          Your email
        </label>
        <input
          id="email"
          type="email"
        />
      </div>
      <div>
        <label htmlFor="password">
          Your password
        </label>
        <input
          id="password"
          type="password"
        />
      </div>
      <button>Submit</button>
    </form>
```

```
    );
  }
export default Form;
```

6. Add state and event handler functions to register and store entered **email** and
    password values:

```
import { useState } from 'react';
function Form() {
  const [enteredEmail, setEnteredEmail] = useState('');
  const [enteredPassword, setEnteredPassword] = useState('');
  function changeEmailHandler(event) {
    setEnteredEmail(event.target.value);
  }
  function changePasswordHandler(event) {
    setEnteredPassword(event.target.value);
  }
  return (
    <form>
      <div>
        <label htmlFor="email">
          Your email
        </label>
        <input
          id="email"
          type="email"
          onChange={changeEmailHandler}
        />
      </div>
      <div>
        <label htmlFor="password">
          Your password
        </label>
        <input
          id="password"
          type="password"
          onChange={changePasswordHandler}
        />
      </div>
      <button>Submit</button>
    </form>
```

```
    );
  }
export default Form;
```

7. Add a form submission handler function to **Form**.

8. Inside that function, validate the entered **email** and **password** values (with any validation logic of your choosing).

    The validation results (**true** or **false**) for the two input fields are then stored in two new state slices (one for the email's validity and one for the password's validity):

```
import { useState } from 'react';
function Form() {
  const [enteredEmail, setEnteredEmail] = useState('');
  const [emailIsValid, setEmailIsValid] = useState(true);
  const [enteredPassword, setEnteredPassword] = useState('');
  const [passwordIsValid, setPasswordIsValid] = useState(true);
  function changeEmailHandler(event) {
    setEnteredEmail(event.target.value);
  }
  function changePasswordHandler(event) {
    setEnteredPassword(event.target.value);
  }
  function submitFormHandler(event) {
    event.preventDefault();
    const emailIsValid = enteredEmail.includes('@');
    const passwordIsValid = enteredPassword.trim().length >= 6;
    setEmailIsValid(emailIsValid);
    setPasswordIsValid(passwordIsValid);
    if (!emailIsValid || !passwordIsValid) {
      return;
    }
    // do something...
    console.log('Inputs are valid, form submitted!');
  }
  return (
    <form onSubmit={submitFormHandler}>
      <div>
        <label htmlFor="email">
          Your email
```

```
        </label>
        <input
          id="email"
          type="email"
          onChange={changeEmailHandler}
        />
      </div>
      <div>
        <label htmlFor="password">
          Your password
        </label>
        <input
          id="password"
          type="password"
          onChange={changePasswordHandler}
        />
      </div>
      <button>Submit</button>
    </form>
  );
}
export default Form;
```

9. Use the validation result state values to conditionally add the **invalid** CSS class (defined in **index.css**) to the **<label>** and **<input>** elements:

```
function Form() {
  // ... code didn't change, hence omitted ...
  return (
    <form onSubmit={submitFormHandler}>
      <div>
        <label htmlFor="email" className={!emailIsValid &&
'invalid'}>
          Your email
        </label>
        <input
          id="email"
          type="email"
          onChange={changeEmailHandler}
          className={!emailIsValid && 'invalid'}
        />
      </div>
```

```
      <div>
        <label htmlFor="password" className={!passwordIsValid &&
'invalid'}>
          Your password
        </label>
        <input
          id="password"
          type="password"
          onChange={changePasswordHandler}
          className={!passwordIsValid && 'invalid'}
        />
      </div>
      <button>Submit</button>
    </form>
  );
}
```

This example does not use CSS Modules; hence, the CSS classes are added as string values and no special CSS import syntax is used here.

The final user interface should look like this:

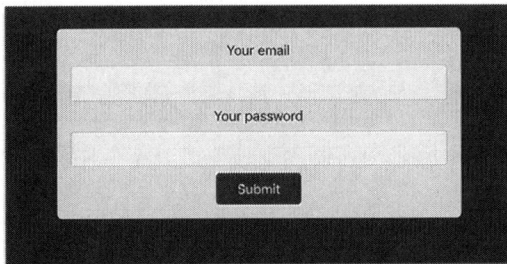

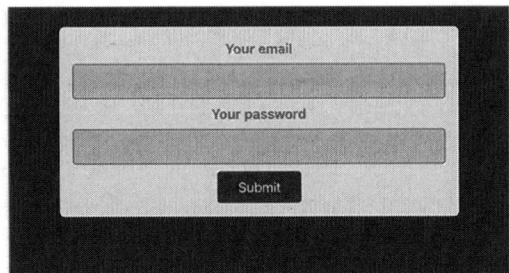

Figure 6.7: The final user interface with invalid input values highlighted in red

> **NOTE**
>
> You will find all code files used for this solution at https://packt.link/1iAe9.

ACTIVITY 6.2: USING CSS MODULES FOR STYLE SCOPING

Solution:

Perform the following steps to complete this activity:

1. Finish *Activity 6.01* or use the provided code on GitHub.

2. Identify all **Form**-related CSS rules defined in **index.css**. The relevant rules are as follows:

Form-related CSS rules	Relevance
`form { ... }`	This rule sets the general styling for the form.
`input { ... }`	This rule sets the general `<input>` styles.
`label { ... }`	This rule sets the general `<label>` styles.
`button { ... }` and `button:hover { ... }`	These rules set the `<button>` styles.
`label.invalid { ... }` and `input.invalid { ... }`	These rules control the conditionally added styles.

Figure 6.8: Table for Form-related CSS rules

You could, of course, argue that the **form, input, label,** and **button** styles should be global styles because you might have multiple forms (and inputs, labels, and buttons) in your app—not just in the **Form** component. This would be a valid argument, especially for bigger apps. However, in this demo, all these styles are only used in the **Form** component and therefore should be migrated.

3. Cut the identified styles from **index.css** and add them into a newly created **components/Form.module.css** file. The file must end with **.module. css** to enable the CSS Modules feature. Since CSS Modules need class selectors, all selectors that don't use classes right now must be changed so that **form {** **... }** becomes **.form { ... }, input { ... }** becomes **.input {** **... },** and so on.

The leading dots (.) matter because the dot is what defines a CSS class selector. The class names are up to you and don't have to be **.form, .input,** and so on. Use any class names of your choice, but you must migrate all non-class selectors to class selectors. For consistency, **input.invalid** is also changed to **.input.invalid** and **label.invalid** is changed to **.label.invalid**.

The finished **`Form.module.css`** file looks like this:

```css
.form {
  max-width: 30rem;
  margin: 2rem auto;
  padding: 1rem;
  border-radius: 6px;
  text-align: center;
  background-color: #eee8f8;
}
.input {
  display: block;
  width: 100%;
  font: inherit;
  padding: 0.5rem;
  margin-bottom: 0.5rem;
  font-size: 1.25rem;
  border-radius: 4px;
  background-color: #f9f6fc;
  border: 1px solid #ccc;
}
.label {
  display: block;
  margin-bottom: 0.5rem;
}
.button {
  cursor: pointer;
  font: inherit;
  padding: 0.5rem 1.5rem;
  background-color: #310485;
  color: white;
  border: 1px solid #310485;
  border-radius: 4px;
}
.button:hover {
  background-color: #250364;
}
.label.invalid {
  font-weight: bold;
  color: #ce0653;
```

```
}
.input.invalid {
  background-color: #fcbed6;
  border-color: #ce0653;
}
```

4. Import **Form.module.css** into the **Form.js** file as follows:

```
import classes from './Form.module.css';.
```

5. Assign the defined and imported classes to the appropriate JSX elements. Keep in mind that you must use the imported **classes** object to access the class names since the final class names are unknown to you (they transformed during the build process). For example, **<button>** receives its class (**.button**) like this: **<button className={classes.button}>**. For the conditional classes (the **.invalid** classes), the final code looks as follows:

```
<label
  htmlFor="email"
  className={
      !emailIsValid ? `${classes.label} ${classes.invalid}` :
classes.label
    }
  >
  Your email
</label>
```

6. Work with extra variables that store the ternary expressions (or replace them using **if** statements) to reduce the amount of logic injected into the JSX code.

The final **Form.js** file looks like this:

```
import { useState } from 'react';
import classes from './Form.module.css';
function Form() {
  // ... other code - did not change ...
  return (
    <form className={classes.form} onSubmit={submitFormHandler}>
      <div>
        <label
          htmlFor="email"
          className={
            !emailIsValid
              ? `${classes.label} ${classes.invalid}`
```

```
            : classes.label
      }
    >
      Your email
  </label>
  <input
    id="email"
    type="email"
    onChange={changeEmailHandler}
    className={
      !emailIsValid
        ? `${classes.input} ${classes.invalid}`
        : classes.input
    }
  />
</div>
<div>
  <label
    htmlFor="password"
    className={
      !passwordIsValid
        ? `${classes.label} ${classes.invalid}`
        : classes.label
    }
  >
    Your password
  </label>
  <input
    id="password"
    type="password"
    onChange={changePasswordHandler}
    className={
      !passwordIsValid
        ? `${classes.input} ${classes.invalid}`
        : classes.input
    }
  />
</div>
<button className={classes.button}>Submit</button>
</form>
```

```
    );
  }
  export default Form;
```

As explained above, the final user interface will look the same on the surface as that of the previous activity:

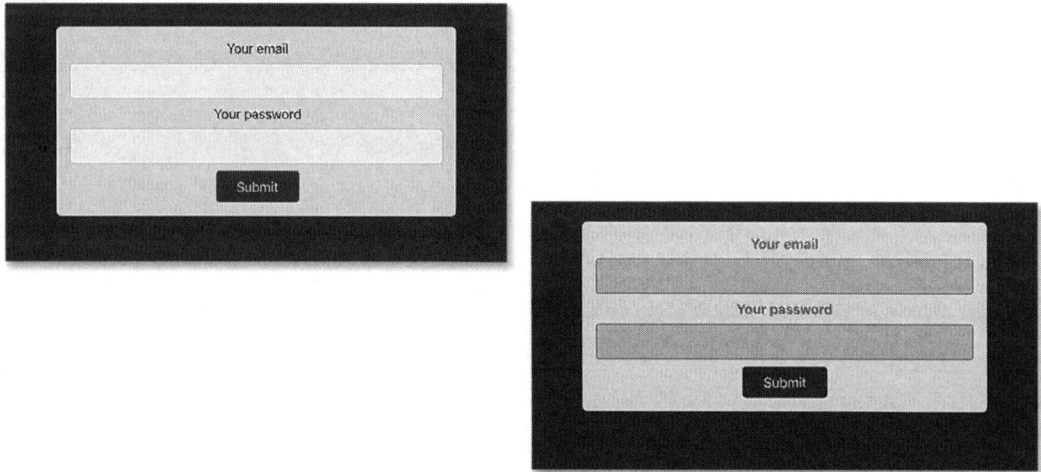

Figure 6.9: The final user interface with invalid input values highlighted in red

Test your new interface to see CSS scoped styles in action.

> **NOTE**
>
> You will find all code files used for this solution at https://packt.link/fPvg1.

CHAPTER 7: PORTALS & REFS

ACTIVITY 7.1: EXTRACT USER INPUT VALUES

Solution:

After downloading the code and running **npm install** in the project folder (to install all the required dependencies), the solution steps are as follows:

1. Inside the **Form** component, create two ref objects via **useRef()**. Make sure that you don't forget to run **import { useRef } from 'react'**:

```
import { useRef } from 'react';

function Form() {
  const nameRef = useRef();
  const programRef = useRef();

  // ... other code ...
}
```

2. Still in the **Form** component, connect the ref objects to their respective JSX elements (**<input>** and **<select>**) via the special **ref** prop:

```
return (
  <form onSubmit={formSubmitHandler}>
    <div className="form-control">
      <label htmlFor="name">Your name</label>
      <input type="text" id="name" ref={nameRef} />
    </div>
    <div className="form-control">
      <label htmlFor="program">Choose your program</label>
      <select id="program" ref={programRef}>
        <option value="basics">The Basics</option>
        <option value="advanced">Advanced Concepts</option>
        <option value="mastery">Mastery</option>
      </select>
    </div>
    <button>Submit</button>
  </form>
);
```

3. In the **formSubmitHandler** function, extract the entered values by accessing the connected ("stored") DOM elements via the special **current** property on the ref object. Also output the extracted values to the console via **console. log()**:

```
function formSubmitHandler (event) {
  event.preventDefault();

  const enteredName = nameRef.current.value;
  const selectedProgram = programRef.current.value;

  console.log('Entered Name: ' + enteredName);
  console.log('Selected Program: ' + selectedProgram);
}
```

The expected result (user interface) should look like this:

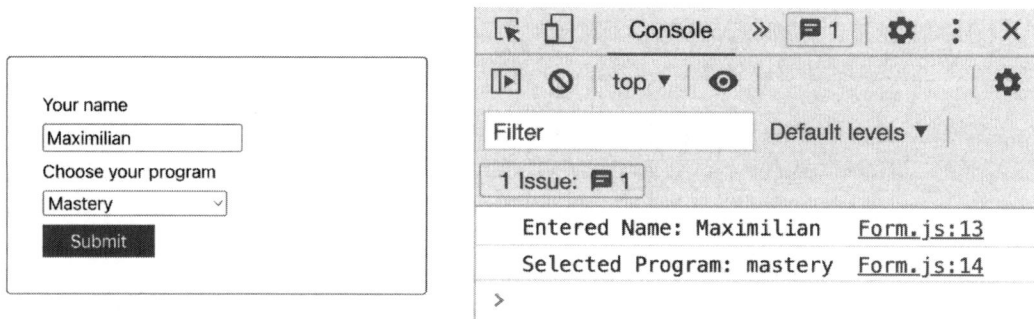

Figure 7.11: The browser developer tools console outputs the selected values

> **NOTE**
>
> You will find all code files used for this solution at https://packt.link/RnnoT.

ACTIVITY 7.2: ADD A SIDE-DRAWER

Solution:

After downloading the code and running **npm install** to install all the required dependencies, the solution steps are as follows:

1. Add the conditional rendering logic by adding a **drawerIsOpen** state (via **useState()**) to the **MainNavigation** component. Set the state to **false** initially and in a function that should later be executed whenever the backdrop is clicked, while setting the state to **true** in a function that is executed upon a click of the menu button:

```
import { useState } from 'react';

import SideDrawer from './SideDrawer';
import classes from './MainNavigation.module.css';

function MainNavigation() {
  const [drawerIsOpen, setDrawerIsOpen] = useState(false);

  function openDrawerHandler() {
    setDrawerIsOpen(true);
  }

  function closeDrawerHandler() {
    setDrawerIsOpen(false);
  }

  return (
    <>
      <header className={classes.header}>
        <h1>Demo App</h1>
        <button className={classes.btn} onClick={openDrawerHandler}>
          <div />
          <div />
          <div />
        </button>
```

```
        </header>
        {drawerIsOpen && <SideDrawer />}
      </>
    );
  }


  export default MainNavigation;
```

2. Pass a pointer to the **closeDrawerHandler** function to the **SideDrawer** component (here, this is via a prop called **onClose**: **<SideDrawer onClose={closeDrawerHandler} />**) and execute that function inside the **SideDrawer** component whenever the **<div>** backdrop is clicked:

```
import classes from './SideDrawer.module.css';

function SideDrawer({ onClose }) {
  return (
    <>
      <div className={classes.backdrop} onClick={onClose} />
      <aside className={classes.drawer}>
        <nav>
          <ul>
            <li>
              <a href="/">Dashboard</a>
            </li>
            <li>
              <a href="/products">All Products</a>
            </li>
            <li>
              <a href="/profile">Your Profile</a>
            </li>
          </ul>
        </nav>
      </aside>
    </>
  );
}


export default SideDrawer;
```

3. To control where the side drawer JSX elements are inserted into the DOM, use React's portal feature. As a first step, add an *"injection hook"* to the **public/index.html** file:

```
<body>
  <noscript>You need to enable JavaScript to run this app.</noscript>
  <div id="root"></div>
  <div id="drawer"></div>
</bod>
```

4. In this case, **<div id="drawer">** was inserted at the end of the **<body>** element to make sure that it would be positioned (visually) above any other overlays that might exist.

5. Use the newly added hook (**<div id="drawer">**) and the **createPortal()** function of **react-dom** inside the **SideDrawer** component to instruct React to render the component's JSX code in this specific place in the DOM:

```
import { createPortal } from 'react-dom';

import classes from './SideDrawer.module.css';

function SideDrawer({ onClose }) {
  return createPortal(
    <>
      <div className={classes.backdrop} onClick={onClose} />
      <aside className={classes.drawer}>
        <nav>
          <ul>
            <li>
              <a href="/">Dashboard</a>
            </li>
            <li>
              <a href="/products">All Products</a>
            </li>
            <li>
              <a href="/profile">Your Profile</a>
            </li>
          </ul>
        </nav>
      </aside>
    </>,
```

```
        document.getElementById('drawer')
    );
}


export default SideDrawer;
```

The final user interface should look and behave like this:

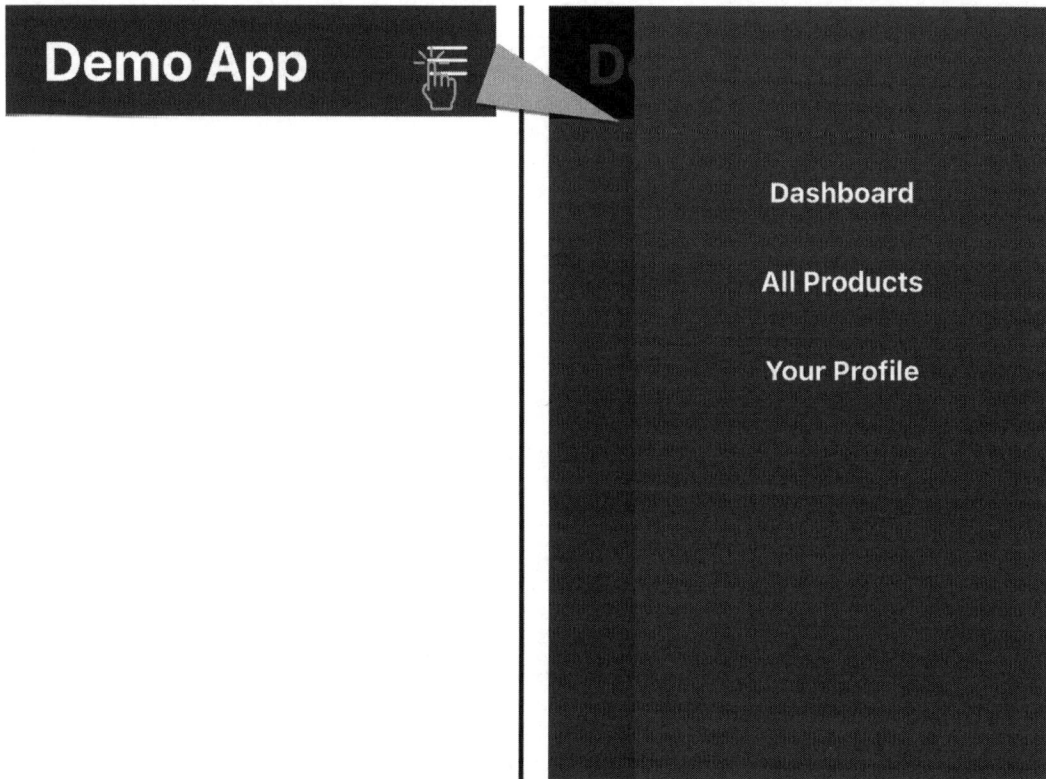

Figure 7.12: A click on the menu button opens the side drawer

Upon clicking on the menu button, the side drawer opens. If the backdrop behind the side drawer is clicked, it should close again.

The final DOM structure (with the side drawer opened) should look like this:

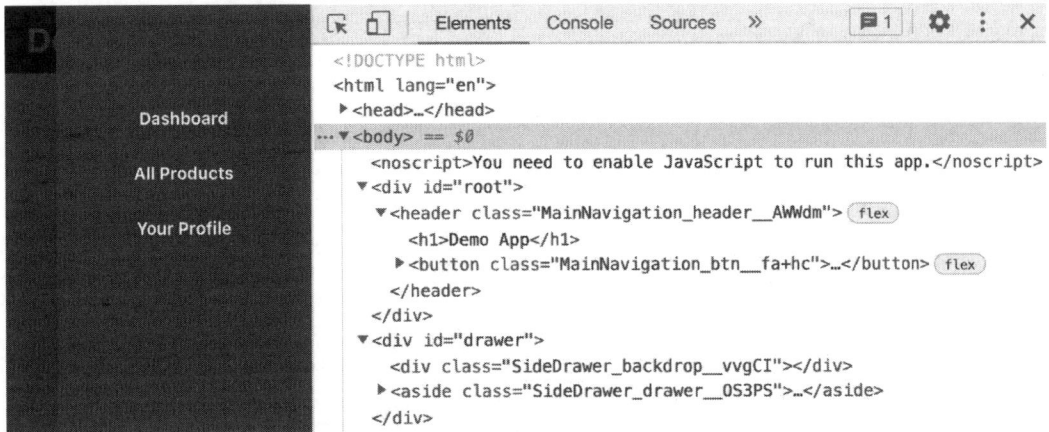

Figure 7.13: The drawer-related elements are inserted in a separate place in the DOM

The side drawer-related DOM elements (the **<div>** backdrop and **<aside>**) are inserted into a separate DOM node (**<div id="drawer">**).

> **NOTE**
>
> You will find all code files used for this solution at https://packt.link/APvHg.

CHAPTER 8: HANDLING SIDE EFFECTS

ACTIVITY 8.1: BUILDING A BASIC BLOG

Solution:

After downloading the code and running **npm install** in the project folder to install all required dependencies, the solution steps are as follows:

1. Inside the **NewPost** component, in the **submitHandler** function, use the **fetch()** function to send a **POST** request to https://jsonplaceholder.typicode.com/posts:

```
function submitHandler(event) {
  event.preventDefault();
  fetch('https://jsonplaceholder.typicode.com/posts', {
    method: 'POST',
    body: JSON.stringify({ title: enteredTitle }),
  });
}
```

You can confirm that everything works as intended and view the network request in the browser developer tools via the **Network** tab:

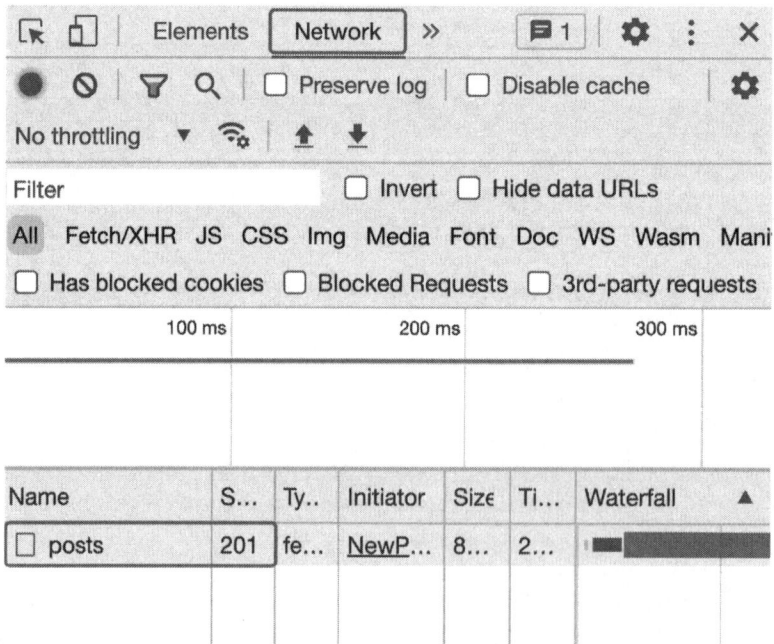

Figure 8.10: The network request is sent successfully

useEffect() is not required for this outgoing request because the HTTP request is not triggered when the component function is invoked but rather when the form is submitted. Indeed, if you tried to use **useEffect()** for this request, you'd have to get creative as using **useEffect()** inside of **submitHandler** violates the rules of Hooks.

2. To fetch blog posts when the app is rendered, you should import **useEffect** from react in **App.js**. Thereafter, inside the **App** component, call **useEffect()** directly in the component function and pass an effect function (an empty function for now) and an empty dependencies array to the effect:

```
import { useEffect } from 'react';
import BlogPosts from './components/BlogPosts';
import NewPost from './components/NewPost';
function App() {
  useEffect(function () {}, []);
  return (
    <>
      <NewPost />
      <BlogPosts />
    </>
  );
}
export default App;
```

3. Inside the effect function (in the **App** component), send a **GET** request via the **fetch()** function to https://jsonplaceholder.typicode.com/posts. To extract the response and response data in a convenient way, wrap the HTTP request code in a separate **async function loadPosts** (defined as part of the effect function), which is called in the effect function. **await** both the response as well as the data extracted from the response (via the **json()** method):

```
useEffect(function () {
  async function loadPosts() {
    const response = await fetch(
      'https://jsonplaceholder.typicode.com/posts'
    );
```

```
        const blogPosts = await response.json();
    }

    loadPosts();
}, []);
```

Keep in mind that the effect function itself must not be turned into an **async** function since it must not return a promise.

4. Add a state value (named **loadedPosts** here) to the **App** component and set the state value from inside **loadPosts()** (the function in the effect function) to the fetched **blogPosts** value. Pass the **loadedPosts** state value to **<BlogPosts>** via props (for example, via a **posts** prop):

```
import { useState, useEffect } from 'react';

import BlogPosts from './components/BlogPosts';
import NewPost from './components/NewPost';

function App() {
  const [loadedPosts, setLoadedPosts] = useState([]);

  useEffect(function () {
    async function loadPosts() {
      const response = await fetch(
        'https://jsonplaceholder.typicode.com/posts'
      );

      const blogPosts = await response.json();
      setLoadedPosts(blogPosts);
    }

    loadPosts();
  }, []);

  return (
    <>
      <NewPost />
      <BlogPosts posts={loadedPosts} />
    </>
  );
```

```
  }

  export default App;
```

5. Inside of **BlogPosts**, render the list of blog posts received via props by mapping all blog post list items to **<li>** elements. Output the blog post titles in the list:

```
function BlogPosts({ posts }) {
  return (
    <ul className={classes.posts}>
      {posts.map((post) => (
        <li key={post.id}>{post.title}</li>
      ))}
    </ul>
  );
}
```

6. For the bonus task, inside of the **NewPost** component, add a new state value called **isSendingRequest** via **useState()**. Set the state to **true** right before the **POST** HTTP request is sent and to **false** thereafter. Wait for the request to complete by turning **submitHandler** into an **async** function and await the **fetch()** function call:

```
import { useState } from 'react';

import classes from './NewPost.module.css';

function NewPost() {
  const [enteredTitle, setEnteredTitle] = useState('');
  const [isSendingRequest, setIsSendingRequest] = useState(false);

  function updateTitleHandler(event) {
    setEnteredTitle(event.target.value);
  }

  async function submitHandler(event) {
    event.preventDefault();

    setIsSendingRequest(true);

    await fetch('https://jsonplaceholder.typicode.com/posts', {
```

```
    method: 'POST',
    body: JSON.stringify({ title: enteredTitle }),
  });


  setIsSendingRequest(false);
  setEnteredTitle('');
}


// JSX code didn't change...
}


export default NewPost;
```

7. Still inside **NewPost**, set the **\<button\>** caption conditionally based on **isSendingRequest** to either show "Saving…" (if **isSendingRequest** is **true**) or "Save":

```
return (
  <form onSubmit={submitHandler} className={classes.form}>
    <div>
      <label>Title</label>
      <input
        type="text"
        onChange={updateTitleHandler}
        value={enteredTitle} />
    </div>
    <button disabled={isSendingRequest}>
      {isSendingRequest ? 'Saving...' : 'Save'}
    </button>
  </form>
);
```

The expected result should be a user interface that looks like this:

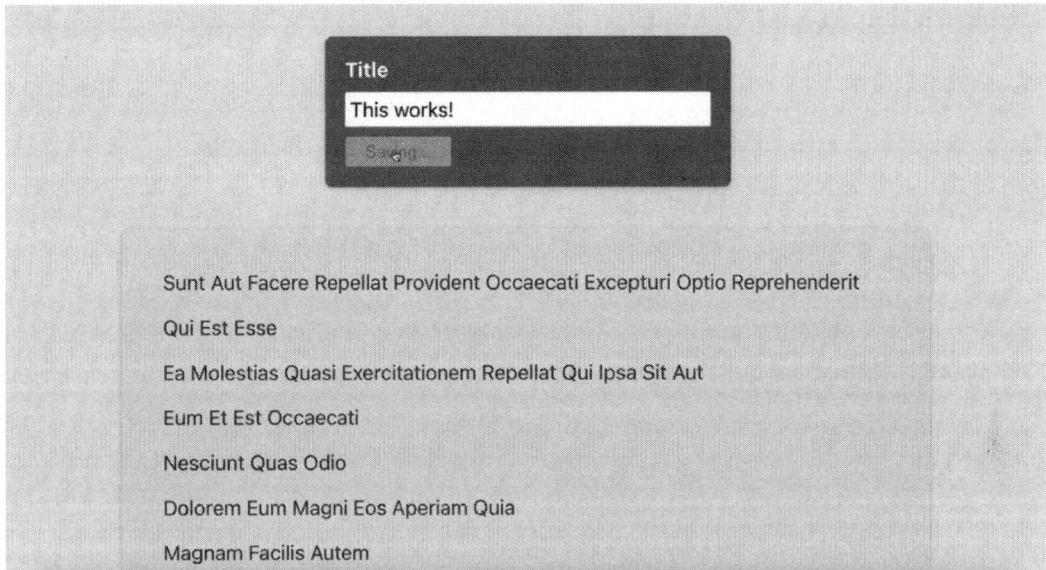

Figure 8.11: The final user interface

> **NOTE**
>
> All code files used for this solution can be found at https://packt.link/NoEZz.

CHAPTER 9: BEHIND THE SCENES OF REACT & OPTIMIZATION OPPORTUNITIES

ACTIVITY 9.1: OPTIMIZE AN EXISTING APP

Solution:

Naturally, for an activity like this, chances are high that every developer comes up with different ideas for optimizing the app. And indeed, there will be more than one correct solution. Below, you will find solution steps describing the optimizations I would implement. Definitely feel free to go beyond those steps. For example, in the solution provided below, the code structure will not be changed (that is, components will not be broken apart, etc.). You could absolutely consider such measures as well though.

Four areas of possible improvement were identified for this solution:

- In the **Authentication** component, the app allows for switching between the **Login** and **Signup** forms. While the **Login** form is always loaded (it's the first thing every page visitor sees), the **Signup** area will not always be needed—existing users will very likely not create a new account after all. Therefore, loading the code for **Signup** lazily makes sense, especially since the **Signup** component also **internally** uses the **Validation** component, which is rather complex and even includes a third-party package (**react-icons**). Being able to load all that code only when it's needed ensures that the initially loaded code bundle is kept lean.

- In the **Validation** component, both the email addresses and the password are validated. While the email validation is relatively simple and straightforward, validating the password involves various regular expressions (that is, matching for text patterns). Avoiding unnecessary execution of the password validation code therefore makes sense.

- In addition, the **Validation** component function will be re-executed whenever the **Signup** component function is invoked. Since **Signup** also includes state for conditionally showing or hiding extra information (via the **More Information** button), ensuring that the **Validation** component is not re-evaluated unnecessarily is another important step.

- The last identified area of improvement can be found in the **Login** component. There, the **ResetPassword** component code should only be loaded when it's needed. Typically, resetting a password involves quite a bit of code and logic (for example, asking a security question, checking for bots, etc.), therefore only loading that code when it's really needed makes sense, especially since most users will not need that feature for most of their visits.

As mentioned, you could identify other areas of improvement as well. However, as explained throughout this chapter, you should be careful not to overoptimize.

Below are the solution steps to tackle the four problems described above:

1. To load the **Signup** component lazily (in the **Authentication** component), you must import two things from react: the **lazy()** function and the **Suspense** component:

```
import { useState, lazy, Suspense } from 'react';
```

2. As a next step, the **Signup** component import (**import Signup from './Signup/Signup'**) should be removed from **Authentication.js**. Instead, add code to store the lazy-loaded component in a variable or constant named **Signup**:

```
const Signup = lazy(() => import('./Signup/Signup'));
```

3. It's important that the variable or constant is called **Signup**, not **signup**. It must start with a capital character since it's used as a JSX element.

4. This constant can now be used like a component in your JSX code. However, since it's loaded lazily, the component must be wrapped with the imported **Suspense** component (in **Authentication**'s returned JSX code). The **Suspense** component also needs a fallback JSX element (for example, **<p>Loading...</p>**, passed to **Suspense** via its **fallback** prop). The final **Authentication** component looks like this:

```
import { useState, lazy, Suspense } from 'react';

import Login from './Login/Login';
import classes from './Authentication.module.css';

const Signup = lazy(() => import('./Signup/Signup'));
```

```
function Authentication() {
  const [mode, setMode] = useState('login');

  function switchAuthModeHandler() {
    setMode((prevMode) => (prevMode === 'login' ? 'signup' :
'login'));
  }

  let authElement = <Login />;
  let switchBtnCaption = 'Create a new account';

  if (mode !== 'login') {
    authElement = <Signup />;
    switchBtnCaption = 'Login instead';
  }

  return (
    <div className={classes.auth}>
      <h1>You must authenticate yourself first!</h1>
      <Suspense fallback={<p>Loading...</p>}>{authElement}</Suspense>
      <button
        className={classes.btn}
        onClick={switchAuthModeHandler}>
          {switchBtnCaption}
      </button>
    </div>
  );
}

export default Authentication;
```

5. Next, in order to avoid unnecessary code execution in the **Validation** component, start by importing the **useMemo()** Hook from **react** (in the **Validation.js** file):

```
import { useMemo } from 'react';
```

6. Use the **useMemo ()** Hook to wrap the password validation code (the code between lines 12 to 20 in **Validation.js**) with it. Extract that code into an anonymous function that is passed as a first argument to **useMemo ()**. Make sure to return an object that groups the three-password validation Booleans together. Also, pass a second argument to **useMemo ()**. It's the dependencies array and should contain the **password** variable, since changes to **password** should cause the code to execute again. As a last step, store the value returned by **useMemo ()** in the **passwordValidityData** constant. The final code looks like this:

```
const passwordValidityData = useMemo(() => {
  const pwHasMinLength = password.length >= 8;
  const pwHasMinSpecChars = specCharsRegex.test(password);
  const pwHasMinNumbers = numberRegex.test(password);
  return {
    length: pwHasMinLength,
    specChars: pwHasMinSpecChars,
    numbers: pwHasMinNumbers,
  };
}, [password]);
```

7. To ensure that the **Validation** component function itself is not executed unnecessarily, wrap it with React's **memo ()** function. To do this, as a first step, import **memo** from **react** (still in **Validation.js**):

```
import { useMemo, memo } from 'react';
```

8. Thereafter, wrap the exported **Validation** function with **memo ()**:

```
export default memo(Validation);
```

9. To improve the code in the **Login** component, add lazy loading for the **ResetPassword** component. As a first step, import both **lazy** and **Suspense** from **react** (in **Login.js**):

```
import { useState, lazy, Suspense } from 'react';
```

10. Next, replace the **ResetPassword** import with a constant or variable that stores the result of calling **lazy ()** and passing a dynamic import function to it:

```
const ResetPassword = lazy(() => import('./ResetPassword'));
```

11. Finally, wrap **ResetPassword** in your JSX code with React's **Suspense** component and pass an appropriate fallback element (e.g., **\<p\>Loading...\</p\>**) to **Suspense**. The final **Login** component function looks like this:

```
import { useState, lazy, Suspense } from 'react';

const ResetPassword = lazy(() => import('./ResetPassword'));

function Login() {
  const [isResetting, setIsResetting] = useState();

  function loginHandler(event) {
    event.preventDefault();
  }

  function startResetPasswordHandler() {
    setIsResetting(true);
  }

  function finishResetPasswordHandler() {
    setIsResetting(false);
  }

  return (
    <>
      <form onSubmit={loginHandler}>
        <div className="form-control">
          <label htmlFor="email">Email</label>
          <input id="email" type="email" />
        </div>
        <div className="form-control">
          <label htmlFor="password">Password</label>
          <input id="password" type="password" />
        </div>
        <button className="main-btn">Login</button>
      </form>
      <button className="alt-btn" onClick={startResetPasswordHandler}>
        Reset password
```

```
      </button>
      <Suspense fallback={<p>Loading...</p>}>
        {isResetting && <ResetPassword
                          onFinish={finishResetPasswordHandler} />}
      </Suspense>
    </>
  );
}


export default Login;
```

You can tell that you came up with a good solution and sensible adjustments if you can see extra code fetching network requests (in the **Network** tab of your browser developer tools) for clicking on the **Reset password** or **Create a new account** buttons:

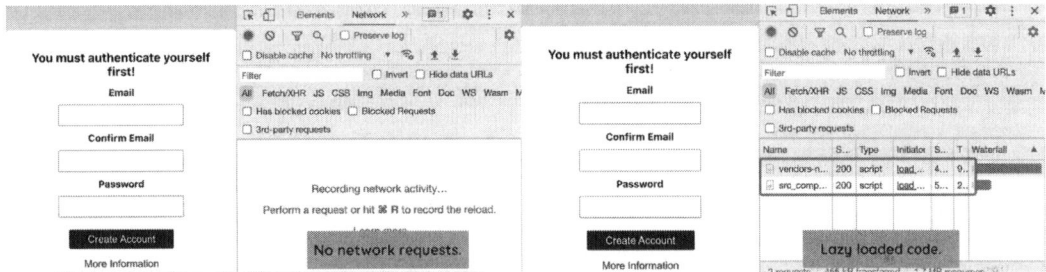

Figure 9.22: In the final solution, some code is lazy loaded

In addition, you should see no **Validated** password. console message when typing into the email input fields (**Email** and **Confirm Email**) of the signup form (that is, the form you switch to when clicking **Create a new account**):

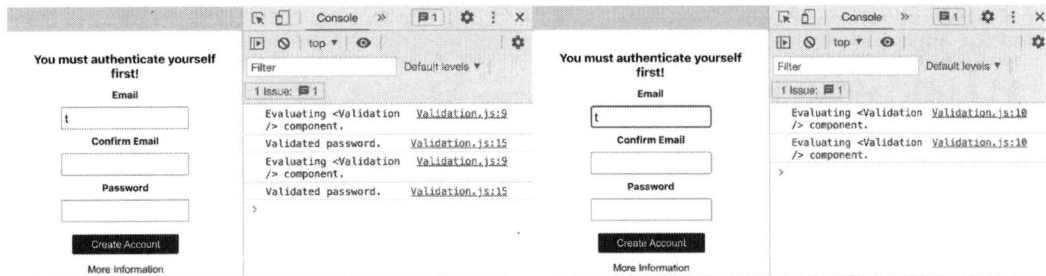

Figure 9.23: No "Validated password." output in the console

You also shouldn't get any console outputs when clicking the **More Information** button:

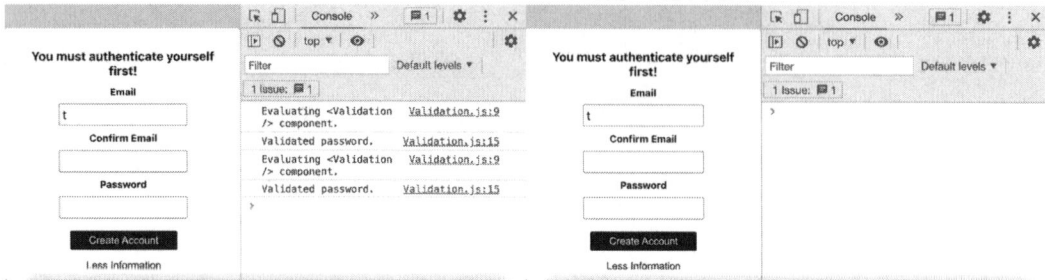

Figure 9.24: No console messages when clicking "More Information"

> **NOTE**
>
> All code files used for this solution can be found at https://packt.link/gBNHd.

CHAPTER 10: WORKING WITH COMPLEX STATE

ACTIVITY 10.1: MIGRATING AN APP TO THE CONTEXT API

Solution:

Perform the following solution steps to complete this activity:

1. As a first step, create a **store/cart-context.js** file. This file will hold the context object and the **Provider** component that contains the cross-component state logic (which is exposed via the **Provider** component).

2. In the newly added **cart-context.js** file, create a new **CartContext** via React's **createContext()** function. To get better IDE auto-completion, the initial context value can be set to an object that has an **items** property (an empty array) and two methods: an (empty) **addItem** and an (empty) **removeItem** method. The created context also must be exported, so that it can be referenced by other project files.

    This is the final cart-context.js file content (for the moment):

    ```
    import { createContext } from 'react';


    const CartContext = createContext({
      items: [],
      addItem: () => {},
      removeItem: () => {},
    });


    export default CartContext;
    ```

3. To provide the context, the **CartContext.Provider** component will be used. To manage the cross-component state in a central place (and not bloat any other component with that logic), you should add an extra React component to the **cart-context.js** file: a **CartContextProvider** component. That component returns its **children** (i.e., content passed between its opening and closing tags), wrapped by **CartContext.Provider**:

```
export function CartContextProvider({ children }) {
  return (
    <CartContext.Provider>
      {children}
    </CartContext.Provider>
  );
}
```

4. The **Provider** component requires a **value** prop. That **value** prop contains the actual value that is distributed to all components that subscribe to the context. In this project, the **value** prop is set equal to an object that contains an **items** property and the two methods defined in the initial context value previously (in *Step 2*). The two methods (**addItem** and **removeItem**) are empty named functions for the moment but will be populated with logic over the next steps, as follows:

```
export function CartContextProvider({ children }) {
  function addItemHandler(item) {
    // to be added ...
  }

  function removeItemHandler(itemId) {
    // to be added ...
  }

  const contextVal = {
    items: cartItems,
    addItem: addItemHandler,
    removeItem: removeItemHandler
  }

  return (
    <CartContext.Provider value={contextVal}>
      {children}
```

```
      </CartContext.Provider>
  );
}
```

5. To make the context value dynamic, the **CartContextProvider** component must start managing state (via **useState()**) and distribute that state via the context value. In order to trigger state updates, appropriate logic must be added to **addItemHandler** and **removeItemHandler**. The final **cart-context. js** file therefore contains the following code:

```
import { createContext, useState } from 'react';

const CartContext = createContext({
  items: [],
  addItem: () => {},
  removeItem: () => {},
});

export function CartContextProvider({ children }) {
    const [cartItems, setCartItems] = useState([]);

    function addItemHandler(item) {
      setCartItems((prevItems) => [...prevItems, item]);
    }

    function removeItemHandler(itemId) {
      setCartItems(
        (prevItems) => prevItems.filter((item) => item.id !== itemId)
      );
    }

    const contextVal = {
      items: cartItems,
      addItem: addItemHandler,
      removeItem: removeItemHandler
    }

    return (
      <CartContext.Provider value={contextVal}>
        {children}
      </CartContext.Provider>
```

```
    );
  }


export default CartContext;
```

6. Now that all cross-component state management logic has been moved into the **CartContextProvider** component, that code must be removed from the **App** component (where cross-component state was managed before, when it was lifted up).

   You also must remove all props (and their usage) that were used for passing cart-item-related state down to other components. For the moment, the App component looks like this:

```
import Events from './components/Events/Events';
import MainHeader from './components/MainHeader/MainHeader';


function App() {
  return (
    <>
      <MainHeader />
      <main>
        <Events />
      </main>
    </>
  );
}


export default App;
```

7. The **CartContextProvider** component must be wrapped around that part of the overall application component tree that needs access to the context. In this example app, that means that all JSX code in the **App.js** file should be wrapped (since both **MainHeader** and the **Events** component need access to the context value):

```
import Events from './components/Events/Events';
import MainHeader from './components/MainHeader/MainHeader';
import { CartContextProvider } from './store/cart-context';


function App() {
  return (
    <>
```

```
      <CartContextProvider>
        <MainHeader />
        <main>
          <Events />
        </main>
      </CartContextProvider>
    </>
  );
}


export default App;
```

8. Now, all components that need context access (either for reading the context value or for calling one of the exposed context value methods) can subscribe to the context via React's **useContext()** Hook. In this example project, the **MainHeader**, **EventItem**, and **Cart** components need access. The **MainHeader** component therefore uses the **useContext()** Hook (and the received context value) like this:

```
import { useContext, useState } from 'react';

import CartContext from '../../store/cart-context';
import Cart from '../Cart/Cart';
import classes from './MainHeader.module.css';

function MainHeader({ cartItems }) {
  const cartCtx = useContext(CartContext);
  const [modalIsOpen, setModalIsOpen] = useState();

  function openCartModalHandler() {
    setModalIsOpen(true);
  }

  function closeCartModalHandler() {
    setModalIsOpen(false);
  }

  const numCartItems = cartCtx.items.length;

  return (
    <>
```

```
      <header className={classes.header}>
        <h1>StateEvents Shop</h1>
        <button onClick={openCartModalHandler}>Cart
({numCartItems})</button>
      </header>
      {modalIsOpen && <Cart onClose={closeCartModalHandler} />}
    </>
  );
}


export default MainHeader;
```

9. Ensure the **EventItem** component looks like this:

```
import { useContext } from 'react';

import CartContext from '../../store/cart-context';
import classes from './EventItem.module.css';

function EventItem({ event }) {
  const cartCtx = useContext(CartContext);

  const isInCart = cartCtx.items.some((item) => item.id === event.
id);

  let buttonCaption = 'Add to Cart';
  let buttonAction = () => cartCtx.addItem(event);

  if (isInCart) {
    buttonCaption = 'Remove from Cart';
    buttonAction = () => cartCtx.removeItem(event.id);
  }

  return (
    <li className={classes.event}>
      <img src={event.image} alt={event.title} />
      <div className={classes.content}>
        <h2>{event.title}</h2>
        <p className={classes.price}>${event.price}</p>
        <p>{event.description}</p>
        <div className={classes.actions}>
          <button onClick={buttonAction}>{buttonCaption}</button>
```

```
        </div>
      </div>
    </li>
  );
}


export default EventItem;
```

10. And confirm that the **Cart** component contains this code:

```
import { useContext } from 'react';
import ReactDOM from 'react-dom';

import CartContext from '../../store/cart-context';
import classes from './Cart.module.css';

function Cart({ onClose }) {
  const cartCtx = useContext(CartContext);

  const total = cartCtx.items.reduce(
    (prevVal, item) => prevVal + item.price,
    0
  );

  return ReactDOM.createPortal(
    <>
      <div className={classes.backdrop} onClick={onClose} />
      <aside className={classes.cart}>
        <h2>Your Cart</h2>
        <ul>
          {cartCtx.items.map((item) => (
            <li key={item.id}>
              {item.title} (${item.price})
            </li>
          ))}
        </ul>
        <p className={classes.total}>Total: ${total}</p>
        <div className={classes.actions}>
          <button onClick={onClose}>Close</button>
          <button onClick={onClose}>Buy</button>
        </div>
```

```
        </aside>
      </>,
      document.getElementById('modal')
  );
}

export default Cart;
```

> **NOTE**
>
> All code files used for this activity can be found at https://packt.link/vjkCr.

ACTIVITY 10.2: REPLACING USESTATE() WITH USEREDUCER()

Solution:

Perform the following solution steps to complete this activity:

1. Remove the existing logic in the **Form** component that uses the **useState()** Hook for state management.

2. Import and use the **useReducer()** Hook in the **Form** component. For the moment, pass an empty (newly added) reducer function as a first argument to **useReducer()**. Make sure to create the reducer function outside of the component function. Also, pass an initial state value as the second argument to **useReducer()**. That initial value should be an object containing values and validity information for both the **email** and **password** fields. Overall, for the moment, the code in **Form.js** looks like this:

```
import { useReducer } from 'react';

import classes from './Form.module.css';

const initialFormState = {
  email: {
    value: '',
    isValid: false,
  },
  password: {
    value: '',
    isValid: false,
```

```
    },
  };

function formReducer(state, action) {
  // to be added
}

function Form() {
  useReducer(formReducer, initialFormState);

  const formIsValid = true; // will be changed!

  function changeEmailHandler(event) {
    const value = event.target.value;
  }

  function changePasswordHandler(event) {
    const value = event.target.value;
  }

  function submitFormHandler(event) {
    event.preventDefault();

    if (!formIsValid) {
      alert('Invalid form inputs!');
      return;
    }

    console.log('Good job!');
    console.log(formState.email.value, formState.password.value);
  }

  return (
    <form className={classes.form} onSubmit={submitFormHandler}>
      <div className={classes.control}>
        <label htmlFor="email">Email</label>
        <input id="email" type="email" onChange={changeEmailHandler}
/>
      </div>
      <div className={classes.control}>
        <label htmlFor="password">Password</label>
```

```
            <input id="password"
                type="password" onChange={changePasswordHandler} />
        </div>
        <button>Submit</button>
    </form>
  );
}


export default Form;
```

3. As the next step, fill the reducer function. It must handle two main types of actions: an email address change and a password change. In both cases, the state value must be updated appropriately (i.e., the newly entered value must be stored and the validity of the input must be derived and stored as well). You also must return a default value in case of unknown action types. The updated reducer function looks like this:

```
function formReducer(state, action) {
    if (action.type === 'EMAIL_CHANGE') {
        return {
            ...state,
            email: {
                value: action.payload,
                isValid: action.payload.includes('@'),
            },
        };
    }


    if (action.type === 'PASSWORD_CHANGE') {
        return {
            ...state,
            password: {
                value: action.payload,
                isValid: action.payload.trim().length > 7,
            },
        };
    }


    return initialFormState;
}
```

Please note that the **type** values you want to support (**'EMAIL_CHANGE'** and **'PASSWORD_CHANGE'** in the preceding snippet) are up to you. You can use any identifier values of your choice. You can also assign a different name to the **type** property (e.g., use **action.identifier** instead of **action.type**). Similarly, you can also use any other name than **payload** for the extra data required by the state updates. If you do choose different identifier values or property names, you must use the same values and names in the following steps.

4. Update the code where **useReducer()** is called. That Hook returns an array with exactly two elements: the current state value and a function that can be used for dispatching actions. Store both elements in different constants (or variables):

```
// ... more code ...
function Form() {
  const [formState, dispatch] = useReducer(formReducer,
initialFormState);
  // ... more code ...
}
```

5. Dispatch the actions in the appropriate places. **'EMAIL_CHANGE'** is dispatched in the **changeEmailHandler** function and **'PASSWORD_CHANGE'** is dispatched in the **changePasswordHandler** function. Both actions also need payload data (the value entered by the user). Pass that data along with the action via the **payload** property:

```
// ... more code ...
function changeEmailHandler(event) {
  const value = event.target.value;
  dispatch({ type: 'EMAIL_CHANGE', payload: value });
}

function changePasswordHandler(event) {
  const value = event.target.value;
  dispatch({ type: 'PASSWORD_CHANGE', payload: value });
}
// ... more code ...
```

6. Lastly, use the state managed via **useReducer()** in all the places where it's needed (in the **Form** component) to derive the **formIsValid** Boolean and log (via **console.log()**) the entered values inside the **submitFormHandler** function. The finished **Form** component code looks like this:

```
function Form() {
  const [formState, dispatch] = useReducer(formReducer,
initialFormState);

  const formIsValid = formState.email.isValid && formState.password.
isValid;

  function changeEmailHandler(event) {
    const value = event.target.value;
    dispatch({ type: 'EMAIL_CHANGE', payload: value });
  }

  function changePasswordHandler(event) {
    const value = event.target.value;
    dispatch({ type: 'PASSWORD_CHANGE', payload: value });
  }

  function submitFormHandler(event) {
    event.preventDefault();

    if (!formIsValid) {
      alert('Invalid form inputs!');
      return;
    }

    console.log('Good job!');
    console.log(formState.email.value, formState.password.value);
  }
```

```
  return (
    <form className={classes.form} onSubmit={submitFormHandler}>
      <div className={classes.control}>
        <label htmlFor="email">Email</label>
        <input id="email" type="email" onChange={changeEmailHandler}
/>
      </div>
      <div className={classes.control}>
        <label htmlFor="password">Password</label>
        <input id="password" type="password"
onChange={changePasswordHandler} />
      </div>
      <button>Submit</button>
    </form>
  );
}
```

NOTE

All code files used for this activity can be found at https://packt.link/Ua7VH.

CHAPTER 11: BUILDING CUSTOM REACT HOOKS

ACTIVITY 11.1: BUILD A CUSTOM KEYBOARD INPUT HOOK

Solution:

Perform the following solution steps to complete this activity:

1. As a first step, create a **hooks/use-key-event.js** file. This file will hold the custom Hook function.

2. Create the **useKeyEvent** Hook function in the newly added **use-key-event.js** file. Also, export the **useKeyEvent** function so that it can be used in other files (it will be used in the **App** component later):

```
function useKeyEvent() {
  // logic to be added...
}


export default useKeyEvent;
```

3. Move the **useEffect()** import and call (and all the logic inside of it) from the **App** component body to the **useKeyEvent** function body:

```
import { useEffect } from 'react';


function useKeyEvent() {
  useEffect(() => {
    function keyPressedHandler(event) {
      const pressedKey = event.key;

      if (!['s', 'c', 'p'].includes(pressedKey)) {
        alert('Invalid key!');
        return;
      }
      setPressedKey(pressedKey);
    }


    window.addEventListener('keydown', keyPressedHandler);


    return () => window.removeEventListener('keydown',
keyPressedHandler);
```

```
  }, []);
}


export default useKeyEvent;
```

4. Make sure to remove that **useEffect()** logic (and the **useEffect** import) from the **App** component file. At the moment, the **useKeyEvent** Hook won't work correctly as there are multiple problems:

   • Inside the effect function, it's calling **setPressedKey(pressedKey)** without that function existing in the Hook function.

   • The custom Hook does not communicate with the component in which it might be used. It should return the key that was pressed (after validating that it's an allowed key).

   • The allowed keys (**'s'**, **'c'**, and **'p'**) are hardcoded into the custom Hook.

   These issues will be fixed over the next steps.

5. Start by adding state to the **useKeyEvent** Hook. Import and use **useState** to manage the **pressedKey** state:

```
import { useEffect, useState } from 'react';


function useKeyEvent() {
  const [pressedKey, setPressedKey] = useState();


  // ... unchanged rest of the code
}
```

6. Add a **return** statement at the end of the custom Hook function and return the **pressedKey** state value. Since it's the only value that must be returned, you don't need to group it into an array or object:

```
function useKeyEvent() {
  const [pressedKey, setPressedKey] = useState();


  useEffect(() => {
    // unchanged logic ...
  }, []);


  return pressedKey;
}
```

7. Make the Hook more reusable by converting the hardcoded list of allowed keys (**['s', 'c', 'p']**) to a parameter (**allowedKeys**) that is received and used by the **useKeyEvent** Hook function. Don't forget to add the parameter variable as a dependency to the **useEffect()** dependencies array since the value is used inside of **useEffect()**:

```
import { useEffect, useState } from 'react';

function useKeyEvent(allowedKeys) {
  const [pressedKey, setPressedKey] = useState();

  useEffect(() => {
    function keyPressedHandler(event) {
      const pressedKey = event.key;

      if (!allowedKeys.includes(pressedKey)) {
        alert('Invalid key!');
        return;
      }
      setPressedKey(pressedKey);
    }

    window.addEventListener('keydown', keyPressedHandler);

    return () => window.removeEventListener('keydown',
keyPressedHandler);
  }, [allowedKeys]);

  return pressedKey;
}

export default useKeyEvent;
```

8. The custom Hook is now finished and hence can be used in other components. Import and use it in the **App** component like this:

```
import useKeyEvent from './hooks/use-key-event';

function App() {
  const pressedKey = useKeyEvent(['s', 'c', 'p']);

  let output = '';

  if (pressedKey === 's') {
    output = '😊';
  } else if (pressedKey === 'c') {
    output = '😺';
  } else if (pressedKey === 'p') {
    output = '🎉';
  }

  return (
    <main>
      <h1>Press a key!</h1>
      <p>
        Supported keys: <kbd>s</kbd>, <kbd>c</kbd>, <kbd>p</kbd>
      </p>
      <p id="output">{output}</p>
    </main>
  );
}

export default App;
```

> **NOTE**
>
> All code files used for this activity can be found at https://packt.link/LzxOO.

CHAPTER 12: MULTIPAGE APPS WITH REACT ROUTER

ACTIVITY 12.1: CREATING A BASIC THREE-PAGE WEBSITE

Solution:

Perform the following steps to complete this activity:

1. Create a new React project via **npx create-react-app** as explained in *Chapter 1, React: What & Why?*. Then, install the React Router library by running **npm install react-router-dom** inside the project folder.

2. For the three required pages, create three components: a **Welcome** component, a **Products** component, and a **ProductDetail** component. Store these components in files inside the **src/routes** folder since these components will only be used for routing.

   For the **Welcome** component, enter the following code:

```
// src/routes/Welcome.js


function Welcome() {
  return (
    <main>
      <h1>Welcome to our shop!</h1>
      <p>
        Please explore our products or share this
        site with others.
      </p>
    </main>
  );
}


export default Welcome;
```

   To create the **Products** component, run the following:

```
// src/routes/Products.js


import products from '../data/products';


function Products() {
  return (
    <main>
```

```
      <h1>Our Products</h1>
      <ul id="products-list">
        {products.map((product) => (
          <li key={product.id}>
            {product.title} (${product.price})
          </li>
        ))}
      </ul>
    </main>
  );
}

export default Products;
```

The code for the **ProductDetail** component will look as follows:

```
// src/routes/ProductDetail.js

function ProductDetail() {
  return (
    <main>
      <h1>PRODUCT TITLE</h1>
      <p id="product-price">$PRODUCT PRICE</p>
      <p>PRODUCT DESCRIPTION</p>
    </main>
  );
}

export default ProductDetail;
```

3. At the moment, no routing logic has been added yet. Therefore, dummy content such as "**PRODUCT TITLE**" is output in **ProductDetail**. This will change later.

4. With the components added, it's time to add route definitions. For this, you must first enable React Router by importing and using the **BrowserRouter** component (in the **App** component):

```
import { BrowserRouter } from 'react-router-dom';

function App() {
  return (
    <BrowserRouter>
```

```
      // ...
    </BrowserRouter>
  );
}


export default App;
```

5. Between the **BrowserRouter** tags, add the route definitions for the three routes. This is done via the **Route** component. Keep in mind that the individual **Route** definitions must be wrapped in the **Routes** components. For each route definition, you must add a **path** and an **element** prop—the latter of which should render the respective component that belongs to the route:

```
import { BrowserRouter, Routes, Route } from 'react-router-dom';

import ProductDetail from './routes/ProductDetail';
import Products from './routes/Products';
import Welcome from './routes/Welcome';

function App() {
  return (
    <BrowserRouter>
      <Routes>
        <Route path="/" element={<Welcome />} />
        <Route path="/products" element={<Products />} />
        <Route path="/products/:id" element={<ProductDetail />} />
      </Routes>
    </BrowserRouter>
  );
}


export default App;
```

6. The paths are up to you, but with the provided page descriptions, **/**, **/products**, and **/products/:id** are sensible choices. Though, instead of **:id**, you could, of course, use **:productId** or any other identifier.

7. The website should also have a main navigation bar. Therefore, as a next step, create a **MainNavigation** component and store it in an **src/components/MainNavigation.js** file. It's not a component that will be assigned directly to a route, and therefore it does not go in the **src/routes** folder. Inside the **MainNavigation** component, you should render a **\<header>** element that contains a **\<nav>** element, which then outputs a list (**\<ul>**) of links. The actual links, however, will be added in a later step:

```
function MainNavigation() {
  return (
    <header id="main-nav">
      <nav>
        <ul>
          <li>
            Home
          </li>
          <li>
            Our Products
          </li>
        </ul>
      </nav>
    </header>
  );
}

export default MainNavigation;
```

8. Import the newly created **MainNavigation** component into the **App** component file and output it right above the routes:

```
import { BrowserRouter, Routes, Route } from 'react-router-dom';

import MainNavigation from './components/MainNavigation';
import ProductDetail from './routes/ProductDetail';
import Products from './routes/Products';
import Welcome from './routes/Welcome';

function App() {
  return (
    <BrowserRouter>
      <MainNavigation />
```

```
        <Routes>
          <Route path="/" element={<Welcome />} />
          <Route path="/products" element={<Products />} />
          <Route path="/products/:id" element={<ProductDetail />} />
        </Routes>
      </BrowserRouter>
    );
  }


  export default App;
```

9. It's time to add some links. Place one link in the **Welcome** component. There, the text "our products" (in **'Please explore "Our Products" ...'**) should be turned into a link. Since it's an internal link, use the **<Link>** element:

```
import { Link } from 'react-router-dom';


function Welcome() {
  return (
    <main>
      <h1>Welcome to our shop!</h1>
      <p>
        Please explore <Link to="/products">our products</Link>
        or share this site with others.
      </p>
    </main>
  );
}


export default Welcome;
```

10. In the **MainNavigation** component, use **NavLink** so that the navigation items reflect whether or not they are linked to the currently active route:

```
import { NavLink } from 'react-router-dom';


function MainNavigation() {
  return (
    <header id="main-nav">
      <nav>
        <ul>
          <li>
```

```
                    <NavLink
                      to="/"
                      className={({ isActive }) => (isActive ? 'active' :
'')}
                    >
                      Home
                    </NavLink>
                  </li>
                  <li>
                    <NavLink
                      to="/products"
                      className={({ isActive }) => (isActive ? 'active' :
'')}
                    >
                      Our Products
                    </NavLink>
                  </li>
                </ul>
              </nav>
            </header>
          );
        }


        export default MainNavigation;
```

11. More links must be added to the **Products** component. In the list of products that's rendered there, ensure every list item links to the **ProductDetail** component (i.e., to the **/products/:id** route). The link, therefore, must be generated dynamically with the help of the product **id**:

```
import { Link } from 'react-router-dom';

import products from '../data/products';

function Products() {
  return (
    <main>
      <h1>Our Products</h1>
      <ul id="products-list">
        {products.map((product) => (
          <li key={product.id}>
            <Link to={`/products/${product.id}`}>
```

```
                    {product.title} (${product.price})
                </Link>
            </li>
        ))}
        </ul>
    </main>
    );
}


export default Products;
```

12. To finish this project, dynamic product detail data must be output in the
ProductDetail component. For this, use the **useParams()** Hook to get
access to the product **id** that's encoded in the URL path. With the help of that
ID, you can find the product that's needed and output its data:

```
import { useParams } from 'react-router-dom';

import products from '../data/products';

function ProductDetail() {
    const params = useParams();
    const prodId = params.id;
    const product = products.find((product) => product.id === prodId);

    return (
        <main>
            <h1>{product.title}</h1>
            <p id="product-price">${product.price}</p>
            <p>{product.description}</p>
        </main>
    );
}


export default ProductDetail;
```

The finished pages should look like this:

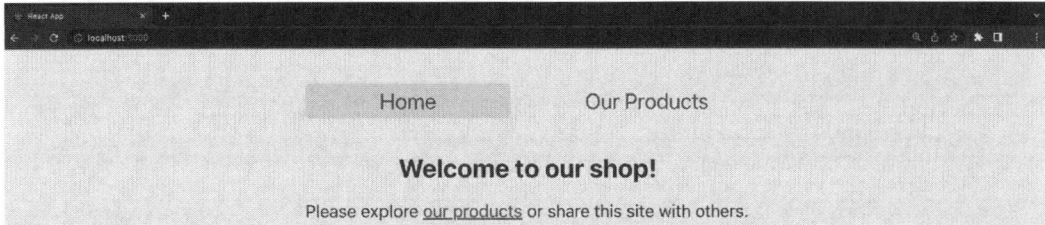

Figure 12.16: The final welcome page

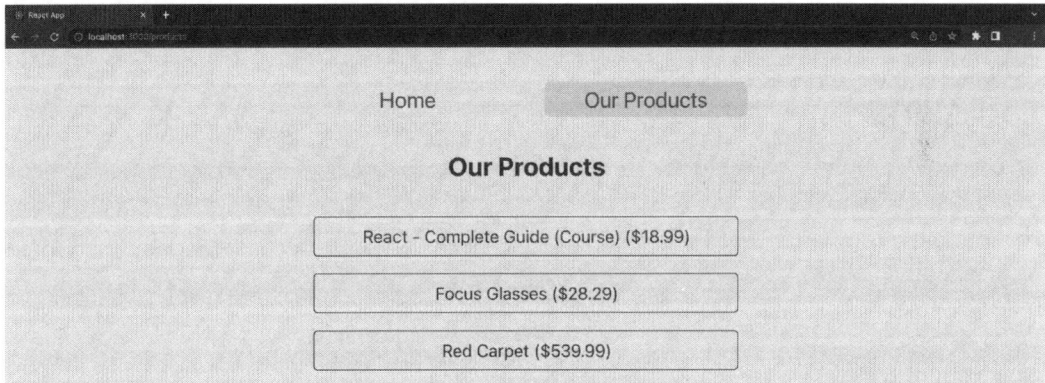

Figure 12.17: The final products page

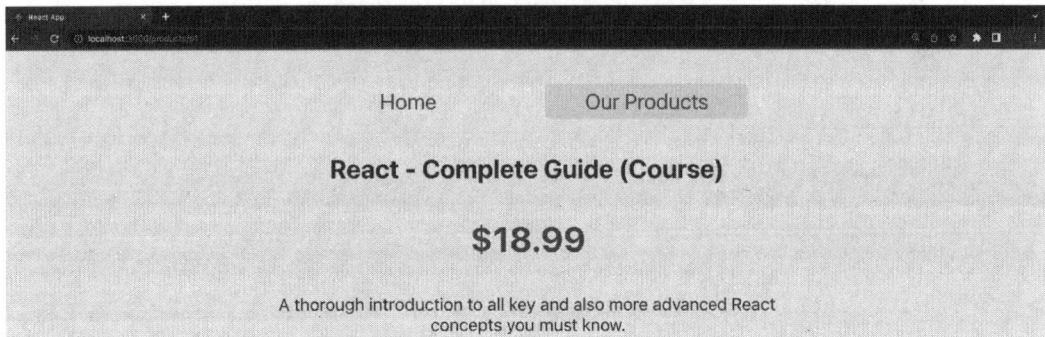

Figure 12.18: The final product details page

NOTE

All code files for this solution can be found at https://packt.link/wPcgN.

ACTIVITY 12.2: ENHANCING THE BASIC WEBSITE

Solution:

Perform the following steps to complete the activity:

1. Create a new **Layout** component in the **src/components** folder. In that component, include **MainNavigation** (remove that component from the **App** component), as well as a **<main>** element, which should be wrapped around the **special children** prop:

```
import MainNavigation from './MainNavigation';

function Layout({ children }) {
  return (
    <>
      <MainNavigation />
      <main>{children}</main>
    </>
  );
}

export default Layout;
```

2. Since you are using React Router's nested routes feature, you must also add a new route component—e.g., a component named **Root**. Add it in the **src/routes** folder and make sure it outputs the **Layout** component, wrapped around the special **Outlet** component:

```
import { Outlet } from 'react-router-dom';

import Layout from '../components/Layout';

function Root() {
  return (
    <Layout>
      <Outlet />
    </Layout>
  );
}

export default Root;
```

3. Next, add a new route definition to **Routes** in the **App** component. The definition for the **Root** route should wrap all other routes (i.e., the other routes are now nested into the **Root** route). Since the existing routes are converted into nested routes, you must change their paths to relative paths. You also should remove the path from the **Welcome** route and instead add the **index** prop to it:

```jsx
import { BrowserRouter, Routes, Route } from 'react-router-dom';

import Root from './routes/Root';
import ProductDetail from './routes/ProductDetail';
import Products from './routes/Products';
import Welcome from './routes/Welcome';

function App() {
  return (
    <BrowserRouter>
      <Routes>
        <Route path="/" element={<Root />}>
          <Route element={<Welcome />} index />
          <Route path="products" element={<Products />} />
          <Route path="products/:id" element={<ProductDetail />} />
        </Route>
      </Routes>
    </BrowserRouter>
  );
}

export default App;
```

4. Add code splitting to the application by importing **lazy** and **Suspense** from React in the **App** component file. Thereafter, replace the existing imports for **Products** and **ProductDetail** with the code to load these components lazily. Don't forget to use the **Suspense** component as a wrapper around your route definitions:

```jsx
import { Suspense, lazy } from 'react';
import { BrowserRouter, Routes, Route } from 'react-router-dom';

import Root from './routes/Root';
```

```
import Welcome from './routes/Welcome';


const ProductDetail = lazy(() => import('./routes/ProductDetail'));
const Products = lazy(() => import('./routes/Products'));


function App() {
  return (
    <BrowserRouter>
      <Suspense fallback={<p>Loading...</p>}>
        <Routes>
          <Route path="/" element={<Root />}>
            <Route path="" element={<Welcome />} index />
            <Route path="products" element={<Products />} />
            <Route path="products/:id" element={<ProductDetail />} />
          </Route>
        </Routes>
      </Suspense>
    </BrowserRouter>
  );
}


export default App;
```

Lazy loading makes a lot of sense for **Products** and **ProductDetail** since their routes are not necessarily visited by users (at least not immediately). It makes no sense for the **Root** component as this component wraps all other routes and is therefore always loaded. The **Welcome** component is the starting page and so does not significantly benefit from code splitting either.

5. For the *"Not Found"* page, first add a new **NotFound** component and store it in **src/routes/NotFound.js**. Add the content shown in *Figure 12.15* in the activity description:

```
function NotFound() {
  return (
    <>
      <h1>We're really sorry!</h1>
      <p>We could not find this page.</p>
    </>
  );
```

```
}


export default NotFound;
```

6. Thereafter, add a new (nested) route definition in your **App** component and use the special "catch-all" path (*****) to ensure that this route becomes active when no other route is matched. Since this page should rarely be shown, you can load it lazily:

```
import { Suspense, lazy } from 'react';
import { BrowserRouter, Routes, Route } from 'react-router-dom';


import Root from './routes/Root';
import Welcome from './routes/Welcome';


const ProductDetail = lazy(() => import('./routes/ProductDetail'));
const Products = lazy(() => import('./routes/Products'));
const NotFound = lazy(() => import('./routes/NotFound'));


function App() {
  return (
    <BrowserRouter>
      <Suspense fallback={<p>Loading...</p>}>
        <Routes>
          <Route path="/" element={<Root />}>
            <Route path="" element={<Welcome />} index />
            <Route path="products" element={<Products />} />
            <Route path="products/:id" element={<ProductDetail />} />
            <Route path="*" element={<NotFound />} />
          </Route>
        </Routes>
      </Suspense>
    </BrowserRouter>
  );
}


export default App;
```

The final *"Not Found"* page should look like this:

Figure 12.19: The final "Not Found" page

> **NOTE**
>
> All code files for this solution can be found at https://packt.link/HChZi.

CHAPTER 13: MANAGING DATA WITH REACT ROUTER

ACTIVITY 13.1: A TO-DOS APP

Solution:

Perform the following steps to complete this activity:

1. Create a new React project via **npx create-react-app** as explained in *Chapter 1, React—What and Why?*. Then, install the React Router library by running **npm install react-router-dom** inside the project folder. Check the **package.json** file to confirm that you have at least version 6.4 of the **react-router-dom** package installed.

2. For the three required pages, create three components: a **Todos** component, a **NewTodo** component, and a **SelectedTodo** component. Store these components in files inside the **src/routes** folder since these components will only be used for routing.

3. For the **Todos** component, enter the following code:

```
// src/routes/Todos.js

function Todos() {
  const todos = [];

  let content = (
    <main>
      <h1>No todos found</h1>
      <p>Start adding some!</p>
      <p>
        <Link className="btn-cta" to="/new">
          Add Todo
        </Link>
      </p>
    </main>
  );

  if (todos && todos.length > 0) {
    content = (
      <main>
```

```
            <section>
              <Link className="btn-cta" to="/new">
                Add Todo
              </Link>
            </section>
            <ul id="todos">

            </ul>
          </main>
      );
    }

    return (
      <>
        {content}
        <Outlet />
      </>
    );
  }

  export default Todos;
```

4. The code for the **NewTodo** component should look like this:

```
// src/routes/NewTodo.js

import Modal from '../components/Modal';

function NewTodo() {
  return (
    <Modal>
      <Form method="post">
        <p>
          <label htmlFor="text">Your todo</label>
          <input type="text" id="text" name="text" />
        </p>
        <p className="form-actions">
          <button>Save Todo</button>
        </p>
```

```
        </Form>
      </Modal>
   );
}


export default NewTodo;
```

5. The code for the **SelectedTodo** component will look as follows:

```
// src/routes/SelectedTodo.js
import Modal from '../components/Modal';

function SelectedTodo() {
  return (
    <Modal>
      <Form method="patch">
        <p>
          <label htmlFor="text">Your todo</label>
          <input type="text" id="text" name="text" />
        </p>
        <p className="form-actions">
          <button>Update Todo</button>
        </p>
      </Form>
      <Form method="delete">
        <p className="form-actions">
          <button className='btn-alt'>Delete Todo</button>
        </p>
      </Form>
    </Modal>
  );
}


export default SelectedTodo;
```

6. At the moment, the route definitions are missing, and no data loading or submission logic has been added. Please note, however, that the components already use **<Link>** and **<Form>**.

7. With the components added, it's time to add route definitions. For this, you must first enable React Router by importing and using the **RouterProvider** component (in the **App** component):

```
import { RouterProvider } from 'react-router-dom';


function App() {
  return <RouterProvider />;
}


export default App;
```

RouterProvider requires a value for its **router** prop. That value must be an array of route definition objects. These objects can be created directly by you, or indirectly via the **createRoutesFromElements()** function. For this solution, use the direct approach (in **App.js**):

```
import { createBrowserRouter, RouterProvider } from 'react-router-dom';

import Todos from './routes/Todos';
import NewTodo from './routes/NewTodo';
import SelectedTodo from './routes/SelectedTodo';

const router = createBrowserRouter([
  {
    path: '/',
    element: <Todos />,
    children: [
      { path: 'new', element: <NewTodo /> },
      { path: ':id', element: <SelectedTodo /> },
    ],
  },
]);


function App() {
  return <RouterProvider router={router} />;
}


export default App;
```

8. Please note that the **/new** and **/:id** routes are child routes of the **/** route. The **/** route is thus a layout route, wrapping these child routes. That's why this layout route (**Todos** in **Todos.js**) renders an **<Outlet />** element.

9. To load and display to-dos, add a **loader()** function to the **Todos** route. As a first step, export such a function in the **routes/Todos.js** file:

```
// other imports ...
import { getTodos } from '../data/todos';

export function loader() {
  // getTodos() is a utility function that uses localStorage under
the hood
  return getTodos();

}
```

10. Thereafter, assign it as a value for the loader prop on the **/** route definition:

```
import Todos, { loader as todosLoader } from './routes/Todos';
// other imports ...

const router = createBrowserRouter([
  {
    path: '/',
    element: <Todos />,
    loader: todosLoader,
    children: [
      // child routes ...
    ],
  },
]);
```

11. **getTodos()** from the previous step is a utility function that reaches out to **localStorage** to retrieve and parse stored to-dos. Implement this function using the following code:

```
function getTodosFromStorage() {
  return JSON.parse(localStorage.getItem('todos'));
}



export function getTodos() {
  return getTodosFromStorage();
}
```

12. To use the loaded to-dos data, use the **useLoaderData()** Hook inside the **Todos** component. The loaded to-dos are then output via an unordered list (**<ul>**):

```
import { Link, Outlet, useLoaderData } from 'react-router-dom';

import { getTodos } from '../data/todos';

function Todos() {
  const todos = useLoaderData();

  let content = (
    <main>
      <h1>No todos found</h1>
      <p>Start adding some!</p>
      <p>
        <Link className="btn-cta" to="/new">
          Add Todo
        </Link>
      </p>
    </main>
  );

  if (todos && todos.length > 0) {
    content = (
      <main>
        <section>
          <Link className="btn-cta" to="/new">
            Add Todo
          </Link>
        </section>
        <ul id="todos">
          {todos.map((todo) => (
            <li key={todo.id}>
              <Link to={todo.id}>{todo.text}</Link>
            </li>
          ))}
        </ul>
      </main>
    );
```

```
    }

    return (
      <>
        {content}
        <Outlet />
      </>
    );
  }
```

13. Another route that needs to-do data is the **/:id** route. There, a single to-do item must be loaded as the route is activated. You could reuse the to-dos data from the **/** route (via **useRouteLoaderData()**) but for practice purposes, use a separate **loader()** function for this activity. This **loader()** function, which is added to and exported from **routes/SelectedTodo.js** has this shape:

```
import { getTodo } from '../data/todos';
// ... other imports

export async function loader({ params }) {
    return getTodo(params.id);
}
```

14. **getTodo()** is yet another utility function. Implement it as follows:

```
export function getTodo(id) {
    const todos = getTodosFromStorage();
    const todo = todos.find((t) => t.id === id);

    if (!todo) {
        throw new Error('Could not find todo for id ' + id);
    }

    return todo;
}
```

15. Please note that this function throws an error if no to-do is found for the specified **id**. For that reason, error handling will be implemented in a later step.

16. Inside the **SelectedTodo** component, access the selected to-do item data via **useLoaderData()**. Then, use that data to set a default value on the form input:

```
function SelectedTodo() {
  const todo = useLoaderData();

  return (
    <Modal>
      <Form method="post">
        <p>
          <label htmlFor="text">Your todo</label>
          <input
            type="text"
            id="text"
            name="text"
            defaultValue={todo.text} />
        </p>
        <p className="form-actions">
          <button>Update Todo</button>
        </p>
      </Form>
      <Form method="delete">
        <p className="form-actions">
          <button className='btn-alt'>Delete Todo</button>
        </p>
      </Form>
    </Modal>
  );
}
```

17. To ensure users are able to submit new to-dos, export an **action()** function in the **NewTodo** component file, as shown here:

```
import { addTodo } from '../data/todos';
// ... other imports

export async function action({ request }) {
  const formData = await request.formData();
  const enteredText = formData.get('text');
  addTodo(enteredText);
```

```
    return redirect('/');
}
```

18. This function extracts the submitted form data, retrieves the entered text value, calls the **addTodo()** utility function, and then redirects the user back to the main page (**/**). Since the **NewTodo** component uses **<Form>** instead of **<form>**, React Router will automatically prevent the browser default and call the **action()** function assigned to the route that contains the form (**/new** route, in this case).

19. Implement the **addTodo()** function (defined in **data/todos.js**) by running the following code:

```
function saveTodosToStorage(todos) {
  const serializedTodos = JSON.stringify(todos);
  localStorage.setItem('todos', serializedTodos);
}

export function addTodo(text) {
  let todos = getTodosFromStorage();
  const newTodo = {
    id: new Date().toISOString(),
    text,
  };
  if (todos) {
    todos.unshift(newTodo);
  } else {
    todos = [newTodo];
  }
  saveTodosToStorage(todos);
}
```

20. To allow React Router to execute the preceding **action()** function when the **<Form>** in **NewTodo** is submitted, register the action in the route definition:

```
import NewTodo, { action as newTodoAction } from './routes/NewTodo';
// ... other imports

const router = createBrowserRouter([
  {
    path: '/',
    element: <Todos />,
    loader: todosLoader,
```

```
         children: [
             { path: 'new', element: <NewTodo />, action: newTodoAction }
         ],
      },
   ]);
```

21. To allow users to update or delete to-do items, add an **action()** function to the **SelectedTodo** component file. In that function, use **request.method** to differentiate between **PATCH** and **DELETE** requests. This is required because inside the **SelectedTodo** component, two forms are created via **<Form>** (see *step 3*): one **<Form>** creates a **PATCH** request (for updating to-do data), and the other **<Form>** creates a **DELETE** request (for deleting a to-do). The **action()** function is implemented like this:

```
import { deleteTodo, getTodo, updateTodo } from '../data/todos';

// ... other imports

export async function action({ request, params }) {
  const todoId = params.id;

  if (request.method === 'PATCH') {
    const formData = await request.formData();
    const enteredText = formData.get('text');
    updateTodo(todoId, enteredText);
  }

  if (request.method === 'DELETE') {
    deleteTodo(todoId);
  }
  return redirect('/');
}
```

22. Once again, define **updateTodo()** and **deleteTodo()** in the **data/todos. js** file:

```
export function updateTodo(id, newText) {
  const todos = getTodos();
  const updatedTodo = todos.find((t) => t.id === id);
  updatedTodo.text = newText;
  saveTodosToStorage(todos);
}
```

```
export function deleteTodo(id) {
  const todos = getTodos();
  const updatedTodos = todos.filter((t) => t.id !== id);
  saveTodosToStorage(updatedTodos);
}
```

23. Finally, to make React Router aware of this **action()** function and ensure that it gets executed as the respective forms are submitted, register the action created in *step 16*, as follows:

```
import SelectedTodo, {
  action as changeTodoAction,
  loader as todoLoader,
} from './routes/SelectedTodo';
// ... other imports

const router = createBrowserRouter([
  {
    path: '/',
    element: <Todos />,
    loader: todosLoader,
    children: [
      { path: 'new', element: <NewTodo />, action: newTodoAction },
      {
        path: ':id',
        element: <SelectedTodo />,
        action: changeTodoAction,
        loader: todoLoader,
      },
    ],
  },
]);
}
```

24. To handle any errors that have occurred, add a new **Error** component that is displayed when things go wrong. This component is stored in **routes/Error. js**:

```
import { useRouteError } from 'react-router-dom';

import Modal from '../components/Modal';

function Error() {
  const error = useRouteError();

  return (
    <Modal>
      <h1>An error occurred!</h1>
      <p>{error.message}</p>
    </Modal>
  );
}

export default Error;
```

25. This component uses React Router's **useRouteError()** Hook to access the error that was thrown. The error is then used to output the error message.

26. To use this **Error** component as a fallback, add it as a value for the **errorElement** property in your route definitions:

```
import Error from './routes/Error';
// ... other imports

const router = createBrowserRouter([
  {
    path: '/',
    element: <Todos />,
    errorElement: <Error />,
    loader: todosLoader,
    children: [
      { path: 'new', element: <NewTodo />, action: newTodoAction },
      {
        path: ':id',
        element: <SelectedTodo />,
        action: changeTodoAction,
```

```
        loader: todoLoader,
      },
    ],
  },
]);
```

27. Here, **Error** is set as an **errorElement** on the main route and is used by React Router for all errors occurring anywhere in the entire app.

> **NOTE**
>
> All code for this solution is available at https://packt.link/oaFoZ.

HEY!

I am Maximilian Schwarzmüller, the author of this book. I really hope you enjoyed reading my book and found it useful.

It would really help me (and other potential readers!) if you could leave a review on Amazon sharing your thoughts on *React Key Concepts*.

Go to the link https://packt.link/r/1803234504.

OR

Scan the QR code to leave your review.

Your review will help me to understand what's worked well in this book and what could be improved upon for future editions, so it really is appreciated.

Best wishes,

Maximilian Schwarzmüller

INDEX

A

access: 15, 57, 66, 76, 96, 165, 168-170, 172, 175, 189, 191, 198, 222, 262, 268, 281-282, 285-286, 290, 298, 302, 304, 306, 308-309, 314, 330, 365-366, 371, 394, 400, 409, 411, 420, 431

adding: 5, 12, 42, 45, 61, 72, 86, 92, 113, 129, 156, 158, 167, 187, 201, 209, 211, 220-221, 230, 241, 248, 250, 266, 268, 347, 352, 364, 366, 368, 372, 376, 378, 392, 399, 434-435, 441

advanced: 40, 238, 318, 326, 433, 443

api: 6, 116, 142, 199-200, 208, 226, 228-229, 234, 284-285, 290, 295, 306-307, 393-394, 399-400, 416-418, 434

app: 8, 15-16, 28-31, 34, 37-41, 44-46, 56, 58-61, 67-68, 73, 84, 86-87, 94-99, 106, 113, 125, 127-128, 136-137, 139, 144, 147, 152, 158-159, 162, 168, 172, 186-187, 191, 198, 200, 208, 212-214, 218, 226, 228-229, 234, 237-239, 242, 245-246, 254, 262, 264-265, 267-268, 270, 272-274, 280, 282, 284, 286, 297, 302-304, 307, 315-316, 320, 327-328, 332-335, 337, 343-353, 355-357, 359-361, 364-366, 373-374, 376-380, 391, 393, 396-397, 399-400, 402, 434, 443-446

approach: 4-5, 8-10, 12, 14, 23, 39, 54, 69-70, 86, 109, 113-114, 117, 119, 121, 123, 129-130, 141, 143, 149, 152-153, 171, 182, 190, 216-217, 230, 268, 348, 397-398, 407, 417, 425

arguments: 30, 40, 53, 141, 182, 188, 205-206, 225, 300-303

array: 38-39, 75-78, 82-83, 92, 98, 116-123, 126-129, 141, 148-149, 206-207, 209-211, 213, 220, 225, 228, 232-233, 243, 256, 286, 292-293, 299, 303, 306, 324-325, 332, 334-335, 397, 419-420

arrays: 28, 39, 56, 79, 82, 84, 98, 123, 129, 250, 324

async: 198-201, 204, 207, 230-231, 299, 304, 315, 327, 329-331, 333, 388, 391, 395, 398, 400, 405, 407, 413-414, 417-418, 425, 429-430, 432

await: 198-201, 204, 207-208, 230-231, 299, 305, 315, 327, 329-333, 388, 391, 395, 398, 400, 405, 407, 413-414, 417-419, 425, 430-432

B

back: 4, 8, 12, 17, 34, 89-90, 111, 128, 160, 167, 273, 342, 372, 426, 443

batching: 245-246

benefits: 297

binding: 88-90

blog: 37, 78, 105, 200, 205, 208, 234, 298, 305, 316, 327, 333-334, 342, 356-357,

365, 386-388, 390, 397, 403, 406, 408, 445-446

building: 2-3, 17-18, 22-24, 26, 30, 33, 37, 43, 50, 52, 57, 66, 74, 79, 95, 99-100, 136, 138, 147, 150, 166, 168, 181, 184, 231, 233-234, 267, 280, 313-314, 317, 335, 367, 374, 376, 429, 433, 440-442, 444-445

bundle: 259-260, 262-263, 265-266

C

challenges: 280, 306, 441-444
checkboxes: 175-177
checking: 75, 92, 115, 256
child: 31, 35-36, 40, 50-51, 77, 90, 98, 181, 186, 201, 238-241, 246-247, 251, 258, 271, 284, 288, 373, 375-376, 401, 404, 406-407, 431
children: 31, 54-55, 57-58, 60, 114-115, 148-151, 154, 186-187, 296, 360,

373, 401, 404, 408-410, 412

class: 26, 135, 143-144, 146-155, 157, 159, 162, 359
classes: 25-27, 135-136, 142-155, 159-162, 167-168, 170-171, 176-178, 180, 182-183, 188, 198-199, 201-202, 204, 207-208, 247-249, 257-258, 260-261, 283, 290-292, 358-359, 363, 368, 370, 382, 434
classname: 144, 146-152, 154, 159, 167-168, 170-171, 176-178, 180, 182-183, 188, 199, 202, 204, 208, 247-249, 257-258, 261, 283, 291-292, 354-355, 358, 363, 368, 370, 389, 391, 394, 427
code: 2-18, 21-46, 50, 52-53, 55-56, 58-61, 67-77, 81-82, 84-89, 91, 94, 96-97, 100, 106-113, 115-116, 118-122, 124-125, 128-129, 131, 136-139, 141-144, 146, 148, 152-154,

156, 158-159, 162, 167-170, 172, 176-178, 180-181, 184, 188-189, 191-192, 197-202, 205-206, 209-210, 216-219, 221-226, 228, 230, 234, 237-238, 241-242, 244-246, 248, 251, 254-256, 259-260, 262-268, 272-276, 284, 286-289, 291, 293-295, 298-304, 306-310, 314, 316-317, 320, 323, 325, 331, 333, 335-337, 343, 345-348, 350-353, 355-356, 358-364, 366, 368-371, 373, 375, 377-379, 382-383, 386, 390-404, 408-409, 413, 415, 417, 422-423, 427-428, 431, 442-444

colors: 144
complex: 3-8, 10, 12, 14, 17-18, 24, 41, 59-60, 69, 86, 91, 95, 98, 101, 121, 126, 129, 181, 189, 243, 245, 250-251, 273, 279-280, 283, 295, 300, 305-306, 314, 316, 322,

326-327, 333-335, 342, 346, 376, 379, 392, 429, 433, 441, 443-446

component: 15, 24-27, 29-35, 39, 41-46, 50-62, 66-70, 73-75, 77-81, 84-85, 89-92, 94-99, 101, 106-107, 109, 111, 113, 115-116, 118-120, 122-124, 127-128, 131, 140, 142, 147, 150-152, 154, 156-159, 161-162, 167-169, 172-179, 181-184, 188-192, 198-203, 205-208, 210-214, 216-219, 222-229, 231-234, 237-242, 244-260, 262-273, 275, 280-288, 290-298, 300, 302-304, 306, 308-311, 314, 316-317, 319-321, 323, 328, 330, 332-337, 343-348, 350, 352, 354, 356-365, 367-368, 371, 373-379, 383, 386-387, 390, 392-395, 397-399, 401-402, 405, 407, 411-416, 418-421, 423, 428-432, 434

components: 9, 15-16, 18, 21-28, 30-34, 37, 41-46, 49-56, 58-62, 66, 71, 74,

77, 81, 84, 90, 94-96, 98-101, 104, 114-116, 127, 129, 135-136, 140, 142, 145, 147, 150-153, 155-156, 158-160, 165, 175, 177-178, 181-182, 184, 187-192, 198, 201, 205, 212, 231, 233, 240-242, 245, 247, 251-252, 260, 262, 264, 266, 268-269, 271-273, 279-287, 290, 293-297, 306-309, 313-314, 316-317, 319-321, 323-325, 328, 330, 332-336, 341-346, 356-362, 365-366, 372, 374-380, 382, 386-388, 392, 395, 397, 401-405, 407, 409, 415, 432, 435, 440-441, 443

computer: 201
concepts: 2-3, 13, 18, 22, 26, 29, 38, 40, 44, 61, 99, 104, 129-130, 136, 145, 151, 160, 190, 197-199, 201, 233, 237-238, 273-274, 280, 307, 309, 314, 335-336, 379-380, 386-387, 390, 433, 440, 445-446
const: 4, 8, 24, 28, 31, 40-41, 56-57, 59, 67, 69-72, 74-76, 78, 80,

82, 84-91, 93-94, 96, 107-108, 110-111, 113, 115-117, 119-121, 127-128, 145, 148, 156, 167-176, 178-180, 183, 198, 201-202, 204, 207-208, 212, 216, 218, 221-223, 225, 227, 229-231, 239, 245, 247, 253, 255, 257, 259-262, 264, 286-294, 296, 299, 301, 303-305, 314-315, 318-319, 322-334, 337, 349, 351, 365-366, 369-371, 377, 388, 390-391, 394-398, 400-401, 404-405, 407-414, 417-419, 422-425, 427, 430

context: 160, 166, 199-200, 256, 270, 284-288, 290-298, 301, 306-309, 311, 314, 321, 342, 344, 349, 385, 402, 440-441
controlled: 14, 181-184, 190
core: 2-3, 6, 8, 11-13, 29, 39, 44, 58-59, 74, 79, 94, 104, 110, 114-115, 135, 156, 158, 198-199, 204, 280, 314, 372, 379, 433, 440, 445
coverage: 29
create: 1, 3, 5-6, 8,

11-15, 17-18, 22, 29,
31-32, 35, 42, 44-45,
56, 61, 123, 161,
179, 191, 202, 206,
231, 276, 285, 290,
296-297, 302, 306,
308, 335-337, 341,
344, 360, 366-367,
376, 380, 382-383,
385-386, 397, 417,
434-435, 442-443

creating: 3, 14, 32,
44-45, 58, 61, 179,
184, 199, 204, 218,
226, 295, 366-367,
376, 380, 382,
416, 442-443
creation: 4, 14, 17,
44, 137, 368
custom: 16, 26, 28,
30, 32-34, 42-43,
53, 57-58, 74, 97,
115-116, 127,
136, 156, 159,
208, 231, 250-251,
307, 313-314,
316-319, 321-324,
326, 328, 331,
335-337, 346, 376

D

data: 5-6, 42, 51-57,
59-60, 66, 73-75,
77, 79, 84, 90,
92, 98, 103-105,
116-119, 121-123,
127-131, 141, 156,
165, 173, 175, 181,
198-201, 203, 217,

233-234, 243, 266,
269-270, 275, 279,
291, 293, 298,
300-301, 303-305,
311, 314-316, 326,
328, 330, 332-334,
342, 362-366,
368-369, 380, 382,
385-388, 390,
392-395, 397-400,
402-403, 405-409,
411, 413-421,
423-435, 442-444

declaring: 68
default: 25-26, 29-30,
34, 57, 83, 89,
92-93, 97, 115, 119,
147-148, 150, 152,
154, 157-158, 175,
178-179, 181-182,
188, 199, 202, 204,
207-208, 212-213,
219, 224-227, 249,
251, 253, 256-257,
261-262, 264-265,
284, 286, 291-294,
297-298, 302, 304,
310, 313, 315,
318, 320, 322,
324, 326, 329,
333, 335, 343-344,
346, 348, 350-353,
356, 359-361, 366,
368, 372, 378-380,
391, 395, 398,
402, 405, 409,
411-412, 414-416,
421, 423, 425
definition: 3, 53,
200-201, 217, 221,

336, 344, 346, 364,
366, 373, 379,
383, 391, 393-397,
399, 410, 415,
421, 425, 428

dependency: 16,
206-207, 210-211,
213, 216-222, 224,
226, 228, 232, 256,
259, 299-300, 332
developer: 2, 4-5, 10,
12, 25-26, 28-29,
32, 34, 56-57, 59,
68-69, 72, 76, 78,
90-91, 108, 124-125,
127, 129, 136, 140,
142, 144, 154,
156-157, 169, 181,
191, 198-199, 214,
229, 237, 244, 253,
256, 260, 263, 268,
272-273, 276, 284,
306-307, 343, 368,
379, 394, 400, 411,
416, 433, 440
document: 4-6, 11,
28-29, 31-32,
67, 70-71, 139,
142, 155, 157,
159, 166-167,
188, 192, 350
dom: 5-13, 17, 29-31,
33, 35, 68, 70, 72,
75, 77, 92, 108-109,
121, 123, 126-129,
136, 139-141, 155,
165-166, 168-170,
172, 175, 177,
181, 184-192,
194, 216, 232,

237-238, 241-246,
272-273, 350

domain: 342-343,
346, 374
down: 8, 11, 68, 97,
121, 156, 207, 222,
259, 282-283, 390

E

effects: 128, 190,
197, 200, 202-207,
212, 216-217, 221,
230, 232-234, 255,
267, 299, 314, 317,
321-322, 324, 335,
386, 388, 390, 443
ejs: 23
element: 5-6, 10,
12, 14, 27, 29-31,
33, 35-40, 42, 45,
50-51, 57-59, 66,
70-71, 76-78, 82-83,
88-90, 97-98, 101,
106, 108-109, 112,
114-116, 126,
128-130, 141-142,
145-148, 150-152,
154-155, 157, 159,
165-166, 168-170,
172, 177, 185-189,
191, 243, 267,
303, 335, 344-349,
351-354, 356-357,
359-361, 363-365,
373-379, 392,
396-398, 401-402,
404, 408-412,

415-417, 421, 423,
425, 428, 431

elements: 5-6, 8-9,
11-14, 23, 28,
30-33, 35-36, 38-40,
43-44, 50-51, 55,
67-72, 75-77, 82,
84, 92, 94, 98, 101,
103-104, 108-109,
112, 115-118,
120-121, 126-131,
135-136, 138,
140-142, 144, 147,
155, 159-160, 162,
165-166, 168, 170,
172, 175, 183-192,
194, 201, 241-242,
303, 306, 314, 320,
324, 345, 348, 350,
352, 354, 357, 359,
368, 376, 379, 382,
397, 402, 415,
417, 431, 434
embedded: 9, 23
enhancing: 101, 382
entity: 42
entry: 15, 28-29, 139
error: 6, 29, 38, 52,
67-68, 70, 77,
79, 87, 104-105,
130-131, 184-187,
189, 210, 220,
226-229, 247-249,
251, 257-259, 267,
271-272, 299-305,
314-318, 326-334,
369, 388-391, 395,
398, 405, 407,

409-412, 418, 420,
430, 434-435

evaluation: 246,
271-272
external: 55-56, 73,
199-200, 210-211,
213, 222, 232, 332,
352, 357, 379

F

feature: 9, 12, 23-24,
30, 32-34, 37, 43,
57, 66, 70, 73, 75,
98, 110, 156, 168,
175, 183-184, 187,
189, 192, 238,
242, 254, 267,
285-286, 290, 293,
295, 314, 317,
319, 321, 335-336,
368, 372-373, 376,
378-379, 382-383,
385-386, 399,
402, 441, 443
features: 2-3, 8, 13,
15, 17, 26-27, 29,
45, 66-67, 69, 71,
74, 98-99, 119, 136,
160, 177, 189-190,
197-198, 233, 238,
244, 267, 273-274,
307, 309, 311, 336,
343, 345, 362, 377,
379, 382, 386-388,
391, 395-396, 412,
415, 433, 441-444
fetch: 198-204, 207,

234, 298-299, 301, 303-305, 314-316, 326-334, 385-388, 391, 394-395, 398-400, 405, 407, 413-414, 417, 419, 430

file: 7, 11, 14-16, 23-25, 28-29, 32-34, 42, 44-45, 68, 137-140, 142, 146, 152-156, 159, 161-162, 187-188, 210, 246, 263-264, 286, 291, 296, 319, 328, 337, 359, 382, 391-393, 395, 405, 417, 428, 434

files: 11, 15-16, 25, 34, 39-40, 45, 69, 138-140, 142, 147, 152-153, 155-156, 159, 266, 362

flow: 240

follow: 2, 28-29, 34, 42, 69, 81, 230-231, 295, 417

form: 22-25, 80, 92-94, 104-105, 130-131, 144, 150, 160-162, 166-172, 175, 177-189, 191, 223-224, 227-229, 234, 241, 247-248, 257-259, 271, 275-276, 280, 289, 298, 300, 309-311, 368-370, 387,

411-423, 425-429, 432-433, 444-445

forms: 84, 92, 190, 416-417, 423

fragment: 39, 397

fragments: 402

function: 4-5, 8, 10, 24-27, 29-31, 33, 35-42, 44, 52-59, 61, 66-72, 74-78, 80, 82-94, 96-98, 106-111, 113-116, 119-123, 141, 145-151, 154, 156-158, 167-171, 173-184, 188, 191, 198-234, 237-242, 244-267, 270-273, 275, 283, 285-294, 296-306, 309-311, 314-320, 322-335, 337, 344, 347, 349, 351, 353, 355-356, 358-360, 363, 365, 368-369, 371-373, 375, 377-379, 388, 390-403, 405, 407-408, 411-432

functional: 26, 28, 160, 298, 300

functions: 9, 13, 25-28, 30, 32-34, 38, 40, 45, 50, 52-54, 60, 69, 73-75, 77-78, 81, 84-85, 87, 97-98, 116, 156, 165, 173, 177-178, 181, 183, 200,

206-207, 209-211, 213, 216-217, 219, 222, 229-232, 238, 240-242, 246-247, 251, 256, 258, 262, 267-268, 275, 282, 285, 289, 293-295, 301-302, 314, 317-318, 320, 322-323, 335, 355, 392, 399-400, 406, 418, 420-422, 426, 432-435

future: 92, 182, 203, 266-267

G

github: 6, 10, 16, 137, 155, 158, 162, 188, 213, 218, 223, 228, 248, 254, 265, 284, 294, 298, 323, 325, 345, 356, 361-362, 366, 373, 383, 390

H

handle: 4-5, 14, 32, 81, 92, 127, 129, 197-198, 233-234, 279-280, 285, 294, 308, 314, 316-317, 321, 343, 386, 409, 412-414, 416, 423, 433

handling: 9, 32, 71, 97, 136, 167, 190,

197, 299, 318, 366,
376, 386, 388, 390,
409, 411, 418, 433,
435, 443-444

history: 442
hook: 74-75, 78, 80,
98-99, 167-168,
187-188, 192, 197,
204-205, 224,
231-233, 254,
275, 280, 288,
290, 300, 303,
306-307, 310-311,
314, 317-324, 328,
330-333, 335-337,
365, 371, 379, 386,
391, 393, 399,
407-409, 411, 419,
422-423, 426, 444
hooks: 26, 74-75,
98, 187, 205, 225,
231, 237, 302,
306-307, 309,
313-314, 316-319,
321-322, 324, 326,
328, 332, 334-337,
343, 440, 445
how: 2-5, 7-8, 12-13,
17-18, 22, 24, 32,
34-35, 38, 42-44,
50-52, 55-56, 58,
60-61, 66-69, 73,
75-76, 78, 83,
91-92, 98-99,
104-107, 109-110,
117-118, 121-122,
127, 129-130, 136,

138-139, 151, 157,
160, 172, 179,
190, 198, 205,
207, 216, 219,
233-234, 237-238,
240, 243-244, 246,
268-269, 273, 286,
293, 295, 301,
303, 306-307, 314,
328, 335-336, 342,
347, 354, 359, 365,
370, 380, 386-388,
409, 421, 433,
439-440, 445

html: 5-6, 9, 11-12,
14-15, 23-24, 27-30,
32-34, 37, 39-40,
42-45, 50-51, 54-55,
71, 80, 94, 114, 116,
136, 138-143, 153,
159, 169, 187-188,
192, 242, 343, 347,
349, 354, 360

I

ide: 294-295
imperative: 4-5, 8,
12, 18, 68-69,
71, 172, 181
import: 8, 24-26,
28, 42, 46, 73, 75,
107-108, 110-111,
116, 121, 138-140,
153-156, 158, 168,
174, 188, 198, 201,
204, 207, 212,

223, 225-227, 249,
255, 257, 260,
262-264, 267, 283,
285-288, 290-292,
297, 318-319, 322,
324, 328, 332,
334, 343-344, 347,
350-352, 355,
358-360, 365, 371,
375, 377-378,
388, 390, 392,
394-396, 398, 402,
405, 408-409, 411,
414-415, 419, 422,
424, 426-430

inspecting: 139, 205
integrated: 294

J

javascript: 1-15, 17-18,
23-30, 32-41, 43, 54,
56-58, 68-72, 75-79,
82, 84, 92-94, 97-98,
108-110, 112-115,
117-119, 125-126,
129, 136-137,
139-142, 144, 149,
152, 154-156,
158-159, 166-168,
174, 181-183,
187, 199, 210,
214-215, 217, 219,
226, 228-229, 234,
242-243, 258-259,
262-263, 265,
317-320, 322, 324,

335, 368, 382, 397, 399, 432, 434, 444

jest: 14, 16
jsx: 9, 11-13, 15, 18, 21-22, 24, 26-41, 43-46, 50, 52-54, 58, 70-71, 75-76, 80, 82, 87, 94, 98, 103-104, 108-112, 115-121, 127-131, 135-136, 140-141, 144-145, 152, 159, 162, 165, 168-169, 177, 180-181, 188, 190, 192, 201-202, 217, 225, 238, 241-242, 244, 254, 264-265, 314, 317, 320, 333, 344, 346, 360, 368, 371, 382, 397, 434, 441

K

keyword: 26, 38, 43, 94, 144, 178, 205, 230, 432

L

language: 27, 32, 54, 113-114, 136, 160
layers: 59, 283, 306
legacy: 267
let: 38-39, 69, 71-72, 76, 91, 107-108,

110, 146-151, 154, 172-174, 189, 214, 292-293, 337, 389, 419

library: 2-3, 13-14, 17, 27-28, 32, 34-35, 135-136, 152, 156-159, 234, 260, 262, 265, 343-344, 350, 355, 371, 378-379, 399, 443-444
links: 50, 58, 341-342, 347-348, 350, 352, 356-358, 366-368, 372, 379-380, 382, 435
lists: 45, 59, 99, 103-105, 116, 121, 126, 129-130, 137, 149, 169, 184, 254, 441-442
literal: 149, 156-157, 368
loader: 391-401, 403-410, 412, 414-416, 418, 420, 422, 426-435
loading: 24, 104, 259-260, 265, 298, 300, 305-306, 316, 318, 327, 330, 333-334, 364-365, 368, 377-380, 382-383, 385, 389-390,

393, 397, 399, 407, 413-414, 422, 429-431, 433-435

locally: 16
locators: 342

M

management: 4, 6-7, 74, 273, 295, 298, 300, 306-307, 310, 314, 316, 321, 337, 433, 441, 443-444
manager: 2, 14
managing: 2, 69, 73, 78-79, 81-84, 101, 182, 267, 286, 293-298, 300, 306, 361, 385, 411
map: 103, 114, 119-122, 128-129, 199, 202, 204, 208, 253-255, 291-292, 363, 368, 389, 391, 394, 399, 420, 423
mapping: 119, 121
means: 4-5, 7, 9, 14, 17, 30, 68-69, 91, 104, 112, 136, 140, 200, 284, 296, 317, 342, 346, 364, 368, 395
method: 28-30, 35-36, 93, 119-122, 129, 181-182, 200, 291, 397, 409, 413-417,

419, 421, 423-428

mode: 151-152, 154,
237, 246, 267, 273
model: 5-6, 51,
139, 150, 166
module: 153-155,
188, 198, 201, 204,
207, 249, 257, 260,
283, 290, 292, 358
modules: 16, 25,
135, 152-155,
158-159, 162, 359
multiple: 6-7, 14, 25,
33-34, 39-42, 45, 50,
54, 56, 58-62, 78-81,
83-84, 95, 99, 101,
105, 109, 112, 114,
126, 128-129, 142,
148-149, 187, 208,
212, 214, 216-217,
220, 237, 241-242,
245-246, 252, 254,
265-266, 272,
279-281, 283-284,
293, 297-300, 306,
314, 316, 321-322,
324, 330, 335-336,
342-345, 357, 361,
374, 377-378, 392,
406, 410, 432

N

native: 3, 13, 30,
36, 445
navigation: 22-23,
59, 96, 104-105,
116, 143, 192,

344, 347-348, 350,
352-355, 358-359,
361, 366, 368,
370-372, 376,
379-380, 382-383,
403-404, 408,
421-423, 426, 435

need: 2, 5-6, 10, 12-16,
18, 25, 40, 44, 51,
54-56, 59-60, 67,
72, 76-77, 79, 81,
91, 96, 100, 104,
126-127, 129, 136,
160, 170, 181,
184, 187, 190,
198-199, 203, 206,
216, 224, 233-234,
241, 244, 247,
251, 260, 280-287,
290, 295, 297-298,
302, 306, 308-309,
316, 322, 324-325,
335, 343-344, 352,
364-365, 367, 369,
372, 375, 382-383,
386-388, 395, 397,
402, 413, 421,
423, 426, 434,
441-443, 445-446
nested: 12, 23, 30,
35-37, 59, 95, 109,
111, 169, 175,
186, 192, 231,
238-240, 242, 245,
247, 251-252, 269,
282-283, 285-286,
288, 290, 293-294,
300, 318, 335, 341,

372-376, 379-380,
383, 394, 401, 410,
419, 421, 428, 434

nesting: 12, 112,
283, 295, 372
network: 205, 259,
263, 276, 346
node: 2, 14-16, 126,
156, 189, 194, 443
npm: 2, 14-17, 34,
44, 156, 191-192,
234, 259, 274, 308,
310, 337, 343-346

O

object: 5-6, 29, 35, 38,
53-54, 57-58, 60,
68, 80-84, 88, 93,
101, 115, 123, 131,
139, 141, 145, 149,
153, 166, 168-169,
172, 179-180, 203,
210, 217-219,
226, 228-230, 232,
242-243, 250, 259,
285-287, 290-291,
294, 300, 303-304,
306, 309-310,
318-320, 324-325,
330, 333-335,
355-356, 366,
372, 393-394,
397, 399-400,
414-418, 422,
426-427, 430-431
objects: 30, 56, 79,
82-84, 97-98,

117-118, 120, 123, 126, 131, 144, 149-150, 172, 210, 217, 222, 226, 228-229, 243, 250-251, 258-259, 300, 302, 324, 397-398

operator: 58, 112-115, 123, 129, 149

P

package: 2, 13-17, 28, 30, 35, 54, 242, 341, 343, 345, 378, 382, 386, 391, 433, 435

page: 3, 5, 10-11, 14-17, 23, 29, 35, 44-46, 50, 62, 73, 100-101, 105, 108, 116, 131-132, 138-139, 142, 144, 150, 162, 166, 175, 192, 194, 235, 241-242, 259, 268-272, 277, 297, 309, 311, 336, 338, 341-343, 345-350, 352, 354, 360, 362-364, 366-372, 375-376, 380-383, 385-388, 392-393, 400, 413, 418, 421-422, 426, 428-429, 434-437, 440-441, 443

parameters: 178,

301, 322-323, 364-366, 399-400

pascalcase: 33-34, 43

passing: 42, 51, 61, 69, 75, 88, 90, 145, 148, 213, 295, 304, 397, 416

past: 256, 266, 444

path: 14-15, 328, 342-349, 351-354, 356-357, 359-361, 363-367, 373-374, 376-379, 392, 396-399, 401-402, 404, 408-410, 412, 415, 421, 428

personal: 44, 121, 156, 222, 267

point: 17, 29, 41, 43, 50-51, 59, 61, 66, 79, 92, 99, 104, 113, 121, 136-138, 172, 187, 190, 206, 233, 238, 260, 262, 289, 293, 295, 342, 354, 383, 402-403, 409, 429

portal: 187, 189, 192

portals: 27, 160, 165-166, 184, 187, 190, 231

post: 105, 199, 202, 204, 208, 234, 365, 386-387, 389, 391, 394, 397-399, 403-405, 407-409, 412-417, 419-421, 423-424,

426-428, 431

prior: 15, 177, 402

profiler: 270-272

project: 9, 12-18, 24-25, 28-29, 32, 34, 41, 44-45, 52, 137-138, 152-153, 158-159, 161, 186, 191, 234, 274-275, 307-310, 319, 336-337, 343, 357-358, 382, 435, 441-443, 445

promise: 199-200, 230-231, 393-394, 417, 430-432

promises: 199, 230-232

prop: 54-60, 71-72, 85, 89, 92, 94, 97-98, 113, 115, 127, 129, 141-142, 144-145, 147-152, 159, 168-169, 171, 179, 182, 218, 228-229, 248, 250-251, 253-254, 256-259, 265, 272, 284, 287, 290, 294-296, 306-307, 345-346, 352, 354-357, 360, 364-365, 368, 372-374, 379, 392, 397, 411, 415-416, 421, 431

properties: 53-54, 82-84, 115, 141-142, 149, 153, 179-181,

229, 289, 291, 304,
306, 320, 333, 366,
399, 417, 427

props: 42, 49, 51-62,
66, 71-73, 77, 80,
90, 92, 96-99, 104,
115-116, 136, 147,
150-151, 158,
178-179, 182-183,
198, 201, 207,
209, 226, 228-229,
238, 241, 248,
250-251, 269, 272,
280, 282-285, 293,
295-296, 306, 335,
342, 354-355,
360, 363-365,
373, 440-441
pure: 7, 330
purpose: 39, 112,
115, 147, 191, 206,
357, 380, 433
put: 40-42, 66, 68,
124, 177, 216-217,
286, 440
putting: 216

R

react: 1-4, 8-18, 21-45,
49, 51-61, 65-79,
81, 83, 85-86,
88-92, 94-95,
97-100, 103-104,
106-117, 121-124,
126-131, 135-139,
141, 143-145, 152,
155-156, 158-162,
166, 168-175,
177-178, 180-182,
184-185, 187-192,
197-202, 204-207,
209-212, 214-216,
223-227, 229-234,
237-238, 240-246,
249-251, 253-255,
257, 260, 262-268,
270, 272-275, 280,
283-288, 290-291,
293-295, 297, 300,
302-303, 306-307,
309, 311, 313-314,
316-319, 321-322,
324, 328, 335-336,
341-346, 350, 352,
355, 357, 359,
364-366, 371-372,
374, 376-379,
382-383, 385-388,
390-393, 395-402,
406-407, 409-412,
414-416, 418,
421-423, 426,
428-435, 439-446
reactdom: 28,
30-32, 44, 139
redirects: 372
reducer: 300-303,
306, 309-311, 328
refactor: 336, 358
refs: 27, 160, 165-166,
168, 170, 172,
174-175, 177,
181-182, 184,
189-191, 201, 231,
314, 322, 415

render: 28-31, 54, 68,
70, 99, 103-104,
108, 112, 116, 129,
139, 188, 190, 192,
201, 203, 206, 234,
267, 271, 343, 346,
348, 374, 376, 399,
401, 410, 428-429
renderable: 27-28, 43
rendering: 103-104,
106, 109, 112,
126-127, 130,
137, 149, 167,
169-170, 184, 198,
201-203, 233, 350,
368, 401, 442
repository: 7, 191,
234, 274, 307,
309, 336, 383
request: 92-93,
199-204, 206,
208-210, 212, 214,
216-217, 226,
228-229, 232-234,
266, 298-299, 303,
314, 316, 318, 326,
330, 332-333, 346,
349-350, 386, 390,
393-394, 399-400,
407, 409, 413-414,
416-418, 425
requesting: 166
requests: 198-202,
205, 230, 234, 263,
275-276, 316, 332,

386-388, 399, 421, 441, 443-444

resource: 72, 210, 234, 342, 352, 367

retrieving: 256

returns: 27, 58, 75-76, 82, 98, 112, 115, 123, 157, 200, 226, 285, 290-291, 302-303, 306, 310, 320, 322, 324, 334, 349, 366, 390, 408, 430

reuse: 66, 295, 317, 324, 335, 363

router: 14, 341, 343-344, 350, 352, 355, 364-366, 371-372, 374, 376, 378-379, 382-383, 385-388, 390-393, 395-402, 404, 406-412, 414-416, 418, 421-423, 426, 428-433, 435, 441

routes: 341, 343-353, 355-357, 359-362, 364-367, 372-380, 383, 385, 392, 396-398, 401-404, 406-408, 410, 421, 428, 432, 441-443

routing: 14, 17, 344, 346, 357, 359, 363, 365, 374, 377-380, 382, 386-388,

433-435, 440

rules: 38, 41, 44, 137, 222, 231, 295

S

sending: 93, 199-201, 203, 212, 229-230, 232-234, 314, 316, 318, 350, 386-388, 393, 409, 413, 416, 418, 421, 425, 444, 446

server: 6, 16-17, 34, 44, 92, 104, 167, 169-171, 274-275, 308, 310, 337, 346, 349, 386, 390, 393-394, 399, 416, 443

setup: 15, 18, 32, 152, 404

side: 3, 11, 104, 123, 128, 190, 192-194, 197, 200-206, 216, 224, 228, 232-233, 255, 267, 271, 299, 314, 317, 321-322, 324, 335, 337, 386, 388, 390, 393, 399, 401, 406, 434, 443

simple: 5, 7-8, 10, 12, 41, 58, 69, 77, 79, 95-96, 98, 100, 106, 109, 129, 167, 190, 214, 219, 222, 251,

266, 280, 300, 306, 326, 349-350, 376, 379, 397, 411, 417, 429, 442-443, 446

single: 8, 14-15, 17, 23-24, 29, 33-34, 40-43, 52, 57, 60, 80-82, 84, 95, 99, 101, 109, 114, 141, 240, 242, 285, 297-298, 300, 309, 314, 324, 336, 342-343, 346, 349, 397, 407, 409

slices: 80-81, 83-84, 94, 101, 300

source: 15, 88-89, 125, 364, 386, 403

sources: 86, 89

spa: 14, 16, 18, 343, 378

spas: 17, 342

splitting: 7, 25, 42, 260, 263, 266, 272-273, 357, 361, 377, 383

spread: 58, 115, 123, 149, 158

spreading: 57, 59, 115

state: 6-7, 9-13, 17, 26, 41, 60, 65-66, 68-70, 73-88, 90-92, 94-99, 101, 104, 107, 121-123, 126-129, 136, 144-146, 166-167, 170-171, 173-177, 180-184,

189-191, 197-198,
200-203, 206-209,
211, 213, 216,
218-219, 222, 224,
226, 228, 231-233,
237-238, 240-241,
243-249, 251,
258-259, 267, 269,
272-273, 279-291,
293-296, 298-311,
314, 316-318,
321-323, 326-328,
330-337, 342-343,
349-350, 352, 355,
393, 413, 422-423,
429, 440-444

stateful: 121, 316-317,
321, 335
statements: 25, 28,
40-41, 109, 111,
113-114, 119, 129,
140, 147, 199, 216,
231, 263, 390
states: 8, 12, 17, 60,
183, 216, 245,
318, 321, 411
stop: 14, 259, 270
storage: 76, 198,
203, 232-233,
328, 387, 393
strict: 237, 246,
267, 273
string: 10, 55, 75,
77-79, 82, 89-91,
108, 116-117, 120,
128, 141, 148-149,

157, 251, 285, 300,
324, 368, 371, 422

strings: 28, 82, 98,
100, 118, 153,
159, 172, 368
strong: 12
sugar: 32, 34,
37-38, 43, 108
suspense: 264-266,
272, 377-378,
430-431
switching: 79, 182, 350
system: 15-16, 346,
393, 442-443

T

template: 149,
156-157, 368
templates: 23, 156
testing: 14
throwing: 72
tools: 2, 9, 14, 41,
69, 72, 104, 108,
124-125, 129, 140,
144, 154, 157,
190-191, 214, 229,
237-238, 256, 263,
268, 272-273, 276,
280, 295, 306,
386, 441, 445
two-way: 88-90
type: 5, 25, 28, 66-67,
70-71, 73-74,
78-80, 82-83, 88-91,
93-94, 96, 114,

130, 145, 167-168,
170-172, 176-177,
179-180, 182, 184,
208, 219, 223-224,
227, 248, 258,
261, 301, 303-306,
310, 314-315, 324,
326-334, 370, 411,
413-414, 418-419,
423, 430, 441

U

under: 3, 69, 76, 94,
104, 153, 273
uniform: 342
uploading:442
url: 14, 207-208,
211, 316, 330-333,
341-347, 350, 352,
354, 356, 364-366,
376, 379, 383,
386, 399-400
urls: 316, 332,
342, 347, 363
usecontext: 290-293,
298, 306
useeffect: 197,
204-209, 211-214,
216-226, 228-233,
255, 299, 304-305,
315-317, 324,
327-332, 334,
385-386, 388,
390, 393, 409
usefetch: 328-334
usememo: 237,

254-256, 259, 268, 272-273, 275

user: 2-7, 9-10, 12-14, 17-18, 22, 24, 28-29, 35-37, 41, 43, 45, 49-50, 57, 60, 62, 65-67, 77-79, 81, 84, 88-92, 94, 98, 100-101, 103-106, 112, 120, 125, 129-132, 136-137, 145-146, 160-162, 166, 170, 174-175, 181-182, 184-185, 190-191, 193, 198, 201-203, 208, 211, 235, 238, 241-244, 250, 272, 274-275, 280-281, 294, 297, 306, 308-311, 316, 321, 337, 341-342, 348, 350, 352, 354-355, 362, 364, 368-370, 372, 374-377, 379, 385-387, 406, 415, 418, 420-423, 425-426, 429, 431, 441-445

usereducer: 300-304, 306-307, 309, 311, 314-317, 321, 324, 327-331, 333, 335

useref: 168-170, 172-175, 178-180, 205, 231, 324,

369, 371, 412

usestate: 8, 24, 26, 73-78, 80-94, 96, 98-99, 107-108, 110-111, 121-122, 145, 167, 169, 171, 173, 176, 179, 182-183, 198, 200-202, 204-205, 207-208, 211-212, 216, 218, 223, 225, 227, 231, 239, 245, 247, 257, 260, 262, 264, 280, 288-289, 293, 296, 298, 300, 303, 306-307, 309-310, 317-318, 321-324, 335, 349-351, 385, 388

using: 2, 4, 8, 10, 12, 14, 17, 21-22, 25, 30, 32-34, 36, 43-44, 51-54, 57-58, 68-69, 72, 75-76, 78, 80, 84, 86-87, 96-97, 100, 109, 111, 113-115, 119, 121, 123, 128-130, 136-137, 139-142, 144, 147, 149, 152-153, 155-156, 158-159, 162, 166-168, 171-172, 178, 180-184, 187, 189-191, 200-201, 203, 213, 224,

228, 230, 238, 246, 251-253, 260, 266-268, 282, 285-286, 288, 290, 293-294, 300, 304, 306-307, 315, 318, 321, 327, 337, 352, 355, 357, 359, 366, 368, 372, 378, 385-386, 388, 397-398, 402, 409, 414, 417, 423, 425, 428-429, 431, 441-442, 444-445

V

values: 8-9, 28, 38-40, 43, 53, 55-57, 72, 75-84, 90-92, 97-100, 104, 108-109, 113-114, 116-120, 123, 126-128, 130, 145-147, 149-151, 153, 159, 161, 166, 168, 170, 172-173, 175, 177, 180-181, 183-184, 188-189, 191, 209-211, 213, 216, 219, 222, 224, 228-230, 232-233, 241, 245-247, 250, 254, 257, 262, 279-280, 282-283, 285-287, 290, 293-294, 297-300,

302, 306, 309,
320, 322-325, 330,
332-333, 335,
342, 355, 357,
360, 363-365,
368, 379-380,
397, 416-420,
422, 430-431

vanilla: 2, 4-6, 9-12,
17-18, 28-29, 33-35,
37, 68-69, 75, 79,
93, 129, 139, 141,
167-168, 174, 181
variable: 7, 9, 40-41,
52, 70, 75-78, 91,
108-109, 116, 121,
173-174, 210, 215,
226, 232, 259, 285,
294, 298, 319
variables: 25, 40, 57,
75-78, 97, 108-109,
116, 173, 207, 213,
219, 222, 442
versions: 16, 266
virtual: 13, 17, 35, 237,
241-246, 272-273

259, 263, 268, 342,
346, 368, 372, 386,
394, 400, 416, 434,
441, 445-446

welcome: 31, 380-381,
396-397, 401, 404,
408-410, 412
working: 2, 4-6, 9, 12,
23-24, 26-28, 33,
39-40, 44, 51, 55,
58, 60, 65, 69-70,
75, 78-79, 82, 84,
91-92, 95, 100, 107,
121, 123, 127, 136,
141, 144-145, 149,
152, 168, 173, 181,
185, 190, 200, 231,
233, 244, 260, 273,
279, 282, 295, 298,
307, 314, 386-388,
415, 440-442

W

waiting: 431
web: 1, 3-4, 6, 10,
13-14, 23-25, 33-35,
50, 57, 66-69, 72,
79, 99, 104-105,
129, 136, 138-139,
142, 156, 160,
166, 169, 198-199,
233-234, 238, 242,

Printed in Great Britain
by Amazon